Constructing Civilizations

CONTEMPORARY STUDIES IN SOCIOLOGY, VOLUME 5

Editor: John Clark, *Department of Sociology, University of Minnesota*
Series Editors: Robert Althauser, *Department of Sociology, Indiana University,*
John D. Kasarda, *Department of Sociology, University of North Carolina,*
Clark McPhail, *Department of Sociology, University of Illinois*

CONTEMPORARY STUDIES IN SOCIOLOGY
Theoretical and Empirical Monographs

Editor-in-Chief: John Clark
Department of Sociology, University of Minnesota
Series Editors: Robert Althauser, Department of
Sociology, Indiana University, John D. Kasarda,
Department of Sociology, University of North
Carolina and Clark McPhail, Department of
Sociology, University of Illinois

Volume 1. **THE ENTREPRENEURIAL BUREAUCRACY: BIOGRAPHIES OF TWO FEDERAL PROGRAMS IN EDUCATION**
Ronald G. Corwin, Department of Sociology,
Ohio State University

Volume 2. **TRANSITION TO THE 21ST CENTURY: PROSPECTS AND POLICIES FOR ECONOMIC AND URBAN-REGIONAL TRANSFORMATION**
Edited by Donald A. Hicks, School of Social
Sciences, University of Texas at Dallas and
Norman J. Glickman, Departments of City and
Regional Planning and Regional Science,
University of Pennsylvania

Volume 3. **ORGANIZATIONS AND THEIR ENVIRONMENTS: ESSAYS IN THE SOCIOLOGY OF ORGANIZATIONS**
Charles K. Warriner, Department of Sociology,
University of Kansas

Volume 4. **INTERDISCIPLINARY THEORIES OF RURAL DEVELOPMENT**
Frank W. Young, Department of Rural Sociology,
Cornell University

Volume 5. **CONSTRUCTING CIVILIZATIONS**
Carl J. Couch, Department of Sociology,
University of Iowa

To the Memory of My Father

My father was far too perceptive to conclude all lawyers
and preachers were devoid of merit; he also excused some
of the behavior of liars. He simply recognized that
specialists in the manipulation of words often deliberately
misused words for personal benefit. Had he had more than
an incidental acquaintance with professors he would have
categorized them with lawyers and preachers. However, the
only professor he knew was one of his own children. His
perception of his children was always rose tinted.

Constructing Civilizations

by CARL J. COUCH
Department of Sociology
The University of Iowa

 JAI PRESS INC.

Greenwich, Connecticut   *London, England*

Library of Congress Cataloging in Publication Data

Couch, Carl J.
  Constructing civilizations.

  (Contemporary studies in sociology ; vol. 5)
  1. Civilization. 2. Social structure. 3. Time
perception. I. Title. II. Series: Contemporary studies
in sociology ; v. 5.
HM101.C73 1984   909   83-48085
ISBN 0-89232-438-4

Copyright © 1984 JAI PRESS INC.
36 Sherwood Place
Greenwich, Connecticut 06830

JAI PRESS INC.
3 Henrietta Street
London WC2E 8LU
England

ISBN NUMBER. 0-89232-438-4
Library of Congress Catalog Card Number: 83-48085
Manufactured in the United States of America

CONTENTS

Preface

This account of the emergence of complex social structures that link together millions of persons presumes that sometime in the past the human inhabitants of the earth lived in self-sufficient, small nomadic bands. No account of a transformation of this magnitude can be complete. Many facets of the transformation are not considered here. This book focuses in particular on the formulation of temporal structures and the elaboration of forms of sociation.

The issue is not that explanations of the transformation are selective, but rather are the selected dimensions critical? Or, are they epiphenomena? The presumption of any scholar offering an explanation is that the series of events he or she has selected are critical and prototypical. Only the subsequent responses of others can validate or invalidate the selection.

The selection of temporal structures and forms of sociation as the phenomena to be analyzed is a considerable departure from traditional accounts of the emergence of civilizations. Many have noted features of the temporal structures of societies, but few have held that they are critical dimensions of social structure. More often they have been regarded as intriguing epiphenomena. In contrast, my position is that only by acquiring a better understanding of temporal structures will it be possible to generate a greater understanding of human life and acquire more command over future developments.

Several social scientists have advocated the examination of social forms. Several held that the analysis of variation in social forms is the key to understanding of the human condition. Marx held that the control of the means of production was the fundamental variable; Innis claimed the form of communication was the significance variable; and many anthropologists hold that the basic social forms are egalitarian and authoritarian.

Each of these positions and the positions of others have merit. Social forms are ways that human beings act with each other, toward each other, against each other, for each other, and are ways that they share experiences. One of the critical consequences of various social forms is the quality of life they allow. Some generate boredom, others excitement, others pain, others security, and others opportunities. The forms of social relations that have been constructed, imposed, adopted, and discarded all provide opportunities and exercise constraints. The elementary forms have been combined in many ways. The variation and complexity of social forms that are possible make it difficult to specify with more than a modicum of certainty the consequences of different forms. Nonetheless the effort is made.

The focus on temporal structures and forms of sociation necessarily implies that some features of human life that have been assigned significance by others are given minimal attention. For example, little attention is given to tools and technology, none to ceramics. Civilizations could not have emerged without tools. However, the significance of tools is a consequence of the social structure that encases them. It is the temporal structures and forms of sociation that establish the function of tools. The typewriter facilitates communication only among literates; it may be a resource among illiterates, but not a tool. The obsidian spear point is a nice decoration in a modern middle-class home, but not a tool.

The widely used transformation sequence based upon type of tool is ignored. The neolithic age was preceded by the paleolithic and in turn followed by the bronze and iron ages. However, the use of a particular material does not specify the nature of the life of the users. The Huns and the Phoenicians were iron age societies. They had other similarities. But the differences in their social structures were so profound that it borders on the absurd to place them in the same category. While the development of tools was a significant set of transformations, the significance of this development has often been overstated. Meaningful assessment of the significance of tools for human experiences and conduct can only be assessed by placing them within a social context.

The classification of evolutionary stages on the basis of material used for tool construction stemmed from the fact that these tools are the artifacts most readily available. They are the most common tracings of ancient groups available for examination. Consequently they have occupied a dominant position in the reconstructions of ancient societies. In contrast, transformations of temporal structures and modes of sociation are emphasized in this reconstruction of ancient societies.

No one sentence definition of civilization is offered, nor is there a listing of the cultural traits that constitute civilization. Such an exercise is possible, but of questionable merit. The specification of when civilization appeared is similar to the specification of when the cat first appeared as a distinct species. In both cases it is possible to specify a series of incremental changes, but the designation of a given occurrence as the watershed point for the transformation is always arbitrary.

The word "civilizations" in the title instead "civilization" is not capricious. Both the Athenians of 500 B.C. and the Aztecs of 1500 A.D. merit the designation. However, the differences between the two are so great that the plural seems preferred.

Many persons have had a significant impact upon my thinking. The writings of George Herbert Mead, Georg Simmel, Harold Adams Innis, Marshall McLuhan, and Alexander Marshack are the source of many of the ideas expressed. The influence of Manford Kuhn was profound. Robert Stewart and Hideya Kumata were sources of ideas for many years. My intellectual indebtedness to Dan Miller, Robert Hintz, Glenda Sehested, Marilyn Leichty, and Marion Weiland is greater than can be indicated. They formulated a frame of thought that completely transformed my own. Hopefully they will some day receive recognition for the paradigm they have provided for social scientists.

This statement rests upon principles of coordinated behavior that were formulated on the basis of extensive laboratory studies of social action (Couch and Hintz, 1975). These principles, the presumption that simpler forms of coordination necessarily preceded more complex forms, and data provided by archaeologists, ethnographers and historians are combined to offer an account of the emergence of civilizations. The argument is advanced that through transactions between human collectivities and transactions between human beings and their environments, complex temporal structures and complex composite forms of sociation emerged that transformed the nature of human existence.

Chapter I offers the frame of analysis employed. Chapter II attends to the acquisition of simple temporal structures by infants; Chapter III deals with how children acquire more complex temporal structures, the ability to produce the basic elements of sociation, and the ability to symbolically sequence their behavior. Chapter IV presents ethnographic accounts of the temporal structures of contemporary primitive groups and Marshack's (1972) analysis of ancient calendric systems. These four chapters emphasize temporal structures.

The next section—Chapters V, VI, VII, and VIII—focus on the emergence of more complex elements of sociation. Consideration is given to bargaining, the emergence of markets, sedentary communities, and urbanism. The emergence of these forms of sociation allowed for the expansion of interdependence and transformed the nature of relatedness between collectivities and within collectivities. The emergence and expansion of the exchange relation was accompanied by the rise of individualistic temporal structures and an attenuation of solidary relatedness.

Chapters IX, X, XI, and XII detail the establishment of food production, the growth and expansion of agriculture, and forms of relatedness associated with agricultural production. Chapter IX specifies how sedentism provided the social and ecological conditions necessary for the domestication of grains and animals. Chapter X argues that agriculture became a pervasive way of life primarily through colonization. In Chapters XI and XII a reconstruction of the social structures of ancient agricultural communities is offered. Special attention is given to the extension of temporal structures and the position of specialists in timekeeping in these societies.

The emergence of more complex temporal structures and modes of sociation were accompanied by the formation of abstract symbol systems—arithmetic and geometry. These symbol systems allowed for the development of complex bodies of information. Chapters XIII and XIV offer an account of the growth of these symbol systems and bodies of abstract knowledge. The bodies of knowledge were generated by specialists who were supported by their communities and communal concerns.

Chapters XV, XVI, and XVII address the emergence of enduring authoritarian and totalitarian social structures. Chapter XV reconstructs the rise of administrative units; Chapter XVI assesses the part conflict, coercion, and conquest played in the formation of complex social structures; and, in Chapter XVII, the merger that occurred in some ancient civilizations of specialists in timekeeping, administrative specialists, and specialists in centralized coercion is examined.

Chapters XVIII, XIX, and XX move into the "historical" eras. Chapter XVIII examines how the amount and nature of information available was transformed with literacy. Special attention is given to the emergence of classical Greece in Chapter XIX. The civilization of the ancient Greeks had some distinctive features, but its emergence had many parallels with the emergence of other more ancient civilizations. The last chapter examines modern civilization. Its emergence and spread followed much the same pattern as that of several other ancient civilizations. One of its distinctive features was the mechanization of time.

Many have read parts or all of earlier drafts. Those I am aware of include Frank Kohout, Stephen Wieting, Monica Hardesty, Michael Katovich, Marvin Krohn, Frank Kosier, John Fixx, Norman Denzin, Glen Vernon, Barbara Sink, John O'Shea, Thomas Charleton, Robert Hulbarry, Paul Durenberger, Jeanette Sherboundy, Joel Powell, Lloyd Gehring, Glenda Sehested, Mary A. Smith, Clark McPhail, David Maines and Joan Lind. Some expressed strong disagreements with some ideas. I appreciate that. They stimulated thought. If in this draft I have failed to convince them of the merits of my formulation, that is my deficiency. Rebecca Couch provided information about and interpretations of Egyptian-Greek contacts; several of the ideas offered in Chapter XIX are hers.

A special note of thanks is due those archaeoastronomers and archaeologists whose data I have used. I am sure some of them will think I have abused and misused their data. There are several instances where I have offered an interpretation of data that is at some variance with either an explicit or implicit interpretation that was offered by those who uncovered and offered data about ancient ways of life. I make no apology for such reinterpretations. New understandings can be acquired from both a close familiarity with data and examining data from some distance. It is the latter standpoint that I have taken.

A few years ago I attended a conference of Mesoamerican archaeology. At the end of one of the sessions I engaged one of the archaelogists in a conversation, querying him about some details of the site he had excavated. I had introduced myself by name, but after a few questions he asked "What's your name?" He then followed up with asking where I had been in the field. I confessed that I was not an archaeologist, but one of those who some referred to as a grand synthesizer. "Oh, a slinger of bullshit" was his response. I appreciate his position, but am convinced that reconceptualization is as important a part of the intellectual enterprise as is the accumulation of data.

Carl J. Couch

Chapter I

Frame of Analysis

The central theme of this statement is that the temporal structures and forms of sociation that human beings have constructed are two of the keys to an explanation of both the emergence and the nature of civilizations. All human behavior except the most primitive responses to impingements has a temporal dimension. All social activity also has a relational dimension. All relations have a temporal dimension. The many varieties of social structures that human beings have constructed reflect various intertwinings of temporality and forms of sociation.

All structured human behavior is timeful. Walking, conversing, celebrating, and building a house all have duration. In addition, to move from one location to another in a structured manner or to converse with another requires using the past in the ongoing present to project a future. The production of structured activity requires that persons relate the ongoing present to a projected future. When persons cannot project a future or cannot relate the present to the projected future action becomes disorganized. The production of all structured activity from learning to walk to the coordination of the affairs of a nation requires the prior acquisition of sequenced pasts. Sequenced pasts provide the foundation necessary for the projection of a structured future.

The production of coordinated action by a dyad or larger unit requires that those who are jointly organizing their activity to use their pasts in the present to project a shared future. Coordinated activity is only possible when persons indicate to each other a future line of action and detect each other's projected future. Projected shared futures are necessary for all organized social action. This is the case if the action undertaken is as simple as two persons walking together or as complex as a nation readying itself for an invasion.

It is the ability of human beings to project distal futures—futures beyond the immediate encounter—that allows them to construct social structures. Those without the ability to project distal futures are capable

1

of coordinating their actions with another in the immediate encounter, but they cannot create a social structure. Coordinated social action is dependent upon the projection of at least a proximal—immediate—future, but the construction and maintenance of social structures requires in addition the establishment of distal futures (Hintz and Couch, 1975).

Before individuals or groups can structure their action they must acquire sequenced pasts. Series of sequenced pasts allow for the anticipation of sequenced futures. After sequenced pasts have been acquired, then they may be used to structure or organize action. When it is impossible to anticipate the future it is impossible to produce organized action. Activity becomes chaotic. If human beings cannot project shared futures the only possible social action is apathy, panic, the chase, or conflict. The projection of a shared future is a necessary element of all coordinated action.

There are many levels of temporality. They range in complexity and duration from a young infant moving his head to avoid the approaching nipple, through an athletic team practicing its timing, to complex programming of the future by the administrators of a factory. When human beings cannot or do not temporally structure their activity, no social order is possible. Or, when there is no temporality there is no social structure.

Human beings have devised many different levels of temporality. The complex intertwinings of these levels provides one of the foundations for the many different types of social order. The complexity of the social order of a group or society is constrained by the complexity of the temporal structures at the command of the members. If only temporal structures of limited duration are available then only a simple social structure is possible. However, the presence of complex temporal structures within a group or society does not assure the construction of a complex social structure.

Not only does temporality provide the foundation for ordered human activity, but there is a sequential order in the acquisition of levels of temporality. In the development of each person and the evolution of the human species simple levels of temporality are acquired before complex levels of temporality are established. The infant must learn to time his activity with his environment before he can learn to project shared futures with another. The complex levels of timing of activity based upon numeric calendars was preceded by millennia during which societies used observations of celestial bodies to structure their activities.

The establishment of a more complex level of temporality both transformed, and to an extent replaced, the simpler forms of temporality. The acquisition of the ability to symbolically sequence the future not only establishes an additional procedure for structuring activity, but it also encases or contextualizes simpler forms of timing, and to an extent replaces the more primitive forms of timing. In a similar manner when societies developed numeric calendars, observations of the winter solstice were transformed and to an extent replaced.

The various levels and forms of temporality were the backbone of the social structure of the societies that developed and used them. If all the procedures for timing activity were removed from a group, the persons constituting the society would remain, but they would be incapable of coordinated action. The situation would be similar to removing the backbone from a vertebrate. The bulk of the organism would remain, but it would be incapable of organized behavior. In a similar manner if all temporality were removed from a society, the bulk of the social organism would remain, but it would be incapable of acting with directionality. The system would collapse.

A second set of dimensions is how persons fit their individual lines of action together to construct courses of social action. Both the slave and master and two friends project immediate and distal futures when they coordinate their activity. However, the nature of the relatedness that prevails between the two sets of dyads is fundamentally different (Miller, Weiland, and Couch, 1978).

All forms of coordinated action require that the units producing the coordinated action attend to each other, be responsive to each other, and project lines of action that are detected by the other. Furthermore, they must establish a shared focus, or a series of them, and a social objective (Miller, Hintz, and Couch, 1975). However, there is tremendous variation in how these primitive elements of sociation can be combined. The attentiveness and responsiveness of each to the other may be relatively symmetrical or they may be highly asymmetrical. Friends typically are equally attentive and responsive to each other. The slave is typically highly attentive and responsive to the master with the master only attentive and responsive enough to the slave to assure retention of control of the slave's behavior.

Many combinations of forms of association have been developed. For example, the basic forms of sociation that constitute cooperative behavior can be combined with the elements of competitive behavior to construct mixed motive encounters. Bargaining is both a cooperative and a competitive act.

Asymmetrical forms of sociation may be encased by a distal future. The slave-master relation may endure for a lifetime. Or, an asymmetrical form of sociation may be limited to an immediate future. In an emergency one person may assume command of the situation and direct the behavior of all others. Symmetrical forms of sociation may be encased by a projected future of extended duration or of exceedingly short duration.

It is the complex intertwinings of stabilized temporal structures and forms of sociation that constitute the basic elements of all social structures. However, as human action is continuous, social structures are constantly changing. Some elements of a social structure endure for generations and even millennia. Other elements change rapidly. On many occasions social structures that have endured for extended durations collapsed catastrophically. Social structures are only relatively enduring modes of relatedness that have been established and used by human beings to coordinate their actions. They are human constructs and thereby continuously subject to change and transformation.

PARADIGMS

Those who have attempted to ferret out abstract principles to array their experiences have developed many different conceptual frameworks. These include formulations of magical, religious, and scientific principles. All are efforts to detect, understand, and articulate complex sets of experiences. They differ not so much in what they attempt to explain, but in how they attempt to explain observed events. Each offers a standpoint to take toward phenomena (Couch, 1982).

One of the distinctive features of the scientific framework is the priority assigned to phenomena. The magical and religious paradigms assign greater priority to nonsensory elements, regarding the sensory experiences as but crude manifestations of more fundamental but nonobservable phenomena. A scientific paradigm presumes that if a phenomenon can be repetitively observed but fails to fit with established dictums it is necessary to reorganize the formulations that have been offered to incorporate the phenomena. Empiricism is the cornerstone of scientific explanations.

Many paradigms have been developed to provide an explanation of empirical events. The most ancient and comprehensive one is the cyclical (mechanistic) paradigm. In its modern form the cyclical paradigm derives from Newton. However, it has a more ancient tradition.

The cyclical paradigm is sometimes characterized as timeless. It is not. However, the temporality of the cyclical paradigm is of a special sort. Namely, that each present and each future is a re-occurrence of a past: sequences of events are completely repetitious. The cyclical paradigm denies the phenomena of transformations, emergences, and disintergrations—the future is closed.

The cyclical paradigm does provide a framework that allows for the detection and articulation of many principles. However, some changes are not completely redundant. Noncyclical changes have been noted since the recording of history. The cyclical paradigm can only be retained as viable by the denial of many phenomena, or by the characterization of some phenomena as insignificant.

The cyclical paradigm was challenged by the research of early geologists and chemists. They noted that not all changes were cyclical, that some changes were transformations. The early formulations of this paradigm specified that some events occurred in a linear manner instead of cyclically; namely, A must occur before B and B must occur before C and when A and B combine to form C, it is not necessarily followed by A.

Perhaps the most distinctive contribution of the transformational paradigm was the implicit presumption that a greater understanding of phenomena could be acquired by giving special attention to the processes of transformation, by noting the sequences of events that are critical when one form transforms into another. This development directed concern from the observation and specification of the nature of objects and events to the observation and specification of the processes of transformation.

The evolutionary paradigm incorporated noncyclical transformations. It acknowledged novelty; that is, events and objects emerged that were distinct from previous events and objects. In addition, it explicitly attended to emergence and disintegration. It was originally formulated to account for organic phenomena. It was developed and accepted as it became recognized that neither the cyclical nor the transformational paradigms offered an adequate framework for the study of organic phenomena.

It noted that chaos or variability, to use Darwin's term, was ever present; that chaotic events combined with ordered events and novel forms appeared. One of the central questions became: How does order—regularity—combine with variability—chaos—to produce a new order?

It was by combining Mendelian principles with Darwinian principles that it was possible to provide an explanation for both emergence and continuity. The explanations offered were in terms of the transmission of information from one generation to the next and the interaction between a species and its environment. This mode of thought specifies that not only do organisms exist in time, but that in addition, the genetic code of past generations informs the present generation. Yet at the same time there is the recognition that as species interact with their environment the content of the information undergoes some transformation which gives rise to novel forms.

Many of the early social scientists offered explanations by applying the evolutionary paradigm to human conduct. The paradigm became discredited among social scientists. In part its demise was the consequence of a vulgar interpretation of the paradigm. Specifically, the intepretation that the paradigm inherently implies progress, that movement toward greater complexity was predetermined, and that evolution was unilinear. Consequently many observers of human conduct rejected it as viable for the analysis of human activity.

However, devolution is a significant feature of the evolutionary paradigm. Some transformations are in the direction of simplicity. The emergence of a more complex form does not assure that that form will endure. It may devolve into a simpler form. However, before devolution can occur, evolution must have taken place.

Directionality is not an inherent part of the paradigm; it does not predict the future. The only prediction, and it is an implicit one, is that transformations will continue, that constancy will not prevail. This feature of evolutionary thought is captured in the statement of three wise men when charged with the task of formulating an everlasting truth. They offered: "This too will pass."

Multilinear changes were an integral facet of Darwin's formulation. He only presumed that all life stemmed from a common source, not that all life had evolved in the same direction.

More or less simultaneous with the emergence of the evolutionary paradigm, the positivistic mode of thought came to the fore. It equated scientific analysis with determinism: all scientific propositions must reflect a predetermined order. Positivism was transformed into logical positivism. This development stressed the "logical" structure of propositions, the correspondence of propositions to "reality," and that reality consisted of the simplest observable phenomena. Phenomena that could not be fitted into this framework were defined as epiphenomena. Variability (chaotic events) and emergences were denied significance.

The evolutionary paradigm and the positivistic mode of thought competed for center stage. Positivism became predominant among philosophers. Many social scientists attempted to force their observations of human conduct into the positivistic mode of thought. Nonetheless the evolutionary paradigm changed human consciousness about the past. It extended the past and called for the sequential ordering of the past. Perhaps more importantly the belief in an ever-changing world posited by it was followed by the development of a consciousness that perhaps it was possible to exercise some control over future developments.

The evolutionary paradigm has been effectively used by many students of social life. However, it became apparent that the evolutionary paradigm did not provide an adequate account of the continuity and changes of societies. It was combined with the learning paradigm to provide a more adequate account.

In the latter part of the nineteenth century and the early part of the twentieth century the learning paradigm emerged. It was developed partially in response to the failure of other paradigms to provide an adequate explanation of behavior. To the extent that behavior had been previously attended to, it had been explained as flowing from the "nature of the organism." Cats hunted mice because that was their nature; some human groups were peaceful and others were warlike because that was their nature. Many of the earliest attempts to explain both the behavior of other animals and human beings attempted to specify associations between behavior and biological variables. These efforts achieved a degree of success, but it became evident that not all behavior flowed from the "nature of the organism."

The learning paradigm made its unit of analysis an organism capable of movement within an environment. Organisms acquired structured behavior through their transactions with their environment (Mead, 1934). Many different theories of learning were formulated. They ranged from those of Freud, who attempted to explain the variation in behavior of different individuals on the basis of dramatic childhood experiences in conjunction with mechanisms of repression, to the classical conditioning theory of Pavlov. In all there was the presumption that behavior acquired structure in transactions between organisms and their environment.

Nearly all theories of learning, ranging from the classical conditioning theories to Freudian theories, presume the stucture acquired through organism-environment transactions operates in the same manner as the genetic structure. Namely, the past organizes or structures the future. Once the structure was acquired, subsequent behavior was presumed to directly reflect that structure, just as growth patterns after birth were regarded as directly reflecting the genetic information the organism acquired as the consequence of the intermix of genes acquired from its parents, plus any variation that was the consequence of mutations.

However, no concept equivalent to mutation was made a viable part of the learning paradigm. Rather the presumption was that organisms acquired structures in the form of habits or personalities. These structures were different from the structures of genetic information only in how they were acquired.

Many theories of learning have been combined with the genetic structure aspect of the evolutionary paradigm to explain human behavior. One offshoot of these efforts has been the continuing quarrel between those who offer an explanation of behavior on the basis of genetic information and those offering explanations based upon learning processes.

The learning paradigm is a powerful framework for explaining much of human conduct. All social scientists (there may be an exception or two) accept some form of the learning paradigm as a framework for explaining some human conduct. Others take the position that the learning paradigm offers an adequate framework for a complete understanding of human conduct.

One of the deficiencies of most theories of learning is their failure to incorporate the functional equivalent of mutations. Most theories of learning instead incorporate the determinism of the cyclical paradigm—the tenet that all sequences of events are completely repetitious. The failure to demonstrate complete predictability is commonly regarded as an inadequacy of measurement or failure to specify the correct phenomena.

One possibility for explaining variations in behavior is to note changes in the genetic structure. That may provide a means for explaining variations in the behavior of rats, pigeons, and dogs, but it is not adequate for an explanation of the emergences and disintegrations of social structures. There have been no modifications of genetic structures that could account for the emergences of cities or the demise of nations. Explanations of these phenomena require the formulation of a more comprehensive paradigm.

THE CONSTRUCTIONARY PARADIGM

Social activity is not ordered on the basis of mass-energy transformations, nor is it structured by genetically transmitted information, nor can social order be accounted for on the basis of habits acquired in organism-environment transactions. The social structures constructed by human beings are constrained by mass-energy limitations, their genetic structure, and learning capacity; but these dimensions neither structure social activity nor determine the form of social structures.

The constructionary paradigm presumes that human beings use their pasts to organize their futures. The past informs the present and future, but does not determine either. The learning paradigm implicitly acknowledges that locomoting organisms equipped with distance perceptors—sight, sound, and smell—acquire sequenced pasts that are used to anticipate the future. Further, that when the future can be anticipated action is organized in part on the basis of the anticipated future.

That particular feature of behavior is excluded from many studies of learning. Electric shock and air puffs are two of the favorite stimuli of experimental psychologists. One of the distinctive features of these two stimuli is that they cannot be anticipated with precision or certainty. The impingement stemming from these two stimuli are always somewhat of a surprise.

The design of many studies of experimental psychologists excludes anticipations and intentions. The only temporal dimensions operative are the past and the present. The future is excluded. The informational structure attended to is equivalent to that attended to by those who study the transmission of genetic information. The participants in the study, whether mice, rats, or human beings, can only use their past to respond to the present. The design of the studies attempts to rule out the future. Of course, the designs are not completely successful. All organisms that have acquired sequenced pasts almost continuously project futures and organize their actions in part on the basis of the projected future. The unsophisticated cat may leap to where the mouse is a few times, but it quickly learns to anticipate futures, and to use those anticipated futures in the organization of its behavior.

Human beings, like all other organisms capable of learning, learn to anticipate and to organize themselves on the basis of those anticipations. They thereby construct their action and act upon their environment as well as respond to it.

Furthermore, human beings are capable of anticipations of considerable duration. They can anticipate distal futures as well as proximal futures and initiate actions to bring distal futures to fruition. In addition, through the use of significant symbols, human beings are capable of projecting distal shared futures and jointly organizing their actions to facilitate the occurrence of the projected futures.

Some behavior is merely a response that is the combination of a structure acquired in the past (a habit) and the stimulus in the ongoing present. However, much behavior is intentionally produced. Namely, the organism projects a future and then organizes its action in part on the basis of that projected future. Not all behavior is merely patterned responses to unfolding events that is structured by habits.

Intentionality is a viable part of much of human conduct. However, not all human conduct is isomorphic with intentions. Incompetency and the impingement of unanticipated events frequently prevent the completion of the intended action. One consequence of the interface between intentions and accomplishments is that intentions are constantly reformulated.

Each time there is a clash between intentions and an unanticipated impingement a historical accident occurs. The scope of historical accidents range from when a person who is solving a problem for the hundredth time has his intention deflected and notes something he had not previously noted, to citizens of two nations making unintended contact. Usually nothing of significance flows from historical accidents. However, on occasions historical accidents are followed by sweeping transformations that become stabilized. Columbus's attempt to establish a trade route with China was an intentional act. However, it culminated in a historical accident of major proportions that had great consequences for humanity.

Historical accidents are analogous to mutations. When a mutation occurs it combines with an established genetic structure to produce a new biological form. When a historical accident occurs, intentionally organized activity combines with unanticipated events to produce novel behavior. Very few mutations and very few historical accidents are consequential.

Both are predictable only within broad probabilities. It is unlikely that a rattlesnake will hatch that has five legs; the birth of five-legged mammals is not unknown. The series of historical accidents that culminated in ancient totalitarian states did not occur among nomadic food gatherers. Several totalitarian states emerged, but each time they emerged in large sedentary communities with a pre-existing social structure of considerable complexity.

Only a few mutants survive, of those only a very few are capable of reproduction. Very few historical accidents are followed by the establishment of a new pattern of behavior; of those, very few are transmitted to subsequent generations or diffused to other social units. Most mutations and historical accidents fade with no trace. However, a very few endure.

The establishment of a given structure does not assure the survival of a society or its members. Some structures facilitate survival more than others. The formulation and use of novel temporal structures and forms of sociation sometimes allows human beings to render their existence somewhat less problematic.

All social structures evidence both continuity and change. Although a few have endured for millennia, continuity is more problematic than variation. Sometimes transformations occur in an incremental fashion; other times transformations, especially disintegrations, have been cataclysmic. The civilization of the Olmec emerged through a series of incremental changes, but its demise was a cataclysmic event.

Not all transformations are the consequence of historical accidents. On occasions human groups have intentionally formulated alternative social structures and then organized themselves to produce those social structures. Even then some unanticipated events usually occur.

When human beings intentionally construct novel social structures they use their individual and collective pasts to project alternative futures and then use their imaginations to assess the consequences of the pro-

jected alternatives. They are thereby recombining information and re-
soures to construct novel social structures.

Continuity of social structure is maintained largely through learning.
Each generation acquires much of the information of their ancestors
and uses that information to structure their life. Biological evolution and
social development have produced human organisms that have a tremendous capacity for learning. Learning has replaced biological inher-
itance as the procedure for maintaining continuity. During periods of
dependency the young are exposed to a social order that they accept
and use to organize their lives.

Collective memories and learning within a social context that provides
sustenance and protection are essential facets of human life. If each
human organism were required to learn the behavior necessary to survive through transactions with the nonhuman aspects of its environment,
the human species would not survive.

Once a pattern of behavior has been established within a group, then
it is possible not only to transmit that pattern to following generations,
but to transmit it to other social units. Diffusion then is a special type
of learning. It is learning that crosses social boundaries, not generations.
The transmission of information across social boundaries often stimulates additional formulations.

Human beings both respond to their environment and construct it.
In general, the more complex the social structure they have constructed,
the less vulnerable they are to the nonconstructed elements of their
environment. However, lessened vulnerability to the nonconstructed elements sometimes prevents human groups from being responsive enough
to the nonconstructed elements to survive in the changing environment.

A NOTE ON METHODS

The specification of temporal sequences is a necessary feature of all
scientific principles. Astronomers specify the order of celestial events,
chemists specify the sequence of events that constitute a transformation,
and biologists specify the temporal order of genetic transformations. An
explanation of the emergence of civilizations must specify the sequential
appearance of the critical phenomena. That is often difficult.

Recent developments allow for far more accurate specification of sequence than was possible a few decades ago. However, many problems
remain. There are many disputes that center on dating. These disputes
are not addressed. Future work may result in a somewhat different
sequence than that presented. One of the sources of difficulty is that

some of the critical developments may have occurred simultaneously. For example, the assessment is made that sedentary life, which was a critical junction in the emergence of civilizations, rested primarily on a foundation of intercommunity trade, not agriculture, and further that agriculture followed trade. It may prove to be the case that the long-held tenet of anthropologists that the domestication of plants and animals was the foundation for sedentary communities is valid. It is also possible that agriculture and intercommunity trade networks appeared simultaneously.

The emergence of these two traditions may be a case of the chicken and the egg. The two traditions may have been twin born. However, it seems more likely the development was on the order of whether reptiles or mammals appeared first. It was reptiles that provided the foundation for the subsequent emergence of mammals, not mammals for reptiles. Similarly it appears that intergroup trade networks provided the foundation for the development of agriculture.

When mammals appeared reptiles did not discontinue evolving. They continued to evolve, but now their evolution occurred within an environment that included mammals. Consequently their evolution took a somewhat different form. In a similar manner with the establishment of food producing communities, trade centers and trade networks continued to evolve, but now their developments took a different form.

Devolution complicates the task. The residents of Rome in 1000 A.D. retained some social forms that reflected the social structure of the Roman Empire; these items were intertwined with elements that had recently developed. Those groups that are descendants of ancestors with more complex social structures are comparable to feral plants. Feral plants are the descendants of domestic ones that have escaped from human care and have reproduced in the wild. They complicate the efforts of botanists to specify the wild ancestors of domesticated plants and to determine the stages of the transformation from a wild plant into a domestic one.

A similar problem is created by diffusion. Simpler societies have frequently taken on elements acquired from more complex ones. The practices acquired in this manner may be maintained by a society so long as it has contact with a more complex one without the host society having the ability to produce or maintain the item. For example, several relatively simple societies of Southeast Asia used the Chinese calendar to adjust their own simpler calendar. These societies did not develop a numeric calendar, yet they routinely used a numeric calendar. The general trend has been from simple societies to complex ones, but devolution and diffusion combined with uncertainty of dating often makes it difficult to determine sequences with certainty. The specification of the sequential order of the appearance of temporal structures and forms of sociation among human groups is based on limited data. Only a few artifacts and tracings remain of ancient societies. The more ancient the group, the fewer tracings. These tracings do not provide us with much information about the social structures of those who made the artifacts and tracings. Ethnographic descriptions of contemporary primitive groups are used to "flesh out" the archeaological data. The use of ethnographic data to characterize the lives of those who made the artifacts and tracings is fraught with many pitfalls. Similarity of artifacts does not necessarily indicate similarity of social structure.

These factors render the specification of the sequential order of the development of temporal structures and forms of sociation analogous to attempting to determine the relative location of a number of objects by viewing them through a maze of shifting mirrors. Future research will stabilize some of the mirrors through which we view the past, but a large element of uncertainty will remain an inherent part of reconstructions of the past.

SUMMARY

The theme developed in this statement focuses on temporal structures and forms of sociation to explain the formation of complex social structures. Any statements of principles of human conduct must attend to temporal dimensions. Not only does human action occur over time, but social processes and relationships are produced by human beings using their pasts in the present to project futures. The nature of the past both constrains and facilitates the projection of futures.

The world of human beings is in part one of their own construction; human beings both impinge upon and are impinged upon by their environment. Both the construction of social relations, and the construction of relations between human beings and their environment, entail human beings acquiring and developing several forms of timefulness. The development of complex temporal structures was accompanied by the creation of more elaborate forms of sociation.

The emergence of civilizations followed an evolutionary trajectory. The evolution of biological species took place through a series of incremental changes over millions of years. Many of the changes that resulted in the emergence of civilizations also took place through a series of incremental changes. However, the fact that human beings can acquire vast amounts of information in a multitude of ways allows them to construct cataclysmic changes within an extremely short period.

Novel social structures were often the outcome of historical accidents interacting with extant social structures. However, some modifications of social structures have been the consequence of intentional action. Human beings can use their past to inform the present and imagine alternative social structures. That allows them to intentionally construct novel structures. Whether novel structures were created as the consequence of historical accidents, or by intention, or by a combination of the two, the simpler structures necessarily preceded the more complex. However, the transformations did not always precede from the simpler to the more complex; devolution from complex structures to simpler ones has been a common occurrence.

Chapter II

The Infant and His Environment

Animals are not timeful at birth. They become timeful by transacting with their environment. Temporality emerges as organisms experience two sequential events — two differentiated experiences in tandem. The production of sequences of experience requires either movement on the part of the organism, or on part of the environment, or both. Some sequences are the consequences of two or more experiences derived through the same sensory mode; others are based on experiences derived from different sensory modes (Leichty, 1975). The infant may first experience a slight touch followed by firm tactile contact, or he may first visually note a movement followed by tactile contact.

The most primitive sequences of experiences are based upon tactile contact with the environment. All animals, even the most simple one-celled animals, respond to experiences based on tactile contact. Tactility is the first external sensory mode to develop, both in evolution and in the life trajectory of animals. Newborn infants respond to tactile contact. However, so long as the behavior is only a response to tactile contact it is not timeful. Behavior only becomes timeful after repetitive sequences of tactile stimulation. Repetitive sequences allows organisms to anticipate event 2 upon experiencing event 1 of a sequence.

Temporality based upon sequences of tactile experience provide only a very limited structure for the organism's subsequent experiences. However, with the acquisition of temporality on this restricted level the organism can, upon experiencing event 1 of a sequence, organize itself in anticipation of a future event. The degree of control the organism exercises over its experience, when sequences are limited to tactile experiences, is very small. Yet, to the extent an organism can organize itself to avoid or to receive the anticipated second event, the action is timeful.

With the development of the visual and auditory modes, sequences based upon a combination of experiences acquired through visual, auditory, and tactile modes can be acquired. Those sequences that include

15

experiences acquired through the distance perceptors can have greater duration than those acquired from only tactile contact. Subsequent to participating in sequences of events wherein a specific visual experience is followed by specific tactile experience, the infant, upon visually detecting an event, can then organize himself for the anticipated tactile experience. This is but one of several possible combinations.

The infant is exposed to a multitude of experiences involving complex combinations of the sensory modes that are highly varied in their complexity and order. Sometimes he experiences tactile contact with another before seeing or hearing the other; other times he sees or hears the other before tactile contact. If the infant is to become timeful, some of the sequences of events must be repetitive. It is by participating in repetitive sequences that the infant acquires ordered pasts. His experiences thereby acquire a temporal structure.

Through the participation in repetitive sequences of experiences involving at least one of the distance perceptors, the infant acquires the ability to organize himself for impending tactile contact. When the infant, upon experiencing the first event of a repetitive sequence, responds with a level of excitation greater than previously displayed in response to the event, he can be said to have acquired timefulness. For example, when the parent appears in the visual range of the infant, and the infant wiggles in anticipation of forthcoming tactile contact, he is responding to an anticipated future. His behavior is no longer simply a response to the immediate ongoing present. Rather, he is using his past to organize himself toward the future.

The earliest acquisition of timefulness by the human infant is highly dependent upon repetitive movement in the external environment. The human infant plays a relatively passive part in the acquisition of his original temporal structures. The human infant is not only dependent upon others for protection, material needs, and nurturing, but is also dependent upon others producing repetitive sequences of experiences for him if he is to acquire a temporal structure of any complexity. If the activity the infant's caretakers take toward the infant is chaotic, then the infant cannot acquire a sequenced past. He would remain incapable of anticipating future events.

The original anticipations of the infant are of extremely short duration and consist of two differentiated experiences. Through participation in sequences of greater complexity the duration of anticipations is extended. Early and simple anticipations become elaborated and modified by continued participation in the transactions between the infant and his environment.

Once acquired, anticipations are subject to extinction. When a particular event 1 is no longer followed by event 2, then subsequently the infant will no longer anticipate event 2 when event 1 occurs. Temporal structures are not fixed. They are continually modified, elaborated, and extinguished.

The original timefulness of the human infant is largely dependent upon sequences of activity occurring in its environment. Most, but not all of these early repetitive sequences are initiated by the caretakers of the infant. Other repetitive sequences also occur as the infant interacts with his environment. When these are repetitive, they too can be the basis for the acquisition of anticipations.

INTENTIONALITY

Some sequences of experiences are the consequences of initiations of the infant. The infant produces movement, flailing his arms and crying, then has a subsequent experience. The helplessness of the newborn human infant greatly restricts the complexity of sequences of experiences resulting from his own movement. Nonetheless when the infant moves his limbs or cries and has subsequent experiences, the movement provides a base for the acquisition of sequenced events that are different than those provided by the other initiating action toward him. Temporal structures based on the infant's initiation provide the foundation for the development of intentionality.

Some of these movements, especially crying, are assigned significance by caretakers. When the infant cries, he sometimes elicits activity on the part of his caretakers. When the activity of the infant is responded to in a repetitive manner the infant can acquire the ability to produce a particular act at time 1 to produce a particular consequence at time 2. Intentionality is the consequence of a sequence resulting from action by the infant that is repeatedly followed by a specific experience, whereas simple anticipations are based on sequences of experiences provided by the external environment.

The original activity that provides the foundation for intentionally produced sequences are responses to internal and external stimulations—they are not timeful activities. It is only when the infant produces event 1 of a sequence with the anticipation that event 2 will follow that the activity is intentional.

The content of these sequences is varied. The significant dimensions for the emergence of intentionality is not the content of the behaviors. Rather, it is that they are part of a repetitive sequence. Namely, a given act produced by the infant is subsequently followed by a specific experience by the infant. Most, but again not all, of these sequenced experiences are dependent upon the infant being a part of a social environment that is organized to be responsive to the initiations of the infant. If other human beings are not responsive to the activity of the infant only extremely limited intentionalities can be acquired.

When the infant moves his arm and experiences contact with a facet of his material environment a degree of intentionality can be acquired. He can learn that if he moves his arm in a given manner a certain experience follows. The duration of intentionality acquired in this manner is quite limited. The earliest intentionalities of any substantial duration acquired by the human infant necessarily involve sequences of activities produced by others. The sequences based on subsequent contact with the material environment tend to be limited to simple sequences; those that involve the responses of adults can be very complex.

The contribution of the human infant to the early sequences that provide the basis for the emergence of intentionality is relatively minor in comparison to that of mammals capable of considerable mobility early in life. For example, the newborn calf is capable of much more complex activity shortly after birth than is the human infant. Consequently, the temporal structure acquired by mammals capable of considerable movement shortly after birth is to a greater extent the consequence of their own movement than is the case for the human infant.

When a sequence is initiated by movement on the part of the infant, kinetic experiences are an integral part of the sequences. In the production of activity the infant not only acquires a sequence based upon the external sensory modes — sight, sound, and tactile contact — but also on the basis of internal sensory modes, especially the kinetic sense. By acting the infant provides part of his subsequent experiences for himself. He feels, hears, or sees himself move as well as experiencing his external environment. His own activity, whether crying or flailing his limbs, becomes a part of his environment (Liechty, 1975).

With the acquisition of ordered sequences that are keyed to his own initiations, the infant no longer simply anticipates. He continues to organize his activity in part on the basis of anticipations, but now these anticipations are framed by an awareness that he can exercise some control over his future experiences. When crying is produced, it is now intentionally organized to elicit a specific future. He attempts to produce a future, not simply to prepare himself for impending contact. Not only does the infant have an awareness of ordered sequences, but he has, in addition, an awareness that he can initiate a sequence.

When the infant acts and the act produced is followed by the same or similar activities on the part of others toward the infant, the infant is exercising control over his subsequent experiences on two levels. When he cries and receives attention from someone, he acquires awareness that he can influence, if not determine, some of his experiences. In addition, he also hears and feels himself cry and thereby acquires awareness that some dimensions of his experiences are the consequences of his own actions, that he can stimulate himself.

The acquisition of temporal structures is not entirely restricted to the activities of others and to self-stimulation. As the infant acts on other facets of his environment and is impinged on by his environment he also experiences sequential sets of experiences. For example, when the child grabs and holds a blanket in his hand and presses it to his face he acquires sequenced experiences. The sequences acquired in this manner are many and varied. The immobility and helplessness of human infants makes it impossible for sequences acquired in this manner to be of sufficient complexity to allow infants to acquire the complex temporal structures necessary for survival. The acquisition of complex temporal structures required for human survival is dependent upon the infant being a part of a social system that provides the necessary protection, care, and complex sequenced responses by caretakers.

A major transformation occurs when infants acquire mobility. Both biological maturation and the continual acquisition of repetitive sequential experiences underlie the emergence of mobility. Neither biological maturation nor the acquisition of repetitive sequential experiences is sufficient for the emergence of the infant's ability to exercise greater control of his own activity and experiences; both are necessary. Temporal structures are a prerequisite for the development of mobility that has directionality. With the emergence of directed mobility, sequences of greater duration and involving larger numbers of discrete experiences can be obtained.

When infants acquire mobility and temporal structures that allow them to move intentionally from location to location, then those blessed with sight and hearing can learn to organize themselves to initiate complex sequences. Immobile infants—those severely handicapped—are extremely dependent upon others to produce complex sequences if they are to acquire the ability to project futures of considerable duration. In a similar manner, those without sight or hearing are highly dependent upon others to produce complex sequences if they are to become capable of anticipating and projecting complex futures.

The acquisition of the ability of an infant to time his activity with external movement is not dependent upon any given sensory mode. However, the acquisition of sequences of any great duration is dependent upon some combination of the infant's sensory equipment, his mobility, and the activity taken by others providing a multitude of discrete experiences that are repetitive. The range of the timefulness is a function of the complexity, variety, and repetitiveness of the sequences.

The content of these sequences shapes the specific acts performed, but the content per se is relatively inconsequential for the acquisition of timefulness. What is important is the repetition of discrete and orderly sequences of experiences of different duration. It is that quality of the experiences that allows the infant to organize his action.

The ordering of the sequences is determined by neither the environment nor by the infant; rather it is the consequence of the interactions between the infant and the environment. Both are necessary for the production of sequenced experiences, and neither is sufficient for their production. The infant produces one-half of the equation and the environment produces the other half. Furthermore, the acquisition of sequences does not assure that the infant will subsequently and automatically produce his "half" of the equation when an event occurs in the environment, nor that the environment will produce its "half" of the equation when the infant initiates a sequence.

Once the infant has acquired the ability to anticipate and to act with intentionality, not all subsequent activity becomes orderly. All through life human beings continue to have experiences that are distinct from previous sequences. However, once temporal structures have been acquired with a fair degree of complexity, and an unanticipated event occurs, we usually attempt to "make sense" of the event by ferreting out its temporal location. When we hear an unanticipated loud noise we attempt to make sense of it by determining what preceded the noise— what caused the noise; and/or by attempting to assess the future consequences of the event. Not all unanticipated events become of concern. Some are judged to be of no consequence and dismissed with no attempt made to locate them in a temporal sequence.

To locate an event within a temporal sequence requires an active effort. The infant, or other organism, that has the ability to locate events sequentially does not always temporally locate events. Even as adults we sometimes float through our experiences without attempting to place them in a sequence. In short, the acquisition of temporal structures does not automatically make all subsequent experiences timeful.

CONSCIOUSNESS OF TEMPORALITY

If the sequences of experience of an organism were entirely redundant, an almost impossible condition, an organism could acquire the ability to anticipate, but it could not become conscious of its sequenced experiences. The acquisition of consciousness (awareness) of sequenced experiences requires both repetitiveness and variation. If all sequenced experiences were redundant, the organism could acquire the behavioral pattern of responding to event 1 by organizing itself for event 2, but would be unaware of organizing its behavior. A habit could be acquired but not consciousness. It is the interface between variation and repetitiveness that is critical for the emergence of consciousness.

Repetitiveness and variation are a matter of degree. Some of our experiences are very repetitive and others are unique. The repetitive experiences provide the base for the acquisition of temporal structures, but it is sequences that contain some variation that provide the base for conscious sequencing. As adults we produce the repetitive sequence of turning a doorknob and pulling the door open before attempting to proceed through the door. The acts produced in this sequence are so repetitive that we typically produce them without consciousness of the sequence. We produce such activity habitually. On occasion, either due to our incompetency or external conditions, the habitually projected sequence is not completed. When it is not completed, we become conscious of the necessary sequence.

When there is variation in a habitually produced sequence it allows the projection of alternative future sequences. However, before awareness of the production of sequences can arise, the infant must have a past of participating in repetitive sequences. Then with the occurrence of variation, awareness of sequencing can arise. When there is awareness of variation, a necessary condition for the projection of alternative sequenced futures is then present. With awareness of alternatives the infant can, when a given activity is not followed by an anticipated sequence, produce a modified version of an act in an effort to initiate the sequence. If upon crying, the anticipated experiences do not occur, he can organize himself to cry in a different manner—louder or in short bursts.

Consciousness of alternatives allows the infant to instruct himself, to organize himself in a different way to elicit the desired future. When this level of sophistication is reached the infant can be said to have a will. He can then willfully organize himself in an effort to produce a specific future. Behavior is no longer simply habitual or a response to external developments, it is now consciously organized. Willful action requires the projection of futures that are in part the consequence of one's own effort. The exercise of will ranges from relieving an irritating sensation by itching it, to the person who organizes himself to become the world's most famous statesman.

The exercise of will involves the conscious selection from alternatives. When activity is organized willfully the infant is a conscious initiator. He is a subject as well as an object. He consciously selects an alternative. The conscious selection of acts does not assure that the projected sequence of activity will follow. The conscious attempt to control the future provides some control of subsequent experiences, but the control is only partial. We never achieve complete control of our experiences. Unanticipated events, some of which are not controllable, frequently impinge on us.

However, with biological maturation and increasing awareness of alternatives, the human infant acquires greater control of his future. The development of the ability to manually manipulate objects, and to locomote from location to location in conjunction with increased ability to use information acquired visually and auditorily, produces a tremendous transformation in the nature of the sequences of experiences. The sequences become much more complex and of far greater duration.

MULTIPLE SEQUENCES

As we impinge on our environment and are impinged upon by it, we partake in multiple sequences. While we may be conscious of only a single sequence, other experiences also occur. It is the ability to experience multiple sequences simultaneously that provides the necessary base for acquiring awareness of duration. Some sequences consist of only two events and have a very short duration; others consist of many discrete events of considerable duration.

The ability to simultaneously experience more than one sequence allows human beings to become aware of overlapping experiences. The simultaneity of sets of sequenced experiences also provides a base for awareness that some experiences are of greater duration than others. For example, the events composing the experience of being caressed may be encased within experiences of sitting on the parent's lap—one experience occurs and fades while a second one is sustained. Multiple sequences allow for the comparison of one set of experiences with another and the development of awareness that some are of greater duration than others.

Some simultaneous sets of sequences are the consequences of multiple sets of events impinging on the infant; others are the consequences of initiations of the infant. For example, when the infant detects the presence of an object and organizes himself to crawl toward it, a sequenced future of some complexity is projected. In the process of completing the act of making contact with the object, a multitude of other sequences are produced. The sequences of placing one limb in front of the other as he locomotes toward the object are encased within the relatively long-range sequence of noting the changing relation between himself and the object.

The emergence of the most primitive awareness of duration requires simultaneously experiencing two or more sets of sequences with some overlap but of different duration. When such activities as locomoting from one location to the other are produced, the actor usually has awareness of only the extended sequences. Typically there is no awareness of the subsequences that make up the larger sequence. If a subsequence is not completed then, of course, the actor becomes conscious of the subsequence. When the subsequences are produced successfully, usually there is no awareness of them.

When there are sequences of experience of different duration and different complexity produced, then those of greater duration encase those of shorter duration. In the example given, as the child crawls, each movement of his limbs consists of a subsequence encased within the sequence of greater duration—that duration bracketed by first detecting the object and subsequent contact with the object.

Those subsequences that are encased within larger sequences become habits. As the child learns to walk, consciousness of the activity necessary to take a step recedes. These subsequences might be thought of as analogous to the inner layers of an onion encased by the outer layers. However, there is a profound differences; namely, upon the unsuccessful completion of one of the subsequences of a larger sequence, consciousness of the subsequence comes to the fore.

Through the manual manipulation of objects, the manipulation of self, and noting the consequences of his own action for his experiences and his environment, the infant acquires complex sequences of experience. Some of the sequences are in relative isolation from other experiences; others are complexly intertwined and encased within one another.

The above formulation has been presented as if sequences of experiences consisted of discrete events. Not all experiences are equally distinct. Some occur in an acute fashion and are clearly discrete from preceding and following experiences, whereas others fade from one another. Just as there is a twilight zone between day and night there is a twilight zone for many of our experiences. Some beginnings and endings of sequences are relatively definitive; others fade from one into the other.

INTERPERSONAL TIMING

Interpersonal timing underlies all social activity. The earliest activity of the infant is not social. The infant does not become a social being until he can detect and respond to the intentions of another. When two individuals note and respond to each other's intentions, they produce social activity. The construction of social activity requires that each project a sequence of activity that the other detects, and both fit their actions with the projected intentions of the other.

When the infant first intentionally organizes his acts toward another, he attempts to produce sequences of behavior in a tyrannic manner; he initiates and anticipates compliance. He cries and anticipates attention. If the caretaker is always or nearly always responsive, then the infant may become a little tyrant. This type of social activity requires the caretaker to subordinate himself to the intentions of the infant. Reciprocal behaviors are produced, but the infant is not responsive to the intentions of the caretaker.

In his interaction with his environment, the infant notes, vaguely to be sure at first, that some facets of his environment are more responsive to his initiations than others. In general, it is other human beings that are most responsive. Further, he notes that on some occasions persons are more or less immediately responsive, while on other occasions the responses of others are not immediate. The differential responsiveness of others informs the infant that others control their own actions, that the actions of others are not automatic reactions to his initiations. These variations provide the foundation for infants becoming capable of distinguishing between the human and nonhuman facets of his environment.

An important type of activity for the production of this awareness is the caretaker offering insertions. Insertions indicate that the called-for activity will not be immediately forthcoming, but may be produced later. For example, one of the earliest reciprocal acts between an infant and his caretaker might be the infant crying and then being fed by the caretaker. Subsequently, the infant may cry and the caretaker may make vocal sounds that are followed by feeding the infant. Through participating in a series of these kinds of reciprocating acts the infant becomes aware that some acts "promise" other acts will be delayed but subsequently forthcoming.

When the caretaker is differentially responsive to the initiations of the infant, the infant becomes aware that others are not automatic responders. He learns that some of the behavior of others are willfully organized by others. He learns that others control their own behavior toward him and thereby his experiences. When this level of sophistication is achieved, reciprocal activities are no longer limited to the infant initiating a sequence with the anticipation of immediate compliance. Rather a sequence is initiated and then an assessment is made by the infant of the intention of the caretaker. When the assessment of the other's intention becomes a part of the reciprocating activities, persons are then producing interpersonal timing.

To a large extent, but not entirely, the emergence of the ability to produce interpersonal timing is dependent upon the initiations of the infant and the responses of the caretaker. The helplessness of the human infant inhibits his responsiveness to the initiations of others. The caretaker may attempt to initiate sequences of acts between him and the infant, but the infant is severely limited in the responses he can make. Most of the extended sequences of acts produced between the infant and caretaker early in life are keyed to the initiations of the infant.

After the infant has acquired the ability to assess the intentions of the caretaker, then the original sequences can be elaborated. For example, the caretaker may approach the infant as if to pick him up, which may elicit the response of joyful anticipation; then the caretaker may withhold the completion of the act until after the infant has vigorously wiggled. Such "teasing" extends the number of specific acts that are produced in sequence. The projected future of the infant then is no longer restricted to an AB sequence; they can be extended to an ABABAB sequence. The temporal span of the infant is extended.

Much of the playful activity between children and their caretakers is an effort to entice children to willfully participate in extended sequences of interpersonal timing. When parents teach their children to play patty-cake, they are enticing them to take part in extended sequences of interpersonal timing. As the child learns to take part in extended units of interpersonal timing he learns on three levels. One, he learns the sequences that he is to produce; two, he learns the sequences the other is to produce; and three, he learns the sequences of activity *they* are to produce.

In the process of becoming incorporated into extended sequences of activity, the child learns both that his experiences are dependent upon the other willfully relating to him; and, the other's experiences are dependent upon his activity. Consciousness of mutual dependency emerges. The child becomes aware that not only can the other provide him with stress and joy, but also that he can offer the other stress or joy.

After a minimal level of competence in the production of interpersonal timing has been acquired, if the adult fails to produce the anticipated next act, the act is "officially" absent (Schegloff, 1968). When this first occurs the child typically reacts with the assessment that the adult failed due to incompetence. The child then often attempts to instruct the adult. The child takes a third-party standpoint toward the missing act; the same standpoint the adult has previously taken when the child failed to produce his "half" of the sequence.

As the child acquires consciousness that adults sometimes produce disruptions intentionally, he learns that he too, can disrupt the sequence. Then it is possible for both the child and adult to tease. He can then project a sequence, and when the other indicates anticipation of the projected future, withhold the promised sequence. Teasing is a complex social act that requires awareness that others anticipate and intentionally organize their behavior.

The earliest interpersonal timing is based upon sequenced and differentiated acts. Subsequent to acquiring the ability to participate in this form of social activity, and in conjunction with acquiring control of his body, the infant becomes capable of producing activity that is parallel with the activity of the caretaker. Parallel sequences are produced when both the caretaker and infant act in a similar manner more or less simultaneously. The earliest instances of parallel action often take the form of the caretaker imitating the child. An example is when the caretaker "coos" whenever the infant does.

Caretakers often entice children to act in a parallel manner with them. Examples range from attempting to get the child to babble with them through grasping the child under his armpits and attempting to get the child to "walk" with them. The degree of similarity in the action in the beginning is small. But eventually the child will acquire the ability to walk with his parents and they may make the same sounds more or less in unison.

With the acquisition of the ability to produce parallel and sequential activities with another, the child and the other acquire shared pasts. Previously when producing differentiated activities, the child acquired an individualistic past, not a shared past. It is through the joint production of parallel sequences that human beings acquire shared pasts. Consciousness of interdependency is generated when reciprocal and differentiated activities are produced. Embeddedness with others is generated when parallel sequences are produced.

Through the production of extended parallel sequences of activity, the infant acquires greater autonomy. After the child has participated in a series of these joined activities with another that center on walking, he become capable of walking by himself. He becomes independently mobile. He can than move from location to location. The child acquires a host of abilities in this manner. They range from learning to manipulate objects in the same manner as adults do, to acquiring command of vocal sounds. It is by incorporating complex sequences of behavior offered by others through the parallel alignment of behavior that each child becomes capable of acting autonomously.

Extended sequences of activity then can be produced by the individual as an individual or in conjunction with the others. For example, when the child learns to walk he can act as an individual or walk with another. The production of extended sequences of acts becomes automatic or habitual. A prototype of this phenomenon is military recruits learning to march. Those without prior skill must be told time and again how to act in unison with others. The production of coordinated sequences is at first an extremely self-conscious activity. However, after sufficient practice, extended sequences can be produced in unison with another or as an individual with little difficulty.

The acquisition of the ability to produce extended sequences allows for the emergence of long-range anticipations and intentions. Anticipation is originally restricted to the next act of a sequence. Similarly, intentionality is originally limited to the next act. However, by acquiring complex sequences of acts that can be produced habitually, then anticipations and intentions can span complex sequences of activities. The child can then project a future of considerable duration and organize himself to achieve the projected future.

SUMMARY

Timefulness is a quality that organisms with an internal source of energy that can be organized to produce movement are capable of acquiring. It is not a quality that human infants have at birth, nor is it a quality that emerges as the consequence of biological maturation. Rather, it emerges as the consequence of the transactions between the infant and the environment. The emergence of timefulness of any complexity in human infants is dependent upon a protective environment that provides the infant with repetitive sequences of experiences.

The emergence of the ability to anticipate future sequences does not require activity on the part of the infant. Anticipations can emerge as the consequence of the infant experiencing repetitive sequences provided by others. However, the emergence of intentionality of even the most primitive sort requires movement on the part of the infant that initiates repetitive sequences. The simplest and earliest forms of intentionality require that someone responds in a rather consistent manner to the initiations of the infant. If there is no consistency in the responses of others to the infant's initiations, then complex levels of intentionality cannot arise.

Through the emergence of simple anticipations and intentions in conjunction with biological maturation, the infant acquires greater control over his experiences. With the development of the ability to manually manipulate the environment and himself within the environment in conjunction with the distance perceptors—sight and sound—the infant becomes aware of relatively long-range sequenced pasts and futures. He can, then, coordinate his activity with events occurring in his environment. He thereby becomes a subject as well as an object, and he can exercise his will upon his environment.

Multiple and overlapping experiences provide the necessary base for the infant to acquire awareness of duration. Multiple and overlapping experiences also provide the base for conscious activities to become habitual activities as shorter sequences of activity become encased within longer sequences. After the shorter sequences have become habitual, they tend to become conscious activities only when unanticipated events occur that disrupt the habitual sequence.

The timefulness acquired by infants in their transactions with their environment underlies all other more complex forms of temporality. These transactions provide the first organized experiences, but in turn they are subsequently reorganized and encased within large temporal structures. It is the acquisition of temporality that allows human beings to produce structured or organized conduct. When neither anticipations nor intentionalities can be formed, there is no organized human action.

The acquisition of the awareness that others organize their activity with intentionality is dependent upon the others offering insertions. Insertions inform the other that the called-for reciprocating act is not immediately forthcoming, but may yet be produced. From a series of experiences of this sort, the child can acquire consciousness that his experiences are partially dependent on the other, and that the other's experiences are partially dependent upon the child's activity. Awareness of mutual interdependency can then emerge.

Awareness of interdependency emerges through the participation in sequences of reciprocating acts wherein each assesses the intentions of the other. When the joined activity produced is differentiated and reciprocal, no sharing can emerge. The production of joined parallel action provides the base for shared experiences. The production of parallel activities provides the foundation for persons to become embedded with each other as well as dependent upon each other. When two persons "babble together," or sing together, they are both dependent on each other and share experiences. Parallel activities involve persons acting "with" each other, as opposed to reciprocal activities involving persons acting "with respect" to each other.

Through the production of complex parallel activities children acquire the ability to project sequences of acts of considerable complexity. These extended sequences can then in turn be used to produce still more complex sequences of reciprocal acts. Parallel sequences provide a temporal span greater than sequences restricted to reciprocating and differentiated acts. Parallel sequences of interpersonal timing provide the foundation for the emergence of temporal structures of great complexity and duration.

Chapter III

Cooperative Behavior and Symbols

The complexity of cooperative behavior undertaken is limited by the complexity of the temporal structures at the command of the interactors. Children are capable of producing only simple cooperative acts. As they acquire more complex temporal structures they become capable of producing more complex units of cooperative behavior. The development of complex temporal structures and the ability to produce complex units of cooperative activity are intertwined. Human beings first learn to produce simple units of cooperative behavior, then acquire symbols which they then use to symbolically sequence their activities. The first sequences of cooperative behavior are simple coordinated acts of limited duration. These provide the foundation for the acquisition of significant symbols. Once significant symbols are mastered, they can be used to symbolically sequence futures. Only then is it possible for human beings to project complex futures of extended duration.

THE STRUCTURE OF COOPERATIVE BEHAVIOR

Cooperative behavior is a triadic phoneomen. The transactions between the infant and his environment are dyadic phenomena. More than two units may be involved, but need not be. At the minimum, the production of cooperative behavior requires two organisms capable of independent action fitting their activities together while simultaneously acting toward a third event or object—a shared focus—to achieve a social objective. When persons cooperate, they are simultaneously or intermittently attentive and responsive to each other while maintaining a shared focus. In addition, each projects a line of forthcoming activity that is noted and taken into account by the other. When future lines of action are linked to a shared focus a social objective is established. Each party is aware of the other's intention and adjusts his own activity to make it congruent with the other's intentions. When two or more persons produce units of cooperative behavior they are: (a) reciprocally attentive, (b) mutually responsive, (c) project congruent lines of action, (d) establish a shared focus, and (e) project a social (shared) objective (Miller, Hintz, and Couch, 1975).

When two persons cooperatively hunt game these elements of sociation must be established and maintained. Each hunter must be attentive and responsive to the other, project congruent futures, focus on the same object and project the social objective of killing game. If any of the elements of sociation are absent then cooperative behavior distintegrates. If one person ignores the activity of the other, he may kill the game, but he will complete the act independent of the other. The objective is achieved by an individual, not as a consequence of a cooperative effort.

Cooperative action may be parallel or differentiated. When two persons pull together on a rope to move an object they produce parallel lines of action; when one frightens the game toward the other with the intention of providing the second person an opportunity for killing the game, differentiated action is taken. In both cases congruent lines of action are produced that are linked to a social objective. In all instances the production of cooperative action is predicated upon the projection of a shared future—a social objective. Congruent futures are a necessary condition for the production of cooperative action. Before congruent lines of action and a social objective can be produced a shared focus must be established.

Shared Foci

A shared focus is established when two or more persons are attentive to the same event or object and are mutually aware of that condition. Two persons may be attentive to the same event without the event serving as a shared focus. For example, two hunters might at the same moment detect the presence of game. A shared focus can be established by one turning to the other and asking, "Do you see it?" Or it may be established by them making eye contact and through reciprocating gestures informing each other that both have sighted game.

Adults routinely establish complex sets of shared foci. However, it is very difficult to establish shared foci with young infants. Both maturation and extensive socialization are necessary before a caretaker and a young child can establish shared foci. The first attempts by caretakers to establish shared foci with children are only minimally successful. In the beginning the degree of sharedness is limited. As the child acquires the ability to note what others are attending to, it becomes easier to establish shared foci and the degree of sharedness becomes greater.

Even the establishment of shared foci by adults is often problematic.

Sometimes adults fail to establish a shared focus even when both actively attempt to focus on the same event or object. On occasions the degree of sharedness is minimal, as when one adult is only vaguely aware of the focus of attention of another. The production of shared foci requires coorientation and mutual awareness of attending to the same event or object.

Efforts to establish shared foci permeate early socialization. The efforts take one of two basic forms. One is when the caretaker is attentive to the child's orientation, orients himself toward the same event or object, and attempts to inform the child they have a parallel orientation. The second is for the caretaker to manipulate and entice the child to attend to an event or object selected by the caretaker.

The early efforts to establish shared foci by the caretaker subordinating himself to the child's orientation are failures. When the caretaker attempts to inform the child that they have a parallel orientation, it typically results in the child reallocating his attention to the caretaker and discontinuing to attend to his original focus. It is only after many repetitious efforts that the child becomes capable of maintaining his original focus, while simultaneously recognizing that he and the caretaker are attending to the same event or object.

Other early efforts to etablish shared foci involve the caretaker manipulating either the child or a third object or both. When these efforts are undertaken the caretaker attempts to entice the child to attend to a focus provided by the caretaker. For example, the caretaker may have the child in his lap, and then place a toy or other object in front of the child, and attempt to elicit mutual awareness from the child that both of them are attending to the same object. The first efforts to establish shared foci in this manner are failures. Repetitious efforts and maturation usually culminate in success.

Not all forms of social activity require the establishment of a shared focus. Conflict is possible without a shared focus. All that is necessary to produce conflict is that each is attentive to the other and attempts to adversely impinge on the other. The social activity of mutual avoidance or social accommodation can be produced without a shared focus. To accommodate each other, all that is necessary is that those involved attend to each other and for each to avoid the other. However, the production of all units of cooperative action requires that a shared focus be established. If persons cannot establish a shared focus they cannot cooperate. The establishment of shared foci underlies all complex forms of social action.

Congruent Lines of Action

The establishment of shared foci is a present-centered activity. It does not imply a future course of action. Shared foci establish coorientation, but not sequences of action. Persons must project congruent sequences of activity that are linked to a shared focus before they can produce units of cooperative action.

When the shared focus is a series of events—a process—three sequences of activity are produced. Both A and B produce their individual sequences of action, and, in addition, the two of them together produce a sequence of social activity that is linked to the movement of the shared focus. Two distinct forms of timing are required when cooperative action is taken toward a moving shared focus: one, the timing of responses to each other and two, the timing of their activity toward the shared focus.

An example of fairly complex timing by a dyad toward a moving shared focus would be a young child and his parent attempting to capture a kitten that is avoiding them. When cooperative action of this complexity is first attempted with a child, the child is typically very attentive and responsive to the movement of the kitten but ignores the activity of the parent. When this form of cooperative behavior is successfully produced the child is timing his actions with those of another and with the movement of the shared focus. Timing with the environment and interpersonal timing must be simultaneously produced if cooperative action toward a moving shared focus is to ensue.

The integration of the two forms of timing requires that persons to a minimal degree share anticipations and project congruent intentionalities. They must have somewhat similar anticipations of the forthcoming movement by the shared focus and congruent intentionalities that are linked to the shared focus. Furthermore, if a unit of cooperative behavior is to be produced there must be a degree of consensus of what they plan to do with the shared focus. If one intends to chase the kitten from the house, and the other intends to capture the kitten, they will not produce a cooperative act. A social objective must be established and maintained if persons are to cooperate.

Social Objectives

A social objective is established when a shared future is projected and persons organize their actions to bring to fruition the projected future. Before a social objective can be established, persons must be capable of assessing the intentionalities of others toward a shared focus. If we do not understand what the other intends to do toward a shared focus we cannot be cooperative with him.

Social objectives may be as simple as two persons cooperating to move an object from one location to another, to as complex as a nation organizing itself to construct a replica of the Great Pyramid. It is social objectives that provide directionality for social behavior. A shared focus provides an orientation, but it does not provide directionality. Unless persons can establish a social objective, they may act with respect to each other, but they cannot act *with* each other.

When coorientation is first produced with a child, the child has no awareness of social objectives. Children acquire the ability to cooperate by being enticed by their caretakers to take action with their caretakers toward a series of shared foci. They thereby acquire shared pasts. Then, and only then, do children acquire the ability to initiate units of cooperative action.

Participation in a series of cooperative acts linked to specific objectives is usually necessary before persons are capable of producing complex units of cooperative action smoothly. For example, the person who has never hunted game before usually has difficulty in coordinating his behavior with others when he goes on his first hunt. When persons acquire shared pasts of hunting with others, complex units of cooperative action can be easily produced. Persons who have hunted together several times can produce smoothly complex units of cooperative action while giving only intermittent attention to each other. Experienced hunters can usually accurately anticipate both the movement of the game and each other's activity. They have rather complete awareness of how each will act. In contrast, the naïve hunter often can neither accurately anticipate the movement of the game nor the activity of the other hunters. He often cannot make an accurate assessment of the intentions of others in a given situation. Reciprocally, experienced hunters often find it difficult to assess the intentions of inexperienced hunters.

The acquisitions of numerous and varied shared pasts allows persons to subsequently establish a shared focus, project congruent sequences of activity, and establish a social objective hierarchically. When two experienced hunters spot game, upon establishing the game as their shared focus they may instantly organize themselves to achieve their objective. The prototype of complex units of cooperative behavior being produced hierarchically is the activity of a well-trained medical unit of an emergency ward. As soon as the shared focus of "an emergency" is established, complex units of cooperative action are immediately elicited.

Even when those coordinating their behaviors to take cooperative action have extensive shared pasts, they must still allocate some attention to each other and be, to some degree, responsive to each other's action in the ongoing present. The priest and the altar boy who have performed a ritual a thousand times together must intermittently note each other's activity, and be responsive to the other, if they are to achieve the social objective of successfully completing the ritual.

The successful completion of a cooperative act requires that each monitor his own behavior, the behavior of the other, the fit between the two sequences of behavior, and the movement of the shared focus. Each must project forthcoming sequences of action that are detected by the other and have a social objective. Even when all of these elements of sociation are present, it does not assure the successful completion of a unit of cooperative action. Even the most experienced hunters sometimes fail to bag their game.

All cooperative behavior has a temporal dimension. At the minimum, the production of cooperative behavior requires that persons fit their activities together in the ongoing present and project a shared future— a social objective. In most instances, interactors also have a shared past, a past wherein they have successfully produced units of cooperative action similar to the action they are now taking. When that condition prevails they can use their shared pasts in the organization of their activity in the ongoing present. Pluralities of persons who have an extensive past of cooperating with each other can usually produce complex units of cooperative action without difficulty.

Members of primitive bands and other groups with an extended past rely primarily on their shared past for the organization of their cooperative efforts. However, persons with common pasts can also produce complex cooperative action. For example, five persons who have independently of one another had considerable experience in playing basketball can form a team and produce relatively complex units of coordinated activity. In instances of this sort each presumes all of them have had similar common pasts. Of course, as they practice together, and construct shared pasts, the complexity of the cooperative behavior can then increase.

Contingent Versus Shared Futures

When persons produce units of cooperative action the future of each is to some degree contingent upon the other. They are interdependent. The degree of interdependence may range from those instances where the objective could not be achieved without the cooperation of a specific other to those situations where each person is only diffusely dependent upon others. If one person has control of the necessitites of life and is more powerful than the other, then the future of the weaker person is contingent upon the more powerful person. The future of a young child is highly dependent upon the behavior of his caretaker. At the other extreme are those situations where the projected future is only minimally dependent on the activity of another. For example, the future of a member of a large group that practices sharing food is only minimally dependent upon any given person. It is contingent upon the collectivity.

In some instances the projected future is a shared future; in other instances a differentiated future is projected. Among groups that share the fruits of the hunt, the projected future is that all will feast if the hunt is successful. In other instances the projected future is highly differentiated. Differentiated and contingent futures are projected in trade transactions wherein each of the participants has a monopolistic control of a resource desired by the other. In such transactions only a minimal degree of sharedness is present—only that of consummating an exchange.

When persons produce cooperative action that is predicated primarily on a shared future, they become embedded with each other. Each acquires consciousness of sharing with the other a standpoint toward specific facets of their world. In contrast, when cooperation is based on contingent futures, persons become aware of their interdependency. But persons who cooperate primarily on the basis of contingent futures do not become embedded with each other, although they may be extremely conscious of their interdependency.

THE ACQUISITION OF SYMBOLS

Young children can produce simple units of cooperative action and fairly complex units of individualistic action without benefit of symbols. However, when individuals do not have command of significant symbols cooperative action is limited to the immediate context. The social objectives are proximal; they are directly linked to current activity. After command of symbols is acquired, then it is possible for persons to establish distal social objectives. When there is recognition that current activity is linked to an objective that will be achieved some time after the completion of the current activity, a distal objective structures the immediate activity. When farmers plant in the spring, the activity is organized on the basis of a distal future—a future that is symbolically linked to the act of planting seed.

A distal future can be rather "immediate." It can be the next act after the completion of a relatively simple act of short duration. For example, in some families eating does not begin until after offering thanks. Whether the distal future is long range, one of several months or years, or short range, it provides directionality for the subunits of cooperative action that it encases.

Distal futures also provide a framework for the assessment of current activity. When persons cooperate to build a dwelling they assess and evaluate their efforts on the basis of whether or not their actions move them in the direction of achieving the distal objective. Assessments of the foundation for the building are made on the basis of its consequences for later stages of construction.

It is distal futures that give "meaning" to much of our activity. The significance of the activity of a group of actors memorizing their lines and practicing their performance rests upon the anticipated future of "opening night." The distal future of success on the hunt encases the manufacturing of a bow and arrow. Human beings without command of significant symbols cannot project distal futures. Before complex distal futures can be projected, it is necessary to symbolically sequence the future. Then complex distal futures of considerable duration can be projected.

The acquisition of significant symbols is dependent upon the establishment of shared foci. The emergence of significant symbols and the acquisition of the ability to produce simple units of cooperative action are closely intertwined. In one sense the acquisition of significant symbols is a form of "co" "operation." However, the production of significant symbols does not involve any sequence of activities, only that a shared focus is linked to an act. Most symbolic acts are vocalizations, but they can take many forms.

In the early stages of socialization, the caretaker and the child produce a multitude of acts as they attempt to establish a shared focus. Over time the acts become simplified to the point where only a single act is necessary for the two of them to establish coorientation. A significant symbol is established when a single act by one establishes coorientation for two or more. The acquisition of the first symbols is a rather long and drawn-out process. Furthermore, the first significant symbols usually are idiosyncratic to the caretaker and child; no one else understands them. After several symbols have been acquired then additional symbols are acquired more rapidly. In the process of learning symbols, the child acquires a categorical attitude; he acquires awareness that fields of experience can be designated. The categorical attitude is clearly present when the child asks, "What is that?"

The earliest symbols are limited to the immediate present. For example, the child acquires first the ability to produce the sound "dog" upon the appearance of the family dog. After learning to produce the sound "dog" to establish coorientation in the immediate present, the child can then acquire the ability to produce the sound "dog" when the dog is not present and produce coorientation between himself and another. When an act by one person produces coorientation on the part of two persons and elicits a standardized act from the other toward the shared focus, the shared focus is transformed into a social object (Mead, 1934; Hintz, 1975).

When this level of sophistication has been achieved there is a minimal specification of a future. The child can say dog and anticipate coorientation on the part of another and perhaps the subsequent appearance of the dog. Such a sequence is predicated upon the caretaker taking action on the basis of the child's act that leads to the appearance of the dog. When the act of producing a symbol "touches off" a sequence of activity that has the consequence of the referent for the symbol being produced, symbols are then employed to call for a specific future. Upon acquiring some sophistication in initiating coorientation and calling for desired futures, the child becomes capable of organizing the behavior of others as well as his own.

The earliest symbols are constrained to the immediate ongoing present. They produce coorientation to events and objects that both are capable of experiencing in the immediate context. Considerable sophistication in the manipulation of symbols in the here and now is necessary before children can acquire the ability to symbolically sequence their own activity or to symbolically sequence the joined activity produced by themselves and another. Before this level of complexity can be achieved, the child must acquire mastery of the functional equivalents of "now" and "later" and "first" and "second."

SYMBOLIC SEQUENCES

Symbolic sequences are first imposed on the child. Children are commonly first introduced to symbolic sequences by being told to wait. The typical sequence consists of the child designating a social object with the anticipation that the object will be produced and the caretaker responding with "wait," "in a minute," or "later." The event called for by the child is not immediately forthcoming. The child experiences these early acts of "later" as blockages. They carry no promise that the called-for event will be forthcoming; they are simply frustrating.

However, repetitious experiences of this sort, followed by the production of the called-for event, provide sequences of experience that allow the child to develop anticipations that the called-for activity will not be immediately forthcoming, but will subsequently occur. Statements of "wait" become symbols when the child maintains the anticipatory stance in response to "wait." This is the most primitive form of symbolically sequenced social action.

Children then acquire command of the symbols of "wait." They use them to inform others that a called-for act will not be produced immediately, but will be subsequently produced. Sequences of social action that are organized in part on the basis of the functional equivalents of "now" and "later" are implicitly ordered by symbols. Such sequences do not involve the explicit specification of order of subsequent activities. The symbolic ordering is limited to inserting a period of anticipatory waiting before a given event occurs. There is no other content to the period between the immediate present and the anticipated future.

Social action is explicitly sequenced when there is symbolic specification of two distinct activities and the completion of one activity is necessary before the second can be undertaken. The explicit specification of sequences requires at least a tacit understanding of first and second and that first is a necessary precursor to second. The statement, "We will leave after we finish the dishes" symbolically sequences a future. Specifications of this sort contextualize ongoing action by specifying the content and order of the future.

The acquisition of the ability to symbolically sequence the future has a parallel to the acquisition of the categorical attitude. Instead of asking, "What?" the child now asks, "When?" He has learned there is a temporal order to some activity, and that the occurrence of some events are contingent on the prior occurrence of other events.

SUMMARY

All cooperative activities have several temporal dimensions. The production of cooperative acts requires that each person time his actions with his environment and with the intentions of another person. Furthermore, cooperative acts require the projection of a shared future— a social objective. By acting in unison, persons acquire shared pasts. Once shared pasts have been acquired, they can become taken for granted and used to facilitate construction of complex units of cooperative action hierarchically. Persons with a shared past can upon making contact with each other immediately establish a social objective or organize themselves to achieve the objective.

The complexity of the cooperative acts that can be produced by a group is restricted by the complexity and precision of the futures the group can project. Young children can cooperate, but the complexity and duration of their cooperation is constrained by the complexity and precision of the futures they can project. In contrast, bureaucrats routinely project futures of great duration and elaborate complexity. A series of futures of shorter duration are nested within the long-range future.

Cooperative acts are often nested within larger cooperative acts. For example, a community might establish the construction of a new temple as a social objective. Then within the framework provided by that objective, some persons organize themselves to design the temple. Then a complex series of cooperative acts are produced to achieve a series of subobjectives that are all encased within the larger objective of the community acquiring a new temple. These might range from the acquisition of a water supply for pouring the concrete for the foundation to putting the spire into place.

Once the ability to symbolically sequence events has been acquired, then persons can establish distal futures. Both the programming of extended individualistic futures and extended shared futures is based upon the symbolic specification of a temporal order. The programming of distal and elaborate individualistic futures is predicated upon prior participation in social action that was symbolically sequenced.

The ability to symbolically sequence distal futures allows for persons to produce complex units of cooperative action. They can coordinate actions taken when they are not in each other's copresence. Symbolic sequencing allows persons to specify a distal future and then to organize their individual lines of action while separated to achieve a social objective. Two persons can agree that each of them will take distinctive and separate lines of action with the anticipation of them, thereby accomplishing a task. For example, they can agree that one of them will hunt while the other makes the necessary preparation for cooking. In these instances the actions they are to take both while separated and together are symbolically sequenced. The ability to produce coordinated action while separated requires symbolic sequencing. Persons without the ability to symbolically sequence their actions are only capable of coordinating their actions with each other when copresent.

The programming of distal futures ranges from agreeing on what we are going to do next to the formulation of nationwide ten-year plans. Societies vary tremendously in the complexity of their projected futures. Hunting and gathering societies develop only restricted programs; the bulk of their coordination is achieved by being responsive to developments in the ongoing present. In all human societies there is some programming of distal futures. In those societies that repeat much the same sequence of activities each year, there is only a minimal amount of attention given to the explicit programming of the future. Programs that have been developed are taken for granted and used in the organization of behavior.

Chapter IV

Extending Temporal Structures

The specification of precise distal futures and the production of complex units of cooperative behavior to achieve these futures are taken for granted in modern societies with calendars and clocks. Many significant events are scheduled long before they occur. They range from a family specifying months in advance when they will take their vacation to the scheduling of national elections. The schedule for the election and installation of the next president of the United States is already determined. Between now and then a complex set of intertwined and sequenced events will occur. These include a host of primary elections, party conventions, and a national election.

Neither young children nor primitive groups that lack a numeric calendar are capable of projecting the precise futures required for the production of social activities of this complexity. Before long-range distal futures can be specified with any precision it is necessary for persons to have command of a calendar. Then and only then can a future that extends over months or years be projected with any precision. The scheduling of long-range distal futures does not require that all members of a group or society have command of a calendric system, only that some members of the unit do and that others accept the specification of the future offered by those with command of a calendar.

Future sequences of activity of considerable complexity can be specified without a calendar. A group can construct a program of action for undertaking a hunt by specifying a host of things that are to be done before they leave in search for game. The program might consist of notifying relatives, performing rituals, readying the weapons, and a number of other activities. The program of action specifying the future in these types of efforts consists of putting the necessary activities in a sequential order. The sequence may be rigidly specified or the sequence may be of minimal significance. When the sequence is specified, then the future is temporally structured. Whenever there is a specification

41

that activity X must be completed before activity Y can be undertaken, the future is programmed.

All complex cooperative behavior is programmed to some degree. The program may be quite simple and of limited duration or extremely complex and of extended duration. Hunting expeditions, family visits, and the construction of a temporary dwelling are all structured in part on the basis of symbolically sequenced activities. Prior to the production of these activities by two or more persons there is at least the projection of a future sequence of activity that at least vaguely places the forthcoming activity in temporal order. The five-year plans of the Soviet Union are but one example of the complex and precise sequencing of the future of considerable duration.

Not each instance of complex cooperative action is explicitly programmed. Those groups with an extensive shared past of successfully completing complex cooperative acts use their shared past to project complex futures. Some appreciation of the importance of symbolic sequencing can be obtained by noting the time and attention given to establishing a program when a group plans to take a novel course of action of some complexity that requires several days to complete. Then they must devote a considerable amount of time to the specification of the temporal structure of their forthcoming activity. If they do not, they are almost certain to fail. Even when there is detailed and precise sequencing of the future, groups often fail to achieve their objectives.

When a family holds its first reunion, a considerable amount of explicit programming is required if the reunion is to occur. After the reunion has been held for a number of years, the programming of subsequent reunions need not be explicit. All that may be necessary is the specification of when and where. All other dimensions of the activity that are necessary for the holding of the reunion may be ordered on the basis of their shared pasts. Even then there is usually some discussion of who will do what when to assure the reunion will occur.

If the distal objective is removed by several days from the present, then a calendar of some sort is used to specify the sequence of activities that are to be taken between the present and the achievement of the objective. The calendric specification of future sequences of activities is not sufficient to assure that the future will unfold as programmed.

Whenever a future with any degree of complexity and duration is projected, as persons attempt to follow the program they usually find it necessary to reprogram their future. A previously established program or "game plan" may frame their actions, but usually it is necessary to make adjustments in the face of unanticipated developments. When a complex program of action is undertaken, it is impossible to completely anticipate future developments.

When a group of persons have an extensive shared past, and are more or less continually copresent, very little explicit programming of the future is necessary. Small hunting and gathering societies engage in relatively little explicit programming. They use their shared pasts to organize their actions, and as the action unfolds, through intermittent attention to each other and their environment, they make the necessary adjustments and maintain social unity. Most hunting and gathering groups are quite small. They seldom exceed thirty to fifty persons in size and are often smaller. Groups of this size can coordinate their activity largely on the basis of extensive shared pasts and taken-for-granted futures, as well as by being responsive to unfolding events.

Some hunting and gathering groups do convene at certain seasons. During these periods the social action of the group, or at least some of it, is often explicitly programmed. For example, the Sioux Indians spent most of the year in small bands, but united each year to hunt buffalo. During the periods the bands were united, far more of their activity was explicitly programmed than was the case when they were in small bands.

Most, but apparently not all hunting and gathering groups organize their yearly activity on the basis of at least a general and vague program. The program may be nothing more than the specification of what sort of game will be plentiful in a given season. All groups have communal anticipations of future developments that are relevant to the welfare of the group, but some have only a vague program that is used to organize their communal activity. This feature of their life stands in marked contrast to the complex social programs that encase the cooperative activity of large organizations.

CALENDARS

Nearly all societies have a calendric system. The content, complexity, and precision of calendars varies tremendously (Baity, 1973). At one extreme are those that allow for the projection of a vague yearly cycle; at the other is our modern calendar which, in conjunction with our clocks, allows us to project a future that is decades in duration and specifies intervening sequences in hours, minutes, and seconds. Calendric systems are extended sequences; they allow for the complex and precise structuring of the future and past. All are based in part upon sequenced celestial events.

All human societies anticipate seasonal changes; nearly all make some use of celestial phenomena to form anticipations of those changes. Some groups have only a modest and vague calendar; others have multiple and elaborate calendars. In general, nomadic food gatherers have simple calendars; agricultural groups usually have complex calendars. Anthropologists have long been cognizant of the complex calendars of many ancient civilizations. It is only recently that they have assigned much significance to calendars. Marshack's (1972) work has demonstrated that calendars have an ancient tradition.

Of all the long-term sequenced experiences of human beings, those based on celestial phenomena have the greatest uniformity. The rising and setting of the sun, the lunar cycles, the changes in the location of the sun on the horizon at sunrise and sunset, and the disappearance and reappearance of the stars have great regularity. All the stars except the circumpolar ones disappear from the sky and reappear again at regular intervals. How long a star disappears from view depends upon its latitude and the latitude of the observer. Various combinations of these celestial phenomena have been used in many different ways to construct calendars.

All societies make use of the daily cycle to structure their future and past. "Tomorrow" is the first symbolic temporal unit mastered by children that is based on celestial movement. Subsequent to mastering tomorrow they acquire mastery of today and yesterday. During the evolution of the human species tomorrow was probably the first unit of duration that human beings mastered that was linked to celestial phenomena.

In a few of the simplest societies the duration of projected futures and pasts do not extend much beyond tomorrow and yesterday. The Siriono, a food gathering group of South America, had only the concepts today, tomorrow, yesterday, brother of tomorrow, and brother of yesterday. "The year, with its divisions into months or 'moons', is quite unknown" (Holmberg, 1969:123). All events that occurred prior to yesterday were located as having occurred during the "brother of yesterday." The brother of yesterday referred to events that occurred the day before yesterday and to those that were located far in the past. The same condition held when specifying the future. It seems likely that given a strong interest in making a distinction between the day after tomorrow and three days from now they could have made the differentiation.

Holmberg characterized the Siriono as having little foresight. His description of their day-to-day activities substantiates his characterization. However, they planted small crops of maize which suggests they were capable of at least vaguely projecting a future of considerable duration. The fact that they lived in a tropical area, were primarily food gatherers, and could plant at any time of the year partially explains how they could survive without benefit of a calendar that sequenced the yearly cycle.

Nearly all primitive groups had a calendar that at least specified the yearly cycle. The most common calendars were lunar. Sequences of lunar cycles were noted and named. Each lunar cycle is approximately 29½ days in duration and there are approximately 12⅓ lunar cycles in each year. Consequently all lunar calendars were keyed to either a yearly solar, sidereal, or terrestial phenomenon. A modern exception is the Muslim calendar. It is strictly a lunar calendar that was institutionalized by Mohammed to disassociate Muslims from nonbelievers (O'Neil, 1975).

All other lunar calendars were keyed to some yearly event. Solar-lunar calendars of the northern hemisphere were commonly keyed to the Winter solstice. The keying was accomplished by noting the sun's location on the horizon. When the sun had reached the southernmost point of the horizon and began moving northward another yearly cycle was started. Then each subsequent new moon was noted.

Some lunar calendars are keyed to a sidereal event. The most common keys were the heliacal risings or settings of bright stars. There are approximately 366¼ sidereal days for each 365¼ solar days. The stars visible in the heavens change slightly each night. After a star has disappeared from the heavens it first reappears on the eastern horizon just before sunrise. Then each subsequent night it appears slightly higher in the heavens before sunrise. A star's first reappearance on the eastern horizon is its heliacal rising. For example, at the latitude of thirty degrees North, Sirius, the brightest star in the heavens, is not visible for approximately seventy days each year. It then reappears on the eastern horizon just before sunrise.

Those groups that used the heliacal rising of Sirius as their key noted when the star reappeared and then made note of each subsequent new moon. After the passage of twelve moons they then anticipated the heliacal rising of Sirius. Many groups employed a sidereal-lunar clendar that was keyed to the heliacal rising of the Pleiades (Seven Sisters).

A few lunar calendars have been keyed to a terrestial event. One group keyed their lunar observations on the first sound of thunder which heralded the beginning of the rainy season. Then they noted each new moon, for the next ten moons. Many societies made use of complex combinations of celestial and terrestial events in their sequencing of the yearly cycle. The Greenland Eskimos noted the Winter solstice and the five subsequent new moons until the nights became so bright it was difficult to reckon on the basis of the moon. "Then they reckon by the increasing size of the young of the eiderduck and by the ripening of berries, or along the seacoast by the departure of the tern and the fatness of the seals; when the reindeer shed the velvet from their horns they know that it is time to move into the winter houses" (Nilssen, 1920:52).

The simplest lunar calendars do not use numbers. In the Carolina Islands a "count" of the days in a lunar month was kept "by having a different name for each day and major phase. One remembers thirty names the way we remember the seven days of the week or the names of the twelve months. This is a way of counting, but it is not numerical" (Marshack, 1972:136). The counting of moons was accomplished in the same manner. An orderly sequence of names was applied to each new moon following the event the calendar was keyed on.

The number of new moons that occur between two Winter solstices may be twelve or thirteen. Some groups with a lunar calendar were not aware of the variation in the number of new moons between the solstices, or whatever else served as the key for the calendar. In one group the topic of "What moon is it?" was commonly discussed. Note was made of plant growth and other phenomena, and the lunar sequences were eventually brought in line with terrestial events. The Caffred frequently became confused about which moon it was. In that case the heliacal rising of the Pleiades resolved the issue (Nilssen, 1920). Another group, the Yami, keyed their calendar to the seasonal catching of flying fish. Every twelve moons they held a ritual that summoned the flying fish. They then went out to catch the fish. "If no flying fish turn up to the summons, the Yami do not blame themselves for miscalculating the time—they blame the fish for being late for their appointment. In such years, they extend the flare-fishing season for an extra moon" (Leach, 1954:119).

The variation in the number of moons each year produces an inconsistency from the point of view of those of us who accept the year as 365¼ days in length. However, "the incommensurable motions of the Sun and Moon can give rise to a conceptual framework in which the heavenly bodies are seen as alternately running fast and slow" (McCluskey, 1977:183). Sometimes it takes the sun thirteen moons to return to the same location on the horizon and other years twelve. This variation would only be of concern to those with a belief in the uniformity of motion on the part of celestial bodies.

Many groups were aware that the number of new moons varied from year to year. Some had rather complex formulas for intercalating an extra moon to maintain synchronization between climatic and celestial seasons. In other instances the intercalation of a moon was negotiated. Among the Arabs prior to Mohammed, the calendar was adjusted at the end of the pilgrimage ceremonies. Each year those in charge of the ceremonies agreed among themselves if an extra moon was to be added. Then they informed the pilgrims whether the next year would be one of twelve or thirteen moons. "This procedure they called Nase, or shifting, because every second or third year the beginning of the year was shifted" (Pannekoek, 1961:27). This procedure allowed the various tribes that had convened to coordinate their meeting the following year. Many groups established similar procedures for adjusting their solar-lunar or sidereal-lunar calendars.

Some societies had multiple calendric systems. One calendar was used for programming one set of activity and another for another set. The two systems may or may not be synchronized. Two or more systems may exist simultaneously with no concern about their interrelation. Gladwin (1970) provides an account of pointing out to some South Sea navigators an inconsistency between the two calendars they used. One was employed for navigation and the other for planting and related activities. The navigators were intrigued by the inconsistency between the two systems and excitedly talked about it for a short while and then dropped the subject. To a western European this inconsistency was a problem. For the navigators it was just an interesting observation.

Many groups did not fill out their yearly cycle with moons. The group noted above, which keyed their calendar to the first sound of thunder, only noted the passage of ten moons following the beginning of the rainy season. In a similar manner the early calendar of the Romans only counted ten moons. The period between the tenth moon and the event that marked the beginning of a new year was of variable duration. For groups with this type of calendar the variable period tends to be that part of the yearly cycle wherein there is little productive activity. In the northern hemisphere the period is roughly the months of January and February.

Some contemporary food gatherers use only sidereal events. One group used the heliacal rising of Arcturus to inform them when to begin hunting for the larvae of an ant that was regarded as a delicacy. Another group began their search for the eggs of the Malle-hen at the heliacal rising of Canopus. In many societies a lunar calendar was used for the yearly cycle while other activities were keyed to a yearly sidereal event.

A few groups had systems based on solar alignment with features of the landscape. "The Silhouette of a mountain range is so individual from every view angle that it is not difficult to memorize the place of sunset at the farthest point to the right. When the sun returns to this point— a year has past" (Maistrov, 1974:268). Within the same group no months or weeks were used. Nor was it reported that the waxing and waning of the moon was noted. Rather the number of days that transpired between the sun setting over one mountain top to the next was noted. In this manner various holidays were established and the number of days between holidays was noted.

The calendric system developed by early Mesoamericans was originally keyed to the zenith passages of the sun—the two days of the year that the sun is directly overhead at noon. The 260-day cycle of the Olmec-Maya calendar was based upon an earlier calendar keyed to zenith passages of the sun (Malmstrom, 1978). Calendric systems keyed to zenith passages of the sun could only develop between the topic of Capricorn and the tropic of Cancer.

EARLY CALENDARS

The evolution of lunar calendars probably proceeded from those keyed to terrestial events, to those keyed to heliacal risings or settings of bright stars, to those keyed to the solstices. The detemination of the solstice with any precision at all requires that observations of the location of the sun on the horizon be made from roughly the same geographic location during at least the period near the solstice. It is possible that the earliest lunar calendars were keyed to sidereal events. Even when a group is quite mobile the heliacal risings and settings will occur at about the same time during the yearly cycle. It is more likely that the most ancient lunar calendars were keyed to terrestial events. Neither the location of the sun on the horizon or the reappearance of a star in the heavens impinges upon human beings as much as the beginning of the rainy season, the seasonal floods from the melting of snow or the first snowstorm.

Marshack (1972) has demonstrated that at least as early as 35,000 years ago some groups had developed a calendar. The most ancient calendars were used to predict the return of migrating herds and the termination of pregnancies. "These scratched and engraved bits of bone and stone, dug from the soil layers of all periods of the Upper Paleolithic, roughly 35,000 to 10,000 years old and contemporary with the 'birth of art,' raise profound questions about about the nature of evolved human cognition and intelligence and human culture and society" (Marshack, 1972:109).

The detection, articulation, and use of yearly cycles based on celestial movement is an invention that ranks in importance with acquiring control of fire; it perhaps surpasses it in significance. The ability to anticipate futures of several moons' duration provided extended temporal structures. This allowed human beings far greater control over their lives than was possible prior to the specification of the yearly cycle. Those groups that developed calendars that allowed for the fairly precise projection of distal futures were more likely to endure than those that did not.

It is unlikely that the earliest calendric systems were made by making notches on bones and stone. Less durable material was probably used long before bones and stones were notched. These notchings and drawings analyzed by Marshack indicate that for many generations careful observations of celestial events had been made and their correlation with terrestrial events had been determined.

Some of the paleolithic hunters maintained more or less permanent

camps along mountain passes that herds crossed in their yearly migration. "The campsites are still marked by immense middens" (Childe,
1951:52). In some regions the walls of the valleys were honeycombed
with caves. The survival of these groups depended upon the killing of
game, and they had a calendric system that allowed them to anticipate
the yearly migration patterns of their game.

The most celebrated feature of the life of these groups is the famous
cave drawings and paintings of Southern Europe. The most ancient
drawings are merely profile outlines. The later drawings show greater
sophistication. The earliest drawings and markings were made simply
to record the passage of moons; the later drawings also expressed the
atittude of the artist.

At least some upper paleolithic groups were capable of symbolically
specifying distal futures on the basis of the celestial events they observed.
This provided them the foundation for the development of a fairly
complex social structure. Those groups with this ability were not simply
responding to terrestial changes; they were organizing their lives in part
on the basis of distal futures of considerable duration and complexity.

The method of notation of the passage of lunar cycles by paleolithic
groups were similar to the calendric methods of some primitive contem-
poraries. "A small notched message-stick of the Seneca, . . . looks exactly
like certain Upper Paleolithic notched bones and some Australian mes-
sage-sticks. It contains a marking of days, calling chiefs to a particular
ceremony at a certain time" (Marshack, 1972:139).

All the ancient calendric systems deciphered by Marshack made use
of lunar sequences. It need not have been the case that the earliest
systems were based on lunar movement. Those that did, necessarily
keyed their lunar notations to some other yearly event to achieve a self-
adjusting calendar that would allow for accurate anticipation of seasonal
developments.

The findings of Marshack indicate only that some ancient groups
developed complex calendars, not that all did. It is likely that while some
groups had command of complex calendars linked to celestial changes,
other groups had only vague awareness of terrestial cycles and organized
their lives primarily by responding to terrestial changes.

Many of the primitive calendars, especially those used by nomadic
groups, incorporate both patterns of celestial movement and terrestial
changes. A few groups are reported to believe that there is as much
regularity in the pattern of terrestial events as there is in the pattern of
celestial events (Turton and Ruggles, 1978; Nilssen, 1920). However,
the location of the sun on the horizon and the disappearance and reappearance of stars are better predictors of distal climatic conditions, the
appearance and disappearance of game, and plant growth than are im-

mediate climatic conditions. Whether it will snow within the next ten days can be predicted with greater accuracy by carefully noting the location of the sun on the horizon than it can by noting the current temperature. The farmer who plants on the basis of the location of the sun on the horizon is more likely to avoid crop failure due to an early or late frost than is one who plants whenever the climatic conditions allow.

Complex and precise calendars necessarily were preceded by simpler ones. The long-range trend was toward more complex calendars. But the simpler ones did not automatically transform into more complex ones. So long as the system was adequate for programming critical activities, usually there was no effort to develop a more precise one. The evolution of calendric systems, as with the evolution of biological species, entailed the development of many varieties. Some endured and evolved into complex forms, some complex forms devolved into simpler forms, some disappeared leaving no trace, and a very select few provided the foundation for the development of civilizations.

Eddy (1979) has deciphered several large "medicine wheels" which consist of large circular layouts of stones oriented to the heliacal rising of stars and the summer solstice. These "medicine wheels" allowed for the precise specification of the summer solstice. They are indicative of considerable calendric sophistication. "Yet if we ask Plains Indians today about the sun or stars, or if we examine the oral depositions taken from them during the last century, we find very little, if anything, about practical astronomy" (Eddy, 1979:24).

ORDERING THE PAST

The past as well as the future can be symbolically sequenced. When the past can be arrayed chronologically, then assessments can be made of the significance of various events for subsequent developments. For example, after a hunting group has failed in its effort, they might symbolically order the past and analyze their efforts. They might discuss the temporal order of a number of events. Such activity requires both a shared or common past and the ability to sequentially order that past.

All who have acted together have a shared past; however pasts need not be temporally ordered. Groups may have complex and elaborate pasts with only a minimal ability to sequentially order the past. Many primitive groups had only minimal sophistication in historical thought, but had a richly textured past. Some had elaborate legends that recounted the exploits of their ancestors but were not capable of sequentially ordering the legends.

The term prehistorical is used to refer to groups with no written accounts of their pasts. In one sense this is a correct usage of the term. Without written records it is difficult for a group to develop elaborate historical thought. However, any procedure that allows a group to organize their past in a chronological manner provides one of the foundation stones for historical thought. In most societies without written records the past was only sequenced for a generation or two; all events prior to that were simply "in the days of old." There was an awareness of a distal past that stretched over generations, but efforts to specify the duration between one event and another in the past were typically very limited.

Some nonliterate groups maintained extended genealogies by an oral tradition. These groups had at least a modicum of historical thought; they had a past that was sequenced. A few ancient groups developed complex methods for ordering the past before they acquired literacy. But before this mode of thought could achieve any degree of complexity, both a calendar and some method for noting the order of events had to be present.

SUMMARY

Calendars make it possible to project sequenced futures of considerable complexity and duration. Even the simplest ones allowed members of groups to discuss and plan for a distal future. They provided a means for organizing action toward events that were expected to occur in the distal future and facilitated the achievement of social objectives. Groups that planned for the appearance of migrating herds a moon or two before the herds appeared were more likely to have a successful hunt than those that simply responded to the appearance of the herds.

The formulation of extended temporal structures did not free human beings from unforeseen disasters. On many occasions the anticipated herds did not appear, climatic changes frequently rendered the land incapable of sustaining human life, and catastrophies such as unanticipated storms and raids destroyed many communities. The projection of extended temporal structures only made human existence slightly less fragile.

The original significance of calendars was not that of providing extended futures and pasts per se; rather it was that they allowed for more accurate anticipation of important terrestial events. Neither the reappearance of Sirius nor the Winter solstice was significant as an isolated event. But when it was noted that the reappearance of Sirius in the sky was usually followed by the reappearance of migrating herds, then human beings could more effectively organize themselves for the hunt.

In most nomadic groups, only a small percentage of their total activity was structured on the basis of their calendar. In some, all that was organized was the "spring hunt." Even so the calendar made their life somewhat more secure. The calendar provided them with a means of acquiring slightly more control over their future.

The development of calendars was the foundation for one form of abstract thought. Moons, years, decades, centuries, and millennia are abstract concepts that allow human beings to "chuck up" the past and future. Each moon contained an orderly sequence of days; each year contained an orderly sequence of moons. These and similar concepts specify units of duration that allow for the abstract ordering of the future and the past.

The intricate interrelations between the emergence of complex temporal structures and abstract thought may never be unraveled. However, it is difficult to disagree with Marshack when he claims that the development of timekeeping systems has tremendous significance for understanding the evolution of human thought.

Calendric systems supplemented and, to an extent, replaced more primitive forms of timing. Nomadic groups without a calendric system organized their lives by being extremely responsive to the immediate present; those with a calendar were able to incorporate distal futures into the present which sometimes facilitated the achievement of desired futures. To the extent groups organized themselves on the basis of projected distal futures, they became less responsive to their immediate environment. On occasions this had the consequence of groups becoming so unresponsive to environmental changes that they failed to make the necessary adaptions for survival.

The development of distal futures of several moons' duration made it possible for larger social units to be maintained. It improved the effectiveness of hunting and food gathering. Hunting and gathering groups were still highly dependent on the resources provided by their immediate environment. But calendric systems allowed them to organize their behavior so they could be at a given location when a food supply was likely to be plentiful. Without a calendric system, knowledge of when to be where was severely limited. Calendric systems made it easier for food gatherers to acquire the necessities of life.

Chapter V

Primitive Distribution

In the ancient past all human beings lived in small bands; there were no societies with large populations. Most contemporary food gatherers spend the bulk of the yearly cycle in bands of fifteen to thirty. Contemporary food gatherers have been squeezed into the more impoverished environments, but prior to the emergence of large societies many food gatherers lived in far richer environments. The ancient bands who lived in the richer environments may have been considerably larger than those of contemporary food gatherers. Nonetheless it is unlikely that many, if any, of these bands achieved a relatively permanent population of over fifty to one-hundred persons.

All ancient bands were nomadic or seminomadic. Some moved from site to site more or less continuously, making but brief stops at each encampment. Others were almost continually on the move as they followed migrating herds of animals. Some remained within rather well delineated territories throughout the year. Some were semisedentary. Some groups had a base camp at a site that furnished a plentiful supply of food for several months of the year. For example, some paleolithic groups in Europe camped at passes through which herds of animals passed. They acquired many of the necessities of life by preying on herds of animals that migrated through the passes. Others established semisedentary communities where there was a plentiful supply of fish.

The subsistence base of ancient bands of food gatherers varied greatly. Some eeked out the necessities of life largely by gathering plant materials; others hunted large game and were primarily meat eaters; still others relied heavily on fish and other marine products. Whatever their subsistence base, both their food and the few manufactured items they possessed were obtained through their own productive efforts. They were self-sufficient.

Despite the variations in their size, degree of nomadism, and subsistence base the predominating modes of sociation within these bands were very similar. The basic cycle of activity was shared by all. The search for food was a communal enterprise. There was some division of labor based on sex and age. But for the most part these divisions were encased within an overarching solidarity. The similarity of their concerns, experiences, and activities provided a foundation for a rather robust solidary relationship. When they were successful in wresting the necessities of life from their environment their solidarity was enhanced; when they were unsuccessful it was attenuated.

The solidary relationship that prevailed within each band provided a foundation for the distribution of food and other necessities of life through sharing. When food was plentiful, all ate; when it was in short supply all went hungry. Both the production and consumptive processes were encased by a rather intense solidarity and framed by temporal structures of relatively short duration when food was plentiful.

There was considerable variation in the amount of food available by season and year, however. In some seasons there was an excess of food, in others food was in short supply; some years far more food was available than could be consumed; in other years there were sustained shortages. When there were sustained shortages, members of bands competed and sometimes conflicted with one another for what food was available. During periods of shortage the bands moved on to other locations in search of food and on many occasions fragmented.

SOLIDARITY AND INTERNAL DISTRIBUTION

When human beings act in unison and achieve mutually desired objectives they generate solidarity. Whenever a hunting group, whether a group of modern hunters or the hunters of a nomadic band, coordinate their actions to kill game they produce elements of solidarity. The parallel lines of action and similarity of emotions generated by persons acting in unison produce a shared standpoint. All are aware that they share a concern with the same events and objects and have similar visceral responses to unfolding events. They thereby develop shared standpoints—they become solid (Sehested, 1975). Anytime persons produce identical or similar lines of action in unison toward a shared focus to achieve a social objective, elements of solidarity are generated. Solidarity is generated in such varied activity as walking together, acting in unison to protect one's group from outsiders, and launching outer space vehicles.

If the projected social objective is achieved, then solidary responsiveness is also elicited among those who have acted in unison. When a band of hunters bring down game they joyously celebrate their effort and achievement. They respond with similar emotions to the accomplishment. Both the production of solidary action and solidary responsiveness contribute to human beings becoming embedded with one another. Solidary actions and responsiveness pervaded the lives of ancient food gathering bands. It was the most common form of sociation within each band.

Not all members of ancient bands continuously acted in unison. Nonetheless much of the action taken by members of these bands was encased by a shared concern. When an animal was stalked by an adult male, all members of the band expressed solidary concern toward the activity, and were solidarily responsive upon success. When there is consensual concern about an objective, and when the objective is attempted by a single person, all have much the same response to success or failure. That condition holds whether it involves a hunter of a small nomadic band bringing down an elk, or a community's athletic team emerging victorious over a rival community's team. The production of the necessities of life within bands of nomadic food gatherers was infused with and encased by solidarity. The productive processes thereby provided a solidary context that structured the distribution and consumption of goods. All members of the band shared the spoils of success. When a hunter was successful all ate; when one found a field of wild tubers all harvested and consumed them. The communal consumption of goods further enhanced the solidarity of the group. All were solidarily responsive to their feast.

Solidary responsiveness, action, and relationships are not unique to small bands of food gatherers. In modern life we often are solidarily responsive and frequently take solidary action. Furthermore most are part of a series of solidary relationships of varying degrees of intensity. Some have rather intense solidary relationships with a few persons—their kin, friends, and neighbors. Some small communities have a fairly intensive level of solidarity. In food gathering groups each person had only a limited number of solidary relationships. The more inclusive one was the band. That solidary relationship encased the solidary relationships of families and internal divisions based on sex and age. The solidarity of nomadic bands was often rather intense, but of limited expansiveness. It usually included only a handful of others. In contrast in modern societies solidary relationships are often more expansive but less intense. Most citizens of modern societies are part of a number of solidary relationships and some of these include large numbers. Nationalism is a solidary relationship that includes all fellow citizens.

The intensiveness of solidary relationships is maximized when persons act in unison to achieve a large number of objectives. The intensity of solidarity is further enhanced when persons act in unison to achieve highly significant objectives. There are few objectives of greater significance than the acquisition of food necessary to sustain life. Members of food gathering bands routinely experienced variation in their success in acquiring the necessities of life. The variation in the availability of the necessities of life made their food gathering activities problematic. They undertook a variety of activities to acquire the necessities of life, some of which were successful, others were not. Those who achieved a relatively high level of success developed a robust band solidarity. Consequently members of these bands usually were deeply embedded with one another.

The sharing of the fruits of the hunt was both a consequence of solidarity and reaffirmed the extant solidarity. The distribution of goods, especially the necessities of life, within food gathering groups was primarily achieved through sharing. In some nomadic groups sharing was nearly total. All members were expected to exert effort in the acquisition of food and all shared the benefits. However, if food was in relatively good supply one could survive by consuming the fruits of the more industrious. Those who did not contribute were the targets of jokes, but if one did not care what others thought, it was possible for a person to survive as a drone (Fried, 1967:62).

Some contemporary food gathering bands specified how food was to be distributed. These distribution procedures did not assure that all acquired exactly equal proportions, but generally they assured that all acquired the minimal necessities. Often they specified rather precisely that all should acquire equal proportions. In some bands there was the further specification that the person responsible for killing a large animal had claim to a particular organ or cut of meat that was regarded as the choicest bit. In one group the person with this prerogative was the one who had manufactured the arrow that killed the animal; he had that honor even when he was not on the hunt (Lee, 1972).

Many have emphasized the egalitarianism that pervades food gathering groups. Nonetheless within most contemporary bands of food gatherers individuals accumulated differential prestige. Adult males were ranked on their hunting abilities. Those with reputations as oustanding hunters were sought out, but one's reputation did not free him from the obligation to share his successes with others. Even those with the greatest prestige were expected to share with others; those who did not were criticized. If one refused to share then others applied sanctions to him (Lee, 1972).

Some students of food gatherers have emphasized their intense solidarity and the pervasiveness of sharing. However, a close reading of the descriptions of the distribution procedures of some groups indicates that not all food gatherers maintained a robust solidary relationship. There are many accounts of members of food gathering groups failing to share with one another when confronted with sustained shortages of food. Then members of these groups often competed and were in conflict with one another for the necessities of life. When food was in short supply for long periods persons hoarded what little food they had, and competed and sometimes fought with fellow band members for what was available. Their solidarity eroded.

The failure to acquire the food necessary to sustain life is the ultimate failure. When there was a shortage of food there were few successes to celebrate, few communal feasts to promote communal solidarity, and the unity of the group lessened. Then those who achieved success in their food seeking efforts frequently failed to share with their fellow band members. Fragmentation of the band was a common consequence.

The continuity of some groups was maintained despite a diminution of solidarity. Solidarity is not the only factor that contributes to group unity and continuity. The lack of alternatives and external constraints sometimes results in continuity of a group when the solidarity of a group is mimimal. However, when the continuity of a group is primarily dependent on the lack of viable alternatives and external constraints, then if new opportunities arise or if the external constraints are removed, the group has a high probability of fragmenting.

A shortage of food was not the only factor contributing to fragmentation. An increase in the size of a group inherently contributes to fragmentation. When a group consists of eight to ten persons, acting and responding in unison is relatively easy; when the group consists of thirty or forty, it becomes more difficult for all to act in unison and to be uniformly responsive. Size per se contributes to the dimunition of solidarity. It makes groups more vulnerable to fragmentation. When the solidarity of a group lessens, whether due to shortage of goods or an increase in its size, then minor internal conflicts are more likely to result in fragmentation.

When ancient nomadic bands fragmented, some of the fragments endured, but others faded from existence. A shortage of food and fragmentation sometimes had the consequence of enticing groups into virgin territories and developing somewhat different subsistence bases. However, it did not lead to the formation of new modes of production. These groups still remained food gatherers. They simply sought out the necessities of life in new territories and sometimes gathered different plants and hunted different animals. They had neither the inclination nor resources to formulate alternative modes of production.

So long as a minimal level of solidarity was maintained, sharing was the prevailing mode of internal distribution of goods. However, when there was a shortage of the necessities of life then other modes of distribution emerged. At these times members of the same band also stole and begged from one another. Competition and conflict replaced solidary action as the prevailing mode of sociation. Neither theft nor begging from one's fellow band members or from outsiders contributed to the development of more complex social structures. Both are disruptive modes of sociation. They led to conflict and avoidance, not to the formulation of more complex modes of sociation, or to the emergence of larger groups.

Nor were these groups that were successful in wresting the necessities of life from their environment inclined to formulate new modes of production or distribution. However, those that were successful did endure and some of them accumulated minimal surpluses. Some of these groups had relatively routine contacts with other groups. Some of these contacts in turn provided opportunities for the distribution of goods between groups.

INTERGROUP DISTRIBUTION

There are several ways that the intergroup distribution of goods can be achieved. Hypothetically, sharing across bands is possible, but it is at best a rare phenomenon. The distribution of goods across social boundaries is a far more tentative and fragile affair than internal distribution. Sharing across group boundaries beyond a doubt occasionally occurred between ancient nomadic bands but it was probably a far less common occurrence than theft, begging, and bargaining. Theft and begging are simply forms of social activity than bargaining and have a much more ancient past than bargaining.

To commit theft all that is required is to locate the goods of another and have the ability to extract them. It is not a cooperative act. Moreover, theft engenders resentment and is conducive to conflict. Begging is minimally a cooperative act. One party pleads to another and the other willingly surrenders control. However, begging is an abrasive act—one party imposes himself upon another. The common response is avoidance of the beggar.

A bargained exchange is a much more complex act than either theft or begging. Young children can commit "theft" and beg long before they can consummate a bargained exchange. Before they are capable of bargaining they must have command of a rather complex set of symbols and be taught a sequence of reciprocating acts. All human beings are capable of learning how to bargain for an exchange of goods. That combined with the fact that the various forms of distribution of goods exist simultaneously have enticed some to conclude that all forms of distribution are equally ancient. But it is the simpler forms of activity that have the most ancient past. Persons stole from one another, shared, and begged before they developed the ability to consummate bargained exchanges.

Bargained exchanges have an ancient past. And it is impossible to determine whether bargaining between members of the same band or bargaining across bands has the most ancient past. In any event it was intergroup bargaining that provided the foundation for the expansion of social contacts and the emergence of more complex social structures. Bargaining between members of the same bands has been reported for contemporary food gathering bands (Holmberg, 1969). However, bargaining between members of the same band tends to occur only during times of shortage, when food is plentiful it is shared. During times of stress members of food gathering bands bargain for food with their fellow band members by offering favors in return for food.

The practice of all sharing when food was in good supply, the fact that bargaining between band members tended to be restricted to times of stress, the limited number of possessions controlled by each person, and the fact that most members of a given band "owned" almost identical possessions minimized the significance of internal bargaining. Bargaining between members of the same band did not provide the foundation for the emergence of larger and more complex social structures.

The emergence of bargained exchanges as an important means for the distribution of goods, and as a significant form of social activity, stemmed from intergroup exchanges, not from the internal distribution of goods. There are indications that intergroup distribution of goods through bargained exchanges was widespread prior to the foundation of sedentary communities. Manufactured items have been found hundreds of miles from their point of origin from the Paleolithic Age. Sea shells that originated from the Mediterranean have been found in central Europe in paleolithic encampments. These and similar findings may indicate the presence of elaborate trade networks. But there are other possibilities.

Some groups migrated over long distances each year. One group of the Paleolithic Age followed herds of reindeer from southern Germany to the northern coastal regions of Europe each year and back. The yearly trek covered several hundred miles (Hadingham, 1979). Some of the ancient dispersal of goods probably was the consequence of migrating groups acquiring goods in one region and carrying items with them to distant locations. These items may have been collected by those who transported them, or they may have been acquired through trade or theft. Various combinations could account for the distribution of goods over vast territories.

The importance of expeditions for the dispersal of durable goods has probably been underemphasized. Expeditions to distant locations to acquire valued resources probably have a more ancient past, and probably were of greater significance for the dispersal of goods, than either groups following migrating herds of animals, trade networks, or theft. Prior to western European contact some Australian groups travelled long distances to collect resources. Once a year members of the Dieri travelled about 300 miles to acquire durable goods. When the expeditions left their home territory they posted guards each night. Another group, the Yantruwunta, travelled nearly 500 miles to obtain red ochre and sandstone slabs for crushing grass seeds. In both cases it was sometimes necessary for the expeditions to fight with groups native to the area to acquire the goods (Thurnwald, 1932). In still another group, the expeditioners and the local groups had a friendly relationship, but the intruding group was not allowed to carry off the local resource until after giving compensation in the form of skin bags (Thurnwald, 1932). All the Australian expeditions, both those who encountered antagonistic groups and those who met friendly locals, were collective enterprises. The goods obtained by the intruding group were distributed equally among the members of the intruding bands (Thurnwald, 1932).

It is difficult to assess how the ancient dispersal of material was achieved. All that can be ascertained with certainty is the widespread distribution of manufactured durable goods. However, it seems likely that the general sequence of development was from nomadic groups collecting desired items in a given location and carrying the items with them as they moved on, through mounting expeditions into regions to acquire goods, to the combination of expeditionary enterprises with trade.

When all were nomadic, intergroup trade was necessarily of limited significance. First, nomadism prohibits the accumulation of large amounts of goods. Second, the contact between nomadic groups was too erratic to allow for the development of stable trade networks through which large quantities of goods moved. Third, before intergroup trade could emerge as a major procedure for the distribution of goods, human beings had to develop the ability to construct bargained exchanges.

Many nomadic groups of the historical period traded extensively. Those that did, traded with sedentary groups. Sedentary groups could accumulate larger amounts of goods; further sedentism allowed for the establishment of routine contacts between groups. And, third, but not least, residents of sedentary communities with contact with a number of other groups could become sophisticated bargainers and entice others to trade with them.

When all were nomadic, bargaining and trade were necessarily limited to the exchange of goods that were readily portable. In the historical eras some nomadic groups accumulated large quantities of goods to transport to trade centers during certain times of the year. However, that activity was encased by the anticipation that an exchange could be consummated. When all were nomadic that condition did not prevail, or if it did, it was only to a very limited extent. After the establishment of sedentary communities there was a quantum leap in the significance of trade. The establishment of sedentary communities allowed the residents of these communities to accumulate large quantities of goods. The presence of sedentary communities with trade goods in turn enticed nomads to accumulate quantities of goods during periods of plentitude that they then transported to the sedentary community to trade.

Some groups probably had fairly stable contact with each other and traded fairly extensively long before sedentary communities were established. Significant intergroup trade would only occur between groups that had relatively repetitive and peaceful contact with each other. It is conceivable that on occasions when groups accidently made contact with each other, there was some exchange of goods through bargaining, but at best these exchanges were of incidental significance. Their lack of material possessions, fear, and suspicion combined to prohibit trade of any significance when contact was unanticipated.

It is possible that when all were nomadic, groups congregated solely for the purpose of trade. But it is doubtful. Some nomadic groups of historical periods did routinely travel to specific locations and congregated for trade. However these meetings were focused upon a sedentary community. When all were nomadic the programming of meetings solely for the purpose of trade could have been at best only a tentative arrangement.

Some contemporary nomadic groups, but not all, convened during certain times of the year. Some Eskimo groups convened during the Winter months; during the dry seasons bands of Bushmen congregated at water holes. Some congregations of Eskimos were 100 to 150 in size. During these congregations members of different bands had the opportunity to trade with others. However, these congregations were composed of persons who had nearly identical possessions. Trade, while it occurred, was of minimal importance.

In the ancient past when the richer environments were populated by nomadic groups, if and when similar congregations were held, they were probably populated by a larger number of persons who had a greater diversity of possessions than was the case for contemporary food gathering groups. These congregations, whether for festivals, collective hunts, or other purposes provided a foundation for routinized contact between different groups. At these meetings persons developed the ability to peacefully relate and to bargain with one another. These affairs probably contributed to the development of the ability to construct bargained exchanges and thereby to the establishment and expansion of trade networks.

Intergroup trade was not an automatic consequence of contact between groups with different possessions. For many millennia the distribution of goods over expansive regions was probably a complex intermixture of extraction, visiting, sharing, theft, begging, and trade. In a few instances bargained exchanges emerged as the predominant move of relating between members of different groups. Those groups that followed rather stable migration patterns or routinely mounted expeditionary forces to collect items of value, were those most likely to establish routine contacts with other groups that had control of goods different from their own. Reciprocally those groups native to a region where others came to extract goods tended to have a greater variety of stable contacts than other groups. It appears that it was these repetitive contacts that provided the foundation for the emergence of bargained exchanges as a significant form of sociation between groups.

BARGAINED EXCHANGES

Bargaining is a form of cooperative action; each bargainer willingly relates to the other. However, it is a mixed motive encounter. Each bargainer is primarily interested in acquiring the goods of the other and in enhancing his personal interests. Yet if a bargain is to be consummated each bargainer must acknowledge that his personal interest can be best served by cooperating with the other. Their divergent interests must be transformed into compatible interests if the distribution of goods is to be achieved through bargaining.

When divergent interests prevail within an encounter, it is more difficult to produce a cooperative act than when similar interests prevail. When similar interests prevail, as when two or more hunters are interested in bagging game, cooperative activity is relatively easy to produce. However, when the primary interest of A is to acquire the goods of B and B is reluctant to share with A, those involved do not have shared interests. Before bargaining can occur, B must indicate an interest in some service or goods controlled by A. Then their divergent interests can be transformed into compatible interests. The transformation is achieved when they project a future of transferring control of the services and goods in question. Only then is the necessary context provided for the construction of bargained exchanges.

Compatible Interests

Trade was originally stimulated by a desire for the possessions of another, not by surplus production. Intergroup trade did not emerge by groups producing a surplus and then seeking out others interested in their surplus. Any excess of goods was waste material, not a surplus. However, others often have control of items that are of interest to oneself. The original expression of an interest in the goods of others did not take the form of attempting to initiate an exchange. Rather it was expressed by either "theft" or begging. Through millennia human beings gradually acquired the ability to establish reciprocating interests in the services and goods of others. These reciprocating interests in acquiring the goods of others provided the foundation that allowed bargained exchanges to become a regular means for the distribution of goods.

Many forms of intergroup contact contributed to the establishment of routinized intergroup trade. However, it is likely that those groups that resided in regions that others regularly visited to extract a resource played an especially important part in the growth and expansion of bargained exchanges. They had the most frequent contact with a variety of others; they also had differential access to a commodity of interest to others. Reciprocally some of the incomers had control of items that the locals were interested in acquiring. Over millennia these contacts allowed for the formulation of divergent, but compatible interests that provided the foundation for working out cooperative exchanges. Cooperative exchanges then became a significant form of intergroup contact and supplemented and to an extent replaced other means of distribution.

Ownership

Unless there is mutual acceptance of each others' control of goods—ownership—bargained exchanges will not occur. Either the attitude that all goods are to be shared or the attitude that those with the might have the right prohibits the development of trade. Before bargained exchanges could become a routine form of intergroup contact, members of different groups had to accept the prerogative of others to retain control of their goods.

Bargaining rests upon a foundation of each attempting to entice the other to relinquish control of his goods, not upon coercion. To entice another to relinquish control, something must be offered in return. That stimulated the accumulation of surpluses. As the recognition grew that one could acquire the goods of others through enticements, then goods were accumulated for that purpose. Surpluses were the consequence of trade, not the foundation for trade. The accumulation of surpluses in turn transformed ownership from "in use" ownership to permanent ownership.

Reciprocal Surrender of Control

The transfer of control of goods through bargaining requires the production of a complex sequence of reciprocating acts framed by compatible interests and acceptance of the other's prerogative to retain control. Then one offers to transfer control of a good in exchange for the other relinquishing control of the good he possesses. The process consummating in the reciprocal surrendering of control may consist of only two reciprocating acts, or it may extend over a complex set of reciprocating acts as each makes offers and counter-offers. The first offer by one may be acceptable to the other and the transfer of control may then be consummated, or at the other extreme a complex set of reciprocating acts may be brought to an end by one indicating he is no longer interested in bargaining with the other. Not all efforts to bargain are consummated by an exchange. Each party to the encounter has the alternative of withdrawing from the encounter without completing the act.

Bargaining, like all cooperative acts, involves both parties willingly relating to the other. The process may be aborted at any time. However, for one party to withdraw after beginning to bargain tends to generate resentment from the other. Yet the maintenance of peaceful intergroup contact requires that any resentment that might be elicited be subordinated to a mutual concern with maintaining peaceful relations. However, many trade relationships have been destroyed by one party resorting to violence when unable to acquire the desired goods by bargaining for them.

In complex societies there may be a period of some duration between the reaching of an agreement to exchange and the actual transfer of goods. However, in primitive bargaining the agreement to exchange and the transfer of control are usually achieved more or less simultaneously. The exchange is consummated as soon as an agreement is reached. The most ancient form of bargained exchanges was face-to-face bartering followed by the direct exchange of goods.

Bilateral Benefits

Most bargaining is framed by the anticipation of mutual benefit. Each presumes the welfare of both will be better served by an exchange than if no exchange is effected. However, only the anticipation of bilateral benefit is a necessary condition for the construction of bargained exchanges. The condition of bilateral benefit obtains when each anticipates that his welfare will be served by consummating the exchange and has no awareness or concern with the benefits of the other. The anticipation of mutual benefit is not required. There need be no concern with the benefit or cost for the other.

When bargaining is framed only by the anticipation of bilateral benefits, then each bargainer simply assesses his sacrifice in comparison to the anticipated benefit for himself. There is no concern with the relative sacrifice and benefit of the other. After the recognition emerges that the other's welfare is or may be enhanced as a consequence of an exchange, then each party can assess the difference between his sacrifice and gain and the sacrifice and gain of the other. A concern with what constitutes a "fair" exchange can then become an element of bargained exchanges. But that is not a necessary element of bargained exchanges.

Bargained exchanges are far more complex social acts than many other forms of cooperative behavior. At the minimum there are two share foci that must be attended to—the goods controlled by the other and the goods controlled by oneself—and the future projected is the rather complex act of simultaneously effecting a transfer of the control of these goods. Furthermore, exchange acts are richly textured acts. At the minimum, divergent but compatible interests must be established, the mutual prerogative of control of goods must be recognized, there must be mutual trust that the other will relinguish control of a good if and when oneself relinquishes control, and each must make the assessment that self-interest will be served by consummating an exchange.

These factors, plus the interest of each of acquiring benefit with minimal sacrifice renders bargaining a complex and fragile form of cooperative behavior. The completion of bargained exchanges from which both parties accrue benefit provides the foundation for repetitive contact. If either party makes the assessment that his welfare is best served by not trading, then the exchange relation is terminated. After completing bargained exchanges that provide benefit to both parties, then human beings are able to repeatedly interact despite divergent interests. Through bargaining, human beings learned that divergent but compatible interests could serve as a foundation for a stable relation.

SUMMARY

The distribution of goods can take many forms. In small solidary bands internal distribution is achieved primarily through sharing. The distribution process was subordinated to the solidary relationship that prevailed with small groups of hunters and gatherers. Theft, begging, and bargaining did occur within solidary bands. The emergence of these modes of distribution within a solidary group are indicative of disintegration of the social relationships. They are relatively inconsequential modes of distribution when the solidary relationship is robust. When theft, begging, and bargaining emerge as common activities within a solidary group, that group is approaching the point of fragmentation.

The distribution of goods from one group to another and from location to location occurred in a number of ways. Both the migratory patterns of some groups and the practice of groups sending expeditions from their native territory to other regions to collect a resource contributed to the dispersal of materials. In some instances, the distribution of goods from region to region was accomplished by combining trade with migration and expeditions. Intergroup trade was probably of some significance in some regions of the world during the middle Paleolithic Age.

It was only after routinized contact between groups with access to different resources was established that trade could have emerged as a significant form of contact between groups. Even then a large number of factors disrupted established relations. Shortages of game or drought drove the groups from their territory; on occasions intruders moved in and forced locals from the territory, and resources became depleted. All of these factors disrupted established trade contacts.

Prior to the establishment of sedentary communities some goods were moved through more or less established trade networks. However, these networks were rather fluid and easily disrupted. Goods moved in this fashion had to have been restricted to esoteric items in high demand and portable. It is extremely doubtful that quantities of food were moved.

Nomadic food gatherers were not interested in accumulating large amounts of goods, nor were they driven by the profit motive. They were only interested in acquiring the food necessary to sustain life, nearly all of which they acquired through their own efforts: a few portable tools, clothing, and a few luxury items. Only sedentary groups imbued with the profit motive concerned themselves with acquiring wealth through trade.

When nomadic Indians first encountered Western European traders, they were quite unconcerned with capitalizing on the opportunities to accumulate wealth. "Not only was the Indian frequently unwilling to alter the mix of furs that he brought to the posts to capitalize on shifting market conditions, he did not increase the quantities he offered for sale as prices rose" (Ray, 1978:359). It was only through sustained efforts by professional traders that included solicitations, trickery, and coercion that significant trade was established between them and the simpler nomadic groups. Given this, it is apparent that the original emergence of trade as a procedure for the distribution of goods was a very drawn out and tentative affair.

Not all ancient groups traded. Some lived in almost complete isolation, others had only incidental contact with other groups. Only those with relatively routine contact could have traded at all extensively. Even then the amount of goods transferred from person to person, from group to group, and from location to location through bargaining was minimal. Nonethless, trade became a significant form of intergroup contact in some regions prior to the formation of permanent sedentary communities. As bargaining came to the fore, a new form of sociation was established. Then persons established social contact with each other for the purpose of acquiring goods, or the exchange of goods was the foundation of the social contact.

Chapter VI

Primitive Markets

It has long been a tenet of anthropological lore that domestic plants and animals provided the subsistence foundation for the emergence of sedentary communities. However, the evidence supporting that belief is conspicuous by its absence. The earliest sedentary communities of Western Asia and Mesoamerica emerged simultaneously with or after the establishment of long-distance movement of goods (Webb, 1974). Communities with populations of several hundred and even a few thousand have been excavated in Western Asia that yield no evidence of an agricultural base. "Although it is axiomatic that the development of farming and herding preceded the growth of cities, it is significant that the first cities not only in the Tigris and Euphrates valleys but also along the Nile and Indus rose outside those 'nuclear' areas where agriculture was first practiced" (Oates, 1979:14). Perhaps the axiom is of questionable validity.

Those who posit the domestication of plants and animals as providing the foundation for sedentary communities assume that human beings first modified their means of production and then constructed more complex social structures. The reverse is more likely, namely, that first more complex social structures emerged and then there was a transformation of the means of production. The emergence of more complex social structures was dependent upon the establishment of sedentary communities. The earliest sedentary communities were primitive markets, not agricultural villages.

The establishment of sedentary communities necessarily preceded the emergence of food production. Only after sedentary communities were established was it possible for human groups to develop the sustained relations between themselves and plants and animals that was necessary for the domestication of plants and animals. So long as all were nomadic it was impossible for human groups to sufficiently influence plants and animals to domesticate them. Furthermore, once domestication was achieved it was necessary for human groups to continue to exercise control over domestic plants and animals to assure their survival. If domestic plants and animals are not controlled and protected they either go feral or die out.

The likelihood of human groups becoming sedentary as the consequence of a recognition that food production provided a more stable supply of the necessities of life than food gathering is minimal.

Neither those groups who were successful in wresting the necessities of life through their food gathering activities nor those who were unsuccessful, would formulate an alternative mode of production. Those who were successful had no interest in formulating an alternative; those who were unsuccessful might have had an interest if the alternative was presented, but they did not have the resources. In addition, the consciousness that prevailed among nomads was that when food was in short supply one moved, one did not settle down.

The first enduring sedentary communities probably emerged from intergroup contacts produced by a number of groups travelling to the same location for the purpose of collecting a valued material. The development of intergroup trade was an accidental consequence of bands congregating at the same location to collect or harvest resources. These repetitive congregations of a plurality of bands provided the foundation for the emergence of significant intergroup trade and sedentism. While intergroup trade preceded sedentism, it was the establishment of sedentary communities that transformed intergroup trade from an incidental activity to the predominant form of activity at some locations. Those who travelled to these locations came to anticipate the meetings. They brought some items to trade with them. These repetitive encounters enhanced intergroup trade. But more than repetitive encounters between nomadic bands was required before a sedentary community was established.

Some persons remained for various lengths of time at the locations where bands congregated. Members of nomadic bands occasionally remained behind when the band moved on. In nearly every instance those that stayed behind did not provide the nucleus for the formation of a new community. They either faded from existence or joined another band. However, in a few instances those who remained at locations, where a plurality of bands met, endured.

The early sedentary communities that evolved into primitive markets were ragtag affairs. They were probably composed of a conglomerate of persons from different bands who for various reasons did not move on when their native groups did. The earliest primitive markets that endured were those located at or near a resource that was desired by a number of groups. They did not necessarily become established at the exact location of the resource that attracted the bands to the region. If the resources were in a barren region, then the concentration of bands was greater at a nearby sheltered area with a stable water supply than at the location of the resource. Nebulous sedentary groups were established thousands of times; only a very few endured. Some were driven from their temporary sedentism by intruding bands. Others faded from existence. Some who were sedentary for a short period returned to the nomadic life when their native band reappeared.

The establishment of an enduring community required the presence of a local resource that could be collected and perhaps manufactured, the relatively routine reappearance of bands, the maintenance of peaceful relations between the sedentary residents and incoming bands, and the presence of some residents of the sedentary community with sufficient sophistication in trading to recognize that when other groups arrived they could acquire goods from them by trade. In some communities there were sufficient number of persons who were sophisticated enough to collect the local resource and offer it in trade to incoming groups. Some of the incoming groups found it more convenient to trade for the local resource than to collect it.

The resources that provided the material foundation of the community could be anything desired by others. What was collected, manufactured, and traded was of little significance. The significant development was the repetitious contact between a plurality of groups. When this condition was met, a primitive market was established.

Bargaining became a common, if not the predominant, form of activity at these centers. Trade was no longer incidental to other activities; it became a central activity. The residents came to spend more of their time in the production of items for trade. They organized their activity on the basis of their anticipations of the future appearance of others with an interest in acquiring the goods the incoming groups had to offer.

The earliest primitive markets were the consequence of a series of incremental changes. The first generations of residents of these communities were not aware that they were establishing a new form of social life. They may have been dimly aware that their way of life was different from that of their ancestors. It is certain that the earliest markets were not established intentionally. They could not have been. There was no awareness that trade could be a means of acquiring the necessities of life.

The residents of the earliest sedentary settlements remained heavily dependent upon hunting and gathering. But as a settlement became known among surrounding groups as a location where one could go and trade, then trade first supplemented and then partially replaced hunting and gathering as the means by which the community acquired the necessities of life.

The earliest sedentary clusters of persons were probably composed of those least capable of nomadism. Older persons, children, and women probably constituted a disproportionate percentage of the early residents. There are several indications that women held a dominant position in some of the earliest primitive markets. At Çatal Hüyük, one of the oldest trade centers, which was located in Anatolia, the beds of the women were slightly larger. Prior to the establishment of farming as the dominant mode in the Nile valley, the graves of women were larger and richer than the graves of men; the names of the predynastic towns were feminine. In another instance there were a much larger percentage of female graves than male graves. That probably reflects the fact that women tended to remain at the location while men continued to roam the countryside in search of game.

EARLIEST SETTLEMENTS

It appears the sedentary communities from which urban centers emerged were first established in western Asia. Future research may indicate otherwise. But even so, it seems likely that the earliest sedentary communities that provided the foundation stones for civilizations were communities located at or near a source of durable material that was desired by a plurality of other groups. It is also likely that sedentary communities that endured for generations, if not centuries, were established prior to the development of primitive markets in western Asia. However, these communities did not evolve into urban centers.

One of the earliest sedentary communities, if not the earliest, that became an urban center was Jericho. The settlement was on an oasis with a perennial spring surrounded by an arid countryside. Jericho became a prosperous community. It has been commented that "It is clear that the settlement could not have been supported by the natural resources immediately available in the area" (Oates and Oates, 1976:77). The "natural resources" in the immediate area of Jericho and some of the other earliest sedentary communities were not capable of supporting the residents. However, this is true only if "natural resources" are conceptualized as sources of food.

The early residents of Jericho mined and worked the local flint. They developed a flint industry that included the production of "arrow-heads, sickleblades, burins, core-scrapers, chisels and adzes: small axes and numerous fine points or blades and flakes" (Singh, 1974:39). During this period there were no walls but an innumerable successions of floors have been identified indicating that several generations of persons built their huts on the top of older huts that had collapsed.

At Mureybit, another early settlement in the region, people lived in permanent structures long before they practiced either agriculture or animal husbandry (Singh, 1974:57). Over 70,000 pieces of chert, flint, and obsidian have been recovered from the site. "The chipped stone industry was made up of two components, a heavy industry comprising scrapers, adzes, picks and hammers made of chet and a light tool industry essentially made of flint and consisting of such tool-types as burins, perforators, notched blades, borers, and tanged points" (Singh, 1974:58). In later deposits at Mureybit, sickle blades and grinding stones appear (Singh, 1974:58). It is estimated that about 200 persons lived in the settlement.

The earliest residents at Beidha also seem to have manufactured tools, some of which were traded for dentalia shells brought to the site. The first settlers deserted the site or were driven from it. They were replaced by another group about 8000 B.C. The later residents specialized in different crafts.

Çatal Hüyük, which became one of the earliest urban communities, rested upon a foundation of obsidian. The residents collected nearby obsidian, manufactured tools of obsidian, and traded them with numerous groups. Caches of obsidian spear points and other items have been uncovered at the site. The later generations manufactured a wide range of goods that they traded with surrounding groups.

Beginning about 10,000 B.C. several primitive markets were established in Western Asia. All appear to have been locations where a sedentary group collected and manufactured items that were then traded. Many were temporary, failing to endure. Others endured for a few generations. At several sites, after the community had been deserted or the residents had been driven from the location, another community subsequently arose on top of the ruins of the earlier community.

In the beginning trade was of minimal importance. The local resources were exploited and there was a minimal amount of manufacturing. The earliest sedentary residents were largely self-sufficient. Some communities acquired a reputation among surrounding groups, and more groups came to the location for the explicit purpose of trading. The continuance and growth of these communities depended upon a plurality of contacts with groups that brought foodstuffs to the location to exchange for tools and other material goods.

Both grain and animals appear to have been brought to the settlements. Einkorn wheat was stored at Jericho. Its native habitat was 150 miles to the north (Redman, 1978). Some communities had enclosures that were constructed to retain live animals. These enclosures may have been built to retain animals captured by the local residents, but it seems more likely they were built to retain animals that had been brought to the center by others and traded for the local resources. It is possible that after a sedentary community was established, residents of the community travelled to fields of wild grain and brought the harvested grain back to the community. That would have occurred only after a tradition of sedentarism had been established.

As the trade contacts of these communities expanded, the communities became less self-sufficient. Their continuance was dependent upon others harvesting and bringing foodstuff to the market. Some endured and achieved a permanent population that far exceeded the size of the typical food gathering group.

COMPETITIVE BARGAINING

Since Adam Smith, classical economists have claimed that unrestrained and competitive trade is the foundation of economic wealth and communal welfare. They maintain that a plurality of both buyers and sellers with all sellers in competition with each other and all buyers in competition with each other stimulates the production of material goods. Smith opposed all constraints on the marketplace. He saw governmental constraints as the major constraint.

The constraints on trade at these primitive markets were not governmental. Three of the more important constraints on competitive bargaining were: (a) limitations imposed by difficulties in transporting material goods, (b) the absence of routine and stable contact between three or more parties, and (c) the solidary relations that pervade small bands. The emergence of competitive bargaining required that a series of intergroup relations develop that removed these constraints.

The emergence of primitive markets did not remove the restraints imposed by the difficulties of transporting goods. However, their establishment did facilitate routine contacts. The sedentary communities allowed all to develop much firmer anticipations of future contact. The nomadic groups had assurance that if they took goods to a given location they would have the opportunity to trade. When the sedentary group traded with a series of others they too developed firm anticipations. When one party is stationary all can systematically organize their production activity for the purposes of trade. Bargaining and trading were no longer activities that were incidental to other activities; they became significant activities in their own right.

The sedentary groups served as focal points for several other groups.

Life thereby became somewhat more structured than when all were nomadic. Interdependence between groups became more extensive. Not only did the sedentary groups become dependent upon trade contacts with others, but the nomadic groups came to be somewhat dependent upon the sedentary groups for some items. During the early centuries, perhaps millennia, the sedentary groups were more dependent upon the nomadic groups than the nomadic groups were upon the sedentary groups.

The survival of a sedentary community required that it maintain contacts with a plurality of nomadic groups. If they were dependent upon only a single group, the supply of food would have been too erratic for the community to survive. As the trade contacts expanded each group became somewhat less self-sufficient, but in the process there was a slight improvement in the material well being of all.

The routinization of trade did not automatically result in the accumulation of material wealth. The earliest residents of sedentary communities had no more wealth than their nomadic ancestors; they probably had less. It was the marginal members of nomadic groups who became the first collectors and traders. They were highly dependent upon incoming groups for the necessities of life. They probably begged from them as well as traded with them.

Subsequent generations of residents of sedentary communities did accumulate far more material wealth than was possessed by the nomadic groups. The accumulation of wealth was facilitated by the routinization of trade contacts. But a new and important element was introduced in their trading transactions when competition emerged between the nomadic bands for the resources controlled by the sedentary community.

The earliest bargaining between nomadic groups were probably conducted within a framework of two solidary bands confronting each other. Solidary relationships severely inhibit competitive bargaining. Family members and friends on occasion bargain with each other, but the bargaining that occurs within such relationships is constrained by considerations for the solidary relationship. When bargaining is between members of different social units then competitive bargaining is more likely to come to the fore.

Even then the solidary relationships within each group operate to inhibit competitive bargaining. Keill (1977) provides an insightful description of relatively primitive groups who routinely bargained with each other. The bargaining was between sedentary groups, who in comparison to nomadic groups possessed great wealth. These groups travelled to each other's villages or met at an agreed upon location for the specific purpose of trade. There were no markets.

There were no established relationships between the groups other than sporadic meetings to effect exchanges. "The relationship between the parties to the exchange seem to consist of nothing more than the transfer of goods itself" (Keil, 1977:259). The meetings were organized for trade. This places the activity in a different context than when trade occurs between members of different groups who have congregated to hold a festival. The practice of meeting solely to trade establishes an interdependence based upon compatible interests instead of solidary interests.

The bargaining was limited to intergroup exchanges; there was no bargaining between members of the same group. All members of each group tended to have the same products to offer to the members of the other group. Only two groups bargained at a time. "The structure is that of two solidary groups" (Keil, 1977:266). Members of each group avoided undercutting the offers made by other members of their group. Each person of both groups demanded the same "price" for his products. On occasions when one seller was not able to complete an exchange with someone of the other group, upon the termination of the encounter another seller might step in and attempt to bargain with the person. Efforts to consummate exchanges by underselling other person from one's own group were constrained by a fear of rejection from one's fellow tribesmen. Intratribe solidarity constrained the offers made by members of each group.

The earliest exchanges between sedentary groups and outlanders were probably conducted in a context where the internal solidarity of the outlander group was more robust than the solidarity of the sedentary group. Therefore, if there was undercutting of prices it probably occurred more often among the residents of the sedentary community. To the extent that it occurred, it placed the residents of the sedentary community at a disadvantage.

However, the residents of the sedentary communities were sometimes confronted with two or more outlander groups who were interested in acquiring the items controlled by the sedentary community. That created the condition where members of different outlander bands found themselves in competition with each other. The emergence of competitive bargaining as an important dimension of intergroup trade probably resulted from interband competition for the same goods rather than from intraband competition.

The sedentary residents, more frequently than the nomadic persons, found themselves with the choice of selecting the items offered that were most appealing and rejecting the offers of the other group. The members of the two nomadic bands would all be interested in obtaining, for example, obsidian, but one group would be offering grain and the other dried meat. The members of the nomadic band whose offer was rejected were thereby enticed to increase their offerings.

The residents of the sedentary community thereby had an implicit unilateral monopoly. This transformed the bargaining from dyadic interchanges between two parties interested in acquiring goods from each other to a focused relation with the sedentary residents serving as the focal point.

The focal party, the sedentary resident, came to bargain from an entirely different standpoint from the other parties. When bargaining is dyadic, each party assesses the item offered by the other on the basis of the worth of the object to himself in comparison to the worth of the object that he is offering. An exchange is consummated when there is mutual assessment that the worth of the object offered is greater than that of the item surrendered.

When bargaining is conducted in a context where one serves as a focal point for a plurality of others, assessments of the same sort continue. However, when A, a member of the focal group, was bargaining with B, a member of one of the outlander groups, he assessed the worth of the item offered by B by comparing it to an item that had been offered by C, a member of the second outlander group, or that might be offered by C. When B and C were not interested in each other's goods, they continued to make assessments of the worth of the item offered by A in the same manner that prevailed in dyadic bargaining. B and C thereby established a competitive relation with each other that served the interest of A. In the meantime A retained his position of bargaining without competition.

The early residents of sedentary communities did not intentionally create unilateral monopolies. They had no awareness that it would serve their interest to do so. Their sedentary life simply created the conditions from which this relation emerged. Subsequently communities intentionally organized themselves to present a united front to the outlanders. However, considerable sophistication in trade and communal solidarity was required before that step was taken.

The establishment of sedentary communities, routinization of contact for purposes of trade, and intergroup competition created the minimal conditions for the establishment of primitive markets. When these conditions were met economic transactions became a substantial and important form of social action.

ACCUMULATION OF WEALTH

The earliest sedentary clusters of persons did not discontinue their nomadic ways to acquire wealth. Yet by becoming sedentary and establishing economic relations with a plurality of nomadic groups, sedentary groups thereby established two of the conditions necessary for the accumulation of wealth. However, before the wealth accumulated by sedentary groups could significantly exceed that of nomadic groups, members of the sedentary group had to learn to stockpile both the local resource and the goods they acquired through trade.

They had to stockpile the local resource in order to have the goods necessary for trade when the opportunity arose. They had to stockpile foodstuff acquired through trade in order to remain sedentary. Those who established the earliest markets learned to husband their goods on a larger scale than is common among food gatherers. The fluctuations inherent in trade made it necessary to store food if a group was to remain sedentary. Many incipient markets failed to endure due to the lack of adequate stockpiling. But some overcame this problem.

The practice of stockpiling goods was slow to develop, but as it developed it strengthened the bargaining position of the sedentary communities. Once stockpiling became an established practice, the residents had an additional advantage over the nomadic groups. They were under less pressure to consummate a given exchange than members of the nomadic groups. Yet, the sedentary people had to acquire some of their food from the nomadic groups if they were to maintain their sedentary life. The nomadic groups desired the goods offered by the sedentary residents, but they could continue their way of life without them. In general, however, the movement was in the direction of transforming the early advantages of the nomadic groups into a situation where the sedentary groups held the advantageous position.

ECONOMIC HEGEMONY

The early markets exercised economic hegemony. They did not exercise political control over the surrounding groups or the surrounding territory, but by serving as the focal point for the trade in the region they influenced the activity of surrounding groups. They provided these groups with the opportunity to hunt and collect for trade as well as to obtain the food necessary to sustain life.

The hegemony of the markets was based upon the more stable wealth and greater sophistication of the residents. Food gathering is an unstable way of life. Some years the hunting is good and other years it is bad. Stored surpluses provided sedentary groups with a cushion that made them less vulnerable to erratic changes in the environment than were food gatherers.

Diverse groups congregated at these centers. The markets were centers of information as well as centers of trade. All participants were exposed to a variety of lifestyles and became aware of the goods harvested and controlled by other groups. The sedentary traders acquired more information than those who came to the markets. Compared to the outlanders the sedentary groups were sophisticates. They were more knowledgable about the supply and demand for products and more skilled in bargaining than the outlanders. The same relation holds today between professional traders and amateurs. One consequence was that the members of settled communities came to see themselves as distinct from and superior to the outlanders.

Repetitive trade encounters between the sedentary group and the outlanders informed all of their differences. In trade there is an implicit recognition of mutual dependency; the welfare of each party is contingent on maintaining trade relations. However, as the markets expanded and more outlander groups came to trade, the level of dependency of the traders on any given group became less. Simultaneously the degree of dependency of an outlander party became greater. The dominance of the settled group occasionally became pronounced.

Trade between the two types of groups remained mutually beneficial. Markets allowed the sedentary groups to acquire the necessities of life and they allowed the outlander groups to acquire goods they could not otherwise obtain. However, the trade became more beneficial to the professional traders than to the outlanders. The "profit" of the traders was greater than that of the outlanders.

The accumulation of wealth by the traders was a source of envy among the outlanders. The greater sophistication and skill in bargaining by the traders created resentment among the outlanders. They often felt they had been taken advantage of, but were in a relatively powerless position to correct the "injustice" inherent in the relationship.

These factors accentuated the differences between the residents of the settlements and nomadic groups. The boundaries between the two types of groups were highly fluid during the developing period but over time the boundaries became clearer. Not only did the boundaries become clearer, but the sedentary groups found they could exploit the outlanders. They learned to exercise their unilateral monopoly and made it an explicit unilateral monopoly. Goods were offered to the outlanders on a "take or or leave it" basis.

This development enhanced their ability to acquire wealth. The accumulation of wealth was not an unmixed blessing. It gave stability to their lives, but it also served as a magnet to surrounding groups. The efforts of the surrounding groups to acquire the wealth of the markets were not always restricted to trade. Drought, shortage of game, stretches of bad luck, and envy enticed some to attempt to acquire the wealth even when they had nothing to trade. Some begged for it, others attempted to steal it, and still others raided the centers.

The begging and raiding further crystallized the distinctiveness between the sedentary traders and the outlanders. In most instances begging and raiding became complexly intertwined with complementary trade relations. Residents of the settlements recognized their dependence on the outlanders, yet at the same time were disdainful and fearful of them. Reciprocally the outlanders were envious and disdainful toward the sedentary group.

These factors and others contributed to the residents of the trade centers coming to see themselves as a distinct category of humanity. The collective differentiation that emerged probably was the first form of class consciousness. The traders conceived of themselves as not only distinct from the food gatherers, but superior to them as well. Conversely the nomadic food gatherers had ambivalent standpoints toward the traders. On the one hand the traders were the source of desired goods, but on the other hand they manipulated the relation to serve their self-interest to the detriment of the outlanders.

The antagonistic sentiments intertwined with asymmetrical dependency created a highly volatile condition. The outlander groups had no compunction against raiding and looting the markets. The Old Testament, the Iliad, the Viking sagas, and other sources reflect the pride taken by groups in their ability to extract wealth from centers of wealth, by raiding them. Begging and asymmetrical trading were ways that material goods could be acquired, but often were humiliating. Successful raids were a source of pride.

This difference reflects the difference in the relations. When outlanders trade with residents of a center that exercises economic hegemony over them, they must, to a degree, subordinate themselves to the professional traders. The asymmetry is accentuated when one begs. When they raided them, they subordinated the traders. To attempt a raid is to make a declaration of superiority.

The incursions of the outlanders created a condition that invited the traders to form mutual protection associations. The most obvious manifestation of this is that later markets were surrounded by walls. In ancient China the word for city and wall was one and the same. By one account the walls of Jericho were destroyed sixteen times. No accounts are available of how often the residents of Jericho were successful in repulsing raiders.

The economic hegemony of the early markets was a diffuse and fragile form of dominance. The residents of these centers relied on their focal position, their greater sophistication in trade, and skill in bargaining to accumulate wealth. An asymmetrical relation between them and each surrounding group was created. The creation of asymmetrical relations often had consequences that resulted in their destruction. The early raiders did not take over the markets; they simply destroyed them.

DISEMBEDDING CONSEQUENCES

Bargaining is a dyadic activity dominated by individualistic interests. Bargainers relate to each other on the basis of divergent but compatible interests, not shared interests. Each is aware his future is contingent on the other, but their shared future is limited. When a bargaining encounter is consummated by an exchange regarded as mutually beneficial both parties experience satisfaction. Even so, the degree of satisfaction of one bargainer is often greater when the satisfaction of the other is less.

The satisfaction stemming from bargaining is that of two individuals, it is only to a limited degree a collective satisfaction. In contrast, when a collective hunt is successful the satisfaction is collective. One person may have been responsible for bringing down the game, but all are pleased with the success. All benefit from the outcome.

Experienced bargainers recognize that while their future is contingent on trade contacts, their personal interests are served by making the best bargain possible. Consequently the orientation of experienced bargainers is to attempt to make the best deal possible, yet assuring future trade. When several others desire the goods one has to offer, then only a minimal, if any concern with the satisfaction derived by the other constrains the behavior of the traders. Even when bargaining is constrained by a concern with preserving trade contracts, experienced bargainers attempt to obtain the best exchange possible without threatening future relations.

Bargainers confront each other as antagonists, but with their antagonism constrained by mutual recognition of their interdependence. When the same persons bargain with one another they acquire a shared past and anticipate future encounters. When bargaining is encased by a shared past and an anticipated shared future, the bargaining is constrained and the bargainers may become embedded with each other.

However, when there is a plurality of buyers then bargaining is more often between strangers. The frequency of a given pair of bargainers establishing repetitive bargaining encounters become less. Each then organizes his action largely, if not solely, to achieve the best possible outcome. The other is treated only as an instrument to achieve the desired result. No embeddedness between persons is produced.

Compared to the action of nomadic groups, most of the action within primitive markets was dyadic. Within each dyadic transaction individuals pursued their personal satisfaction; collective action was minimal. Clusters of families and persons lived at these sites, but relatively little of the action involved the community acting in unison. Rather each person acted as an individual in a series of dyadic encounters with antagonists. The residents of these communities not only did not act in a solidary manner with their trading partners, but they took little solidary action with fellow residents.

The increased emphasis on private activity within dyadic encounters and the decreased frequency of solidary action is a universal consequence of the emergence of the marketplace. As these ancient primitive markets expanded, both the sedentary traders and the members of the nomadic groups experienced an erosion of communal solidarity. The impact was most profound among the residents of the centers; they spent a greater proportion of their time bargaining. But the direction of the impact was the same on the nomadic groups. The more involved the nomadic groups became in trade, the greater the impact.

Among the outlanders the transformation was rather limited. In extreme instances, in modern times, when nomadic groups have become intensely involved in trade the transformation has led to the demise of the group. In severe cases it has resulted in nomadic groups hunting game with such intensity that it disturbed the ecology of the region, on occasion, rendering it incapable of supporting them.

Prior to becoming involved in taking items to a market to trade, the typical member of a hunting society hunts to acquire food for himself, his family, and community. When the traditional hunter was successful all benefitted. The development of markets enticed hunters to hunt less for communal benefit and more for personal benefit. When the spoils of the hunt can be exchanged, the hunter organizes his activity more to acquire items that he as an individual can take to the market to trade and less on the basis of the social objective of acquiring food and clothing for his family.

The communal solidarity of the outlander groups eroded as members of these groups became more involved in trade. Members of these societies organized themselves more on the basis of selfish interests and less on the basis of collective interests. The disembedding consequences of trade, which in extreme cases result in the atomization of members of tribal groups, has been noted by several critics of the market place (Polanyi, 1957).

The impact of the earliest markets on the surrounding groups was minimal. However, the direction of the change was the same as among historical primitive groups who became a part of a trade network centered on trading posts established by traders from industrial societies.

In extreme instances within a generation or two, members of hunting and gathering groups have become so disembedded from each other that the protection and support stemming from communal solidarity was destroyed. Members of primitive groups then were extremely vulnerable to exploitation by professional traders.

Societies have experienced this transformation in historical times. The commercial development of the Greeks and Meccans that occurred when these societies developed into trade-centered societies changed their social order from one determined primarily by kinship into a social order that was based largely on economic relations. The societies become more diversified and homogeneity was replaced by heterogeneity. Family and tribal solidarity was replaced by complex symbiotic relations. When this transformation occurred among the Meccans the real functional units became clusters of rich merchants and their dependents (Wolf, 1969). The Meccan and Greeks underwent the transformation within a few generations. The transformation took far longer when primitive markets first emerged.

The primitive markets that endured developed a new social structure. Instead of organizing themselves on the basis of their embeddedness with one another, these societies came to recognize that they had common interests based on their trade. Instead of relating to one another primarily on the basis of a solidary relationship, they constructed "rationalistic" associations. These associations were formed on the basis of mutual recognition that the interests of all could best be served by presenting a united front to the outlanders. The association was based on a mercenary assessment of the situation, not on the basis of communal solidarity that has emerged from extensive solidary action. In most, perhaps all, cases the associations were partially a response by residents of trade centers to intrusions by the outlanders.

The general impact of markets on the outlander groups, then, was in the direction of creating fragmentation within each of them. In extreme cases the demise of collectivities as distinctive units was the consequence. In some instances the outlander groups were transformed from self-sufficient hunting and gathering collectivities into fragmented and atomized units highly dependent on producing trade goods. The consequences of disembedding among the outlander groups were diffuse and often had no great impact on their life, but the general direction of the change was toward atomization.

In comparison the consequences on the residents of markets that endured were substantial, but different. The traders had greater opportunities to form associations based on their economic position that served their collective interests. They consciously joined together, not on the bases of solidary embeddedness, but on the basis of a rationalistic assessment of their economic position. Occupation and residency supplemented and to an extent replaced kinship and band membership as the foundation for their social structure.

MODIFICATION OF TEMPORAL STRUCTURES

Bargaining changed the temporal structures of the residents of the markets. They developed long-range individualistic futures; shared futures became less significant. Distal futures were projected by hunters and gatherers, including individualistic distal futures. However, within nomadic bands individualistic futures are subordinate to the collective future. Both the activity of bargaining and the accumulation of goods for the purpose of bargaining are organized on the basis of the anticipations and intentions of individuals—not groups.

Bargaining, like all forms of cooperative behavior, is framed by a shared future. But the shared future of bargainers is a proximal one. The only shared future necessary for bargaining is that of the possibility of consummating an exchange. The proximal future of an exchange structures offers and counter-offers of bargainers, but bargainers recognize that when the bargaining process is aborted, or when the exchange is consummated, they may not have any more contact with each other. A distal shared future may encase bargaining, but it is not a necessary feature of the activity. Bargaining between strangers who have no intention of ever seeing one another again is a common activity at markets.

Bargaining does not require the projection of a distal individualistic future, but the projection of a distal individualistic future is usually a viable part of the bargaining process for professional traders. Some exchanges ae completed by one or both parties acting impulsively. However, as persons acquire experience in bargaining, they learn to assess the potential consequences of an exchange in terms of its distal consequences for their personal welfare. Those who project distal individualistic futures of considerable duration and complexity are more likely to be successful than those who bargain impulsively. Those who bargain impulsively are less likely to remain traders; they lose out to those who are more rational in their efforts.

The duration of the futures projected by primitive bargainers was no greater than the duration of the futures that structured the food gathering activity of hunters and gatherers. But they were distinctly different. The distal futures of bargainers were individualistic, not collective. Bargaining generates a concern with personal futures, not collective futures.

The establishment of routinized trade also encouraged the elaboration of individualistic futures during the productive process. The production process among hunters and gatherers is encased within a collective future. With the development of markets, persons produce less to provide necessities for themselves and other members of their solidary unit and more with the intention of acquiring goods to subsequently take to the market to trade. Consequently production and consumption become separated by periods of considerable duration. Within food gathering groups there usually was little duration between the act of production and consumption. When an animal was slain, it was consumed shortly afterwards. As persons became involved in trade, some produce was saved to be traded later for other items. The production-consumption process became extended.

This transformation was most pronounced among the sedentary residents of the primitive markets, but it also occurred to a lesser extent among those who traded regularly at the marketplaces. Those most effective in organizing their day-to-day activity on the basis of long-range individualistic futures tended to be more successful. The hunter who accumulated furs to trade for obsidian not only was a more effective trader, but in addition he acted to maximize the likelihood of acquiring obsidian tools that perhaps made him a more effective hunter.

The temporal structures that ordered the activities of some food gathering bands were quite complex. Most organized their movement from location to location on the basis of a yearly cycle. This required a temporal structure of at least a few moons' duration. However, the distribution of most goods was accomplished within a temporal frame of limited duration. All ate when food was available. Distribution was accomplished within relatively short-range temporal structures. With the emergence of markets, the distribution processes became organized on the basis of extended temporal structures.

The development of bargaining as a common form of social action extended the individualistic temporal structures of both the traders and those who came to the markets. However, the development was more pronounced among the traders. To remain a trader it was necessary to program a future of considerable duration and complexity. Goods had to be accumulated before the arrival of interested parties. If a number of groups were anticipated, then if futures of considerable complexity were formulated, one was likely to be successful in his trading enterprises. Those individuals most adept at planning their personal futures were those who acquired the resources that allowed them to continue their lives as traders; those less adept lost out. Some returned to the nomadic way of life. Others became subordinates to the more successful traders.

The individualistic futures of the members of the nomadic groups also were extended. However, the change in this direction was much less than among the sedentary communities. Nomadic groups, upon accumulating goods, could go to the markets and attempt to trade. It was not necessary for them to develop individualistic temporal structures as elaborate as the traders in order to trade. However, the fact that their activity was less effectively planned often put them at a severe disadvantage in their bargaining with the traders.

SUMMARY

The establishment of primitive markets was the beginning phase of one of the major transformations in humanity's movement from a nomadic life style that was highly responsive to the environment, to a sedentary and rationalistic life. It allowed human beings to accumulate material wealth, to expand the networks of interdependency and to form rational associations that in part replaced the solidary base of prior structures.

A key transformation occurred when a sedentary group found themselves confronted by two or more other groups interested in obtaining the same goods. The resulting implicit unilateral monopoly provided one of the necessary conditions for the emergence of competitive bargaining. Competition between outlanders allowed sedentary groups to accumulate greater wealth and to establish a more stable life than was possible among nomadic hunting and gathering groups.

Bands of food gatherers differentiate themselves from one another. However the differentiation is basically egalitarian. The emergence of markets provided the base for an asymmetrical differentiation. Residents of the settlements exercised economic hegemony over the surrounding groups, placing the outlanders in a subordinate position. Antagonistic relations between traders and the outlanders affirmed and enhanced the differentiation.

The combination of accumulated wealth, acquiring sophistication in trade, and repelling the incursions of outlanders provided a foundation for the formation of a new kind of human association. Residents of those markets that endured formed associations with one another, not on the basis of solidary action, but on the basis of mutual recognition that they had in common mercenary interests. Private interest thereby became the basis for social action.

Not all residents of the primitive markets were traders. Even those who traded extensively continued to hunt and gather foodstuff. But as these markets emerged, those most involved in trading activity became the central persons in the social structures of these communities. As trade became an important means of acquiring goods, those most involved in trade became the dominant persons of their communities. Their experience allowed them to acquire the ability to develop complex and elaborate temporal structures. They developed more precise and complex temporal sequences than those only minimally involved in trade. They became the key persons in programming the future of the community.

Human beings do not become embedded with each other through bargaining. Therefore, trade relations are broken with the greatest of ease when a new opportunity presents itself to one of the parties. At the marketplace each bargainer respects the integrity of the other and his possessions, but at the same time is unconcerned with the other's welfare. The expansion of social relations associated with early markets was based upon utilitarian assessments of the contact. So long as the association was mutually beneficial it was continued, but when one party assessed the relation as nonutilitarian the contact was broken. Rationalistic and individualistic interests displaced communal solidarity as the foundation for the social structures.

The emergence of trade and markets transformed the nature of human interdependence. Members of self-sufficient food gathering groups are dependent on one another, but they are dependent upon kith and kin. To the extent persons became involved in a market economy they became dependent upon strangers. Within solidary units individuals can expect support and aid in times of stress; when the primary mode of relating with others is via bargained exchanges then no support or aid can be expected. Each person is thrown on his own resources at the marketplace. There are no established and enduring relationships, only a variety of contacts.

Chapter VII

The Growth of Trade Centers

Some of the early markets became communities of substance. Settlements with populations of thousands emerged. Some established routine contacts with other communities several hundred miles away. Those primitive markets that endured and established contacts with other sedentary communities were transformed into trade centers. They traded with nomadic groups and each other. Some persons became wholesalers and they specialized in the movement of quantities of goods from one location to another.

The original linkage between sedentary communities was probably forged by groups who followed a regular migratory pattern that brought them into contact with two or more settlements. The migratory groups served as conduits for the movement of goods from one market to another. Fluid networks of trade were probably established between some groups before sedentary communities were established. However, until sedentary communities were established, the contact between groups was quite erratic. The founding of sedentary communities stabilized contact between members of the settlement and nomadic groups, and eventually contact between sets of sedentary communities was routinized. The growth of the sedentary communities and the increase of trade contacts between them occurred simultaneously. Trade between sedentary communities became viable and supplemented the trade between nomadic groups and the sedentary communities.

It may be that the emergence of the first primitive markets was dependent upon the prior existence of fluid trade networks that were fairly routinized. Some of the earliest markets may have been spinoffs of previously established trade networks. Before sedentary communities were established at Jericho and Beidha, two of the earliest markets of western Asia, these locations were stopping-off places for nomadic groups on migratory treks. These communities, and perhaps many others, may owe their origin to the practice of some migratory groups stopping at the locations when they trekked through an area.

Other early trade centers seem to have been the consequence of a plurality of groups trekking to the same location to harvest or collect a local resource. In some instances a plurality of groups came to the same location to acquire the same resource. In such instances contact was established between the groups who came to the location and any local groups that remained in the general area during most of the year. Çatal Hüyük may have originated from such a background. The population of the city was a mixed lot. It had at least three distinct racial groups. Euroafricans, who descended from an upper paleolithic type, were the largest ethnic group; they formed a little over half of the population. Two other racial groups composed the bulk of the remaining population (Mellaart, 1975:99). The group that composed the largest segment of the population were probably descendants of a group or set of groups who lived in the area prior to the founding of the community; the other two racial groups were probably descendants of groups who travelled to the area to collect obsidian before a sedentary community was established.

During the period when sedentary communities were being established, the contact between the sedentary communities was of minimal importance. However, as the settlements grew, contact between the different sedentary communities became more important. The growth of a settlement and its endurance was dependent upon trade contacts with other sedentary settlements.

Jericho may have been one of the earliest trade centers of western Asia. By 8000 B.C. it had an estimated population of 2,000. During the ninth millennium, obsidian from Anatolia, a distance of a few hundred miles, was reaching Jericho. It is conceivable that residents of Jericho mounted expeditions to Anatolia to acquire obsidian, but it seems more likely that it was brought to Jericho by others to trade for local products. Several other trade centers of substance were established in western Asia at approximately the same time and during the following millennia.

These communities rested upon a foundation provided by trade. They did not rest upon subsistence agriculture. At these sites "there is no evidence whatsoever of the domestication of any plant or animal" (Mellaart, 1975:32). Some residents may have practiced horticulture to a limited degree, but the settlements did not rest upon horticulture. Horticulture was of very limited significance during the early millennia; it became more important in the following centuries. The expansion of the early trade centers did not rest upon the development of horticulture, but was dependent on the stabilization and expansion of trade and the manufacturing of trade items. Horticulture was more of an offshoot of becoming sedentary than the foundation for becoming sedentary. Of course, once horticulture became established, it contributed to the further growth of these centers.

The growth of the early trade centers was primarily dependent upon: (a) the expansion of markets, (b) the development of techniques for the storage of perishables, (c) the formation of new forms of communal action, (d) the emergence of professional traders and (e) overcoming the limitations imposed by transportation difficulties. As these constraints were removed some of the primitive markets populated by a dozen or so families living in huts and hovels became not villages, but small cities. Not many of the primitive markets became cities. Some were deserted, others destroyed, while still others stagnated and faded away. Growth is not automatic for any community.

EXPANSION OF MARKETS

After a market had been established it would expand as more of the surrounding nomadic groups learned of its existence and journeyed there to trade. However, so long as the market was restricted to nomadic groups, the growth of the settlement was limited. Nomads have little interest in accumulating large quantities of goods. The population of these centers, when trade was restricted to nomads, could not have been greater than a few hundred.

Interlinkage between settlements provided all of them with more trade items. That enticed larger numbers of nomadic groups to some of those settlements. In addition, trade between settlements contributed to the growth of each. Some of these centers had far-flung contacts and traded a variety of goods. Jericho traded "turquoise from the Sinai region, cowry shells from the Red Sea, and obsidian and greenstones from Anatolia" (Redman, 1978:78). Pre-agricultural communities of the Nile Valley have yielded artifacts that include "copper, Red Sea and Mediterranean Sea shells, hard and attractive gemstones from the eastern and western deserts, and ceramic vases from Palestine" (Hoffman, 1979: 338). A settlement along the Wadi el Tih (Maadi) off the Nile River served as a waystation between the trade centers of western Asia and those along the Nile River. The residents had elaborate storage facilities and some of the houses were of foreign design, suggesting the presence of a multiethnic community.

The elaboration of intercommunity contacts was originally based upon specialized access to local resources and in turn led to considerable community specialization in the collecting, mining, and manufacturing of products. Some of the settlements specialized in extracting minerals, especially obsidian; others specialized in collecting and exporting sea shells; others in collecting and manufacturing luxury items. Malachite, a copper carbonate with a distinctive greenish color, was widely traded in western Asia.

The only tracings we have of the extensive trade networks are of the durable items. Undoubtedly however, perishable items were traded as well. A settlement along the Missouri River in central North Dakota had routinized trade contacts with another trade center located in the southwestern corner of Wyoming, a distance of nearly 1,000 miles. Prior to western Europeans entering the area, the Crow Indians made a yearly trek from one trade center to another. The Crow brought dressed buffalo hides decorated with plumage, porcupine quills and various dyes to the settlement that they traded with the Mandans for grain and beans (Verendry as quoted in Ewers, 1968:19).

The Mandan settlement was agricultural. Yet ancient trade centers may have had trade contacts that were equally extensive. The significant point is that the trade between the Mandan and the Crow was based primarily, but not entirely, on the exchange of perishable items. Such may have been the case for many of the ancient trade centers.

For example, the residents of the lower Nile traded extensively with nomads of the Sahara long before farming was established in the valley and before pastoralists with their domestic herds reached the Sahara. The communities along the Nile traded wild grain to the nomads. Presumably the nomads offered in exchange many other goods to the residents along the Nile that were also perishable. Trade between these two types of populations was established on the Nile by 6000 B.C. Subsequently, about 4000 B.C., pastoralists with domestic herds replaced the nomads of the Sahara. Trade continued between the pastoralists and the Nile Valley settlements.

The establishment of the trade centers elicited a degree of specialization from the nomads. However, the specialization among the nomads was less than that among the sedentary communities. Most of the nomadic groups probably harvested more of the available resources that they found they could exchange than they did prior to the emergence of the trade centers.

The early trade probably was based largely on durable material for tools and distinctive shells and minerals for luxury items. As these trade centers grew, the trade in perishables probably increased. Most of them probably did not achieve a size much larger than large nomadic bands. Like nomadic bands, the settlements fragmented. During the early millennia when they fragmented, most of the segments that left returned to a nomadic life. Later as sedentism became established, more of the groups that fragmented left their native settlement, not to return to nomadism, but to establish new settlements. A multitude of factors contributed to fragmentation. Some left following internal conflicts, others when the trade opportunities lessened, others because they thought it possible to find a better way of life at another location and some when driven from their settlements by raiders.

The collectivities that fragmented and established new settlements were the first colonists. They did not claim territories other than the small amount necessary for a settlement. Many new trade centers were probably established in this manner. The fragmentation that resulted in the forming of new settlements expanded the markets of the older communities. Some of the colonists maintained ties with the residents of their native communities. In most cases there was two-way movement of both people and goods between the new settlement and the mother community. In addition, some of the new communities established contact with other nomadic groups.

Like the original primitive markets many of the new communities probably endured but a short time. But some of them prospered and surpassed the mother community. Complex interlinked trade centers and markets were established in western Asia, in the Nile Valley, around the eastern Mediterranean and into Central Asia. Trade networks between sedentary communities and between the sedentary communities on the one hand and nomadic groups on the other were well-established millennia before agricultural villages emerged.

The development of trade networks and sedentary communities may have occurred somewhat differently in the New World than they did in the Old World. They were a much later development and their emergence seems to have been more closely linked to agriculture. It is possible that their development was stimulated by Old World contact.

Sedentary communities engaged in long-distance trade appeared along the Gulf Coast of Mexico in the third millennium B.C. These communities were the precursors of the Mayan civilization. The Maya claimed they originated in 3111 B.C. No communities that are linked to the Maya have been uncovered that are that ancient. Furthermore, the date of 3111 B.C. is a date that specifies a particular astronomical alignment. Nonetheless the date may be a relatively accurate specification of when the first significant community of the ancestors of the Maya was established. We date our calendar from the birth of Christ; it is now agreed that the original specification of the birth of Christ was slightly in error. There is no archaeological evidence for Christians until about a century or two later. It is not inconceivable that the first Mayan community was founded about 3000 B.C.

Trade centers and extensive trade networks were widespread in Mesoamerica before monumental centers were first established by the Olmec. Tikal, which became one of the major monumental centers of the Maya, served as a trace center with "far-flung trade contacts" long before it became a monumental center (Adams, 1977:17). As in the Old World there is evidence that long-distance trade networks preceded the appearance of agricultural communities.

A similar sequence of development occurred on the coastal region of Peru (Cohen, 1977). Between 12,000 B.C. and 2500 B.C., the region was inhabited by nomadic groups. There are no indications of any permanent settlements during that period. About 5000 B.C. quarry sites display "an increase in the frequency of cobble flakes (sickles?) and grinding equipment suggesting an increased reliance on the harvesting and grinding of seeds" (Cohen, 1977:158). One site that dates about 4000 B.C. yielded "seeds of grass in enormous concentrations" and grinding stones. About 2500 B.C. sedentary communities were established at quarry sites. By 2000 B.C. there was extensive trade between inland communities and coastal communities. The coastal people traded fish and other marine products to the inland farmers for agricultural products. (MacNeish, 1977:788). In addition, the coastal people acquired obsidian from the inland people and the inland people acquired shells from the coast (MacNeish, 1977:789).

Maize, which had been domesticated earlier in Mesoamerica, was first cultivated on the Peruvian coast at about the same time (Pickersgill and Heisier, 1977:806). In Peru the establishment of sedentary communities and grain production appears to have occurred more or less simultaneously. In general the establishment of sedentary communities and the production of grain were more closely affiliated in the New World than in the Old World. In the Old World many communities of substance were established thousands of years prior to the emergence of agriculture; in the New World agriculture was introduced when sedentary groups appeared or shortly after.

STORAGE OF PERISHABLES

Most years the food resources of a given locality were capable of supporting a much larger population than inhabited the region. The food available for nomads varies tremendously from year to year and season to season. The population of a region is limited by the food supply that is available during the leanest times. It was the irregularity of food resources that constrained the population when all were nomadic, not the total amount available. The nomadic inhabitants of the regions where the first markets and trade centers were established lived in a far richer environment than most contemporary food gatherers. Even so the population density of the region was quite low.

An increase in population density was contingent on the development of techniques of storage that provided food during the lean seasons. Some nomadic groups preserve some food, but the amount they preserve is very small. Techniques of storage and preservation of large quantities of food were developed by sedentary groups. The continuation and growth of these communities depended upon the storage and preservation of food. Only those settlements that developed storage techniques endured. Many failed to last because they failed to solve this problem.

The residents of the earliest sedentary communities did not have storage facilities. But some developed procedures for preserving perishables. Unlike nomads who move on when food is in short supply, sedentary communities preserve food for future consumption. The storage of food requires that persons organize their activity to acquire food that will not be consumed for several months.

Sophisticated buildings for storing grain were developed by the eighth millennium in western Asia. "The earliest well-documented type is the so-called grill plan, in which narrow foundation walls were probably spanned by a floor of clay covered saplings, reeds or even stones, leaving ventilation spaces below" (Oates and Oates, 1976:80). These buildings served as granaries and insulated the stored grain from the damp. Villages of northern Syria had roasting pits to parch grain over heated stones. One "effect of this treatment was that it could then be stored without danger of sprouting" (Oates and Oates, 1976:72).

Many of the dwellings of the early trade centers had vats in the floor. Other procedures for the storage of food were also developed. Some had pens for animals. The development of storage facilities proceeded hand in hand with the emergence of more substantial dwellings. The dwellings underwent a series of transitions from crude huts and hovels to larger and more substantial homes. At Beidha there is an "unbroken development from round hut to round house and from there to a polygonal phase into proper rectangular structures; all except the first were built of stone" (Mellaart, 1975:57). At Mureybet the transitions from round dwellings to rectangular ones occurred between level II and level III.

The earliest storage of perishables seems to have been practiced by families. Their homes were not only residences, but also their storage bins. Communal storage of food was a later development. Whether practiced by families or by the community, the storage of perishables required the organization of behavior on the basis of a distal future. As techniques for the storage of food became perfected, the residents of these centers no longer traded simply to acquire immediate necessities, but began trading to acquire food that was not consumed for several months.

The development of communities of several hundred or of a few thousand required the organization of activity to assure food for a distal future. If that practice was not followed, the community failed to endure. Even then some of these communities experienced famine. Then the residents deserted their community. Some communities solved the problem sufficiently to allow large populations to remain at the same location for several generations. The residents of these communities were somewhat less subject to the vagaries of nature than those who remained nomadic.

Population growth was a response to becoming sedentary and solving the problem of storing perishables. Population growth could not have enticed persons to become sedentary. When one is out of food then the only alternative is to search for it—to remain nomadic. A shortage of food within a sedentary community often rendered the community nomadic, but a shortage of food never led nomadic groups to establish a sedentary community.

COMMUNAL ACTION

The residents of the early markets took less communal action than the typical nomadic groups. The earliest settlements did not constitute a community. They were little more than clusters of persons who happened to be at the same location. They were an aggregation, not a community. A few of them sought out food together now and then and took other forms of collective action. But in general they acted more as individuals than did the typical member of a nomadic group. For one thing they no longer moved from location to location in unison. There was probably little or no communal solidarity in the earliest sedentary settlements.

However, new forms of collective action and communal solidarity emerged within these communities. The solidarity that emerged had a different foundation than the solidarity of nomadic bands. The prevailing form of communal action in food gathering groups was based upon the objective of acquiring the necessities of life—food and clothing. This form of collective action decreased in the sedentary communities. The residents of these communities acted primarily as individuals as they traded, collected, and manufactured goods.

The communal orientation that emerged within the settlements was "forced" upon them. It was largely a response to intrusions by nomadic groups. The nomadic groups raided these communities as well as traded with them. An individual or family can attempt to defend their possessions when confronted by a band of raiders, but the likelihood of success is not great. The successful defense of these communities required that the residents organize themselves to deal with their common problem.

The earliest settlements were not especially vulnerable to raids. Their wealth was no greater than that of the typical nomadic groups. In some instances they had possessions that were desired by others, and the incoming group attempted to take the desired goods from the locals instead of collecting it themselves. The conflict that ensued was similar to the conflict between two nomadic groups. The very earliest sedentary persons were no more wedded to their possessions than members of nomadic groups. In the face of a more powerful group a common response was probably flight.

Conflict between groups antedated the emergence of trade centers by eons. But as the trade centers became established the nature of intergroup conflict was transformed. Prior to the establishment of the practices of stockpiling trade goods and storing perishables when conflict arose between a sedentary group and a nomadic one, each party was equally prepared to flee the scene. As the residents of these settlements acquired an investment in their stored food, the stockpiled goods, and their homes, they became less willing to flee when attacked. Intergroup conflict was transformed from skirmishes between groups to "warfare." One group attempted to extract the possessions of the other; the other defended their possessions. Those defending the communities adopted a defensive posture and those attacking an offensive posture.

Intergroup conflict became more intense. Skirmishes between nomadic groups can be intense, but often they are limited to one group frightening another away or conducting a raid with limited objectives. The wealth of these sedentary communities enticed the attackers to sustain their efforts until loot was acquired. Reciprocally the accumulated wealth and the threat of its loss motivated the residents of the community to fight with greater intensity. In time the raiders became more organized in their attacks and the defenders more organized in their defenses. Only those communities that developed communal procedures for fending off the attacks endured; often they did not. Sustained warfare slowly replaced sporadic attacks as a form of intergroup hostility.

The survival of these communities depended upon the development of defensive measures. The development of defensive procedures required the residents to take a new form of communal action. The survival of these communities required that they band together to confront outsiders as a unit. Before they could accomplish this they had to overcome the individualism that is inherent in trading. The development of this form of communal action required millennia. The first two settlements at Jericho did not have walls. The residents of these two settlements either deserted the location or were driven from it. By the eighth millennium Jericho was surrounded by a wall that encompassed an area of about ten acres. Other trade centers underwent similar developments.

The construction of a wall for the community indicates that rather elaborate forms of communal action were possible. It is doubtful that the first form of communal action was the construction of defensive walls. Probably long before that some of these communities had developed procedures to defend their communities when threatened by attacks. Walls were not constructed until after communities had acquired an extended past of being the targets of raids.

Not all trade centers built walls that encircled the community. But nearly all, if not all, of the larger trade centers took steps to defend themselves from raiders. At Çatal Hüyük the residential quarters abutted each other; the houses were aligned to present a solid front to outsiders. Residents left and entered the enclosed city by ladders. Entry into each home was through the roof. These techniques provided a degree of security from raiders.

The fact that some of these centers were destroyed several times gives the impression that they were centers of conflict. Warfare between the cities and raiders was common. However, there were extended periods of peace during which the trade centers and the outlanders peacefully traded. It was the accumulation of wealth by the trade centers during the peaceful periods that served as the magnet to attract raiders.

Some of the early trade centers appear to have conducted their trade with other groups outside of the city proper. In later millennia the large cities had guarded gates that regulated traffic into the city. The evolution of the trade centers was from simple clusters of sedentary persons with their primitive markets to settlements of considerable size, perhaps communities of a few hundred without walls or other defensive fortifications; to large cities with walls to protect the residents from raiders, with the trade between the natives and the outlanders conducted outside the city; to walled cities with markets inside the cities.

The size of the walls indicates extensive planning and a considerable expenditure of energy by some communities. One trade center was surrounded by a stone wall that was five feet thick which was in turn surrounded by a ditch twenty-five feet wide and over six feet in depth (Redman, 1978:8). The presence of a wall of this substance indicates both that raiding was common and that the settlement was capable of taking large-scale defensive measures.

The communal activity of these centers was probably not limited to defensive enterprises. However, it is the defensive fortifications that are the most dramatic evidence we have of the ability of these communities to act as a unit. In at least some of the early centers there was a "community building." In a few instances a high level of technological expertise is evident. One building of Jericho contained a large room with a broad central chamber that "was floored with high polished terrazzo-like pavement of patterned salmon-pink and with stone chips" (Oates and Oates, 1976:80). Çatal Hüyük had several elaborately decorated and finely worked buildings. These and other edifices of these communities indicate that large-scale communal endeavors were possible by the residents of the larger trade centers.

It is a relatively simple task to coordinate the activity of a few persons, but the coordination of the activity of hundreds of persons requires considerable deliberation and planning. In addition, the completion of a project requiring the energies of a few hundred requires that a few act as supervisors or directors of the effort to assure success. New forms of sociation emerged at these centers.

The nature of the coordination of effort for these undertakings was quite different from those of nomadic groups. When communal action is taken within a food gathering society, it is focused on a specific and relatively immediate objective. Once the objective is achieved the program is complete. Communal hunting efforts are at an end when the game is killed or it escapes. The social objective of constructing a defensive wall is distal. One never knows if and when an attack may occur and one never knows if the ultimate objective has been achieved. The ultimate objective is not to construct a wall, but to keep out raiders. The social objective of defensive action has constancy, but is never consummated. Eternal vigilance is necessary, but there is never certainty that vigilance will produce security.

The early trade centers did not mount military campaigns to conquer surrounding groups or territories. Mellaart (1975) suggests that Çatal Hüyük controlled the surrounding territory. He offers no evidence supporting his position other than that the artifacts that originated at Çatal Hüyük are common at some surrounding locations. It is far more likely that Çatal Hüyük had economic hegemony in the region. It was the central trading center. The earliest cities were bastions of defense, not centers of military expansionists. Later cities raided other cities and conquered territory, but the early cities were populated by traders, not warriors.

The communal action that emerged within trade centers had a different foundation than the communal action of nomadic groups. It was based on a common mercenary interest, on a concern with each retaining his possessions, and not on a concern with the collective acquisition of the necessities of life. In addition, it was predicated on an indefinite and distal future, and not a definite and immediate one. The communal action of the trade centers was less exciting than that of nomadic groups. Discussions of whether or not to build a wall and where and how to build it may become heated, but neither the discussion nor the construction of the wall is as exciting as hunting game. The communal action of the trade centers was more rational or deliberative and less emotional and impulsive than the communal action of nomadic food gatherers.

The communal action of the early sedentary communities did not evolve from within the communities. It was, in a sense, forced upon them by the intrusions of others. In the long run residents of the trade centers acquired more conscious control of their lives by more systematically programming their collective future. To an extent the world moved from one of fate to one of conscious choice. An integral facet of this shift was the more precise and clear delineation of the distinction between the emerging urban world and the uncivilized world. Residency supplemented and to a degree replaced kinship as the basis for the specification of membership. Eventually criteria for "citizenship" were formulated.

PROFESSIONAL TRADERS

A new type of individual—the professional trader—emerged in the trade centers. Those who mined obsidian and traded it for grain, tubers, or meat were producers and traders. Their relation to their environment and others was much the same as that of members of nomadic groups who on occasion harvested an excess of grain or meat to trade. At the trade centers a few became adept in bargaining, planning for future trade, and making and sustaining contacts with diverse others. Some of these persons achieved a position where they no longer produced any material goods. Rather they acquired material goods from one party that were in turn traded to another party. Middlemen or petty capitalists appeared on the scene.

The maintenance of their position required that they formulate elaborate plans for future developments and acquire information about where and when goods could be acquired cheaply and sold dearly. They acquired goods at one time or location and sold them later, or at another location, and thereby acquired the necessities of life. They specialized in the accumulation and movement of goods, not production.

The earliest professional traders may have emerged from nomadic groups who served as conduits between centers or they may have been heads of families at the sedentary communities who specialized in bargaining. In either case professional merchants emerged whose productivity rested upon the movement of goods and effective use of information about supply and demand across time and space. Their profit was derived from the mutual benefit of trade.

In the ideal world of distributive justice all three parties to the transaction—the two producers and the middleman—would acquire equal proportions of the benefits of trade. However, the middlemen occupied a position that allowed them to acquire more information than either of the producers. That provided them with the opportunity to take advantage of the two producing parties. Consequently they tended to acquire more benefit from trade than either of the producers. The position of middlemen also provided them with opportunities to control the flow of goods and to manipulate prices to their own benefit. This was both the source of their wealth and their reputations as connivers.

Once the position of middleman has been established then some recognized that the expansion of trade would be to their benefit. This led to the deliberate expansion of trade. New markets and new sources of goods were sought. They became entrepreneurs. It was they who wove together trade centers and established new trading outposts. Persons imbued with the trade ethic were the first to systematically search out new markets and resources. They located opportunities and founded new communities.

When and exactly how a professional merchant class emerged cannot be specified precisely. However, at some centers some of the residents probably specialized in the organization of long-distance trade by the eighth millennium. The presence of goods at trading centers like Jericho several hundred miles from their point of origin indicates that at least a few persons were planning and mounting long-distance expeditions to acquire trade goods. Not many residents of these early centers were directly involved in the planning and execution of long-distance trade. However, a small number of entrepreneurs would have a significant impact on a community. It was the successful entrepreneurs who became the focal persons of the social structure of their community. These ancient capitalists, like their later counterparts, were the elite of these communities. They not only organized, financed, and supervised the expeditions, but they also had considerable influence on the internal affairs of their communities. It is likely that the internal affairs of these communities was largely in the hands of the wealthy merchants, much as was the case in the Phoenician cities.

A popular image of ancient trade is that it flourished under monarchs. However, such was not the case. In fact, the indications are that when the first dynasties were founded intergroup trade declined. During the predynastic period and the early dynastic period of both Mesopotamia and Egypt foreign trade was extensive, but in the following periods foreign trade declined.

Some of the cities of early dynastic Mesopotamia had established trade contact with distant ports. The merchants of Eridu, located at the southern end of the Mesopotamian area near the sea coast, sent ships around present day Saudi Arabia to Quseir. "Quseir was 3,506 miles from the head of the Persian Gulf. The distance is half as much again as the passage of Columbus from the Canaries to San Salvador" (Divine, 1973:32). The merchants of Mesopotamia dealt with communities in Iran, Anatolia, the Mediterranean coast, the Nile Valley, the Indus Valley, and the "immense coastline of the Arabian Peninsula and whatever civilization it had harbored as the 'Great Unknown' " (Oppenheim, 1977:63).

Ships from Dilmun, Makan, and Meluhha were docking at Ur in 2300 B.C. during the early dynastic period. Two hundred years later, after countless battles between dynasties and widespread destruction of cities, only voyages to Makan are recorded. An additional 200 years later only a single voyage to Dilmun is recorded. After that there are no references to overseas trade. Trade that had been established and maintained for centuries declined as warfare and monarchies emerged. It was partially replaced by the exchange of gifts between kings that were conveyed by royal emissaries (Oppenheim, 1977:64). Merchants had been replaced by monarchs and their functionaries as the focal persons of communities.

A similar sequence occurred in Egypt. Prior to the unification of the Nile at least the merchants of the lower Nile were in contact with distant trade centers. Foreign trade continued to be important for the Nile Valley during the first few dynasties. One sailor of the Fourth Dynasty is recorded as having traveled to Punt eleven times. As the monarchy achieved dominance, foreign trade declined. The foreign trade that continued was conducted by delegates of the state, not private merchants.

The development of large-scale and long-distance trade did not occur without many setbacks. As the wealth of these traders increased, they became the targets of attacks of nomads and later pastoralists. Yet many of the cities in the period between the formation of the early trade centers until the time of the dynasties became the centers of large-scale trading enterprises. All the indications are these developments occurred without the benefit of autocratic political systems.

The early entrepreneurs planned, organized, and financed trading expeditions. There was a continual, if unsteady, growth in trade during the millennia from the formation of the first trade centers to the establishment of large agricultural city-states and nations. The foundation of large agricultural communities provided a new and major impetus to the growth of trade. However, the subsequent formation of autocratic state systems was associated with a decline in the importance of inter-community trade.

TRANSPORTATION

The difficulties of moving large quantities of goods constrained the expansion of trade. The early trade networks of the Old World were over land; trade centers and networks developed before human beings mastered the intricacies of water transportation and before the domestication of beasts of burden. All the goods were transported by human energy during the first few millennia following the establishment of sedentary communities.

It is possible to move considerable quantities of goods by human transport. One Australian Aborigine group transported seventy pound bags of red ochre over long distances (Hadingham, 1979:169). The extensive inland trade network of the Olmecs, Mayas and other Mesoamerican civilizations were maintained by human transport.

Over-water transportation of goods and the use of beasts of burden to move goods emerged by the seventh millennium. It is certain that rafts were employed in some areas by that time; the domestication of animals was underway at about the same time. It is likely that animals were first domesticated, not to provide a more stable supply of food, but to serve as beasts of burden. This theme is developed in Chapter IX.

Rafts were used earlier and more extensively to transport goods than is commonly recognized. Crete and Cyprus were first inhabited about 6500 B.C. The easternmost edge of Crete is 100 miles from the mainland. It can be reached by island hopping with the longest distance between islands of thirty miles. The only way human beings could have reached these islands is by rafts or boats. The most ancient artifacts of Crete indicate the early residents of the island originated in western Asia. Large rafts were in use on the Nile by 6000 B.C. (Landstrom, 1970:12). Predynastic pottery and rock drawings in the Nile Valley depict wash-through vessels of various sorts, many of them with oars. Some of the vessels are shown carrying fifty persons; others have cattle and large animals aboard.

Rafts and boats were extensively used on the Tigris, Euphrates, and their tributaries. All the early references in the later literate material to the canals refer to their importance as arteries of transportation and communication. None of them make reference to the canals serving as irrigation ditches (Adams, 1966:56). It is likely that the earliest canals of the region were constructed to facilitate the movement of goods, not to irrigate fields. The two uses are not mutually exclusive. The importance of water travel for early Egypt is indicated by the words used to denote travel. To travel was expressed as to "sail downstream" or to "sail upstream."

The first form of water transport were rafts, not boats. The construction of a hollowed-out vessel so that it achieves buoyancy by air replacing water is quite an abstract endeavor. The construction of a raft is a much simpler accomplishment. The early water craft were wash-through vessels made of reeds and wood that were highly buoyant.

When rafts were first used to transport goods on rivers, seas, and oceans is unknown, but it is an ancient practice. The largest rafts had platforms atop them to keep the crew and cargo dry. Illustrations of these rafts have been found in Mesopotamia, the Nile Valley, on Malta, and the Atlantic coast of Morocco.

The Sumerians and Egyptians had large and complex rafts for both rivers and the open seas. Movement up and down the Nile was facilitated by the prevailing wind condition. The rafts floated downstream, with the current; they moved up the river under sail. Travel up river required considerable sophistication in both vessel construction and sailing techniques. These techniques were perfected long before the emergence of the Egyptian dynasties. Similar developments occurred on the Tigris and Euphrates rivers and probably in other regions.

The Sumerians and Egyptians designed reed rafts that were seaworthy. Other coastal centers also used large seagoing rafts. They were constructed in a flexible manner so that they would give with the swells of the sea and yet return to their original shape. Some of the devices of these vessels indicate considerable sophistication. For example, one device allowed the bindings that held the rudder in place to break when hit with a heavy swell and yet retained the rudder. When he built Ra II, Heyerdahl made the two ropes retaining the rudder in place of equal strength. Occasionally when the rudder was struck by a strong wave it broke. Upon re-examining the drawings of the ancient reed rafts he noted that one of the ropes holding the rudder in place was considerably larger (stronger) than the other. This technique allowed the weaker rope to break when a strong wave struck the rudder and the stronger rope to retain the rudder. The rudder could then rather easily be tied back into place. It is very doubtful that such a device would have been developed for sailing the Nile.

There are many indications that some communities of Mesopotamia and along the Nile were conducting long-distance overseas trade prior to the dynastic period. Seagoing ships of ancient Ur and the valuable cargoes from foreign lands are constantly referred to in the earliest Sumerian clay tablets (Heyerdahl, 1978:9). In the Third Dynasty, Egypt built overseas ships of 100 tons. Obviously, ship construction had a long history on the Nile.

Overland trade expanded as water transportation developed. Some of the early trade centers were primarily oriented to the sea, whereas others relied on overland routes. Some inland communities specialized as trade centers between groups with different traditions. "Sippar, famed as the oldest of the Babylonian cities, (was) probably a port of trade between the sheep nomads of the desert and the inhabitants of the urbanized stretches along the Euphrates" (Oppenheim, 1977:116).

Whereas the early large trade centers of the Old World appear to have been inland communities, the earliest ones of the New World were established on the coastal areas of Mesoamerica and the northern coast of Peru. The movement of goods between Mesoamerica and Peru by rafts probably occurred by 2500 B.C. There was extensive sea travel between the two regions at the time of the Spanish conquest.

Sea travel was and remained a high-risk endeavor until relatively recently. This was less inhibitive of overseas travel than might be thought. Those who died at sea did not return to tell the horrors. In contrast, those who were successful returned to tell tales of distant lands. Some also became wealthy. The tales and wealth of the successful venturers stimulated sea travel.

Many relatively primitive groups had complex bodies of knowledge of sea travel. The navigators of the South Seas had a wealth of information that allowed them to sail from island to island. They knew the location of key stars to steer by and of favorable winds and currents. They kept their knowledge from outsiders, but there was "a free exchange of experiences between acknowledged professional colleagues, even if they came from different islands" (Akerblom, 1968:142). All groups that regularly sailed adjusted their sea travel to take advantage of the most favorable wind and ocean currents. It seems reasonable that the ancient sailors of these trade centers also developed bodies of knowledge about overseas travel.

As warfare between cities emerged, it probably contributed to overseas colonization and trade. The colonization of Iceland was motivated by the emergence of an authoritarian system in Scandinavia. The defeated left to found a new community rather than submit to the victors. On some occasions Polynesian groups set out for unknown lands by sea after defeat. The losers "preferred the hazards of the sea to the almost certain prospect of meeting death or humiliation on land" (Akerblom, 1968:92). It is likely that overseas colonization and trade was stimulated both by adventuresome persons in search of excitement and wealth and by flight from impending disaster.

SUMMARY

Childe's formulation that civil life emerged from farming villages is established canon. Mellaart suggests the two revolutions occurred simultaneously. Jacobs argues that a revolution in the distribution of goods preceded the revolution in the means of production. The sequence posited by Jacobs is consistent with the formulation implicitly offered by Adam Smith. The formulations of Smith and Jacobs fit the data better than either the formulations of Childe or Mellaart.

It is certain that the emergence of trade did not rest upon the production of surplus. Rather it rested on an interest in acquiring the goods of others. Imports, not exports, were the original stimulus for trade. Awareness that imports could be acquired through offering something in exchange led to the accumulation of surpluses to acquire imports.

The acceptance of Childe's formulation of the sequential order is probably linked to the emphasis given to the "products" of human activity by students of ancient societies. Tools, bits of durable material, traces of foundations, their wastes, and pieces of pottery give us tantalizing glimpses of the accomplishments of the ancients. The tracings of traders are few and scattered; those of farmers are substantial and concentrated. This has enticed some to overemphasize the importance of agriculture for the establishment of cities.

On the basis of improved archaeological dating it is now apparent that communities of considerable substance preceded the cultivation of fields of grains and totalitarian states. The emergence of trade centers entailed the expansion of social contacts between groups of people. Not all groups became sedentary. Most remained nomadic food gatherers as towns and cities emerged. But even their lives were modified as trade centers and networks expanded and touched them.

The establishment of stable exchange relations, sedentary markets, and then interconnected markets represent movements toward more complex social structures. The establishment of primitive markets and trade centers necessitated the development of long-range individualistic temporal structures that allowed human beings to exercise greater planning. In the process, human beings acquired greater control over their experiences and established a more orderly, if less responsive, mode of life.

The continuation of human life across generations requires interdependence. The transformation from the nomadic way of life to a sedentary one did not change that condition. Although the transformation did change the nature of the interdependence. The interdependence that prevailed in self-sufficient hunting and gathering groups was based on functional solidarity and sharing. The interdependence between traders was based on the mutual assessment that trade enhanced the welfare of all. Trade centers and networks widened the interdependence of all. Each person's welfare became somewhat dependent on others exterior to his immediate community. Interdependence between persons became more extensive and somewhat less intensive. Human life became slightly less vulnerable to the whims of nature and more dependent upon strangers.

Stability and security became dependent on the marketplace. The marketplace replaced interpersonal embeddedness as a security blanket. The replacement was not total. Human beings were still embedded with their family members and friends, but the embeddedness was less communal.

In the process human beings had not merely transformed their forms of sociation; they also transformed themselves. They no longer were the same type of persons they had been. Human beings had not only constructed new social relationships, but in the process constructed new identities—and lost old ones.

Chapter VIII

Urbanism

The market is the cornerstone of urbanism. There have been many compact human settlements that were not urbane. Concentration camps have contained hundreds of thousands of persons, but one would not characterize them as urban centers. Nor would one characterize the administrative centers of some nations as urbane. Ancient Egypt has been characterized as a nonurban nation. Egypt, like all ancient nation states, had concentrations of populations, but the marketplace did not dominate the cities of Egypt. Other ancient civilizations also had cities that were not dominated by the marketplace. In many civilizations the marketplace was subordinated to centralized administration. Egypt was more urbane during the predynastic period than she was after the dynastic age was established.

Urbanism developed and was well established in several locations before the emergence of centralized political structures that controlled territories. At least an incipient urbanism was established in some locations by 8000 B.C. At that time Jericho had a wall that enclosed ten acres. By 6000 B.C. Çatal Hüyük was a thriving center encompassing thirty-two acres. These and other cities rested on a foundation provided by their markets. Urban life consists of more than the marketplace, but an open market populated by a plurality of both buyers and sellers is the core of urban life.

Urbanism did not spring forth when the first primitive markets were established. It came to the fore through a series of incremental changes over millennia. Traces of urbanism first appeared at those markets when a variety of groups congregated to trade. As the markets became linked together and transformed into trade centers urbanism came to the fore. These communities were composed of persons with minimal embeddedness with each other and few committed relationships. It was a highly fluid world that was easily penetrated. Constancy was provided by the market.

These communities were dependent upon the continuation of the market. Some endured for a few generations, others for millennia. They were composed of diverse peoples, and additionally diverse people came to the centers to acquire goods. They were filled with variety. They were islands of concentrated humanity surrounded by nomadic groups. They were first and primarily centers of trade, but they were also centers of communication. The communication networks that centered on the markets were the consequence of the trade. The marketplaces provided the conditions necessary for a wide variety of persons to mingle and learn from one another.

Their continuation was dependent upon the residents accumulating surplus. Some of the residents possessed extensive wealth in comparison to the wealth possessed by the typical nomad. Yet at the same time the centers were rife with poverty. The misfits, incompetent, and the outcasts congregated at markets as well as the wealthy.

A new and distinctive type of congregation was formed at the marketplace of the trade centers. Congregations of relatively large numbers may have been formed earlier for collective hunts or rituals. These earlier congregations took collective action, but were of relatively short duration. In contrast, the congregations at the marketplaces were not formed to take collective action. Rather they were clusters of individuals, families, and other small units who all came together to reap the benefits of trade. Despite the individualistic orientation of the participants the congregations were relatively permanent.

The market allowed for a diffuse and extensive interdependence, but there was little communal solidarity and only minimal accountability. Each was on his own. The number and variety of persons who met at these locations provided opportunities for fleeting and noncommitted encounters. Each encounter was an opportunity for self-enhancement, but it carried with it the threat of loss. Each party was a relatively autonomous agent left to do as he would so long as he did not infringe on others.

"Buyers beware" was the prevailing ethic. Those in need of aid could count on little support or concern from their fellow traders. Each was an autonomous agent surrounded by many others who were relatively indifferent to his welfare.

Variety and lack of embeddedness is the hallmark of all open markets. The urbanite interacts with a fellow retailer one moment, then with a wholesaler, then with a potential buyer, deflects the plea of a beggar, and notes the appearance of a strange family. He is aware of a large number and wide variety of others, but has little involvement with any of them, at least not while at the market.

The marketplace is one of the most viable, volatile, attractive, and yet one of the ugliest institutions ever invented. Long before Adam Smith, many viewed the market as the generator of wealth, personal freedom, civility, excitement, and creativity. One of the ancient Sumerian texts that praises the city asserts that even a native of Marhasi—a nearby mountain region—becomes civilized after living in Ur (Oppenheim, 1977:111). Reciprocally others have seen the marketplace as the locus of evil. The Old Testament claims there is a lack of morality among those affiliated with the market. Traders and others associated with the market have long been viewed as untrustworthy. Those embued with the morality of band, or tribal or village solidarity are appalled by the impersonal conniving of those who associated with the market. Despite the antagonistic attitude of the non-urban to the marketplace, many found themselves attracted to it.

The emergence of markets and the subsequent urban centers provided the foundation for profound changes in humanity. The nature of human interaction was altered, individual and collective consciousness changed, distinctive personalities emerged, and new and distinctive procedures of collective action were established.

A WORLD OF STRANGERS

The urban world is a world of strangers (Lofland, 1973). Most urban residents have enduring relationships with some others. They have friends, although they may be few in number, and are usually family members—although they might not be. Embedded relationships, if present, are "behind the scene"; they are not public. Public activity is with strangers, or if not with strangers, others whom one treats little differently than he treats a stranger.

Members of solidary groups, whether primitive nomads, serfs, or miners, become guarded when approached by strangers. The urbanite is open to any encounter that promises personal benefit, but suspicious of all. Men of the market are prepared to bargain, but reluctant to become involved; they are capable of interacting with diverse persons, but the interaction tends to be restricted to instrumental encounters. Members of solidary groups tend to avoid contact with strangers. If contact is forced upon them they often become fearful or hostile.

The difference in the orientation of traders and members of solidary groups toward contact with strangers is indicated by the different response of the Maya to the first Spanish sailors they encountered and the response of the Tiwi to strangers. The first Maya to contact the Spaniards were a boat load of traders. Despite the fact the Spaniards looked entirely different than any group they had ever encountered before, they immediately attempted to determine if the Spanish were interested in trading.

The Tiwi were a food gathering group who inhabited two small islands off the coast of Australia. They had no reoccurring contact with any other group. They regarded all others as a threat; they were consistently and implacably hostile to all strangers. Outsiders who landed on their islands were resisted or massacred (Hart and Pilling as quoted in Lofland, 1973). Those solidary groups that routinely have contact with traders and merchants often welcome the contacts, but that only occurs after contact has been routinized.

The interaction betwen buyers and sellers at markets has little temporal or emotional depth. Often the interaction occurs between persons who have no shared past and who do not project a shared future beyond the immediate encounter. There is no commitment; the urbanite does not concern himself with locating the other within a network of social relationships. Others are categorized—a potential buyer, a seller, a thief. Behavior towards others is structured on the basis of the categorization. Usually there is little interest in establishing the position of another within a set of relationships.

In contrast, interaction within solidary bands is encased within embedded and committed relationships. Members of solidary bands who have little contact with markets find it difficult to interact with others unless they can place them within a network of relationships. In some groups, strangers who enter their world are assigned a position with the social fabric by being "adopted." Either one is a viable part of established relationships or outside the system.

The interaction that centers upon the market is disembedded. No one is emotionally involved with others. Strong emotion may on occasion be displayed, but if it is, it is typically toward another whom one has become angry at, not emotion expressed with others toward a shared focus. Even when there is the display of strong emotion at another by a sophisticated urbanite, one is often uncertain if the emotion is authentic or a performance.

Not all urbanites live entirely within the market ethos. Although some are so completely a part of it that they are almost entirely creatures of the marketplace. Most have a private world of embedded and committed relationships. This world is behind the scene, it is not located at the marketplace, yet its existence is dependent upon the market.

PRIVACY

The distinction between private and public is not viable in either solidary bands of food gatherers or in monolithic states. In those societies private interests are subordinated to the collective interest. All are expected to act for the collective good. Privacy is not a recognized prerogative. It is an interesting paradox that the distinction between public and private life was enhanced by the emergence of the marketplace. The marketplace is, on the one hand, one of the most public institutions constructed by human beings. It is easily penetrated. Boundaries are minimal. All with resources and inclination could enter primitive markets. Later of course, when markets had achieved a degree of success and accumulated some wealth, walls were constructed to keep out those who threatened the market. However, even then the marketplace itself was inherently a public place. Individuals displayed themselves and their possessions for all to inspect. They made themselves available to all. However, the market was not the total life of most urbanites. They had a private life removed from the market as well as a public one at the marketplace.

A nebulous form of privacy is present in all human groups, although in some nomadic groups very little is private. Members of food gathering bands are almost constantly in the presence of others. The attachments and relationships of all are known by all. In urban societies the openness of the marketplace coexists with a private world that is entered only by invitation or through invasion. The more dominant the market the more clearly the distinction between the public and private world.

Some of the more important features of the market that provide the foundation for making a distinction between a public and private world are: (a) the dyadic nature of bargaining, (b) the noncommittal and fleeting nature of trade contacts, (c) the construction of dwellings that shield individuals from the public arena, and (d) the accumulation of possessions.

Bargaining, in contrast to many other forms of cooperative behavior, is largely a dyadic phenomenon. Several persons can act in unison to gather food or perform rituals. But it is difficult for three or more to bargain. One party may bargain alternately with two others. A may first bargain with B and then turn his attention to C. Each transaction is a "private affair" between the members of the acting dyad. When a third party interjects himself into an ongoing bargaining process he disrupts the transaction. His action is often regarded as an intrusion by both.

Bargaining at markets is conducted in the presence of others, but others are onlookers. Each transaction is a private affair that occurs within a public context. The continuation of a viable market requires that the integrity of bargaining encounters be respected by others. When third parties interject themselves into transactions it creates chaos. Some markets developed the norm that third parties will not interject themselves into encounters in process. The development of this pattern sharpens the distinction between public and private activity. Citizens of the marketplace become conscious of a distinction between public and private affairs, a distinction that is only minimally present in societies without open markets. Dyadic privacy is not limited to the marketplace. However, the marketplace greatly enhances the distinction.

A second feature of the marketplace that enhances the distinction between private and public life is the fleeting and noncommittal nature of the encounters at markets. The establishment and maintenance of a market is dependent upon a variety of persons routinely coming into contact with each other who are not embedded with one another and have no commitments to each other. Markets can only endure as a viable focal point for a society if all, or at least many, congregate for the purpose of achieving material benefit and are relatively unconstrained by embeddedness with others or commitment to others. In the ideal marketplace each participant is an autonomous agent, constrained by no social relationships. In an open market all are free to enter or leave; each has the prerogative of trading or declining to trade on the basis of his personal inclinations. What each visitor does is his business. The greater the variety of participants and the greater the autonomy of each, the more viable the market.

However, the continuation of human beings as a species over generations cannot be accomplished by persons relating solely on the basis of their immediate personal preferences. Fleeting encounters do not provide the stable association that are necessary for mutual protection, the production and socialization of the young, nor a sufficient foundation for the establishment of authentic selves that give stability to behavior over time. The continuation of each human group and the human species requires that at least a minimal level of solidarity and commitment be an integral part of some social relationships.

Embeddedness and commitment places one at a disadvantage at the market. Consequently, if a viable market is to be maintained, it is necessary that both the public world of the market and a private world of embeddedness and commitment be maintained. Only those trade centers that developed these two contradictory but compatible worlds were capable of surviving over generations.

In urban centers fleeting and variegated relations exist simultaneously with enduring and homogeneous relationships. The typical urbanite is active in both the public noncommitted social world of the market and is part of a private committed set of social relationships. The prototype of the latter is the nuclear family of urban centers.

Sedentism allowed for the construction of dwellings of substance. As homes constructed of poles, brush, and hides were replaced by first, huts and hovels, and then homes of substance, each family acquired private territories where they could retreat from others. What occurred within each home was the private affair of each family. Only actions taken in public were regarded as relevant to the larger community, and not all of those.

Private dwellings provided a place for the storage of possessions as well as private territory. Some of the goods that were acquired at the marketplace and elsewhere were stored in the dwellings. Private ownership emerged. It was the combination of the acquisition of goods through bargaining and private dwellings that were the key factors in providing a foundation for the expansion of private property.

Goods acquired at the market were the consequences of individual action. Each successful trader was aware that he acquired his goods as the consequence of his actions, not by communal action. Success in bargaining is a "private" accomplishment. Each bargainer views the material goods he acquires as his. In contrast, hunters in the pursuit of game acquire goods through communal action. When goods are acquired by communal action then a foundation is provided for all to share. When they are acquired through individual actions then a foundation is provided for regarding the goods as those of the individual. The market invites persons to think of the goods they obtain as their personal possessions.

When all action is public, all are aware of the possessions of others. Under such conditions those who have been unsuccessful in the acquisition of goods pressure those who have been successful. With the construction of dwellings of substance, those who have been successful can store and perhaps hide their goods from their less fortunate neighbors. These goods then become thought of as "my" goods, not as goods to be shared with others.

Private ownership was well established in many of the ancient trade centers. In many of the early trade centers each home had storage facilities. In some, each house marked their vats and other containers with a distinctive stamp. Ownership became a static social condition. "Use ownership" was supplemented and replaced by permanent ownership.

DIVISION OF LABOR

The division of labor in the earliest sedentary communities may have been less for the first few millennia than it was within nomadic groups. In the beginning probably all adults did much the same thing. All collected and manufactured the local resource and hunted and gathered in the surrounding territory. However, with the transformation of these primitive markets into trade centers there was a simultaneous elaboration of the division of labor. Persons began specializing in various activities.

The "production units" of these communities were composed of households. Most production units were the residents of a household. Each household probably was composed of a set of interlocking specialists. Some manufactured items, another spent most of his time at the market, and perhaps still another transported goods from their source to the household, or from one market to another. The successful units expanded. As they expanded they became more specialized. When large markets frequented by hundreds of persons appeared on the scene, some residents were specialists in production, others in bargaining, still others in the transportation of goods. Members of the same community began differentiating themselves on the basis of what they spent their time doing. Persons were classified as "weavers" or as "traders." They acquired categorical identities based upon occupation that supplemented and in part replaced family and tribal affiliations.

Social differentiation is a necessary condition for social stratification, but differentiation does not automatically result in stratification. The evidence for stratification at the early trade centers is less than overwhelming. For example, at Çatal Hüyük there were no large and rich homes, all dwellings were of approximately the same size. There is with the exception of a few princely burials no evidence of stratification in the grave goods (Mellaart, 1978:32).

These special burials seem to have been expressions of gratitude by the community for the contributions of the individuals to the welfare of the community. They do not indicate that a stratification system had been established. There probably was some stratification based upon success in manufacturing and trade, but it certainly was not as pervasive as it became in the later agricultural communities.

The offspring of the wealthier families had greater opportunities to acquire wealth than others. But the rankings of lineages on the basis of wealth are fluid. Those with wealth had more influence than those without. And the prestige associated with wealth and the stigma associated with poverty endures after the wealth and poverty disappear. But in societies dominated by the marketplace, wealth followed by sustained poverty or poverty followed by sustained wealth quickly changes one's position within the community. The irregular flow of goods, the changes in demand for goods, natural disasters, and variation in competence at the market make it difficult to maintain a stable aristocracy within a community dominated by the market. Urban centers have not been conducive to the establishment and maintenance of aristocracies; quite the opposite has been the case. The marketplace with its lack of embeddedness and commitment is too volatile.

Some students of ancient societies have assumed that categorical rankings of lineages is a necessary precursor of civilization (Fried, 1967). However the evidence indicates that urban centers of considerable magnitude rose and fell that did not have rigid stratification systems. The social differentiation in some of these centers was extensive and persons were ranked on the basis of their material possessions, but the ranking of lineages was not an inherent part of these social structures.

The development of a stable hierarchical society is dependent upon centralized control of violence and a monopoly of knowledge. Violence is anthithetical to the marketplace. Many markets were destroyed by violence, but none of the early ones were established by violence. The fleeting and varied nature of the social encounters of marketplaces makes it exceedingly difficult to develop and maintain a monopoly of knowledge.

The mixed-motive character of bargaining renders each encounter potentially explosive. To maintain the market, procedures have to be established to restrain the appearance of violence. Most markets of any substance have market police and courts. The police and courts are supported by the traders and charged with the task of constraining and defusing violence. Many ancient markets probably disintegrated as the consequence of uncontrolled conflict breaking out in the marketplace. Some became aware that if the market was to endure, violence had to be contained. Procedures were devised to minimize the likelihood of violence at the market. This development was another form of social differentiation. However, the development of procedures for containing violence did not necessarily lead to greater stratification.

Subsequently when trade became more significant and large differences in wealth emerged, then some of the wealthier employed others to protect their property. However, the early urban centers probably employed persons to prohibit internal conflict and to protect them from intrusions from nomadic groups. The violence associated with the early markets seems to have been primarily that of outsiders raiding and looting the centers, not the exercise of violence by some residents on others.

Almost from the beginning of recorded history traders have received a bad press. The Egyptians characterized the Hyksos, who were traders, as less than human. The ancient Chinese ranked traders as the lowest occupation. Aristotle summed up the attitude of many toward markets when he characterized trading as husterism written large. Pirenne, whose study of the emergence of trade networks in Europe following the fall of the Roman Empire is one of the most insightful ever made, observed, "No scruple had any weight with the Venetians. Their religion was the religion of business men. It mattered little to them that the Moslems were the enemies of Christ, if business with them was profitable" (Pirenne, 1925:86).

According to the Greeks, the Phoenicians lacked moral principles. The Romans competed with the Phoenicians for hegemony and regarded them as conniving and unworthy. However, most communities of the Mediterranean preferred dealing with the Phoenicians instead of the Greeks or the Romans. The Phoenicians were interested in establishing contacts that were mutually beneficial; the Greeks and Romans were interested in looting and extracting tribute. The Phoenician traders may have taken advantage of others in their trade, but at least they did not invade and subjugate communities.

Implicit in many characterizations of trading, such as Pirenne's of the Venetians, is the assessment that the Christians and perhaps the Moslems represented a moral order whereas traders did not. Yet it was the Christians and the Moslems who were killing each other and others in their path. The Venetians in contrast traded with all interested parties. That some of those who benefitted from the trade wished to use their resources to kill other human beings is, from the standpoint of traders' morality, their choice. The morality of the traders recognizes the autonomy of all; it does not call for the imposition of a way of life on others.

The expansion of markets and the associated trade networks undermines solidarity and the morality based on it. The lack of concern with the welfare of others had led some to conclude that the marketplace is immoral. It does transform how persons relate to one another. It leads to less emotional involvement with others, less embeddedness with others. Solidary groups may desert the lame and the halt, but at least some will suffer a pang of sympathy when they do. In the extreme, the urbanite who stumbles over a dying person may only curse him for being in the way.

Variety is the mode at the market. A multiplicity of standpoints are present in urban centers; multiple realities pervade the market. The multiple standpoints and realities not only provide the opportunity for variety and choice, but they also are the basis for tolerance of diversity. Strangeness is an accepted quality at the market. Societies that rest primarily on communal solidarity tend to have homogeneous populations with a monolithic standpoint. All are expected to conform to the monolithic standpoint.

Conformity is antithetical to markets. Variety and personal autonomy are necessary if a viable market is to be maintained. Tolerance of variety and respect for the integrity of others is generated in bargaining and other social encounters associated with the market. Participation in a number of encounters with a variety of others gives persons the ability to adopt a multitude of standpoints without emotional identification with any. The professional trader assesses a variety of standpoints, but adopts none.

Professional traders also display a variety of standpoints. They often put on a performance wherein what is publicly displayed is at variance with their private intentions. Experienced bargainers often project a future of completing an exchange, but simultaneously indicate they may withdraw from the encounter if the other fails to indicate an interest in what is being offered. Deception is inherent to markets.

Deception is a complex activity. The successful completion of the act requires a person to self-consciously control any display of emotions. In addition, while doing so, if the deception is to be effective, the standpoint and reaction of the other must be accurately assessed. Failure to accurately assess the response of another to one's performance often results in failure to achieve one's personal objective. Experienced bargainers routinely display masks that they presume will facilitate their success. The professional trader becomes a multifaceted individual as he self-consciously displays a variety of standpoints and interests at the marketplace. The continuation of a viable market requires that each, or at least most, bargainers acknowledge the prerogative of others to do the same in the name of self-interest. Freedom, not embeddedness or commitment, is a by-product of the market.

Those who completely subordinate themselves to the reified market morality are amoral. They organize themselves solely for personal gain. Greed directs their behavior. They display whatever mask is necessary to acquire material gain. Social unity cannot be maintained when all members of a unit organize themselves solely on the basis of personal greed. The continuation of any social structure requires that occasionally all subordinate themselves to collective objectives. The collective objectives of groups with intense communal solidarity are taken for granted and dominate the individual; the collective objectives of traders are mutually constructed through negotiations.

A NEGOTIATED ORDER

Members of all societies are interdependent. But the interdependence that pervades urban centers is of a different order than that present in many other communities. The interdependence that pervades food gathering bands is not one of conscious choice. One is born into a given group and one's relationships are largely a matter of fate. Persons are also born in urban centers. However, the ethos of urban centers is that each participant can choose to participate or not in ongoing activity. The autonomy necessary to maintain a viable market provides the foundation for the emergence of the issue of personal freedom. That issue has little viability in either a solidary band or a monolithic state. Personal liberty has long been associated with the city. As one of the inscriptions of ancient Babylonia expressed it, "Even a dog is free when he enters the city" (Oppenheim, 1964:121).

Yet the residents of urban centers often find themselves confronted by contingencies that they cannot manage as individuals. These range from protecting the market from raiders, through constraining violence at the market, to the problem of maintaining an adequate water supply. The disembedded residents of the very earliest primitive markets were ill-equipped to confront and manage these contingencies. But over millennia the residents of these centers developed the ability to take community action and deal with them. The communal action rested upon a social foundation that was distinct from that of solidary bands. The ability to construct a negotiated order emerged.

Bargaining and negotiating have many similarities. Both are mixed-motive encounters. Negotiators have mutually recognized disagreements about how the future is to be structured, but at the same time they project a distal future of cooperation. They desire different futures, but at the same time acknowledge they have a shared future. When persons indicate they are willing to negotiate their relatedness, they indicate they will subordinate their disagreements to a mutual concern for establishing a structured future that is acceptable to both. Persons with mutually recognized disagreements do not automatically begin negotiating. They often either disaffiliate or conflict. If they project a shared future despite their disagreement, then they establish their future relatedness as their shared focus.

Then in a manner similar to the offer and counter-offer sequences of bargaining, proposal and counter-proposals are offered in an attempt to construct an agreement. However, in contrast to bargaining where, when an agreement is reached and the exchange consummated the bargainers disaffiliate, the construction of an agreement by negotiators specifies how the negotiators are to relate in the distal future, the future beyond the immediate encounter. Whereas bargaining is structured by the proximal future of the possibility of consummating an exchange, negotiating is structured by a distal future of continued relatedness.

The projection of a distal future and the establishment of future relatedness as the shared focus makes negotiating a more complex form of cooperative behavior than bargaining. The give and take, the offer and counter-offer process of bargaining provided the foundation for the emergence of negotiations as a procedure for the resolution of differences between persons. The development of the ability to negotiate allowed for the construction of large communities composed of persons with diverse interests.

Human beings probably constructed rather complex instances of negotiated order long before sedentary communities were established. But it was with the establishment of sedentary communities populated by diverse persons that negotiating came to the fore as a significant form of human interaction. Residents of these trade centers had diverse interests. The obsidian trader and the tamer of hides who resided at the same location had different interests, yet at the same time came to recognize that they also had common interests. Over millennia these residents developed the ability to resolve their differences through negotiations and thereby increased the likelihood of the continuation of their community. They all had the shared concern of protecting themselves from the uncivilized.

Negotiating is inherently an egalitarian form of social action. Each must acknowledge and respect the other's standpoint and interest. Failure to do so aborts the negotiating process. Many communities fragmented or experienced internal conflict when they were unable to resolve their differences through negotiations. The fact that negotiating is inherently an egalitarian form of interaction does not mean that each participant has an equal say in structuring the future. In most egalitarian communities of any size a few members emerge as the community leaders. It is these persons who construct the negotiated order of that community. These persons served as representatives of their respective families, or other corporate groups, and constructed an order for both themselves and their respective constituencies.

The diversity of marketplaces provided a condition that facilitated the establishment of a negotiated order. Through bargaining with diverse others, all learned to tolerate and acknowledge the standpoints and interests of diverse others. The acknowledgement and acceptance of diverse standpoints is necessary before complex negotiations can be consummated.

While the bargaining associated with the marketplace provided the foundation for the emergence of negotiating as a significant social activity, it also provided a background that was somewhat inconsistent with a negotiated order. Deception or closed awareness is an integral part of bargaining. In contrast the construction of negotiated commitments requires an open awareness context. All must negotiate in good faith. The success of maintaining social unity through negotiating rests upon each trusting the other to abide by the commitments made during the negotiation sessions. A lack of interpersonal trust severely inhibits constructing and maintaining unity through negotiating.

The absence of palaces and similar edifices in the ancient sedentary communities indicates that these communities were essentially egalitarian. On the other hand, the evidence of major communal enterprises such as the walls surrounding these communities indicates the communities were capable of complex coordinated activity. It is impossible to determine how the coordination necessary to construct these edifices was achieved. However, in light of comparable undertakings by urban centers dominated by marketplaces during the historical period, it is likely that the coordination was the consequence of a negotiated order.

SUMMARY

Urbanism developed very slowly. Traces of it probably reach back to at least 9000 B.C. Not all residents of the ancient trade centers were urbane. Urbanism first appeared among those clusters of persons closely affiliated with the markets. By at least 6000 B.C. some communities were thriving pockets of urbanism. Hundreds, and in a few cases, thousands of persons were clustered together about markets. These persons made contact with each other to reap the benefits of trade; their associations with each other were not encased within an enduring relationship. Their only interest in each other was as sources of goods and services. These clusters of humanity had learned to peacefully interact, although not embedded with each other. They established a distinctive form of human association that expanded the interdependence of human beings.

These developments affected far more than those who resided at the trade centers. Others who came to the markets were exposed to a new and distinctive set of human relations. Some non-urbanites were attracted to the markets. The markets offered material benefits that could not be acquired elsewhere. Some found the urban centers attractive and migrated to them. Others despised the residents, and some non-urbanites regarded the wealth of the urbanites as a resource to be extracted whenever the opportunity arose.

The marketplace was humanity's first open institution. All who wished to take part were welcome so long as they did not disturb its fluid order and had something to offer that others were interested in obtaining. However, each person who entered the market was on his own. Those with the proper combination of resources, talent, and luck prospered; those without the proper combination fell by the wayside. There was little sympathy for the losers. But excitement and opportunity for material gain was available for the successful.

The urbanism of the early trade centers was not the urbanism of the modern metropolitan centers. The residents were not literate, but they were capable of record keeping. They were not capable of organizing and supervising long-range and complex undertakings, but they were capable of scheming and planning. Some communities developed the ability to organize collective defensive efforts to protect themselves from attacks from the noncivilized. Their livelihood was tenuous, but no more so than that of most nomadic groups.

Through a combination of internal developments at the marketplace and the developments between them and the non-urbanites, a new form of social action emerged; negotiated social structures were established. Human beings thereby intentionally constructed social arrangements designed to make their lives more secure. Some communities were relatively successful and endured. It was these communities that took one of the giant steps toward civilization.

Chapter IX

Domestication

The domestication of the grains, wheat and barley, and the animals, sheep, goats, and pigs was underway by 7500 B.C., perhaps earlier. Cattle were domesticated slightly later. These developments, especially the domestication of grains, provided the foundation for the subsequent emergence of agricultural communities; agricultural communities in turn provided the foundation for the emergence of nations. There was a span of three and one-half, perhaps four millennia, between the domestication of grains and the establishment of nations that contained expansive territories and several cities.

The domestication of grains was accomplished by the sedentary communities of western Asia. Several plants, including at least the bottle gourd, cotton, and tubers, were domesticated earlier. The domestication of gourds, cotton, and tubers probably was achieved by semisedentary communities of other regions. However, the plants that were domesticated prior to grains did not provide the subsistence foundation for the establishment of large social units that exercised territorial control. It was domestic grains that provided the subsistence foundation for the earliest nations.

Sedentary communities were established in western Asia two to three thousand years, maybe longer, before grains and animals were domesticated. The earliest evidence of domestic grains and animals is associated with the sedentary communities, but the domestication of grains and animals rested upon stable trade relations between sedentary communities and nomadic groups. The sedentary communities acquired grains and animals from the nomadic groups and then subsequently established a distinctive relationship between themselves and the grains and animals. The relationship between human groups and the plants and animals was transformed from that of predator-prey to that of husbandman and object of concern. Human groups began caring for and controlling the species. In the process the human groups were harnessed to their objects

125

of concern. Human beings themselves became more domestic as they domesticated other species.

PLANTS

Grains were an important source of food for some groups tens of millennia ago. Grinding stones have been used to grind grain for at least 45,000 to 50,000 years (Kraybill, 1977:495). Some ancient groups were more than incidental consumers of grass seeds at that time. Despite the tremendously ancient history of grain consumption, grains were not domesticated by groups that routinely harvestd them. Those groups that harvested wild grains had little motivation to domesticate them. Harlan and Zohary (1966) note that in the area where wild wheat grew there were thousands of acres of natural stands of wheat that were almost as dense as cultivated fields. Harlan (1967) demonstrated that with only a sickle of flint it was possible for a person to harvest in three weeks more grain than a family could consume in a year.

Many nomadic groups routinely trekked to stands of wild grain to harvest them. During the ripening period camps were established near the fields of grain. The grain was harvested and consumed. Some groups harvested surplus supplies for later consumption, and occasionally harvested surplus grain to trade with others. The quantity of surplus harvested was necessarily limited by their ability to transport the accumulated grain. Some groups remained at the location for several weeks or a few months. However, unless there was another supply of food nearby when the grain was no longer available they moved on.

The yield of the stands of wild grain, like domestic grains, varied from year to year. Those who came to harvest the wild grains were occasionally disappointed. That did not entice the would-be harvesters to domesticate the grains. Their response was to move on in search of an alternative source of food. These nomadic groups had neither the inclination, opportunity, nor resources to domesticate grains.

The residents of the trade centers in western Asia were consumers of grains before the grains were domesticated. Wild einkorn (wheat) and wild barley were consumed at Mureybet II, a community of approximately 200 houses by 9000 B.C. Several sites dating from 9000 to 7000 B.C. had subterranean pits for storing grains (Flannery, 1969). The earliest evidence of storage of these grains was located sixty to ninety miles from their native habitat (Mellaart, 1975). The soil in the regions where the grains were first stored was not conducive to their growth. Neither wheat nor barley were domesticated in their native habitat. They were domesticated in foreign soils.

A limited form of plant husbandry was practiced in some of these communities by 7000 B.C. The residents were not farmers; they were not planting and harvesting fields of grain. They can more accurately be characterized as horticulturalists. Some had gardens that supplemented their supply of food. One of the distinctive features of the crops associated with the earliest sites in western Asia was the wide variety of plants. Many different plants were cared for and harvested. The change in the distribution of the plant species of these communities through time is striking. The changes were an increase in cereal grains that were foreign to the region and a decrease in wild legumes native to the area (Flannery, 1969). These communities moved from a very limited reliance on cereals to considerable reliance on them.

The transformation occurred in a number of interconnected communities, including settlements in Iran, Anatolia, and Syria. Not all communities of the region were directly involved in the transformation. Some practiced little or no plant husbandry. As grains became more important in the diet of these communities, the grains underwent morphological changes. Both wheat and barley were undergoing changes in western Asia by 7000 B.C. Later, in the fifth millennium after the plants were domesticated, settlements that produced large fields of grains appeared in regions where soils were more suited for their growth (Oates and Oates, 1976:83). These later grain producing communities were spinoffs of the earlier settlements where domestication had been achieved. The emergence of these later agricultural communities was dependent upon prior developments in communities that were primarily trade centers.

The first steps toward domestication of grains was not intentional. They were the unintended consequences of trade and sedentism. Sedentism created an ecological condition that allowed for foreign plants to grow outside their native habitat. Wild grains were brought to the communities. They were probably brought by nomadic groups who harvested the grains and traded at the communities.

Mellaart (1975) suggests that grains were domesticated by residents of the early communities travelling to the area where the plants were native and bringing back seeds and planting them. That is very unlikely. It is difficult to imagine persons with no awareness of the benefits to be derived from planting, tending, and harvesting grain to travel sixty to a hundred miles to acquire seeds to establish plots of grain. Even if such an effort was undertaken, the morphological features of wild wheat and barley rendered success of such an undertaking very unlikely. The more likely sequence is that nomadic groups brought some of their harvest to the centers to exchange for other goods.

It is conceivable that residents of these centers trekked to the wild plots to harvest the grain and brought it back to the centers. But if they did, it was not with the intention of planting them so that they could grow their own crops. Rather it was simply to acquire a supply of food. However the wild grain was brought to the centers, it was at the centers that the domestication of the grains was achieved.

The achievement was a by-product of sedentism. Sedentism created ecological pockets that allowed these plants to grow outside of their native habitat. Plants live in ecological niches. When plants are introduced into a foreign region they seldom endure for more than a generation or two. However when the soil of an area is disturbed, then plants that are strangers to an ecological niche often appear. If the disturbance is temporary, their endurance is short-lived; if it is sustained, new plants may become established.

Anderson (1952) provides an insightful account of this phenomenon. He described an arboretum that included a lowland that was dotted every spring with blossoms of cress. A fire line was plowed on the hillsides of the arboretum. "For several years after the plowing was done, there were so many winter-cress plants along the fire line that they made a streak of yellow in the landscape" (Anderson, 1952:147). Then after a few years the grass grew back on the fire line and the cress disappeared from the hillsides.

The cress were strangers or "weeds" from an ecological point of view. They grew in soil that normally was dominated by other plants. This usually occurs when the soil is disturbed. The disturbance may be created by an eroding river, floods, animals, or man. When sedentary communities were established the soil was disturbed. The conditions inviting ecological weeds were created. Plants that did not normally grow in the region had an opportunity to become established. Sedentary communities created dump heaps. "Dump heaps are relatively open habitats, receptive to a good many kinds of plants while other places, such as meadows and mountains are relatively closed habitats in which aliens will have trouble getting a footing" (Anderson, 1952:145).

If an area is continually disturbed for several decades, then plants that are strangers to the region may endure. The dump heaps of these early sedentary communities, in conjunction with human beings transporting grains to the region, created the conditions necessary for the growth of alien plants. Some of these plants that were ecological weeds were harvested. Then some began caring for and ultimately planting some of the plants. Some of the dump heaps were transformed into gardens. Horticulture became established when the plants that were originally weeds from an ecological point of view became the crops of the gardeners. The unproductive or less productive plants native to the regions became weeds from a horticultural point of view; they were removed by the gardeners providing a greater opportunity for the foreign plants.

In the early centuries, if not millennia, of the existence of these sedentary communities, grains were either nonexistent or of very little importance. They were merely another plant that grew in the dump heaps. It seems likely that the grains were first treated as horticultural weeds. Legumes, tubers, and herbs were domesticated before grains were. The amount of food provided by a few stalks of wheat or barley was insufficient to have much of an impact. However, over an extended period these grains came to occupy a position of some importance in some of the sedentary communities.

The domestic grains were not capable of maintaining dominance when human care was withdrawn. They were "genetic misfits." If human care were withdrawn from the fields of maize, wheat, and soybeans of the midwestern United States, within a few decades nearly all of these plants would disappear. Without human intervention domestic plants lose out to wild plants that are better adapted to ecological niches. Some of the descendents of domestic plants might go feral and survive, but no domestic plant is capable of surviving in its domestic form when it must compete with wild plants.

Therefore, the maintenance of domestic plants required that some of the residents of these centers continued to care for them. Thus, the process of domestication of grains was a series of historical accidents that finally culminated in human beings systematically caring for the plants. Subsequently some groups intentionally selected seeds to increase the productivity of their crops. The plants were thereby transformed, but the establishment of the original relationship between human groups and grains that provided the foundation for domestication was not intentionally organized to modify the species.

Exactly how this process occurred for each of the various domestic plants is not known. However, the transformation of wild wheat to domestic wheat is fairly well documented. The specifics of the process of the transformation were distinctive for each plant. Nonetheless the transformation of wheat is illustrative of how the establishment of a relation between sedentary groups and a wild plant changes the environment of the plant and provides the necessary conditions for the emergence of a new species.

One of the major morphological differences between wild and domestic wheat is the difference in the rachis of the plant. The rachis is that part of the stem to which the ears of the wheat are attached. In the wild species the individual spikelets disarticulate from the rachis on ripening. The domestic forms of wheat have a rachis that does not break off until it is threshed.

The tendency of heads of wild wheat to break up over a period of time facilitates the survival of the wild plant. This same tendency limits its usefulness as a domestic plant. The harvesting of wheat by generations of sedentary groups selected those seeds that remained attached to the stem. The selection of seeds that remained on the stems was unintended. But after many generations of harvesting and planting more grains would remain attached until threshed. The long-term selection was in the direction of creating a plant that was more useful to human beings, but less capable of surviving in the wild. When wild stands of wheat were harvested, the selection was in the opposite direction. Those grains that fell off early or late were those most likely to be the seeds for the next year's crop.

Wild wheat had ears as large as the early domestic wheat. "The main developments under domestication were not selection for bigger seed, but the breakdown of the seed dispersal mechanism" (Zohary, 1969:58). The intentional selection of seed for size was a much later development. Then varieties of domestic wheat were established.

Wheat underwent domestication in the seventh and sixth millennia B.C. in western Asia. It then became a major crop in lower Mesopotamia. Domestic wheat reached the Nile Valley in the fourth millennium, India by the third, and China in the second. In northern China it was intermixed with millet; it was intermixed with sorghum and rice in India. Millet may have been domesticated in China before wheat and barley made their appearance there. It is possible that the domestication of millet was an intentional activity that was stimulated by the awareness of other domestic grains, or it could have been domesticated in much the same way as wheat.

Domestic grains provided an additional and more stable supply of food. Those communities that planted and harvested grains had a somewhat more reliable source of food than those that relied on hunting, gathering, and trade. Other domestic plants contributed to the stability of communities, but it was grains that provided the stable subsistence that allowed for the emergence of the first large agricultural communities and nation states that rested upon an infrastructure provided by plant husbandry.

ANIMALS

Sheep, goats, and perhaps pigs were domesticated in western Asia about the same time as wheat and barley. The domestication of sheep, goats, and cattle took a different form than the domestication of dogs and pigs. Dogs and pigs are scavengers and eat much the same food as human beings. The dump heaps of the sedentary communities attracted them. They initiated their relation with human groups. They were parasites on human communities before they were domesticated.

In contrast sheep, goats, cattle, donkeys, horses, and llamas were not attracted to human settlements. The domestication of these animals required that human groups attach themselves to wild herds. To accomplish their domestication it was necessary for human groups to reach out for these animals and encapsulate these species and bring them under control. The process began when the first human groups attached themselves to herds of these animals and followed them. Human groups were parasites on the herds.

A number of different species were hosts to parasitical human groups. Clusters of horse teeth that display evidence of "crib-biting" have been found which date in the Middle Paleolithic Age (Bahn, 1980). When modern horses are confined, they nervously chew on pieces of wood. The incisor teeth become worn in a distinctive fashion from their "crib-biting." It is likely some middle paleolithic groups followed herds of wild horses and preyed on them. Some of the horses may have been trapped and confined to be slaughtered later, or it is possible that colts were captured and kept as pets. Other groups of the Paleolithic Age probably attached themselves to herds of sheep, goats, aurochs (the ancestors of domestic cattle), and other species. The Lapps probably have been migrating with herds of caribou since the Paleolithic Age.

Those groups that followed and preyed on herds of animals were not directly responsible for their domestication. The domestication of a species was dependent upon the relationships between the nomadic groups that followed the herds and the trade centers. None of the nomadic groups that followed herds of wild animals ever established a sedentary community, but some established sustained relations with sedentary communities. It was the combination of the experience of nomads with animals, their trading of some of the animals to residents of sedentary communities, and the confinement of the animals by residents of the sedentary communities that resulted in the domestication of the first animals.

As with the domestication of grains the first steps toward the domestication of animals were not taken intentionally. Trade and sedentism created the conditions that had the consequence of enticing some groups to preserve in confinement some animals and to subsequently breed them. The original intention was not to transform the species, but to retain a supply of food for later consumption.

It is conceivable, but doubtful, that those groups that followed the herds contributed to the transformation of the wild species to domestic ones. There was considerable variation in the intensity of the relationship between relatively contemporary nomadic groups and the herds of animals they preyed upon. This variation is indicated by the variation in the relationships between arctic groups and the caribou.

In eastern Siberia and western North America the natives were heavily dependent upon the herds of caribou. The caribou were heavily hunted and provided many of the necessities of life, but the herds were not closely followed. Further west the herds were more closely followed but the animals were allowed to roam at will. Still further west, the caribou were used as pack animals and to draw sleds, but they were not milked or ridden. The Lapps, the westernmost group, had the most intense relation with the caribou. They migrated with their herds, castrated some of them, used some for transportation, systematically harvested them, and practiced selective breeding. They did not confine them, but did protect them from predators.

It will probably never be possible to specify the nature of the relationship between human groups and the herds they followed for those groups that systematically hunted a given species at the time sedentary communities were first established. It seems likely that the relationship was not a very intense one. However, as the trade centers became established and grew, it is likely that in some cases the relationship intensified. Routine contact between such groups and sedentary communities provided the nomadic groups the opportunity to harvest their herds for trade as well as for consumption. It is very doubtful that any of those groups had as intense a relationship with their herds as the Lapps had with the caribou, although some groups may have established an equally intense relationship with their herds in the millennia immediately following the establishment of trade centers. The Lapps have had a longer and more intense relationship with sedentary groups than the other arctic groups that were highly dependent on the caribou.

None of these groups that followed herds, even those that may have formed an intense relationship with their herds, established sedentary communities. The continuation of the relation between the human groups and the herds precluded a sedentary life. The length of stay of a group in a given location was limited by the food and water available for the herds. When any one resource was depleted, the herd and the group attached to it moved on. They had to remain responsive to ecological and seasonal changes to survive.

A few members of those groups may have on many occasions left the nomadic life to live in sedentary communities. If and when that occurred, they may have made incidental contributions to the domestication of the animals. They had greater experience with the animals than the residents of the sedentary communities. Members of the nomadic groups may have tended herds of the sedentary communities. If that occurred, it probably did not take place until after domestication was well under way.

Sheep

The oldest findings that might suggest domestication of animals dates from about 9000 B.C. At one site a high percentage of immature sheep were slaughtered (Higgs and Jarman, 1972:3). The animals had the same morphological structure as wild sheep. Morphological changes do not appear until about 1,000 years later. These findings only indicate that selectivity was practiced in the slaughtering of sheep, not that domestication was underway.

The distinctive distribution could have come about in a number of ways. It is possible that the residents of the settlement hunted sheep and deliberately killed only younger animals; the meat of the young is more tender than that of the old. It is also possible that younger animals were captured by the residents and brought to the site to be slaughtered later. It is easier to capture and transport immature animals than mature ones. A third possibility, and one that seems more likely, is that nomadic groups who had attached themselves to herds of sheep came to the settlement and traded some young animals for other goods.

The popular image of wild sheep is that of an extremely alert and skittish animal. However, sheep are docile and easily tamed. "It is hard to imagine a wild animal more readily tamed than a mountain sheep" (Geist as quoted in Harris, 1969). Prior to their domestication, some groups probably had established a relatively intense relation with flocks of sheep. They were probably herded to an extent. It is likely that at certain times of the year the herders came to the sedentary communities to trade and brought their flocks with them.

The residents of the communities kept some of the animals alive for a period to preserve a supply of meat. At first the sheep were probably retained for only a short period, until the surrounding meadowland became depleted, before they were slaughtered.

The transition from saving some for short periods to breeding and caring for them was a major transformation. It was probably the consequence of a series of incremental changes that extended over centuries. The transition may have been motivated solely by a concern with assuring a stable supply of mutton. However, it is possible that sheep were originally kept by residents of the communities to serve as beasts of burden. They may have been used as beasts of burden by the nomadic groups before they were put to that use by the residents of the trade centers. Until recently, sheep were still used in some areas of central Asia as beasts of burden. Both a concern with a stable supply of meat and an interest in retaining beasts of burden probably contributed to the domestication of sheep.

Modern sheep are a source of wool. But the original intense relation between sheep and human groups was not established to acquire wool. The wild ancestors of sheep had fleece that was much the same as the fur of deer. Flannery (1969) suggests that wooliness was an unintentional development that was a consequence of the confinement of sheep. In the wild, sheep stay in the shade during the hottest part of the day. In captivity they were often exposed to the hot sun during the day. "Wool acts not only as a reflector to divert light and heat rays, but also as a layer of insulation which allows air circulation to cool the skin without exposing it to the sun" (Flannery, 1969:92). The woolier confined sheep had a greater chance of survival. Once wooliness made its appearance, then sheep were intentionally bred to enhance their wool. The earliest definite indication of wooliness as a trait is about 3000 B.C.

Cattle

The oldest site that has yielded evidence of domestic cattle is in Greece about 6500 B.C. It is likely that settlements in present day Turkey had domestic cattle almost, if not, as early as the settlements in Greece. Domestic cattle rapidly appeared in widely separated locations from Greece to Iranian Khuzistan (Reed, 1969). A complex "cattle cult" that included teasing bulls was established at Çatal Hüyük.

It is certain that cattle were not domesticated for their milk. It is very unlikely that a concern for a stable supply of meat was the motivating factor. It was far simpler and more effective to hunt for meat than to control a herd of wild aurochs. Nor were the first aurochs kept for traction power. Domestic cattle conjure up the image of oxen pulling plows. However, cattle were domesticated before there were any farms large enough to use cattle for traction power. Cattle were not used for traction until after large agricultural communities were founded.

The first aurochs that were retained and cared for were probably kept to serve as beasts of burden. Cattle have been employed by many groups in diverse parts of the world as beasts of burden. It is likely that the first aurochs that were confined were communal property or the property of a group of traders. The care and feed demanded for a single cow is considerable; the productivity of a single family living at a trade center was probably not sufficient to support one. But a village or cluster of traders that was conducting long-distance trade could make effective use of a cow or a small herd of them.

The "cattle cult" of Çatal Hüyük indicates that cattle occupied a central position in the lives of the residents. The widespread sacred cow complex suggests that these animals were a communal concern. The original cattle that were used to transport goods by the community were probably protected by communal edicts. It is possible that the first steps toward domestication were taken by nomads who formed a parasitical relationship with herds of aurochs. Some of the more docile aurochs could have been used to transport the belongings of the band. These may have been protected while the rest of the herd was preyed upon.

One of the most distinctive morphological changes associated with the domestication of aurochs is the smaller size of domestic cattle. It was the smaller and probably more docile females that were first confined. The larger bulls simply were too difficult to manage. The systematic selection of animals that resulted in domestic cattle had to be maintained for centuries to produce a distinction between the wild aurochs and cattle. That process, while perhaps not limited to sedentary communities, was primarily completed by residents of sedentary communities.

A critical part of that process was the designation of some animals as "sacred" or "off limits" except for those who handled them. These animals were confined to assure the preservation of the community's beasts of burden. This interpretation of the domestication process is supported by a study of cattle bones found at two different sites. One of the communities had domestic cattle and the other did not. At the site with domestic cattle only 9 percent of the bones were of immature animals; at the other site 26 percent of the bones were of immature animals. This distribution suggests that the community with domestic cattle did not kill the young for food, but preserved them for other uses.

That the domestication of cattle followed the domestication of sheep and goats by about a millennium suggests that the domestication of cattle was stimulated by the earlier domestication of sheep and goats. The domestication of all of these animals was closely associated with trade. The complex set of intergroup relations that had been established on the foundation of intergroup trade provided one of the necessary conditions for the domestication of animals.

Other Animals

Domestic pigs first appear about 7000 B.C. in Turkey. Wild pigs were distributed over a wide region and lived in forests. "The first finds of domestic pigs were limited to a small region within the total area of distribution, but then the domestic pig was distributed quickly over a large area" (Herre and Rohrs, 1977:259). As with the domestication of cattle, the domestication of the pig was probably stimulated by the earlier domestication of sheep and goats. The domestic pig provided a more secure source of food than the wild pig. Again, like the early domestic cattle, the most distinctive morphological change was toward smaller animals.

The donkey was domesticated after sheep, goats, pigs, and cattle, but before the horse. It was probably domesticated by traders. Excavation of Maadi (an early trade center) has yielded some of the earliest domestic donkey bones known in prehistoric Egypt. Domestic donkeys were used on the Nile Valley before agriculture became established as the prevailing way of life. Even "today in the Middle East, jars of an analogous shape (to those found in conjunction with donkey remains at Maadi) are strapped to the backs of donkeys and transported with ease over long distances" (Hoffman, 1979:205).

It appears that sometime around 7500 B.C. some of the communities of western Asia began caring for both grains and animals. Both stemmed from conditions created by the establishment of trade centers. The emergence of domestic grains and animals seems to have been closely intertwined. The domestication of grain was a far more significant process than the domestication of animals. Several national civilizations were established that did not have any domestic animals of consequence. The Mesoamericans had the dog and turkey, and perhaps the chicken. Domestic llama, vicuna and guinea pig were present in Peru, but of minimal consequence. Domestic animals were of minimal significance during the first millennia of the Chinese civilization.

The domestication of animals had critical consequences for subsequent developments. It provided the foundation for the emergence of nomadic pastoralists with their herds of animals. It is difficult to specify how pastoralists with domestic animals emerged. They may have evolved when the nomads who followed herds of wild animals came to exercise more control over their herds. It is also possible that nomads acquired domestic animals from the sedentary communities and substituted them for their wild herds.

However, a more likely possibility is the suggestion of Jacobs (1970) that the pastoralists, who appeared with domestic animals in the seventh and sixth millennium B.C., were displaced groups who had earlier been sedentary. Either through failure of the region to continue to provide the necessities of life, or from being driven from their communities by nomadic groups, some communities returned to the nomadic way of life. Some of them preserved their domestic animals and became herders of domestic animals.

Pastoralists with flocks of sheep and goats and herds of cattle appeared in the Sahara region by about 4000 B.C.. They replaced natives who had hunted the wild game. Their animals were descendants of those who had been domesticated in western Asia. Other groups of pastoralists appear in other regions. Some of these groups appear to have also practiced plant husbandry part of the time. The indications are that the herders of domestic animals fanned out more quickly over a wider region than did communities that were primarily dependent on grains. The pastoralists' continued responsiveness to the needs of their herds induced them to spread out over wide areas rather quickly.

These groups, or at least some of them, also preyed upon the sedentary communities some of the time. They were far more warlike than the residents of the trade and agricultural centers. From time to time some of these groups must have become nomadic and then later merged with sedentary communities to take up plant husbandry again. On other occasions these groups established sustained peaceful trade relations with the sedentary communities. The pastoralists of the Sahara had trade relations with some of the sedentary communities along the Nile by 4000 B.C., probably a millennium or two earlier.

TRADE AND AGRICULTURE

Those communities that had domestic grains and animals became more secure and self-sufficient than those that remained dependent on trade and food gathering. Not all of the communities were equally agricultural. Some remained primitive markets, others combined intercommunity trade with food gathering, and some combined food production with trade and food gathering. As domestic plants and animals became more significant sources of goods, there was an expansion of trade.

The agriculturalists and the pastoralists, like the earlier traders, accumulated surpluses during times of plenty; they husbanded their excesses. Those communities primarily dependent on grains stored their grains; the pastoralists accumulated surplus animals. In times of need the excess grain and animals were consumed. In most agricultural communities with domestic animals it was standard practice to slaughter excess animals when the barren months of winter approached.

As agriculture came to the fore some communities acquired the ability to produce the bulk of the necessities of life; they thereby became more self-sufficient and less dependent on trade. However, in most communities the domestic plants and animals provided another resource for trade. Some communities specialized in the production of specific agricultural products. For example, some of the communities of western Asia had many kilns that apparently were used to bake bread. Some had far more kilns than necessary to supply bread for the community. Apparently these communities traded the bread for other items. Perhaps specialists in bread baking maintained a monopoly of knowledge of their skill.

Çatal Hüyük probably specialized in woven cloth. They had several weaves but "did not grow flax nor have we any evidence that they kept domestic sheep or goat" (Mellaart, 1975:105). It is unlikely, but possible, that by then sheep had become wooly. The raw material for the cloth was probably imported. They may then have traded manufactured cloth. Or, it is possible that they acquired the raw material solely for their own use.

The manufacturing of products was not limited to the sedentary communities, but it was at the sedentary communities that small industrial complexes were established. The manufactured goods were traded with nomadic food gatherers, pastoralists, and other sedentary communities. These communities had a more stable source of material goods than those who relied upon harvesting wild species and collecting or mining selected items.

Both the sedentary communities and the pastoralists competed with nomadic food gatherers for access to land. However, during the early millennia of domestic species, the competition for land between those groups with domestic plants and animals and nomadic food gatherers was minimal. For the most part the relation was symbiotic and mutually beneficial.

Those collectivities with domestic species experienced greater population growth than the food gatherers. The stability of their food supply and greater resources lessened the likelihood of famine. Of course, on occasions these communities suffered from droughts and other disasters. But in general they experienced greater population growth than those who remained food gatherers. Consequently they began squeezing out the surrounding food gatherers from the richer environments.

TEMPORAL STRUCTURES

The continuation of domestic species required the projection of complex and precise sequences if future generations of the plants and animals were to be assured. Seeds and breeding stock had to be saved. The seeds had to be planted at specific times of the year and the plants had to be protected from incursions by weeds and animals. Domestic animals had to be confined and protected, especially at the birth of the young. Knowledge of gestation periods is an integral part of the care of domestic animals.

The domestication of species required the simultaneous development of new and different temporal structures. Whereas the development of trade was associated with the development of an individualistic orientation toward the future, the development of domestic species reinstituted communal temporal structures. Among those communities that became primarily food producing communities a communal concern with the future came to the fore. The most ancient calendars were designed to foretell the termination of human pregnancies and the reappearance of migrating animals. The residents of the communities that became involved in agriculture developed calendars linked to their food producing activities. A calendric system linked to domestic plants was established at Çatal Hüyük. One of the murals displays stellar constellations in conjunction with the maturation of barley (Matossian, 1980). A mural of these phenomena indicates that a sidereal calendar of some complexity was of considerable significance to the residents. Other communities probably developed functionally equivalent procedures that were used to organize their care of domestic plants.

The domestication of species extended and elaborated the intentional behavior of human beings. Programs of action were formulated that linked the activity of human beings to the welfare of plants and animals. Human beings subordinated plants and animals to their control, but in the process became subordinated to the demands of their plants and animals. Both human beings and their plants and animals were thereby transformed. As these communities became more concerned with domestic species, they became more attuned to time keeping and developed more refined calendric systems. In the process both the plants and animals and their human caretakers became more differentiated from the undomestic species and nomadic groups.

SUMMARY

Neither the domestication of grains or animals was easily completed; both suffered many setbacks. The evidence indicates that the domestication of a number of important plants and animals occurred at approximately the same time, and further, that a number of plants and animals were domesticated in the same region within a comparatively short period. The rapidity of the development suggests the emergence of a new consciousness. A consciousness that greater control could be exercised over the future by creating a more intense relation between human groups and certain species.

The domestication of both grains and animals rested upon human groups taking a different standpoint toward the species in question. The relation between hunters and animals is that of predator-prey. The animals were stalked, chased, and killed; the animals fled. The relations between human groups and fields of wild grain were not exactly that of predator-prey, but were similar. The fields of wild grain were located and harvested. Both animals and plants were conceived of as resources that were to be located and the goods extracted.

In contrast, when grain and animals were brought to sedentary communities, a foundation was there for the establishment of a new standpoint. Some of the grain and animals was preserved. The grain was put in storage bins; some of the animals were either confined or tethered. The nature of the affiliation allowed human groups to develop a different standpoint, specifically, one wherein there was concern with preserving the grain and animals. This standpoint is of an entirely different nature than that of a predator where the concern is to locate and extract the goods. It was a breakthrough that is probably of equal significance to the establishment of a sedentary life style. Plants and animals were no longer simply objects to be harvested and consumed, but objects to be protected for future use. Norms constraining their use were established.

The transition from nomadism to sedentism was a major transformation. The subsequent domestication of grains cemented the transformation. One consequence of the transformation was larger and more stable communities. These communities were somewhat less subject to the vacillations of shortage and plentitude of food. This, plus their sedentary life, allowed some communities to achieve populations much larger than the earlier primitive markets and trade centers. A few of them eventually became large cities with populations of tens of thousands.

Chapter X

The Diffusion of Agriculture

About 4,000 years elapsed between the domestication of grains and the establishment of the Egyptian nation. During the intervening period many agricultural settlements were established in western and central Asia, throughout large areas of Europe and northern Africa. These communities were more self-sufficient, exercised greater territorial control and were more homogeneous than the earlier trade centers. Some of these regions, especially the flood plains, became densely populated. City-states and nations emerged that rested on a foundation of grain production. The prototypical case was the emergence of Egypt in the Nile Valley.

Shortly after the domestication of grains, about 7000 B.C., agricultural villages began to appear in western Asia. The earliest villages that planted fields of grain were but slightly more dependent upon agriculture than the earlier communities. Some of the settlements were in regions where the soil was conducive to the production of grain. In the following centuries some of these communities became largely dependent on their grain. Food gathering receded and almost disappeared as a means for acquiring the necessities of life in the larger agricultural settlements.

The early expansion of agriculture occurred when trade centers brought adjacent land under cultivation. However, the soils of the regions where grains were domesticated were not particularly conducive to grain production. In the following centuries when these fragmented, some of the colonists established settlements in soils that were more receptive to grain production. These settlements were the first communities highly dependent on grain production. Horticulture slowly became agriculture in some regions.

Agriculture spread largely as the consequence of fragmentation and colonization. Collectivities fragmented off from established communities and carried their agricultural knowledge and grains to new locations. Those that moved into the more fertile regions became centers of food production. They continued to trade, hunt, and collect food, but in some regions grains became the primary subsistence base.

Hypothetically agriculture could have spread by nomadic groups becoming aware of grain production and becoming sedentary. However, given the tremendous difficulty of enticing nomads to become sedentary, plus the intricacies of food production, it is very unlikely that much of the spread of agriculture occurred by nomads becoming farmers. Some were absorbed by sedentary communities, but that process was limited to individuals and families. Rarely, if ever, have intact nomadic groups taken up agriculture.

When new productive regions were brought under cultivation, the population of these communities, once a foothold was established, sometimes expanded tremendously in the following generations. A prototype of population growth following agricultural colonization is the foundation and expansion of settlements in North America by western Europeans. The rapidity of the population growth of the agriculture settlements during the millennia after the domestication of grain was much less than that of those founded in historical times. Nonetheless, comparatively speaking, rapid population growth followed the establishment of agricultural colonies.

EARLY COLONIZATION

Agriculture spread primarily through colonization. In most instances agriculturalists moved into areas that had a relatively low population density. They were intruders. They were far more intrusive than those who established new trade centers. They laid claim to the territories that nomadic groups used for hunting and gathering. They brought the land under cultivation and squeezed the natives off the more productive soils. The indigenous groups did not respect the territorial claims of the colonists. The intruders attempted to keep the natives off the land they cultivated. The natives found the restrictions imposed by the colonists offensive. In historical times, conflict between intruder-farmers and nomadic natives had been ubiquitous. It was undoubtedly pervasive in ancient times as agriculturalists moved into new regions.

The earliest contact between the intruders and the natives may have been welcomed by the natives. The natives probably first had contact with traders, not agriculturalists. The traders provided them with an opportunity to acquire new materials. They did not claim the territory, but when they were followed by agriculturalists, the relationship between the intruders and natives was transformed. Then the natives attempted to resist.

Sometimes the natives were victorious and drove the newcomers from the area. Usually their success was short-lived. In the long run the advantages lay with the intruders. Even if the first groups were driven off, others replaced them. The intruders had a stronger vested interest in controlling the territory than the natives. The natives often moved on to another region. Most of the time the intruders had more sophisticated weapons than the natives. Usually, in due time, the agriculturalists became established and dominated the natives. Finally, most of the natives found themselves living on the edges of the territory they once freely roamed.

Warfare was a significant dimension of early colonization, but the colonists were not military invaders. In most instances they moved into an area with relative ease. Then later, when the natives did not respect their territorial claims, conflict between the two became pervasive. Many colonies and native groups were destroyed in the process.

Europe

Agricultural communities were established in eastern Greece by the seventh millennium B.C. These early communities did not have pottery, but they cultivated cereals and had domestic, or partially domestic, animals from the beginning. The morphological features of the sheep, goats, pigs, and cattle of the early sedentary communities in Greece were quite similar to their wild ancestors. The process of domestication continued as agriculture spread.

The early food producing communities of southeastern Europe were composed of intrusive populations. These earliest farming communities lacked any native European mesolithic tools. There were "close similarities in the form and content of the early neolithic assemblages of southeast Europe to the contemporary and immediately preceding assemblages in Greece and the Near East, particularly Anatolia" (Tringham, 1971:70). The domestic wheat associated with the early farming settlements of southeastern Europe originated in Anatolia.

These early communities of southeastern Europe were also part of trade networks. Obsidian was widely traded. Some obsidian was obtained from the island of Melos as early as 8000 B.C. Melos was uninhabited until 4000 B.C., so either persons went Melos to obtain the obsidian or traders traveled to the island and carried it to various communities. The distribution of obsidian from Melos indicates over-water transportation was possible by 8000 B.C.

Many communities were established in various parts of southeastern Europe during this period. A small settlement was established on Crete by about 6500 B.C. The original community consisted of no more than

100 persons. They brought with them domestic sheep and pigs, and there are traces of domestic wheat and barley. Obsidian from Melos has also been found at the earliest site on Crete.

Agricultural communities were established in several areas along the coastlines and on the Danube River. The Danubian settlements spread over much of Europe during the sixth and fifth millennia. These communities were populated by intrusive populations and display a "remarkable homogeneity" (MacKie, 1978). Food producing communities appear on the east coast of Spain before 5000 B.C. In the early centuries the intruders coexisted with native food gatherers. These colonists cultivated barley and had domestic animals which they had brought with them (MacKie, 1978). They had far-reaching trade contacts. Ivory and ostrich shells from Africa have been found at these settlements. Agricultural settlements were established on the coast of Britain by 4000 B.C. (MacKie, 1978).

Mesopotamia

Agriculture spread into the Mesopotamian region about the same time, or perhaps slightly later than it reached Greece. Agricultural villages were established along the Tigris and Euphrates Rivers by the early sixth millennium (Adams, 1981). Irrigation was practiced in some of the communities. One village of the sixth millennium has been excavated that used irrigation. Small irrigation ditches ran along one side of the settlement (Oates and Oates, 1976: 64). At least some of these communities had plots of grains, although evidence for the presence of domestic grains is ambiguous until as late as the fifth millennium B.C. (Adams, 1966:38). It is possible that the earliest grain production of lower Mesopotamia was achieved by planting wild grains. If so, they were then replaced by domestic grains.

A carbon date places the establishment of Ugaid of lower Mesopotamia at 5020 B.C. plus or minus 170 years. The Mesopotamian region was dotted by sedentary communities if not taken over by farmers and traders by that time. The populations that established these settlements were intruders. A new racial group appeared as farming made its appearance in the region. The relations between the natives and the intruders was probably a complex intermixture of trading, conflict, begging, and mutual distrust. One of the ancient Sumerian myths describes the natives as "hovering over the walls of Uruk like flocks of birds" (Oates, 1979:55).

Agricultural communities were probably established in central Asia during the same period they were spreading into Europe and down the Tigris and Euphrates Rivers (Kohl, 1981). Sedentary communities were present in central Asia by 6000 B.C., perhaps earlier.

Egypt

Egypt may have been the first nation state, but large agricultural communities were not established on the Nile until the fourth millennium. There was trade between western Asia and the Nile Valley before food production became a way of life on the Nile and sedentary communities were present in the Nile Valley millennia before food producing settlements were founded. Horticulture was practiced, but these earlier communities were not self-sufficient food producing centers.

Grains and animals that had been domesticated in western Asia reached Merimde, a community of about 5,000, before food producing communities became dominant on the Nile. Storage facilities associated with family dwelling have been excavated. There is no evidence of centralized storage at Merimde during this period. The community appears to have been populated by families that were dependent upon trade, food gathering, and some horticulture. Nearly all of the 125 skeletons found at the site are of women and children. The women probably were sedentary horticulturalists while the men continued a largely nomadic life. The burials were seldom accompanied by grave offerings. Ranking was of minimal significance, if present at all.

A similar condition prevailed at Fayum A near the apex of the delta. The diet of the residents included both domestic and wild animals. Pierced marine shells, from both the Mediterranean and Red Seas, and green anozonite that came from either the eastern desert or from deep in the heart of the Sahara, demonstrates that Fayum A had extensive trade contacts.

About 3600 B.C. a number of changes occur in some centers. New and foreign trade items appear in both the upper and lower Nile. About 100 years later communities populated by new people appear along the Nile. Skeletons indicate that the newcomers were of a different race. They had larger bodies and wider skulls (David, 1980). The newcomers probably first entered the Nile Valley at Maadi, a community that had become a major commercial center. It was located on the Wadi El Tih which reaches out toward the upper arm of the Red Sea.

Along the Nile there are numerous pictographs of two types of boats that date from this period. One type belongs to "Early Nile Dwellers" whereas the others are of boats that are associated with "eastern invaders." These pictures are all over the eastern desert (Winkeler, as quoted in Hoffman, 1979:243). They extend up to sixty-five miles from the river into the eastern desert, which is halfway to the Red Sea. They also extend into the western desert twelve miles. Water transport apparently reached far up and down the Nile and into its tributaries during the predynastic period.

At the same time monumental brick architecture and distinctive art forms appear on the Nile. Both innovations came from western Asia. One of the new motifs was drawings of composite animals with entwined necks. These designs wre not Egyptian in origin. They had close similarities with Mesopotamian motifs (David, 1980:20–21). These new forms were not the culmination of indigenous developments.

In general, the evidence suggests that sometime around 3600 to 3400 B.C., there was an expansion of trade between residents of the Nile and western Asia followed by agriculturalists moving into the Nile Valley. Through trade contacts some residents of established agricultural communities of western Asia learned of the fertile land of the Nile Valley. Groups of colonists migrated to the Nile Valley. They may have come entirely over land or part way by sea and then across the eastern desert. "Such a journey would not have been difficult, since the higher land of the Eastern Desert has always attracted more rainfall than the Western Desert" (Hoffman, 1979:245).

The intruders did not come via the delta. The delta was an unpopulated marsh at that time. Early dynastic Egypt was oriented to the Red Sea, not the Mediterranean Sea. Egyptian contact with other societies through the delta was a later development. Even as late as 600 B.C. Egypt attempted to link the Nile with the Red Sea by a canal.

The foundation for the classical Egyptian civilization was laid during the following century or two. There was a strong continuity between the village farmers of the predynastic period and the farmers of dynastic Egypt. The transformation from predynastic to dynastic society was largely political; no new cultural traits appear with the emergence of the Egyptian nation.

The colonization of Egypt seems to have been accomplished by groups that originated in western Asia, probably the lower Mesopotamian region. The grains cultivated during the predynastic period were not derivatives of grains native to the Nile Valley. They were introduced by colonists (Jordon, 1976:38). Whereas barley had been the primary crop of Mesopotamia, wheat became the primary crop of the Nile. Within a few hundred years, after grain production became common on the Nile, the Egyptian nation was established. It had a larger population and controlled far more territory than any other civilization that was its contemporary. The Egyptian civilization emerged abruptly.

The transformation of the Nile into a food producing region seems to have taken a somewhat different form than the changes that occurred in southeastern Europe and lower Mesopotamia. One reason is probably due to the fact that sedentary communities were well established on the Nile before the agriculturalists appeared on the scene. These communities traded with one another, pastoralists of the Sahara, and probably others. The agricultural colonists came into contact with well established sedentary communities and probably relatively large groups of pastoralists instead of scattered and small nomadic groups. There probably was considerable conflict and intermingling of the populations.

During the predynastic period the communities of the lower Nile were primarily trade centers. There is little evidence of stratification at these centers. The communities of the upper Nile took a somewhat different form. They were more warlike and there was considerable stratification within these communities during the predynastic period. These communities may have been an outgrowth of a merger between farmers and traders with pastoral groups. A merger of these two traditions would account for the more warlike course of development that occurred in the upper Nile.

The thrust for unification came from the upper Nile. The lower Nile was conquered. Maadi, which was the point of contact with easterners during the colonization period and remained a major trade center, was destroyed when unification was imposed. Ash was widespread and human bones scattered over the settlement (Hoffman, 1979:214). Apparently Maadi was a major point of resistance to the conquerors. The political structure that subsequently encompassed the Nile Valley originated on the upper Nile.

The Indus Valley

The early developments in the Indus Valley were similar to those of the Nile Valley. Trading centers were established prior to farming communities. Toward the end of the fourth millennium large tracts of land in the Indus Valley and its tributaries were colonized (Allchin and Allchin, 1968). The settlements were just above the flood line and were populated by intruders.

The Indus flows through a wide alluvial flood plain that is extremely fertile. Wheat and barley matured and ripened without either plowing or manuring. All that was necessary to achieve a harvest was to plant seeds at the proper time of the year. Civilization flourished over a vast area.

It is possible that the earliest agricultural communities of the Indus Valley emerged as the consequence of agriculture spreading over land from western Asia through central Asia into the Indus Valley. But it is more likely that traders from lower Mesopotamia established overseas contact with the Indus Valley, and that subsequently colonists migrated there and established farming communities. Residents of the Mesopotamian region learned of the vast tracts of fertile land and some formed groups to establish new communities. Agricultural colonization followed the earlier trade contacts.

The Harappan civilization took a different form than the Egyptian civilization. Despite the cultural uniformity of the Indus Valley, there are no indications of a centralized political system that united the various cities and regions. Yet there are indications of large-scale coordination between the communities that centered on trade, or at least that some communities served as shipping centers for others. There was a brick basin 710 feet in length and 120 feet wide at Lothal. It was flanked by a landing platform on the landward side. The eastward entrance had a still 23 feet wide that allowed in enough sea water to float the docked ships. "It is the largest 'public work' in the Indus area, but additionally it is the world's first wet dock" (Divine, 1973: 36). The Harappan civilization had an extended maritime trade network. It traded with Mesopotamia, its likely point of origin, and other maritime centers of commerce. It probably exported large quantities of grain.

China

The earliest food producing communities of China were probably established by intruders. Agriculture appears "suddenly" in the Yellow River Valley. "Between 'Upper Cave Man' and the farming villages of the full Neolithic the archaeological record is blank" (Watson, 1961: 36). There is a lack of evidence of incremental changes that culminate in the appearance of agricultural communities. The agricultural way of life was probably established by a series of overland steps that reached from central Asia into the Yellow River region. In the process wheat and barley were supplemented by millet and rice.

Summary

Food producing communities were probably only "invented" once in the Old World. The invention rested upon a complex set of technological achievements, the elaboration and refinement of temporal structures and a complex set of social relationships. The technologies, temporal structures, and social relationships continued to develop as the invention spread into new regions. The continuation of agriculture required human beings to develop a new relation with their environment. "Nature" was not taken as a given, but something that was acted upon and modified.

Agriculture provided a more secure source of food for both the residents of the food producing communities and the trade centers. Some of the food producing communities subsequently became largely self-sufficient. In these, intercommunity trade receded in importance. Egypt was the prototypical example of this transformation. The marketplace was replaced by temples and palaces as the central institution.

THE NEW WORLD

The polemics that focus on the issue of contact between the Old and New World are so intense that it is difficult to evaluate the evidence. What some specialists in the field present as hard evidence of contact, other specialists characterize as figments of the imaginations of the advocates. At one extreme are the isolationists who deny the possiblity of any contact other than the ancient migrations of peoples across the Bering Straits until the time of Columbus. At the other extreme are those who argue that there were a series of contacts between the Old and the New World. All agree that sedentary communities do not appear in the New World until thousands of years after they had been established in the Old World.

Lathrap (1977) argues that central Africans reached the eastern shore of South America by 12,000 B.C. He claims that these contacts brought plants that are native of the Old World to the New World. It is possible that some central Africans of that period were involved in maritime trade. Some may have blown out to sea and arrived on the shores of South America. It is even conceivable that one or more of these rafts made the return trip to Africa.

The bottle gourd, which is an Old World plant, has been found in widely separated sites in the New World. It was present in Mexico by 7000 B.C. Cotton, another Old World plant, also had a wide distribution in the New World. It was first established in South America and reached Central America later.

There may have been contact between the Old and New World prior to 12,000 B.C. Some plants and cultural elements may have been introduced as the consequence of these contacts. Yet the most ancient agricultural centers of the New World did not rest on a foundation provided by the plants or cultural traits introduced then. These contacts, if they occurred, may have contributed to the establishment of horticulture in some regions and been a minor stimulant to trade. But they did not lead to the formation of food producing communities.

Sedentary communities with pottery first appear on the Gulf of Mexico about 3000 B.C. The pottery reflected a mature technology, not a newly emerging one (Hammond, 1977). Pottery which many associate with agriculture, does not indicate the presence of agriculture. Many nonagricultural communities made extensive use of pottery. Pottery reflects sedentism, not agriculture. The source of the pottery that suddenly appeared on the Gulf Coast is unknown, but there are no known sites in the Americas from which it could have stemmed. It is conceivable, given the presence of seagoing rafts of the Old World, that sailors from the Old World landed at one or more coastal sites and established a settlement. Two-way traffic across the Atlantic was within their capabilities.

The earliest food producing communities of the Americas did not emerge from the third millennium sites of the east coast. The Olmecs established food producing communities in a river valley about 1500 B.C., but they represent a different tradition. They probably were an offshoot of a settlement, or set of settlements, on the west coast of Central America. Sedentary communities were established on the western coast of Mesoamerica about 2000 B.C. Carter (1977) develops the theme that the ultimate origin of the Olmec was China. His theory is not widely accepted. However, some of the practices of the Olmec were similar to those of the early Chinese. For example, all the early temples of the Olmec were earthen. The ancient Chinese widely practiced building monuments of tamped earth. An agricultural tradition appears in the valley of Oxacoa about the same time as the Olmec became established on the east coast. Both seem to have originated on the west coast. The Oxacan tradition much later culminated in the Monte Alban complex.

The Olmec were a "megalithic" culture. They were a food producing society and constructed courts with pyramids at each end. The courts were symmetrical. They built gigantic monuments and sculpted mammoth figures at San Lorenze by 1150 B.C. According to Coe and Diehl (1980) the magnitude of the undertakings is staggering when it is recognized that there were probably not more than 1,000 residents at San Lorenzo. Even if Coe and Diehl underestimated the population, the magnitude of the undertaking reflects a complex social organization. The complexity of the social structure in conjunction with the rapidity of its development argues against it being entirely indigenous.

The Olmec were traders as well as food producers. Some Olmec obsidian knives were made of materials that came from a thousand miles away. They may have travelled to obsidian sites or traded for it. They must have had trade contacts with the Maya tradition. The Olmec do not appear until much later than earliest forerunners of the Maya, but the two traditions existed simultaneously for centuries.

The Olmec tradition of constructing gigantic monuments came to a sudden end. They deliberately and violently destroyed their monuments. Then they ceremoniously buried them. The magnitude of the destruction was as awesome as their construction (Coe and Diehl, 1980). The Olmec tradition of monument construction came to an end. However, the Olmec astronomical system became a central and viable part of the later Maya tradition. Perhaps the Maya civilization represented a fusion of the Olmec agricultural tradition with the trading centers of the forerunners of the Maya.

Temples appear on the northern coast of Peru about 2000 B.C. That complex, as well as the Olmec, may have been an extension of the communities that were first established on the western coast of Mesoamerica. There was considerable maritime trade between the west coast of Mesoamerica and the northern coast of Peru. Maize was first domesticated in Central America and then taken to South America. Cotton was cultivated in Peru before it appeared in Central America. It is not possible that maize was diffused over land from Mexico to Peru or that cotton diffused from Peru to Central America over land. The jungles of southern Central America rule out the possibility.

It is impossible to determine the extent of maritime trade on the west coast of the Americas during the second millennium, but it is apparent there was some. It may have begun earlier than 2000 B.C. Maritime trade was important and extensive on the west coast prior to the appearance of the Spanish. Many of the burial sites of Peru have yielded "dagger boards." These boards were the rudders that were used to steer rafts. The pilots of these rafts controlled the steerage mechanism or dagger boards. When a raft pilot died the boards were buried with him. Apparently sea pilots were honored specialists among the ancient Peruvians. They have occupied a special position in all societies that were involved in overseas trade.

The Spanish were impressed with the seafaring abilities of the sailors of the west coast. These sailors helped transport the Spanish to South America and the Spanish relied on the information provided by them. They relayed the legend that those who sailed the balsa rafts would on occasion untie the logs when forced to transport the Inca and push their passengers into the sea to drown while they clung to the balsa logs in joy. The legend may not have much basis in fact. Yet the legend indicates animosity between the sailors and the inland ruling elite.

The maritime settlements of the northern coast of Peru had an entirely different tradition than the Inca. The sailors were traders and fishermen. Heyerdahl (1978) is convinced that they made voyages between widely separated ports and carried tons of cargo. He has developed the argument that Easter Island was part of a maritime trade network that included the northwest coastal regions of South America. Several have attempted to discredit his thesis. However, these sailors had rafts that would carry as many as fifty soldiers and three horses according to a companion of Pizarro. The presence of seagoing rafts of that size indicates that large amounts of cargo were moved from port to port and that the sailors possessed considerable sophistication in sea travel. The navigators of the south seas sailed several hundred miles from island to island in boats less than thirty feet in length.

The agriculture of the New World may not have been the consequence of colonization of the New World by agriculturalists from the Old World. But the evidence is overwhelming that the early agricultural communities of the New World rested upon a foundation provided by substantial intercommunity trade. The old accepted belief that self-sufficient agricultural communities emerged directly from food gathering can no longer be retained. The emergence and diffusion of agriculture was dependent on trade. At the minimum it was necessary for trade centers and networks to be established before agricultural settlements could arise. The trade centers that provided the foundation of the emergence of agriculture in the New World may have been an indigenous development. It is more likely that the first trade centers of the New World were founded as the consequence of Old World contact. Agricultural settlements of the New World may have then developed indigenously in the New World. Even that sequence is questionable. The first agricultural societies of the New World more likely were founded by Old World colonists.

One feature suggesting Old World colonization is that the food producing communities of the New World emerged much more rapidly after the first sedentary settlements in the New World than they did in the Old World. Approximately 4,000 years separate the foundation of sedentary communities and the appearance of agriculture in the Old World, whereas in the New World agriculture appears within a millennium or two after the first sedentary communities.

The original contact may well have been accidental, followed by sailors intentionally returning to the original point of contact. It is within the realm of reason that contact was established around 3000 B.C. by sailors searching for new resources and markets. The sailors of that period were using rafts and boats larger than the boats of Columbus, they were as sophisticated about sea travel as Columbus, and like Columbus they were part of an expanding commercial complex.

Future research on the development of agriculture in the New World promises to resolve the issue of Old World and New World contact. The definitive data that resolves the issue also should yield important information about the intertwinings of the development of intercommunity trade and the founding of agricultural communities. Currently the data indicates that trade between sedentary communities was a necessary step in the movement from a food gathering subsistence to a food producing subsistence. The data may also resolve whether an agricultural complex that provided the substance for large populations was developed but once in the history of humanity.

SUMMARY

Intercommunity trade linked to sedentary communities provided the foundation for the emergence of agriculture. The subsequent expansion of trade networks served as the spear point for the colonization of new regions by agriculturalists. When farmers moved into new regions, they claimed the more productive land and forced the food gatherers to the fringe areas. Some food gatherers were absorbed by both trade centers and agricultural settlements. But the establishment of an agricultural way of life in new regions was largely the consequence of intruders colonizing new regions, not the consequence of natives learning of agriculture and adopting it.

The food production complex allowed for the emergence of societies that were more self-sufficient than trading societies. In that sense they were similar to food gatherers. However, these settlements developed a more complex social structure, in general had a more secure and enduring way of life, and achieved populations far in excess of those of food gathering groups. Small groups of food gatherers could not successfully compete with the farmers. They retreated from them, were destroyed by them, and some of them were absorbed by the colonists.

The foundation of new agricultural communities was in part a response to population pressures, but not to the population pressures stemming from the residents of the immediate region. Persons of the regions experiencing population pressures migrated to a more promising region. The establishment of agricultural communities in North America by western Europeans was not the consequence of the population pressures of the natives of North America. Rather it was due to internal developments, including population pressures of western European nations. In a similar manner the establishment of grain producing communities on the Nile was not the consequence of population growth among the natives of the Nile. It was the consequence of developments in western Asia.

The agricultural colonies that were established in the valleys and flatlands where good yields could be obtained with a minimal amount of effort experienced substantial population growth in the following generations. That population growth in turn led to the farming of the less productive soils. Some of these settlements in turn fragmented and established new colonies.

The continuation of an agricultural settlement at the same location across generations requires both a highly consistent level of production and the development of techniques for constraining population growth. Otherwise, the population growth will outstrip the productive capacity of the region. Sedentary communities produce far more young who reach maturity than do nomadic societies. In that sense the establishment of sedentary communities was the cause of population pressures.

The amount of food that can be produced within a region is much greater when agriculture is practiced. But the constancy of the food supply from year to year is only slightly greater. Crop failures were almost as common among the ancient agriculturalists as was a shortage of the necessary plants and game for nomadic groups. Agriculturalists also experience famine. When the shortage was severe the residents had little alternative but to move in search of food. Many agricultural settlements have been abandoned when the region failed to provide the necessary food. Nonetheless, in some regions of the world agriculture became established as the predominant mode of subsistence. It was these communities that provided the foundation for the subsequent emergence of city-states and nations.

Chapter XI

Agriculture and Timekeepers

The development of agriculture transformed the relationship between human beings and domestic organisms. The transformation was far more complex than is commonly recognized. An integral part of the process was the elaboration of collective temporal structures. The elaboration of temporal structures depended on the construction of edifices (observatories) that allowed for the refinement of observations of celestial events. Specialists in timekeeping emerged; they manned the observatories. In many regions of the world the establishment of agricultural communities, the construction of observatories, and the emergence of specialists in timekeeping emerged more or less simultaneously.

In Mesopotamia and central Asia the ziggurats, which originally were observatories, first appear in conjunction with early agricultural communities. The farmers of ancient Britain "hardly seem to have established themselves in their new land before ponderous funerary and religious structures (observatories) were going up all over the Atlantic coastal areas" (MacKie, 1977:7). Observatories were constructed as the Nile Valley became agricultural. The first Mesoamerican observatories were constructed "to enable the early maize farmers to better understand the sequence of seasons on which his livelihood was so dependent" (Malmstrom, 1978:109).

Specialists in timekeeping were part and parcel of the large agricultural settlements. They constructed and maintained the calendar of their community. They made celestial observations, oversaw the construction of observatories, and programmed the yearly cycle for their community. They accumulated knowledge of the movements of celestial bodies and supervised the celebrations of celestial events. They were an elite who occupied a distinctive position within their communities.

The development of agriculture did not cause the elaboration and refinement of calendars, nor the emergence of timekeepers, nor the construction of observatories. Nor did the development of more precise calendars and the rise of specialists cause the formation of agriculture. These developments reciprocally influenced one another. They emerged as an organic whole in the larger agricultural communities. The specification of precise distal future sequences facilitated agriculture and the expansion of agriculture provided a subsistence base adequate for communities to support the specialists in timekeeping. The timekeepers in turn allowed for the construction of new and more complex calendric systems that increased the productivity of the agricultural settlements. The timekeepers emerged as focal persons in agricultural communities.

Groups that do not have a fairly accurate calendar may attempt to become farmers, but their chances of success are minimal. The continuation of a settlement that is dependent upon the production of plant foods requires a fairly precise calendar and the subordination of plant husbandry to the calendar. The continuation of an agricultural community requires that the distal future of "next spring" be of sufficient significance that seeds for planting be preserved. The planting of seeds must be organized on the basis of a calendar. If it is not, the chances of an adequate harvest are greatly diminished.

All agriculturalists recognize that the yields of their crops are associated with when the seeds are planted, when the plants receive water, and when and how they are cultivated. Domestic plants are a living artifact that will not endure without care at the proper time. Even when care is given at the proper time, it does not assure a plentiful harvest.

Sedentism allowed for precise observation of celestial events. Only after geographic stability had been achieved was it possible for observers of the heavenly bodies to detect precise celestial cycles. While celestial cycles were detected and specified long before this occurred when observations of celestial bodies are made at one location one year and at another the next year, only a vague and variable cycle of celestial movement can be detected.

The residents of the earliest sedentary communities had little interest in the precise observations of celestial phenomena. They were probably less interested in these events than those dependent on migrating herds of animals. However, as horticulture became important, a concern with calendric phenomena came to the fore. There was an increased concern with specifying when seeds should be planted. Recognition grew that some crops had to be planted in the early spring to acquire a good harvest, but that if other crops were planted then they would not survive a late frost.

The spread of agriculture into new regions made groups very sensitive to the seasons. The transfer of domestic plants from one region to another was a less complex process than their domestication. However, it was a more self-conscious activity. The domestication of the first grains was a long series of incremental changes, many of which were unintentional. In contrast, the movement of plants from one region to another made the colonists acutely aware of the importance of planting at the proper time and the difficulty of sustaining domestic plants when they are moved from one ecological zone to another. Crop failures were often due to differences in soil. These factors were beyond the control of the ancient farmers. Failures stemming from differences in growing seasons were subject to some control.

When to plant is a universal topic of conversation among all farmers. Modern farmers discuss and debate the most propitious date for planting various crops. "The time to plant" must have been a pervasive topic of conversation among those who established new farming communities. Then as these communities became established, a consensus was established that specified when each of the crops was to be planted.

Procedures for making accurate observations of celestial events were devised. These observations served as the calendar for these communities. The procedures and observations were of concern to all; the welfare of the community was contingent upon an adequate calendar. All agricultural communities that endured beyond a few years developed calendars that specified the dates for the planting of crops. The content of these calendars varied tremendously, but they all had in common the linking of human activity associated with domestic plants to celestial phenomena.

The calendars of the agriculturalists were different from the earlier calendars of food gatherers. Agriculturalists developed calendars that were based on a series of alignments. Most of the alignments were those of the shadows cast by sunlight. The calendars of nomadic groups were largely those of markings and notches to note the passage of lunar cycles. Sequences of celestial events were still noted by sedentary communities, but alignments came to the fore among agricultural groups and the sequences were tied to specific alignments.

OBSERVATORIES

Nomadic groups may have used simple observatories to measure duration. The simplest observatory is a gnomon. Gnomons range in complexity from a stick stuck in the ground to note the length and angle of the sun's shadow, to the pin of a sundial, to the obelisks of Egypt. Gnomons were probably used before sedentary communities were established. The Australian Aborigines used them (Marshack, 1972). However, it was with the development of agriculture that observatories became widespread.

Some horticulture communities probably built fairly complex naked eye observatories. Many of them had "temples." Many of these temples were probably observatories. Jericho may have had one as early as 9000 B.C. They had a "unique structure which has been interpreted as some sort of sanctuary" (Oates and Oates, 1976:73). It consisted of a rectangular platform that was kept scrupulously clean. Similar edifices have been found at other sites that predate agricultural communities.

Nearly all the early large agricultural settlements constructed elaborate observatories. The "megalithic cultures" were widespread. Their remains have been found in Britain, northwestern Europe, through much of the Mediterranean area, in central Asia, India, northern Africa, and the Americas. Astronomical alignments have not been demonstrated for all megaliths, but they have for many. The research of the archeao-astronomers in Britain, western Europe, and the Americas have consistently demonstrated astronomical alignment for megalithic observatories.

The oldest "megalithic cultures" were probably established in western and central Asia. Most of the early agricultural settlements of these regions built ziggurats. The ziggurats of the region "conform with surprising consistency to a standard pattern of layout and decoration" (Oates and Oates, 1976:13). Their similarity suggests that a set of general principles had been formulated and were widely used to design the observatories and monuments.

The original settlements of lower Mesopotamia were but little different from the earlier communities of western Asia. But as agriculture became more widespread in the region, ziggurat construction and the development of an agricultural economy proceeded hand in hand. At least the larger settlements were also part of an intercommunity trade network. Both the early settlements and their observatories were rather modest affairs. Many of the communities had only a population of 100 to 300.

Some of the communities grew enormously. As the communities grew they replaced their earlier and smaller ziggurats with larger ones. The monumental ziggurats had seven steps or terraces. Each level was painted a different color and represented one of the heavenly bodies that moves in its own distinctive cycle. These seven bodies still provide us with the names of the days of the week—Sun for Sunday, Moon for Monday, through Saturn for Saturday. Each ziggurat was topped by an altar that served as a ritualistic observatory.

Despite their similarity in construction and the widespread adoption of the seven-terraced ziggurat, most communities developed their own distinctive calendar. All the Sumerian calendars used the lunar cycle as the basic unit for the measurement of duration—not the sidereal or solar year (Legrain, 1922:7). The placement of the thirteenth moon to keep the celestial and terrestial seasons in synchronization varied from community to community. The cities of Lagas, Umma, Nippur, and Drehem had four different calendars at the beginning of the literate period (Legrain, 1922:7). Nippur occupied a central position in formulation of the timekeeping systems, but the system or systems developed at Nippur were not imposed on other communities.

The calendar of the Sumerians was agricultural; the names of the months were based on the predominant agricultural activity of the season. They were keyed to sidereal events, specifically the heliacal risings of major constellations. At least some of the communities keyed their lunar cycle to the heliacal rising of the Pleiades. While their lunar cycles were keyed to heliacal risings, the Sumerians also celebrated the Summer solstice; they lit fires when the Summer solstice occurred. This practice was followed in widely scattered regions of Europe, north Africa, and Sardinia until relatively recently.

The reliance of the Sumerians on the lunar cycle as the basic unit of duration indicates a continuity of their calendric systems with the earlier calendric systems of ancient nomadic groups. The later civilizations of Mesopotamia continued the practice of using the lunar cycle as a basic unit of duration. The Egyptians of the early dynastic period introduced the solar day and year as the basic units of duration. As farming and megalithic construction became established in other regions of the world, major modifications of calendric systems were made. Other units of duration and observational procedures were developed. The observatories were aligned to a variety of celestial events. Many of the alignments specified the Winter and Summer solstices and the equinoxes, some incorporated alignments specifying the heliacal risings of major stars; other alignments specified the risings and settings of the moon.

Thom (1967 and 1971) and Thom and Thom (1978) have demonstrated many solar and lunar alignments for the megalithic cultures of western Europe. The megaliths served as the calendars for the communities. Again, as in Mesopotamia, there is variation from region to region and over time in how the edifices were constructed and in their alignments. Nonetheless the megaliths of western Europe display a similarity. Apparently there was widespread diffusion of certain principles of construction. Intellectual similarity, if not unity of thought, was widespread in many regions of the world before political unification was achieved.

The same general sequence of development occurred in Mesoamerica. The construction of observatories on the basis of common principles was widespread before political unification was achieved. In the early period of agricultural development and observatory construction "there is neither direct nor indirect evidence for the arrogation and control of force" (Price, 1977:213). Intellectual unity preceded the political unification in several regions in both the Old and New World. At least some members of the various communities of these regions had to have had contact with each other.

Not all of the early megalithic societies were farming communities. However, in general there was a close association between the establishment of agriculture in a region and the appearance of megalithic observatories. They appear first and become most predominant in the richest agricultural land.

Two major exceptions to the close association between farming and megalithic construction are the megaliths on Malta and the Scilly Islands of Britain. Both of these islands had large megalithic centers. Malta is rocky and "could never have supported a large agricultural population in Neolithic times" (MacKie, 1978:150). The Scilly Islands are too small to support the investment indicated by the large number of tombs (Clark, 1977). The residents of these islands during their most active period had to have been supported by others not living on the island. Perhaps they were supported by contributions from a number of agricultural communities, or they may have been supported by maritime commercial interest. They may have been centers for large-scale fishing enterprises.

Another interesting exception is the so-called medicine wheels of the nomadic Indians of North America. These wheels consist of lines of stones that radiate from a central location to points on the horizon denoting the location of the heliacal risings of major stars and the solstices (Eddy, 1979). Some are quite large; a few of the larger ones are in high altitudes in the Rocky Mountains. They may have been stimulated by contact with sedentary communities, but it is possible they were indigenous to nomadic groups.

The construction of observatories that specify the points on the horizon where the sun reaches its solstices and the heliacal risings of stars demonstrates considerable knowledge about the movements of heavenly bodies. The earliest of these observatories were not constructed to acquire "astronomical knowledge"; they were built to serve as calendars for the community. They allowed for more accurate anticipation of forthcoming events. Nonetheless they indicate that these people were aware of some of the major repetitive cycles of heavenly bodies and used them to structure their lives. The complexity and precision of the observatories of some of the ancient agricultural communities indicates that at least some members of these societies devoted a considerable amount of time to the study of celestial events.

TIMEKEEPERS

There is little specialization based on timekeeping in most food gathering societies. If there is specialization, a common arrangement is that certain families or the elders acquire a reputation for their ability to specify the sequence of celestial events and the significant terrestrial events associated with them. The complexity of the notchings, carvings, and drawings that designate lunar sequences of some paleolithic groups suggests they may have had a degree of specialization. The presence of temples (observatories) at some of the early trade centers indicates that calendric phenomena were of concern and that some devoted attention to them. However, it was in the ancient agricultural settlements that timekeeping concerns came to the fore and the specialty of timekeeper emerged.

Among all relatively contemporary primitive agriculturalists there was concern with noting the celestial events that served as their calendar. In some of the simpler agricultural societies there was little specialization based on timekeeping. In one African group all adults were knowledgeable about calendric affairs. Informants stated that some persons specialized in the study of celestial events but these experts were not located (Turton and Ruggles, 1978). This particular group was only partially dependent on agricultural products. Even among some groups that were highly dependent on food production there was only a limited degree of specialization. Among the Hopi there was "wide dissemination of astronomical lore" (McCluskey, 1977:191).

Other somewhat more complex societies had a "Sun Chief" or functional equivalent who was responsible for observing celestial events. Among the Zuni, in the Spring of the year the Sun Chief watched a solar monolith, Thunder Mountain, and the pillar of the gardens of Zuni. When the three shadows cast at sunrise fell in a straight line the Sun Chief announced it was time to begin field work (Cushing, as reported in Ellis, 1975:77).

The Iroquois used a sidereal-lunar calendar to program their activities. When the new year began the two "BigHeads" went from house to house notifying all. They organized the new year's celebration which began with the first full moon after the Pleiades' zenith. Their degree of specialization was limited. They were not relieved of any mundane tasks, but they received gifts of food. They were accorded special treatment immediately prior to and during the celebration.

Among a southwestern Indian group, the Sun Chief had knowledge of calendric affairs that he shared with only a few who were closely associated with him. When he built a new home others helped him. However, the home also served as an observatory. Many simple agricultural societies had one person or a few who were recognized as experts on calendric affairs. They were focal persons, but they were not categorically differentiated from others. They commanded attention and respect on the basis of personal reputation, not on the basis of incumbency in an official position.

These specialists occupied a special position in the organization of and consummation of community celebrations. These celebrations were more than merely communal performances to reaffirm the communal solidarity. They did fulfill that function, but in addition they demarked periods of duration and informed all of forthcoming events. The famous fertility celebration not only asked for a fertile forthcoming year, but informed all that "tomorrow" was when the planting of the corn should proceed. Among a Pueblo group "during the full moon (of the play moon, which roughly corresponds to our month of January) beans and corn were secretly planted in containers and carried into the Chief Kiva which is kept heated to produce early sprouting and growth" (Ellis, 1975:66). The completion of activities of this sort facilitates the continuation of an agricultural community; they are more than mere rituals. The very livelihood of the community rests upon the successful completion of these acts.

These activities and the other activities associated with the timekeeping specialists reflect communal concerns. When members of the community aided the Sun Chief in the construction of a new house that also served as an observatory, they were not merely showing deference to the Sun Chief. They were also expressing and serving a communal interest. When the Sun Chief organized a festival to celebrate the Spring equinox he was not merely supervising a community ritual, but informing all that it was now the time to plant the corn.

Most of the earliest small agricultural groups probably had timekeeping specialists who occupied a position analogous to that observed among recent primitive agriculturalists. However, in many regions of the world, as large agricultural colonies were established, the specialty of timekeeper was established. In the Nile Valley, "At the opening of the historical period, there was not a single temple, from one end of the valley to the other that did not possess its official astronomers, or, as they were called, 'watchers of the night" ' (Maspero, 1897:206). A similar condition appears to have held for the settlers of western Europe, Britain, and Mesoamerica.

The Sumerians may have been an interesting exception. No titles such as "men of the stars" or "watchers of the sun" have come down to us from the Sumerians. The earliest known specialists among the Sumerians were the *sanga*. They were in charge of economic affairs associated with the temples; they did not specialize in timekeeping. Nor do the cuneiform tablets of the early literate period refer to astronomical phenomena. Most express economic concerns, a few deal with political issues, a few are literary, and some are mathematical.

However, the ziggurats occupied a central position within the Sumerian communities. They were both the calendars and the community centers of these settlements. That, plus the widespread dispersal of ziggurats that were constructed in a similar manner indicates that astronomical lore was widespread in the Sumerian civilization. The astronomical lore of the Sumerians was probably retained and transmitted orally. Several complex societies that were illiterate retained their astronomical knowledge orally. The Inca had astronomer-poets who studied the heavens and specified sequences and duration. The Britons at the time of Caesar transmitted their astronomical lore orally. They refused to put it in writing. The navigators and astronomers of the South Sea Islands transmitted their knowledge orally. It is likely that the astronomical knowledge of the Sumerians was restricted to an oral tradition.

The timekeeping specialists of ancient societies are usually referred to as priests. It would be more accurate to refer to them as professors or men of knowledge. It was they who generated and retained the information that allowed for the prediction of forthcoming celestial events and specified the times for planting crops. In many instances when the communities endured for generations they then became priests—persons who were primarily concerned with maintaining and celebrating the established order. However, prior to that, for generations, they searched for and established temporal sequences that structured the lives of their communities.

The speciality of timekeeper emerged in the large and prosperous agricultural communities. It is impossible to state when they first emerged. They probably were well established in some regions of the world before they appeared in western Europe. It is definite that they were established as specialists when large agricultural communities were established in western Europe. It is also impossible to specify the relationship between the timekeepers and the rest of the community. But it is certain that they constituted an elite at least in the agricultural settlements of western Europe and Britain.

The archaeoastronomical work of Thom, Hawkins, Hoyle, and others on the ancient observatories of Britain, and the archaeological work of MacKie, Hadingham, and others provides us with a suggestive image of the timekeepers of Britain when agriculture became predominant. The position of the timekeepers and their relationship with other members of their communities undoubtedly varied from region to region and across time. However, it is apparent that in the large ancient agricultural centers the timekeepers occupied a critical position. They were *the* focal persons in the social structures of these societies.

The earliest intruders of ancient Britain were probably either traders or fishermen. Agricultural settlements were established along the coastlines of Britain by 4000 B.C., perhaps slightly earlier (MacKie, 1978). Two of the distinctive features of these settlements were observatories and burial chambers. Each region was first settled by farmers. The burial chambers followed shortly after, and the megalithic constructions were undertaken later.

The burial chambers of Britain were preceded by those of Portugal where they appeared during the fifth millennium B.C. The spread of the burial chambers complex "shows a remarkably consistent and straightforward maritime distribution throughout the Mediterranean and Atlantic Europe, extending as far as the North Sea and the Baltic" (MacKie, 1978:146). It was once thought these burial chambers served the total community. "Now that two millennia, perhaps more, are known to have been involved, it is simply not possible to believe that the few hundred individuals found in the chambered cairns and long barrows in Britain and Ireland were other than a very select group" (MacKie, 1978:168).

Most members of these societies were not given special treatment at burial. The evidence on the burial practices for other members of these communities is rather meager, but it indicates that most residents were not given special treatment at burial. The graves of the other residents did not have surface markers; the interments were casual.

Several of the burial chambers of the elite of Britain were oriented to key solar alignments. The Newgrange burial chamber, for example, incorporated solar alignment. "Shortly after dawn on a midwinter day (the winter solstice) the sun shines through the roof-box and light penetrates all the way down the passage, a distance of 62 feet, illuminating the central chamber" (Hadingham, 1975:107). This alignment was not constructed to make astronomical observations, but it indicates that those who designed the chamber assigned special significance to the Winter solstice.

The skeletons disinterred from the burial chambers lack "any deep grooves caused by the attachment of particularly strong muscles" (MacKie, 1978:151). These chambers contain the remains of persons who did not do manual labor. In addition, there is a low incidence of marked tooth wear suggesting a diet that was relatively free of gritty particles (MacKie, 1978:151).

The burials of the elite were not completely uniform; the practices vary with region and over time. What is common is the special treatment at death of a small select category of persons. The graves contain some artifacts, but not the wealth associated with the graves of later monarchs. These elite were given special treatment, but artifacts reflecting material wealth were not placed in their graves.

Special burial practices for a segment of the population of these communities is not the only evidence of a special category of persons. Skara Brae is one of the most distinctive sites of ancient Britain. It consists of nine squarish stone huts that were all interconnected by roofed passageways. The set of buildings were constructed on top of at least four more ancient sets of buildings. "The buildings are commodious and well designed by prehistoric and even recent rural standards; the existence of privies with drains is surely unmatched at that time outside of contemporary Minoan Crete" (MacKie, 1978:176).

The residents of Skara Brae were neither farmers nor traders, but a special group supported by surrounding farm communities. In the middens of Skara Brae the bones of sheep and cattle are numerous and hardly any pig or deer bones were found. A high proportion of the cattle bones were of immature beasts (MacKie, 1978:175). Evidence from other sites indicates that the eating habits of the residents of Skara Brae were distinctive from those of their neighboring communities.

Evidence from other centers of southern England and Portugal suggests that other small groups of elite were supported by the surrounding communities. At Durrington Walls there were almost no skulls found among the 8,000 animal bones recovered at the site. Apparently already slaughtered animals were brought to the site. A spindle whorl, which is the only one known of that age in Britain, has also been found at Durrington Walls. Perhaps the residents wore woven clothes while the clothing of others was made of hides.

MacKie develops the theme that these persons constituted a special caste. They were a special class, but it need not be the case they constituted a caste; they may have. The distinction between college professors and other citizens is rather distinctive in modern societies. However, they do not constitute a caste. The ranks are fairly open. Of course, the offspring of professors have a greater opportunity to join the ranks than most others.

The order of development in western Europe and Britain seems to have been first the establishment of small agricultural communities; then as these communities grew they acquired a specialist or two who served as timekeepers. The timekeepers maintained contact with other timekeepers in other communities. Knowledge was shared among the specialists. As the communities grew and contacts between them were elaborated, intercommunity efforts were undertaken to build large monumental centers such as Stonehenge and Avebury. These developments were underway in western Europe during the fourth millennium B.C.; perhaps they reach back into the fifth and sixth millennium.

The observatories of western Europe differ from those of other regions. In fact, each site has its distinctive characteristics. The variation is analogous to that between modern universities. Each university is unique, yet all are organized to search for knowledge, to transmit it to other generations, and the denizens are supported by contributions. The number supported is quite small. These elite do not maintain their position by coercion. They owe their special position to the generally accepted belief that knowledge is beneficial to all.

The presence of a special class in ancient Britain and western Europe does not demonstrate the existence of similar categories of persons in other ancient agricultural civilizations. However, there are many indications that many of the ancient large agricultural settlements had an elite category of people who dedicated their efforts to timekeeping, the study of celestial events, and the programming of communal activities.

The similarity of the megalithic observatories and the burial practices over a rather widespread region suggests that at least the intellectual elite of these settlements had contact with each other. A Maltese temple and two megalithic sites of Brittany display carvings of boats which suggests sea travel was of some significance to the residents. The intercommunity contact between the centers of western Europe and Britain may have been more tenuous than it is between modern centers of knowledge, but it may have been common.

THE BASIS FOR THE EMERGENCE OF SPECIALISTS

The complexity and accuracy of some of these ancient calendars was far greater than necessary for agricultural purposes. A very precise calendar and adherence to it results in somewhat better harvests than a solar-lunar or sidereal-lunar one, but the difference is not great. The elaborate and precise calendars of these societies cannot be explained as the consequence of recognized superiority of planting by a precise calendar as compared to planting by a vague solar-lunar one.

Instead, the development of complex calendric systems, the emergence of timekeepers as specialists, and the transformation of the observatories into monuments was stimulated by the uncertainties inherent to farming and the ambivalent position of the timekeepers within their communities. Even when crops are planted on the optimal date, a good harvest is not assured. In small agricultural communities timekeepers commanded considerable respect, but when crops were less than desired, they were often blamed for the bad crops. There are many documented instances of timekeepers being replaced as the consequence of a poor harvest.

These specialists received deference, but they were also the target of hostility. They had special responsibilities and when the crops failed they were likely to be blamed. When the seeds were planted as specified and a poor crop ensued, the timekeepers were very likely to be saddled with the responsibility for the community's disaster. McCluskey reports of a group that believed if their timekeeper did not make the correct observations and failed to schedule the festivals at the appropriate time they would have poor crops. Of course, they were correct, because the festivals informed them when to plant crops. One year the Snake Chief was blamed for their poor crops. "After some popular criticism of the Snake Chief's observations, the Antelope Chief began to assist him in watching the sun, and, apparently as a result of this the Snake-Antelope festival was postponed" (McCluskey, 1977:191). In this instance the Snake Chief was not immediately replaced, but he must have found the experience irritating, if not humiliating.

Anticipated criticism and communal concerns motivated the timekeepers to be as accurate as possible. However, accuracy would not always relieve the timekeepers from criticism when a crop failure occurred. Two general developments seemed to have resulted in freeing timekeepers from accountability to the community: (a) they constructed a monopoly of knowledge, and (b) they stressed the significance of celestial events and minimized the signifance of terrestrial events.

Monopoly of Knowledge

When astronomical lore is widespread others have a base for criticizing those who claim expertise. Conversely, when some persons have established themselves as experts and the rest are uninformed, the experts are freed from some criticism. Those groups wherein the specialists were most intensely exposed to criticism were those where others had an independent source of information.

This condition prevailed among the Zuni. Many of the Zuni families had portholes in the east side of their homes. These portholes cast a spot of light on their west walls at sunrise of the Fall and Spring equinoxes. The Zuni also had a Sun Chief who had primary responsibility for noting the Spring equinox. The portholes in the homes provided a base for discussions of what moon it was and when the crops should be planted.

Timekeepers with this degree of specialization can be called into account. When crop failures occur, members of the community can exchange information and make assessments of the "Sun Chief's" ability. Those who specialized in timekeeping became aware that those most informed about celestial events were the most powerful critics. An obvious conclusion is that if others are uninformed then they will not have the knowledge for effective criticism.

The timekeepers of some societies constructed walls of secrecy to free themselves from accountability to the community. There are many accounts of specialists deliberately misinforming the rank and file, thus keeping them uninformed. For example, the South Seas navigators knew the solstices and sometimes the equinoxes and the distinction between stars and planets (Lewis, 1974:136). Their secrets were jealously guarded. It was not until after much of their lore had been lost that they "consented to divulge to me, an outsider, the half-forgotten residium of what a nineteenth-century Tuit once claimed. ..., to be secrets that only (he) and the devil know" (Lewis, 1974:137).

It cannot be determined if monopolies of knowledge were established in ancient agricultural centers. Nor is there any documentation of the nature of the relationships between the timekeepers and others. However, within at least some of the ancient civilizations a monopoly of astronomical knowledge was official policy when they appeared on the historical scene. This was the case among the Egyptians, the Chinese, the Maya, and the Incas.

The development of a monopoly of knowledge was probably the consequence of both unintentional and intentional activities. Those who devoted their time to studying the celestial bodies acquired more information than others. They became aware that their expertise was a source of prestige. This in conjunction with the recognition that criticism from others is muted when the others are uninformed would entice the timekeepers to intentionally withhold information. The end result, in at least some cases, was the establishment of a monopoly of knowledge.

Some younger persons attached themselves to the older specialists to learn their lore and to bask in the reflected prestige. As the calendric systems became more complex, more time and effort was required before a command of the knowledge was obtained. Gradually an arrangement emerged wherein those "in the know" selectively accepted candidates for membership into their exclusive club. The accepted candidates were sworn to secrecy.

The wall of secrecy need not be total for an effective monopoly of knowledge to be maintained. Even if the system suffered from some leakage, the specialists were still able to use their esoteric knowledge to maintain their special postition. So long as others did not have sufficient command of astronomical lore to predict celestial events with the accuracy of the timekeepers, there would be general recognition that it was necessary to rely on the timekeepers. Envy and disenchantment could be quite widespread and yet the timekeepers could maintain their special position. Even those disenchanted with the timekeepers would see no viable alternative.

Stress on Celestial Events

Even with the development of a very precise calendar and rigid adherence to it, it was still impossible to assure a bountiful harvest. The timekeepers were the first to understand that terrestrial events are more erratic than celestial events. At the same time their accumulated knowledge allowed them to predict with considerable accuracy celestial events. A partial resolution to this problem, from the timekeepers' point of view, was to emphasize the significance of celestial events and their own ability to predict them.

A public demonstration of the ability to predict the occurrence of the Winter solstice, for example, would validate the timekeeper's special knowledge. Among groups of the northern hemisphere, with only a solar-lunar calendar, the Winter solstice was often a time of anxiety. There was an increased concern as the sun continued southward along the horizon. When the timekeepers specified when the sun would discontinue its southward movement on the horizon and the sun subsequently began moving northward, their position was validated.

In one group the time for "calling back the sun" was deliberately set incorrectly. It preceded the actual solstice by a few days. Anxiety became widespread as the sun continued to move southward. The timekeepers then put on an act that stopped the sun's southward movement and claimed power over the sun. Among the Pueblo "Predictions of the sun's reversal of its apparent movement along the horizons are politically important; when successful, these predictions increase a priest's power because they demonstrate his 'control' of astronomical phenomena" (Reyman, 1980:43).

Such hocus pocus by the timekeepers was a common practice. In many instances the population came to believe that what the timekeepers specified as necessary for the occurrence of future events was necessary. In some instances after the timekeepers had transformed from men of knowledge to priests, the timekeepers themselves came to believe that it was necessary for human beings to perform certain rituals to assure the future would unfold as desired.

At the time of the destruction of the Aztecs, it was believed, or at least widely accepted as public policy, that human sacrifice was necessary to reassure the continuation of solar cycles. There was widespread concern among the general citizenry and perhaps among the Aztec elite that with the end of each fifty-two-year cycle, the world might come to an end. Elaborate rituals and large sacrifices were offered to prevent this catastrophe. The Aztecs also deliberately rewrote their history to legitimate their rulership. Therefore it seems likely that the intellectual elite were aware of the hoax perpetrated on the citizens. Similar arrangements were the mode in other totalitarian civilizations.

SUMMARY

Timekeepers as a special class and the construction of communal observatories first emerged in western Asia as agricultural communities became established. The position of these specialists in the earliest agricultural communities may have been less centralized than it was in some of the later agricultural communities. In at least some of the early agricultural regions the timekeepers and their observatories were the focal point of the communities. The timekeepers were extremely important elements of the social structure of many of the early agricultural communities of western Europe and in the Nile Valley.

Those communities that relied primarily on agriculture developed elaborate calendric systems. Precise and complex temporal structures were devised by these specialists and used to program the activity of their communities. The timekeepers had the knowledge necessary to maintain agricultural communities. They specified and programmed communal festivities and informed all when crops were to be planted. It is impossible to specify the exact nature of the relationship between these specialist and other members of the community. At least some of the ancient agricultural regions supported a small population of intellectual elite. That this relationship continued for generations in some regions without coercion suggests that the rank and file did not strongly resent the special position of the timekeepers.

The timekeepers did not owe their special position to violence. On the basis of ethnographic data it seems likely that the development and maintenance of a monopoly of knowledge served to ensure their special position. The perceived benefits provided by their knowledge rendered the relationship between them and the rank and file relatively stable. Their "authority" rested on knowledge, not on violence. These conditions appear to have been maintained in some locations of western Europe and Britain for many centuries. The same condition may have endured for equal periods in other regions of the world.

The continuation of these centers was dependent on the ability and willingness of the farmers to support them. In some instances the timekeepers appear to have been displaced. A few hundred years after the establishment of the large Olmec centers the monuments were destroyed by the local population (Coe and Diehl, 1980). Perhaps the citizens found their timekeepers too demanding, or perhaps their crops failed a few years in a row and the timekeepers were blamed for the failure. Other agricultural centers were invaded by raiders and the farmers scattered. The smaller settlements were more vulnerable to destruction by raiders than the larger ones.

The basis for the stability and unity of these centers rested upon their complex temporal structures and the extensive communal solidarity that was linked to these observatories and monuments. Temporal structures of these communities were not mere epiphenomena, but one of the, if not *the*, critical dimensions of their social structure. As has been noted "to pass over the chronovision of the Maya would be to deprive this culture of its soul" (Leon-Portilla, 1973:112). A similar characterization is appropriate for the megalithic builders of Europe, the early Egyptians, and those who built the observatories and monuments of many other ancient civilizations.

The timekeepers were the first stable class of persons who were supported by contributions from their communitites. The relationship between them and other members of these societies was similar to the current relationship between professors and researchers on the one hand and the rank and file on the other. The relationship was (is) regarded by both as mutually beneficial, although the rank and file often have their doubts about the benefits they derive from the relationship.

Chapter XII

Monuments and Communal Solidarity

Many of the ancient agricultural communities that endured and prospered transformed their observatories into monuments. In some instances this culminated in the construction of gigantic monuments that continue to elicit awe. The transformation from simple observatories to gigantic monuments in some cases occurred through a series of incremental changes; in other cases incremental changes were interlaced with cataclysmic changes. Whether the transformation occurred through a series of incremental changes or cataclysmically, the result of monument construction was the replacement of a search for information with dramatic ritualistic celebrations.

The gigantic monuments were designed largely to display knowledge and to make an impression; the earlier and smaller observatories were primarily designed to facilitate the acquisition of more precise knowledge about the movements of celestial bodies. When the monuments emerged the timekeepers and other elite of the community became primarily interested in maintaining the established social order and retaining their special position. Concern with the acquisition of knowledge about the movements of celestial bodies receded to the background. Men of knowledge were transformed into priests. Inquiry was replaced by ritual.

The emergence of gigantic monuments through a series of incremental changes tended to occur in those regions where monarchies were not established. In contrast, the emergence of gigantic monuments through a series of incremental changes interlaced with cataclysmic developments occurred in those regions where monarchies became established. However, it is a mistake to conceptualize the cataclysmic developments as a consequence of monarchs imposing their will upon the community. The earliest gigantic monuments were constructed primarily to dramatize celestial events, not to glorify a person or lineage.

The developments in ancient Britain are an example of the appearance of gigantic monuments through a series of incremental changes over an extended period. Alterations and additions were made at Stonehenge for over five centuries (Hawkins, 1973:24). The transformation from observatory to monument appears to have occurred between Stonehenge I and Stonehenge III. Stonehenge III is the monument commonly thought of as Stonehenge. "Stonehenge I is essentially very simple, a set of marked positions and a few naturally occurring boulders—there may even have been wooden posts instead of boulders in the beginning" (Hoyle, 1977:113). Stonehenge I was sufficient for noting celestial cycles, but Stonehenge III gave dramatic display of selected celestial events. "Once simplicity became replaced with complexity, as in Stonehenge III, one can be virtually certain that science had been replaced by ritual" (Hoyle, 1977:113).

Stonehenge is but one of many gigantic monuments constructed by the ancient Britons. Another impressive monument is the great circle of Avebury. It consists of a large circular area about 365 meters in diameter and is surrounded by a ditch 9 meters deep and 24 meters wide. The builders of Avebury lived in scattered hamlets. Few if any of the villages at the time surpassed a population of 5,000. There is no evidence that the residents of the surrounding region were a political unit. The monument required far more energy to construct than could have been provided by a single village or even a few of them. Furthermore the amphitheater of Avebury is large enough to hold 250,000 people. Apparently residents from many villages of the region united their efforts to construct the monument and then participated in the celebrations held there.

Many of the ancient gigantic monuments were constructed by communities with a monarchy. It has often been asserted that these monuments were built at the behest of the monarch. Nowhere is this idea asserted with greater confidence than in accounts of the construction of the giant pyramids of Egypt. However, the evidence supporting this assertion is far from overwhelming. It is, in fact, almost nonexistent. Herodotus, the Greek historian of the fifth century B.C, reported to the Greeks that the pyramids of Egypt were built to glorify monarchs. Many have since reiterated the statement. Herodotus journeyed to Egypt 2,000 years after the construction of the pyramids. There is very little other evidence that the pyramids were built to glorify kings.

A monarchy had been established in Egypt prior to the construction of the giant pyramids. But there is no evidence that any king was ever buried in any of the pyramids constructed during the Fourth Dynasty. There were more pyramids built during the Fourth Dynasty than there were kings to bury in them (Mendelssohn, 1974a). "Leaving out Zorer's Step Pyramid with its unique burial chambers, the nine remaining pyramids contain no more than three authentic sarcophagi" (Mendelssohn, 1974:74a).

Many gigantic monuments were constructed at the behest of monarchs. They range from the Ramos Monument of Egypt, through the famous ziggurat of Babylonia (which is not to be confused with the earlier ziggurats of the Sumerians), to the temple of Palenque that probably contained the remains of a king. These and many other monuments serve as reminders of the search for glory by ancient monarchs. However, it appears that the earliest ancient gigantic monuments constructed by communities with a monarchy were constucted primarily to dramatize celestial events, not to glorify a person.

The widely accepted belief that these monuments reflect the search for glory of monarchs rests upon the fact that later monarchs did order the construction of monuments in their name. Scholars of ancient civilizations have projected that practice back onto earlier periods. The most ancient gigantic monuments were expressions of communal will, not the will of despots. They emerged from communal concerns and interests and expressed the gratitude of the community for the well-being of the community. They dramatized celestial events that provided temporal structures for communal activity and were expressions of robust communal solidarities. They also served as the focal point for the continued expression of communal unity.

In some instances, as in Egypt, this development occurred more or less simultaneously with the emergence of monarchies. In other instances, as in ancient Britain, monuments were constructed by communities joining together on the basis of their common concern with timekeeping and shared sentiment of gratitude for the welfare of the community. When monarchies emerged the political elite encouraged their construction and affiliated themselves with the efforts, but they were not responsible for their construction. After the establishment of totalitarian regimes monuments were constructed primarily at the behest of the political elite and secondarily as expression of communal sentiments and interests.

The two concerns are not mutually exclusive. When later monuments were constructed to glorify the political elite, such as the Ramos monument and the temple of Palenque, they were also celestially aligned. The construction of monuments that glorified both kings and celestial events was preceded by monuments that dramatized only celestial events.

Before gigantic monuments could be constructed a number of prerequisites had to be met. The region had to be capable of supporting a fairly dense and large population. The natural resources—the soil— had to provide crops that were both bountiful and stable. Only the wealthier agricultural settlements constructed gigantic monuments. Second, the population of the region had to have shared sentiments and interests. These shared sentiments and interests were given expression through a shared focal point. The focal point was provided by their timekeepers. Third, some members of the community had to have the technological expertise to design the monuments. The only persons with that level of sophistication were the timekeepers or persons closely affiliated with them. These factors then were combined into an organic whole that was expressed by the construction of monuments.

THEIR COMMUNAL BASE

Most, but possibly not all, of the most ancient gigantic monuments were constructed by communities that derived the bulk of the necessities of life from agriculture. The gigantic monuments of preclassical and classical civilizations were those of large agricultural settlements. Large monuments did not appear until after large agricultural communities were well established. Many of the communities that endured and expanded constructed a series of monuments. Many of the ziggurats of the Sumerians encased smaller observatories and monuments. The Pyramids of the Sun and Moon at Titeohaucan encased several earlier and smaller efforts. The Chakohian Pyramid on the Mississippi River encased several earlier efforts. The construction of the Great Pyramid of Egypt was preceded by several modest monuments.

Only the larger and more prosperous settlements had the resources to construct gigantic monuments. Those communities that continued to experience prosperity often surpassed the efforts of their ancestors. Apparently both intergeneration and intercommunity competition stimulated the construction of bigger and better monuments. Some of the communities seem to have been been bent upon outperforming both their ancestors and their neighbors.

A similar condition prevailed in medieval Europe when there was an increase in the general well-being. Many of the cities of medieval Europe constructed great cathedrals. These cathedrals were not constructed at the behest of either the kings of Europe or the Pope. The kings and the Pope encouraged their construction, but the motive for their construction sprang from the communal interests of the cities. Not all residents of these cities were interested in building a cathedral, but the overwhelming bulk of the population supported their construction. These cities then hired architects to design and supervise the effort. "These architect-engineers fulfilled one of the ambitions of the medieval cities, which was to have a more outstanding building than any in the neighboring city, with a higher vault, a higher spire. Men of those years were out for world records" (Gimpel, 1976:116).

Many of the ancient communities that constructed monuments were also out for world records. Some of them succeeded. A few built edifices that none of their descendants matched. It is almost a certainty that the timekeeping elite of these communities were more interested in the building of gigantic monuments than were the rank and file. However, in all probability most of the residents of a region took pride in both the construction of the monuments and in the dramatic displays provided by the monuments.

ENGINEERING SKILL

There is a profound difference between making extremely accurate observations of celestial events and the organization of human effort to construct a monument composed of precisely fitted parts to dramatically display celestial events. Making observations is a "passive" activity; the construction of monuments to dramatize events required the projection of elabarote and precise plans of action to fit the constructed artifact to celestial events. Then it was necessary to coordinate the activities of large numbers of persons in a way that brought to fruition the projected objective.

The transition from the accumulation of observations to the formulation of engineering principles was an interactive affair. As more precise observations were made, somewhat more complex observatories were constructed, which in turn allowed for more accurate observations. Then plans could be formulated to build a precise monument that was aligned to the celestial events that dramatically displayed the events. The construction of the first monuments necessarily was made possible by a series of incremental changes as the timekeepers acquired greater command of their astronomical knowledge and transformed it into principles of engineering. After monuments had been constructed, when agricultural settlements developed in new regions, knowledge of monument construction could be imported and used to built monuments tuned to the celestial events in the immediate area.

Some have accused those who credit the ancients with command of astronomical knowledge and engineering principles of mysticism. The charge is ill-founded. To understand how complex and precise monuments were constructed it is necessary to ask: What level of sophistication was necessary for their construction and how were the necessary principles originally formulated? That the monuments reflect astronomical knowledge and engineering principles is the very opposite of mystical;

instead it indicates the designers of the monuments had acquired astronomical knowledge and formulated principles of construction.

Not all citizens of these societies had command of the necessary principles. Only those who specialized in observing celestial movement and articulating its regularity had the knowledge necessary to design the monuments. Only a very few citizens of modern societies have the knowledge necessary to design a bridge that spans the Mississippi River or a skyscraper. The same condition prevailed among the ancients.

The engineering skills represented by these artifacts were the culmination of millennia of systematic observation, notation, computation, and reformulation. It was derived from the observation of celestial events and the construction of observatories to make more accurate observations. This knowledge was then combined with communal interest in observing celestial events. The consequence was the construction of monuments that reflected both the interests of the community and knowledge of the intellectual elite of the community.

Many retain their doubts that the ancient monuments were designed to reflect celestial alignments. Celestial alignments have not been demonstrated for all of the ancient monuments. But a wealth of evidence has been accumulating in recent decades that demonstrates that most, probably all, of the most ancient monuments were celestially aligned. Thom and others have demonstrated innumerable celestial alignments for the megaliths of Britain and western Europe. Aveni, Malmstrom, and Ziduma have demonstrated celestial alignment for many American monuments.

The Step Pyramid and all the pyramids constructed during the Fourth Dynasty in Egypt were celestially aligned. The Egyptians continued to align many, if not all, of their major monuments throughout their history. Part of the inscription of the temple of Dendera, which was constructed late in Egypt's history, specifies that the temple was aligned to a major star. These monuments were not only aligned to celestial events but they dramatized them.

The particular events that were dramatized varied from region to region. Many of them, such as Stonehenge, dramatized the solstices. Others such as those constructed between the Tropic of Capricorn and Tropic of Cancer dramatized the zenith passages of the sun. The Temple of the Sun of Titeohuacan displays the zenith passage of the sun. When the sun reaches zenith, one day each year one section that is in the shadow during the morning becomes illuminated as the sun's rays move from south to north. "The whole effect occurred in 66.6 seconds. A phenomenon which makes the Sun Pyramid a perennial clock, still transmitting its silent message" (Tompkins, 1976:252).

The Monte Alban complex, which is constructed atop a mountain surrounded by three agricultural valleys, contains structures that are aligned to both the zenith passage of the sun and the heliacal risings of the stars. Structure "P" is aligned to the zenith passage of the sun. The sun still shines down a tube onto a small altar on May 8 and August 5, the two days when the sun casts no shadow at noon (Aveni, 1980:253). Structure "J" is oriented to a point on the eastern horizon where the heliacal rising of the star Capella occurred when the complex was constructed. The heliacal risings of Capella coincided with the first zenith passage of the sun when Monte Alban was constructed.

Despite the demonstrations by archeaoastronomers of many celestial alignments for the most ancient monuments of a region, many still cling to the idea that these complex undertakings represent the interests of the military elite. For example, Blanton (1978) interprets the Monte Alban complex as reflecting the interest of a military federation. However, there is no evidence of military activity associated with Monte Alban until period III. Its location atop a mountain argues against its being originally established as either a military or trade center. It is much more likely that the site was originally established as a meeting place for viewing dramatic celestial events, in this instance the zenith passage of the sun. Subsequently monuments displaying the event were constructed.

Not all of the ancient monuments reflect precise astronomical knowledge and sound engineering principles. Some indicate crude designing and clumsy craftsmanship. On occasions, as with modern engineers, the ancient engineers attempted efforts beyond their abilities. The residents of ancient Brittany attempted to erect a megalith that weighed in excess of 150 tons. It lies broken into five pieces. It is possible that it was put in place and then fell. It is more likely that the effort was beyond the abilities of ambitious designers. Engineers of later ancient civilizations also had their problems on occasion. The Temple of Palenque, which was constructed relatively late in the history of the Maya, either partially crumbled during the construction of the temple or shortly afterward.

Even the Egyptians who are the most renowned for their precise engineering skills had their difficulties. The sequence of monument construction for the Egyptians has been studied more extensively than any other. These studies indicate that many of the early efforts of the Egyptians were only partially successful, then an epitome was achieved rather quickly, followed by a decline. The sequence in other regions may not have been the same as in Egypt, yet the Egypt sequence is instructive.

Small monuments were constructed in the Nile Valley long before Egypt emerged as a nation. Shortly after unification the Egyptians began constructing gigantic monuments. The first large monumental effort was the construction of a monumental tomb. "A curious feature of (the) tomb is its irregularity and faulty planning and impressive as it is in size, it is difficult to believe that only a few years separated it from the magnificent Step Pyramid" (Emerey, as quoted by Hoffman, 1979:250).

The Step Pyramid ushered in the pyramid age in Egypt. Several Egyptologists, in addition to Emery, have remarked upon its complexity and precision. But the engineering skill behind the Step Pyramid is far less than that implied by some Egyptologists. In the opinion of an engineer, the designer of the Step Pyramid "was not at all sure of what he wanted done. The whole structure, as well as its details, show that he (the designer) was groping his way, never quite sure of what he was doing" (Sandstrom, 1970:46). The engineers of Egypt of the Second Dynasty did not have sufficient command of engineering principles to design and coordinate an effort that resulted in an elegant and precisely constructed monument.

The engineering skill that lay behind the construction of the Step Pyramid was in all probability imported from Mesopotamia. The pyramid has terraces that are similar to the terraces of the ziggurats of Mesopotamia. Perhaps a native of Egypt went to study in Mesopotamia and returned to Egypt and designed and supervised the construction of the Step Pyramid. Many of the engineers of nineteenth-century North America were trained in Europe.

The collapsed pyramid at Meidum was the next major effort after the Step Pyramid. "It was originally planned as a step pyramid, on an even grander scale than Zoser's (the Step Pyramid), but then the plan was changed and the step pyramid was covered with a smooth mantle which transformed the edifice into a true pyramid" (Mendelssohn, 1974b:392). It collapsed. "The disaster evidently occurred when the building was given a novel, and yet untried, shape by adding the mantle in order to transform it into a true pyramid" (Mendelssohn, 1974:294). The designers reached beyond their abilities.

The designs of the immediately following pyramids were modified to avoid another disaster. Subsequently the engineers acquired sufficient confidence to design and construct the three large pyramids of Giza. The Great Pyramid was precisely constructed. Its four corners are almost perfect right angles. The northwest corner is only 13″ off 90°. "There are few modern buildings where the corners have an accuracy of ± 13″: (Sandstrom, 1970;268). The same degree of precision has been detected in many other facets of the Great Pyramid.

The precision and elegance of the monuments of the Fourth Dynasty emerged quite rapidly once the pyramid age began. The engineers of the period were reaching for perfection and came almost as close to it as the engineers of any subsequent civilization. The level of precision and elegance of the Fourth Dynasty was not maintained. The monuments of the following dynasties were cruder. At times, in the following

2,000 years, Egyptian engineers approached once again the precision and elegance of those of the Fourth Dynasty, but they never matched it.

Many other ancient societies also had the ability to construct complex and elegant monuments with great precision. Avebury, the giant monument of Britain, reflects a precision of one part to a thousand. The precision of the alignments of some of the parallel walls of Mayan temples is within the limits of measurement error of modern surveying equipment. These accomplishments were possible only after the men of knowledge had developed engineering principles and the ability to plan and coordinate large communal endeavors. These monuments reflect both sophisticated engineering skills and a robust communal solidarity. Both the engineering skills and the communal solidarity rested upon a foundation of shared concern with accurate timekeeping and the public display of celestial events.

EXPANDING COMMUNAL SOLIDARITY

The celebration of celestial events has a very ancient history. It reaches back to the time when all were nomadic. Many contemporary food gathering groups celebrated various celestial events: some the reappearance of the moon, others the Winter solstice, and others the heliacal risings of a major star. Many celebrate several different celestial events. The residents of the most ancient sedentary communities also celebrated celestial events. However, it was with the growth of agricultural communities that these celebrations became large-scale communal undertakings. Residents of these communities congregated at specific times and in unison celebrated celestial events.

The planting of seeds, cultivation of crops, and their harvesting does not require that large numbers of persons act in unison. Small numbers of farmers may work in unison, but for the most part farming is an individualistic activity as each attends to his fields. The common interest in planting their crops at the proper time enticed nearly all of the residents of agricultural communities to cluster about the observatories to observe the key events. When a key event occurred, all would celebrate. These events served as shared foci that elicited solidary responsiveness. Even today an element of solidary responsiveness is elicited in modern societies when eclipses occur. Lunar calendars that were keyed to either the solstices or to the heliacal rising of a major star allowed for the anticipation of the key event. However, if the group had only a lunar calendar, the key event could only be vaguely anticipated. There was division of opinion on when the key event would occur. Considerable anxiety was often present prior to the occurrence of the key event among societies with lunar calendars.

In contrast, with the development of agricultural communities and observatories that depicted key alignments, the occurrence of key forthcoming celestial events could be anticipated with precision. Prior to the event, and at its occurrence, extensive solidary responsiveness was elicited as persons congregated to observe the event. Modifications were made to the observatories to allow more to observe the event. Later generations constructed the monuments to heighten the drama of the event. In some instances these celebrations became mammoth undertakings. Hundreds of thousands participated. Widespread and intense solidary responsiveness was produced.

The size of the groups responding to celestial events when the first observatories were constructed by agricultural settlements was but slightly, if any, larger than nomadic groups that observed key celestial events. However, as the agricultural settlements expanded, larger numbers of persons congregated to observe the events. A major stimulus for the transformation of the early observatories into monuments came from a widely shared interest in the events. All wished to participate. Both the timekeepers and the rank and file were interested in constructing edifices that allowed all to experience the occasion.

Elaborations of the observatories were undertaken to allow more to take part and to dramatize the events. The dramatization facilitated the production of celebrations that were enjoyed by all. Even more intense and extensive solidary responsiveness was elicited. In the large settlements large monuments were constructed that produced high drama. The exact drama, the specific events celebrated, and the number participating varied from region to region and across time. But common to all of them was the production of high drama and intense solidary responsiveness linked to celestial events.

The nature of the experiences of those who celebrated these occurrences cannot be recaptured. But accounts of celebrations held in conjunction with celestial monuments in recent times are suggestive. While studying the navigational procedures of the South Sea islanders, Lewis learned of a location where the sunrise at the Summer solstice was observed. The site was a rather simple one. He went to observe the event. No effort was made to recreate the prehistoric observance. A number of the natives congregated at the site. He notes he "was unprepared for the evocative impact of the moment when the sun burst upon the sea horizon, bathing the lintel stone in blinding light, and the low chanting of the people massed below in darkness swelled to a thunderous crescendo" (Lewis, 1974:137).

Elaborate communal celebrations were held in conjunction with the ziggurats of the Sumerians. The most elaborate celebration was the beginning of the new year which lasted several days. The new year's festival was celebrated to announce the beginning of a new cycle of vitality. It was celebrated with great emotional intensity (Frankfort, 1951). Phases of the moon were also celebrated. Nearly all participated.

The Mayan pyramid of Chichen Itza was constructed to dramatize the Spring and Fall equinoxes. Large celebrations were held to note these events. As the sun sets, shadows are cast on the corners of the pyramid in the form of triangles that undulate like a moving snake. The "snake" appears to descend from the top of the pyramid into the earth. The impact on ancient participants cannot be recovered. However, the report of a modern eyewitness to the event is suggestive. Both tourists and local Maya descendants were present. "When the snake was 'in motion' down the balustrade, an hour before sunset, I thought the people would go into a paroxysm of excitement. Or let's put it this way, I thought I would! Even the cool-headed scientist, who had come all the way from Mexico City to explain the event over the P.A. system set up especially for the occasion began to shout into the mike" (Weeks, 1979:23).

The Great Pyramid of Egypt was designed to dramatize the sunrise at the equinoxes. It is now a rather drab edifice, despite its impressive size. Originally it had a casing of highly polished stone that reflected light. The north and south sides are slightly indented. "The indentation is so slight as to be imperceptible in normal light, but for a brief moment twice a year, at sunrise on the days of the spring and autumn equinoxes, the western halves of the north and south faces are sunlit while the east halves are in shadow" (Ivimy, 1974:91). In addition, there was a pyramidion, or capstone, that was probably made of polished granite and precious metals that caught the first rays of the sun just before the sun would appear on the eastern horizon (Tompkins, 1971:203).

It does not take much imagination to conceive of the celebrations held at the Great Pyramid producing high drama. Intense solidary responsiveness was elicited as the sun made its appearance on the eastern horizon and first illuminated the polished capstone followed by the shadows playing across the north and south sides of the pyramid. Similar celebrations were held in conjunction with other gigantic monuments of ancient civilizations.

Participation in these celebrations elicited profound solidary responsiveness. In addition, the celebrations provided a base for subsequent solidary responsiveness. After the celebrations the participants could introduce the celebration as a topic of conversation and solidary responsiveness would once again be expressed. A modern example of this phenomenon is two strangers at a cocktail party discovering that earlier in the day they attended the same exciting football game. Encounters like this provide persons with opportunities to establish or reaffirm their solidary relationship.

The large celebrations encompassing tens and hundreds of thousands were necessarily preceded by smaller efforts. The growth of these monumental centers entailed a complex set of intertwined processes. First there was communal concern with timekeeping and the construction of observatories to allow for precise observations. This was followed by the construction of larger and more elaborate edifices that allowed more to participate. The construction of these monuments was undertaken by communities wherein there was widespread interest in increasing the drama associated with key celestial events. The original stress on increasing the drama did not originate from an elite imposing their will upon the rank and file. Rather, it stemmed from a communal interest and was supported by most.

The construction of these monuments required large expenditures of energy. But it is a mistake to conceptualize the efforts as work. The efforts had no greater similarity to "work" than the activities of the residents of Pasadena, California when they first organized themselves to produce the Rose Bowl. The affair was work for some, but the overarching ethos was that of preparing for a celebration.

These monuments were constructed by the residents of the region volunteering their services. Those who did not volunteer were pressured to do so. Later with the emergence of centralized coercion each region was obliged to provide a contingent of workers for given lengths of time to work on the monuments. The timekeepers and their associates coordinated and supervised the effort. The construction of the monuments rested upon a pre-established communal solidarity, but in turn, the successful efforts reaffirmed and enhanced existing solidarities. As the members of the teams acted in unison to construct the monuments, they produced innumerable units of solidary action to achieve a variety of social objectives. All of the effort was encased by the grand objective of building a bigger and better monument that was a source of pride for all. The residents of regions collectively acknowledged their achievements and all thereby became further embedded with each other.

Not every effort to build a monument had the consequence of expanding communal solidarity. There were probably many efforts to produce a large monument that ended in failure. A number of factors could prevent the successful completion of a monument. The coordinators might be incompetent, those providing the energy might find the directives abrasive and quit, or, what at first appeared to be a good idea might lose its attractiveness as work proceeded. However, the successful efforts reaffirmed and expanded communal solidarity.

Once the monument was constructed, complex units of solidary action would be produced as preparations were made for the celebrations. In Egypt the celebrations were preceded by excited anticipation long after the unification of the Nile. The planning for the yearly celebrations set off widespread hustle and bustle. The ceremonial centers became alive with anticipation for days preceding the event (Frankfort, 1948:79). Then the production of the rituals associated with each event produced complexly intertwined units of solidary responsiveness and action: choirs performed, dances were held, thanks were given. These activities were pervaded with different levels of solidarity. When a choir performs they are producing solidary action, but in addition while performing, and subsequent to their performance, they can be solidarily responsive to their own action when they express mutual satisfaction with their effort. The solidarity associated with the monuments was multitiered.

The intensity of the solidarity varied by region and time. In general, the level of solidarity produced in the rituals linked to newly constructed monuments was more intense than that produced in conjunction with old monuments. The level of involvement by the various participants also varied. Some were deeply involved, others curious newcomers, some indifferent, and some jaded. The populations supporting a given monument were not completely homogeneous. Some were old, others young, some from the immediate vicinity, and others from more distant communities. These and other factors assured that the unity of emotion, action, and thought was not total. Some of the more informed and doubting Thomases might question the importance of the celebrations. But, the presence of a few skeptics would have little impact so long as the celebrations remained joyous occasions for most.

The general impact of the celebrations held in conjunction with a given monument was production of uniformity of emotion, action, thought, and mutual embeddedness. During the celebrations diversity was pushed to the background and uniformity was enhanced. A foundation was provided for the creation of large social units. The residents of the ancient agricultural settlements that constructed large monuments became part of an intensive and extensive solidary relationship that encased large numbers. Residents of these regions developed a collective identity that differentiated themselves from all others. Their relationship to outsiders was similar to that of members of the Catholic Church to non-Catholics, but of much greater intensity.

The communal solidarity focused on monuments provided the infrastructure for nationalism. Members of these communities thought of themselves as constituting a distinct entity and stressed the differences between themselves and outsiders. The settlements that had gigantic monuments were composed of residents with an intense collective consciousness. The monumental centers, and the celebrations associated with them, promoted homogeneity among the participants and stressed the differentiation between the participants and the nonparticipants.

In contrast, those communities that served primarily as trade centers fostered diversity. The homogeneity of the ceremonial centers and the diversity of the trade centers were not entirely mutually exclusive. In many regions the homogeneity associated with the monuments was complexly intertwined with the diversity associated with the marketplace. But in those communities that were primarily food producing, social structures that rested primarily on a solidary relationship came to the fore.

INTERNAL DIFFERENTIATION

As the monuments and the celebrations associated with them became larger and incorporated larger numbers, there were paradoxical consequences. On the one hand, the communal solidarity was extended and intensified; on the other hand, internal differentiation increased. The production of small celebrations requires only a minimal degree of internal differentiation between the programmer of the celebrations and the rank and file. However, as the number of persons who participated increased and the celebrations became more elaborate, the differentiation between the programmers and the rank and file became greater.

The continued celebration of celestial events by large numbers required that some persons direct the behavior of others. An element of authoritarianism became part of the celebrations. The celebrations became more ritualistic. Celebrations publicly extol and honor events. The behavior of the participants is voluntarily produced. The primary focus is the event itself. Rituals emerge from celebrations, but the behavior of participants in rituals is organized in part on the basis of directives. Celebrations and rituals are not completely mutually exclusive. However, when coordinated action is produced on the basis of directives emanating from a focal person, solidary responsiveness among the participants tends to lessen. The focus of attention shifts from the event and from each other to the source of the directives. When celebrations become extremely ritualistic, there is little solidary responsiveness as each focuses his attention primarily on the director of the ritual. Celebrations are transformed into empty rituals when attention has been entirely shifted from the original honored event to the director of the ritual. Then apathy pervades the congregation.

Several of the ancient monumental centers fell into disuse; they appear to have been deserted. It is likely this was the consequence of widespread apathy among the rank and file following the transformation of celebrations into empty rituals. As differentiation between the programmers and the rank and file increased, the programmers stressed the necessity of performing the rituals in a specific manner to assure both the successful completion of the celebration and to validate their special position within the community. Reciprocally the rank and file came to resent the directives and withdrew from participation. The result in some instances appears to have been desertion of the monumental center.

In some instances the monuments, temples, and the celebrations became shrouded with secrecy. The elite associated with the monuments attempted to elicit awe from the rank and file. This was a late development. It was extensively practiced in later Egypt. The early Egyptian monuments were public places; they were not hidden at all; they were built in the open (Ward, 1965:12). Even in the later dynasties "all big city temples had an open, colonnaded court, called at Edfu 'The Chamber of Multitude', designed to accommodate mass-worshippers at the big ceremonies" (Johnson, 1978:126). However, the later temples also had secret places—the holiest of the holy—where only the initiated elite were allowed to enter. Other monumental centers probably experienced similar transformations.

THEOCRATIC?

The social structure associated with ancient monuments is commonly referred to as theocratic. That characterization is misleading. It hides the fundamental base of the social structures of those societies. It implies that religious sentiments provided the foundation for the construction of the monuments. Their origin has quite a different source, namely, a concern with accurate timekeeping.

Religious sentiments did not entice human beings to become concerned with accurate timekeeping. The concern with accurate timekeeping rested upon pragmatic concerns with adequate harvests. Observatories and monuments were constructed to facilitate timekeeping. In some cases specialists emerged; in turn some of these specialists elaborated the timekeeping concerns of the communities. Some of the successful communities transformed their observatories into monuments so that all had the opportunity to take part in joyful celebrations. The monuments were a means for all to collectively participate in the celebration of the passage of significant events and to prepare themselves for the future.

Theocracy emerged with the elaboration of differences between the elite timekeepers and the rank and file. The internal differentiation rested upon a foundation of robust communal solidarity. The communal solidarity combined with communal thankfulness toward the men of knowledge and allowed the men of knowledge to become priests. The timekeeper-priests assumed and were given responsibility for maintaining order. The elite stressed the importance of the ritual for the continued welfare of the community and their own importance. Then, in some instances, a theocracy was established.

These communities did not first worship heavenly bodies and obey the dictates of the priests. Rather they were concerned originally with the more precise specification of temporal sequences. Then priesthoods and ideologies emerged. The religious sentiments associated with these monuments were the consequences of communal solidarity and gratitude, not the cause of them. The timekeeper-priests were in the forefront in the development of ideologies that justified the rituals and special treatment of the priests, but these ideologies could not have been established without a prior foundation of communal solidarity that centered on the timekeeping mechanisms of the community—the monuments. The ideologies followed from communal concerns and activity; they came after the communal celebrations, they could not have preceded them.

In at least some regions the belief developed that the rituals were essential for the continued well-being of the community. In many of the communities of the northern hemisphere elaborate rituals were held prior to and during the Winter solstice to stop the southward movement of the sun. The rituals, of course, worked. The sun subsequently began moving northward on the horizon. All, or at least the articulate majority, probably felt it was necessary to hold properly conducted rituals to assure the northward movement of the sun. That and similar beliefs were sometimes elaborated by the priests. Rituals were specified as necessary to assure order and avoid chaos. At least some of the priests probably thought that properly conducted rituals were necessary to avoid celestial catastrophes, but some of them must have been cynics. Certainly many of the priests of later totalitarian regimes were cynical manipulators of the masses.

The original use of the monuments was to communicate—to share information and standpoint. They served to provide all with the same information. However, in at least some cases, perhaps nearly all, the monuments, the priests, and the rituals became shrouded in mysticism. The elite encouraged the belief that an understanding of the events linked to the monuments were beyond the ken of the rank and file. Mysticism became a quality associated with the monuments, but it does not account for their emergence.

Some contemporary scholars of ancient monuments have been duped by the mysticism of the ancient priests. They presume that some incomprehensible factors led to the construction of the monuments. They claim that an understanding of the monuments is beyond the ken of modern scholars. In contrast, some scholars, such as Thom, advocate that the monuments were intentionally constructed for specific purposes. These scholars deny the mysticism imputed to the monuments by both the ancient priests and their contemporary counterparts.

CIVILITY

Respect, concern, and empathy for others is tentative in most human associations. Indifference, exploitation, and cruelty appear in the best of human conditions. Members of primitive groups, ancient civilizations and modern ones have time and again demonstrated their lack of civility for fellow citizens. Violent and vicious conflict between members of solidary groups has been common in all societies.

Viciousness and indifference toward outsiders has been even more common. Some groups with intensive internal solidarity combine tenderness and empathy toward fellow citizens with extreme cruelty toward outsiders. The pathos of the Greeks of Homer upon the death of one of their friends was combined with taken-for-granted viciousness toward outsiders. The Iroquois were known for their sympathy for each other and their extreme cruelty toward outsiders. One famous and respected Iroquois killed eighty persons from enemy tribes, many of whom he blessed with a slow death by fire.

The violence of more complex societies toward outsiders is well documented. The Spartans exploited, tortured, and killed the Helots for centuries, and western Europeans eradicated the Tasmanians. The Romans, Aztecs, and Incas had systematic and sustained programs of inhumanity. Many of the ancient monarchical civilizations with monumental centers preyed upon surrounding groups. However, there is little evidence that the activity focused on the monuments was conducive to violence and viciousness to outsiders. Quite the opposite was the case. The celebrants of monumental events were more frequently the victims of violence than perpetrators of it. They were willing to allow others to go in peace.

Conquest and subjugation were often associated with monumental centers. Instances range from the Egyptians of the Ramos period, through the Chinese, to the Aztecs. However, this development was associated with the emergence of a totalitarian state. In these states extreme cruelty toward and exploitation of outsiders for the benefit of the elite occurred, but there is little evidence of systematic conquest and exploitation of outsiders during the formative periods of monumental centers.

The early monumental centers extended civility. Solidary relationships were expanded and temporal structures were extended. The expansion of solidary relationships increased the number of others regarded as human beings worthy of respect; the extension of temporal structures brought impulsive responses under greater control. Self-control rests primarily on a recognition of the worth of others and a subordination of immediate behavior to future consequences. These dimensions of human conduct were enhanced by expansion of solidary relationships and extension of temporal structures.

SUMMARY

The most ancient monumental centers were expressions of communal concerns with timekeeping. They emerged from observatories. They reflected the knowledge accumulated by generations of timekeepers and dramatized selected celestial events. They thereby provided the foundation for the expansion and extension of communal solidarity.

One of the distinctive features of some celestial events is that they can be dramatized and thereby provide a shared focus for large numbers of persons. The creation of conditions that allow for large numbers of persons to establish a shared focus provides one of the necessary elements for the establishment of solidarity among large numbers. These ancient monuments provided a means for extending solidarity beyond the immediate family and village. They served as the focal point for celebrations attended by large numbers of persons.

Before large monuments could be constructed, several conditions had to be met: (a) there had to be some persons with command of complex engineering skills, (b) a sufficient population base had to be present to supply the necessary work force, and (c) there had to be widespread concern with accurate timekeeping and the dramatization of events. These conditions did not assure the construction of communal monuments, but they were necessary if a community was to be successful in organizing itself to construct a monument.

It is impossible to determine with any degree of finality the activity produced in conjunction with the most ancient monumental centers. However historic and ethnographic accounts indicate that they were the centers of communal celebrations. These celebrations provided a foundation for the emergence of a new form of human sociation—the coordination of behavior of large numbers of persons that rested upon solidary relationships that encompassed thousands of persons.

Participation in the activity centered on the monuments expanded human embeddedness and extended their temporal structures. Yet simultaneously within the community greater differentiation between the intellectual elite and the rank and file emerged. To a degree the internal differentiation was counteracted by all—both the timekeepers and rank and file—reaffirming their solidary relationship as they took part in the celebration.

In many, if not most cases, attitudes of communal thankfulness and awe toward the timekeepers were generated. These sentiments provided the foundation for the emergence of theocratic social structures. Elements of theocracy developed prior to the emergence of monarchical states. It was with the emergence of monarchies that theocracy became a major tool for exploitation of the rank and file.

Chapter XIII

Quantification and Formalizing Space

Two of the most profound inventions of the ancients were numeric and geometric symbols. Both were the culmination of a series of incremental changes and were millennia in development. Universal numeric systems emerged in conjunction with trade; the formalization of space was affiliated with construction of observatories and monuments by agricultural communities. Both inventions "objectified" experiences. Quantification and formalization of space were creations that established "objects" that represented other objects and events.

Writing, the rendition of discourse into inscriptions, is commonly regarded as one of the distinctive features of civilizations. But towns and cities of considerable size predate literacy. It is certain that numeric symbols were widespread long before a system of writing was established; and it is very probable that geometric symbols preceded writing. Numeric symbols appeared simultaneously with or prior to the emergence of trade centers. Geometric symbols were developed by communities that constructed observatories and monuments. Numeric symbols rested on an infractructure of trade; geometric symbols on an infrastructure of agriculture. The subsequent merging of arithmetic and geometric thought was accomplished by men of knowledge who were supported by the community.

The elaboration and refinement of numbers and geometric forms did not proceed at a uniform pace. Complex number systems were developed and used for millennia before geometric symbols were invented. Geometric symbols were probably developed independently of numeric systems; it is very unlikely that geometric symbols were first developed by persons who were sophisticates in numeric procedures. They were probably developed by persons who organized the construction of ancient observatories and monuments. In a few instances, perhaps only once, mathematical systems that combined numeric symbols with geometric symbols were devised. The combining of the two symbol systems was probably the achievement of specialists in timekeeping who were citizens of regions that had been recently colonized. The reformulation of timekeeping procedures and designing of new observatories and monuments probably stimulated the men of knowledge to develop both a numeric calendar and computational systems that combined numbers and geometric forms.

These developments, especially the invention of geometric forms and the subsequent merger of numeric and geometric systems, seem to have happened rather rapidly. A series of incremental changes appear to have been followed by a series of rapid changes or surges as the implications of the systems were recognized by the men of knowledge of the more successful colonies. A series of dramatic transformations occurred during the first few dynasties of the Old Kingdom of Egypt.

The development of numbers and geometric forms required the prior establishment of complex social relations; they, in turn, allowed for the construction of even more complex social structures. These symbols allowed human beings to store and be reflective about complex bodies of information. These bodies of knowledge then were transmitted to subsequent generations, and in a few instances diffused to other societies.

QUANTIFICATION

Numbers are such an integral dimension of modern thought that we take them for granted. They are so taken for granted that some consider numbers to have an existence independent of human behavior and thought. However, like all symbols, they are human creations that facilitate the classification of experience, the sharing of experience, and the formulation of programs of social action. Quantification facilitates the social programming that is the foundation for such diverse activity as managing a city, organizing a modern factory, international airline traffic, and scientific research.

Not all societies have a universal numeric system. For example, two days might be referred to as "a couple" and two animals referred to as "a pair." The Thimshian language had seven different sets of "number" words. They used one set for flat objects and animals, another for round objects and time, another for counting men, another for counting long objects and trees, another for canoes, and another for measures; they had one set of symbols for counting in general (Dantzig, 1938:6). The last system was probably developed after the others.

There are still traces of this method of "counting" in the English language. We speak of a married couple, a span of horses, a pair of aces, and a brace of pheasants. We readily acknowledge that all share the characteristic of "twoness." However, in some languages where there is more than one procedure for noting pluralities there is no recognition that the symbols used to denote a given plurality have anything in common with other symbols used to denote the plurality of another set of objects.

When a member of an African tribe was asked to count he replied with, "Count what?" Different procedures were used for counting different objects. Counting cows was different from counting cowries (Goody, 1977:13). They applied the same numerical system to different sets of objects. But the same counting procedure was not used for all objects and events. "Two" as a symbol that is applied to all pluralities of objects and events is an abstraction that not all human groups achieved.

Some primitive groups have command of a universal set of symbols for quantification that is of limited complexity. Some can count to five, others to ten, and still others to twenty. These units reflect the digits of the human body. The variation of the base of different numeric systems suggests that complex systems were independently developed on more than one occasion, or that stimulus-diffusion enticed several different groups to develop their own system.

The numeric system of some nonliterate groups was fairly elaborate. However, numeric systems that can specify indefinite quantities in a precise manner appear to have emerged in conjunction with trade. We may never know where and how universal numbers were first invented. But the oldest known were developed by traders. Both the ancient numeric systems of the Old World and of the New World were closely affiliated with trading.

A universal numeric system was established in western Asia by the ninth millennium B.C. (Schmandt-Besserat, 1977). By then a numeric system was used on a series of tokens that designated quantities of items of trade. The early tokens have markings that specified both the type of produce and its amount. In the earliest system a small cone stood for one and a sphere or disc for ten; later a system based on 1, 6, 60, 600, 3,600 and 36,000 was developed. The tokens consisted of markings on pieces of clay.

The earliest tokens were very crude and bore only impressed signs. They were found in a large secular building. "Hearths and evidence of food consumption indicate it was a household, but at the same time numerous jar sealings, bullae and tablets show that some of the rooms were used for business" (Schmandt-Besserat, 1979:23). Simpler and cruder methods for designating quantities necessarily preceded these tokens.

The system or systems of numeration that preceded the use of clay tokens may never be determined. Examples from primitive groups with systems of numeration suggest that prior methods of counting may have used marks on pieces of wood or pebbles. Numeric systems emerged as human beings learned to organize their activity toward large quantities of objects. The development of a universalistic system, one that applied the same symbols to the same quantities irrespective of the nature of the objects, required that large quantities of different kinds of objects were a common focus of concern.

Large quantities of goods can be exchanged through face-to-face bartering without a complex numeric system. The system of counting suggested by these tokens indicates that trade had achieved a high level of complexity. If trade were limited to a few exotic items or to a single product a universal numeric system would not have developed.

A uniform token system achieved widespread use in western Asia and northeastern Africa. The tokens consisted of a series of pictographs that designated a variety of products and the tokens used the same notation system for quantity. The same marking designated sixty whether the items were sheep or wheat. This indicates that an abstract numeric system was established.

A *bulla* system was subsequently developed by these traders. *Bullae* were small clay containers that enclosed a number of small objects that served as counters; on the exterior of the *bullae* were a number of markings equal to the number of sealed-in counters. Evidently these *bullae* were used by traders as bills of lading. Presumably, when a person was in charge of products to be delivered to a trader, he was given a *bulla* that contained a number of counters equal to the number of products, and an equal number of markings were incised on the exterior of the *bullae*. This assured delivery.

The system of counting implied by the *bullae* also indicates that fairly complex trade networks were established. Evidently persons other than the original owners of the goods were assigned the responsibility for delivering the goods to another party. This system appears to have been well developed before farming had achieved a level of productivity that necessitated an elaborate numeric system. Later, after large agricultural communities were established, the same system of notation was employed to keep accounts. But the first complex numeric system appears to have been an achievement of traders.

Sequential Order and Quantification

Elaborate systems of sequential order were developed long before numeric systems emerged. The most primitive calendars consist of a series of interlocking names specifying sequential order. Primitive solar-lunar and sidereal-lunar calendars consisted of a series of names for the moons of the year. The order is similar to our ordering of the months of the year—January, February ... December. This order is supplemented by a series of names for the phases of the moon. In some cases the days of the moon are ordered by a sequence of twenty-eight or twenty-nine names.

This system of thought is not based upon numbers. Those using the system can specify the sequential order of the moons and are aware that the moon of "Tall Corn" is followed by the moon of "Harvesting." However, if those familiar with this system, but without a numeric system are asked, "How many moons in a year?" they are unable to answer. They can specify the order of anticipated events, but cannot quantify the events.

Several complex systems for sequentially ordering events were developed. But they did not quantify the events. Systems of quantification were developed to facilitate the management of objects—not events. After systems of quantification of objects were developed then numeric systems were used to specify the quantity of events and their order. Time thereby acquired another dimension. A sequence of events—a moon— could be specified by noting the number of a set of events of less duration—the days—contained by the larger unit.

There are profound differences between systems of sequential order and numeric systems. One is that at the completion of a sequential order, one begins at the beginning again. Saturday is followed by Sunday. Numeric systems do not consist of cyclical sequences but continue on indefinitely. Every number can be followed by a larger one.

Symbolic sequences—Monday, Tuesday, and so on—provide order, but symbolic sequences are less abstract than numbers. The phrase in "ten days" is a more abstract expression than "when the harvest moon appears," although the latter may refer to a duration of greater length than the former.

Numeric systems make it possible to specify precisely large quantities of both objects and events. They constituted a new means of structuring experiences, sharing information, planning the future, and coordinating action. While numbers were first used in association with trade, they subsequently were used to order a wide range of human activity.

EARLY NUMERIC CALENDARS

The first numeric calendar was probably invented by the Egyptians. During the first dynasties of the Old Kingdom they developed a calendar that specified whenever the heliacal rising of Sothis (Sirius) took place on or before the eleventh day of the month of *wep repet*, an intercalary or extra month was added. The next year then, had thirteen months (Parker, 1971:19). This practice indicates the presence of a complex numeric system and rather precise use of it for at least several decades when making notations of the stars and moon.

The content of this calendar indicates that it was preceded by a vague sidereal-lunar calendar. It seems that as agriculture came to the fore in the Nile Valley timekeepers from different communities compared notes and formulated a more precise calendar. This calendar, however, did not yet specify the length of the year by the number of days. That development occurred shortly after.

The civil calendar of 365 days was introduced between 2937 and 2831 B.C., "with the probability that it was in the direction of the former rather than the latter date" (Parker, 1950:53). The presence of the 365-day year has been interpreted by some as evidence that the Egyptian scholars were not capable of accurately determining the length of the year. This position is difficult to maintain in light of the highly precise engineering feats of the same period. Further, there is incontestable data indicating that the early Chinese and Maya had detected rather precisely the length of the year, and the Egyptians were at least as concerned with the precise notation of celestial events as the Maya and Chinese.

The development of the numeric calendar by the Egyptians was predicated on a numeric system that had been developed in western Asia. The first five digits of the Egyptian language are Hamitic; subsequent digits are Semitic. This suggests that the earliest calendar of the Nile Valley was a sidereal-lunar one that did not use numbers. Then subsequently, with the colonization of the valley by farmers and the emerging of a communal concern with agriculture, a numeric calendar was formulated.

A similar sequence of development occurred in Mesoamerica. Here too, a numeric system was developed by traders to quantify time. The Maya had developed business counting before they created a numeric calendar; one of their terms was *bak*, which stood for 400 things. It was older than the *tun* of 360 days and the *haab* of rain counts of 364 and 365 (Spinden, 1957).

These data indicate that numeric systems were first developed in conjunction with trade, then employed to achieve precision in noting the passage of celestial events. This level of precision may have been achieved in communities that were primarily trade centers where extensive horticulture prevailed. However, it seems more likely it was achieved in association with the development of agriculture.

Not all agricultural groups developed numeric calendars. In fact, numeric calendars that specified the length of the year by the number of days may have only been developed a few times, perhaps only once. All other numeric calendars may be the consequence of stimulus-diffusion. It is possible that once agricultural concerns came to the fore, and if some members of the society had command of a complex numeric system, then a calendar that specified the length of the year by the number of days may have been independently developed.

We take for granted the precise specification of the future locations of the moon, sun, stars and planets. However, those societies with a solar-lunar or sidereal-lunar system do not take the specification of future locations of heavenly bodies for granted. In many societies the movements of the heavenly bodies are regarded as somewhat erratic. Even when there is the belief that a specification of the length of the year by days is possible, and one has the knowledge of how to make the necessary observations, the determination of the length of celestial cycles is not an easy task.

The experience of a southwestern American Indian who studied the calendric system of another society and returned home to make observations illustrates this point. He attempted to predict the day of the Winter solstice. The first year he watched the sun closely, but his calculations for the Winter solstice were early by thirteen days. The next year he was again early, missing the solstice by twenty days. The third year his calculations were two days late. After eight years of study he was able to predict the turning of the sun exactly (Benedict as quoted in Reyman, 1980:1).

The timekeepers who developed the first numeric calendar were unaware that there are a constant number of days in each year. They did not have a belief in uniformity of motion of heavenly bodies. Nor were those who developed the first precise calendars aware that their numeric system would facilitate the specification of future celestial events. McClusky (1979) notes the Hopi seldom use a number greater than sixteen to specify calendric order, although they are capable of using large numbers.

Before the length of the year can be specified accurately by the number of days, it is necessary that the timekeepers have command of a complex numeric system and make controlled observations from a set location. Even when these two conditions are met, a numeric calendar may not be developed. The Hopi were concerned with making accurate observations of the sun. Specific locations were designated as observational sites. "Observations were made of sunset from the rooftop to the matriarchal house of the Bear Clan, a house located near the center of the main house of the Walpi" (McCluskey, 1977:197). Despite their concern with accurate observations, they did not specify the length of the year by the number of days.

The quantification of time could only occur after complex numeric systems had been developed, sedentary communities established, the establishment of a communal concern with when to plant crops, and the establishment of a group of persons who specialized in making observations of celestial events. Not all ancient societies who met these criteria developed numeric calendars. Precise and complex calendars appear to have been developed in those agricultural societies that colonized new regions. When a group moved into a new region, as when agriculturalists colonized the Nile, there was communal recognition that their old calendric system was not adequate. This recognition provided the opportunity for the development of a more precise calendric system. The creation of a new and more precise system was not constrained by tradition.

It may appear strange that not all agricultural groups developed precise calendars. Those societies that organize their agricultural activity on the basis of a solar-lunar or a sidereal-lunar calendar did not plant their crops at the same time of the year from the point of view of the modern method of time reckoning. From their standpoint, of course, they did plant at the same time of the year.

There are many factors that operate to maintain an established system. Prior to the formation of the first numeric calendars, there would be no awareness that a more accurate system was possible. Even if, through contact with other societies, there is an awareness of a precise numeric system, it does not automatically lead to the adoption of a more precise calendar. Whether one plants on the first of May or the second full moon after the Spring equinox usually does not make much difference in the crop yield. It requires careful observation of the crop yield over an extended period before it can be established that a numeric calendar is superior to a solar-lunar one. Over the long run, and it has to be quite a long run, the amount of corn harvested is greater when crops are planted on the basis of a numeric calendar. But there are many other factors that have an impact upon crop yields. Careful observations of the time the corn was planted and the amount of corn harvested have to be made for an extended number of years before a difference can be detected. Most groups with a solar-lunar or sidereal-lunar calendar had neither the ability nor the patience to make the necessary observations. The difference is so slight that some still give credence to the dictum that potatoes planted on Good Friday will produce the best yield.

Most primitive agricultural societies had a complex set of rituals linked to their lunar calendars. Many of these rituals involved communitywide participation and the content of the calendars was in verse. For example, among the Hopi, a chant consisted of twenty nearly identical verses that named points on the horizon where the sun rose or set and the crops to be planted at that time (McCluskey, 1977:176). The replacement of a calendric system of this complexity would require a complete reorientation of members of the society to temporal structures. It would be seen by most at best a risky endeavor. The daily cycle of daylight and dark provides all with a common and fundamental repetitious set of experiences. The yearly solar cycle provides all with a second lengthier cycle. It would not be surprising if several calendric systems that specified the length of the year by the number of days were developed independently. But it also is possible that all calendars that specify the yearly cycle by the number of days stemmed from a single source. The modern western European calendar is a modified version of the calendar developed during the Old Kingdom by the Egyptians.

ORDERING SPACE

Geometric principles are commonly conceptualized as having "truth" value and being capable of "proof" independent of the empirical world; they are thought by some to exist independent of sensate experiences. The foundation for this mode of thought was introduced into the European culture by Thales and Pythagoras and subsequently popularized by Plato. The belief that the symbols, squares, circles, triangles, and so on have an existence independent of human experience and action rests upon the fact it is possible to imagine a perfect circle, but impossible to produce one. On this basis Plato proposed that truth existed in the realm of ideas. In one sense, Plato was correct. Perfect squares, circles, and triangles do not exist anywhere except in the imagination of human beings.

However, these symbols, like all significant symbols, are conventions developed by human beings in their interaction with one another and their environment. They are the culmination of efforts of human beings to structure their experiences. Once developed, these symbols, like all symbols, can be used to order experiences, behaviors, and thought.

Geometric symbols like numeric symbols are highly abstract. Just as many primitives cannot specify large quantities, many cannot specify geometric forms. They do not have symbols for triangle, rectangle, square, circle, sphere, and some do not even have the concept line. They have symbols for direction, but not line; for roundness, but not circle.

Numeric symbols developed in conjunction with trade; geometric symbols developed in association with the observation of the locations of heavenly bodies, the construction of observatories, and the sustained study of the alignments of celestial bodies. Their elaboration was intimately intertwined with the construction of observatories and monuments.

The development of geometric forms proceeded from: (a) the production of a "line" specifying the location of a celestial body on the horizon, to (b) the specification of two locations, to (c) noting the relations between a series of alignments, to (d) the development of means for specifying the similarities and differences between the various relations. Subsequently, the principles formulated were employed to construct observatories, design monuments, specify boundaries, and measure distances, areas, and volumes. To quantify distances, areas, and volumes it was necessary to integrate geometric and numeric symbols.

Concrete symbols such as names of events and objects are established by human beings jointly attending to and acting toward events and objects occurring in the "natural" world. Examples include words of man, dog, tree, and so on. Geometric symbols have a somewhat different base. They are designations of products of human action. First human beings drew lines, sets of lines, and intersecting lines and then designated or named their products.

Geometry is "timeless." It is timeless in that these symbols do not designate sequences of events. Yet geometric symbols emerged from observations of a series of astronomical events. The development of geometry began when lines were drawn to depict the location of celestial bodies. When more than one body was attended to, or when a number of lines depicted the location on the horizon of the sun or moon at different times of the year, a "diagram" was produced. The medicine wheels of the plains Indians are primitive diagrams.

The production of diagrams creates an artifact that can subsequently be examined. The original diagrams were the product of a series of sequenced observations, but the diagrams themselves contained no sequences, Hence, the timelessness of geometric symbols.

A sequenced set of symbols provides a way of ordering the past and the future; numeric symbols provide a means of making precise note of large quantities of objects and can be used to quantify sequences of events; geometric forms are a set of symbols that provide a means for specifying relations. Or, sets of sequenced symbols provide temporal order, numeric symbols quantify objects and events, geometric symbols order space.

The original meaning of the term geometry was "land measurement." The term was used by the Greeks to refer to the procedures used by the Egyptians to resurvey the fields of the Nile valley after each flood. It has come to be used to refer to the study and use of forms; some call it the science of forms. Euclid, a resident of Alexandria, wrote *Elements*, outlining the basis principles of geometry, about 300 B.C. Some credit him with inventing geometry. The principles contained in *Elements* are the culmination of millenia of development. Historians of science are prone to credit the Greeks with inventing geometry. However, recent research demonstrates that principles once thought to have been first formulated by the Greeks were in use thousands of years before.

Sets of geometric procedures were established in a long and drawn-out process of human beings detecting the regularities of the directionality of distal events, the location of distal events in relation to each other, the construction of diagrams of the events, and many other complex activities including applying numbers to the diagrams. The process probably first began a few thousand years after sedentary groups became established. The process involved complex interactions of persons making observations, systematizing their observations by using lines to note them, the formulation of more precise procedures for making more precise directional observations, and finally the construction of monuments to dramatize the observations.

Geometric Forms and Ancient Cities

Not all ancient cities were geometrically aligned, but many were. Some of the centers of the seventh and sixth millennia B.C. appear to have been at least partly geometrically aligned. Some of the later cities in Mesopotamia reflect elaborate geometric patterns, others none at all. It seems likely that the agricultural centers reflect more geometric patterns than cities that were primarily dependent on trade.

The Egyptian cities were geometrically aligned as were those of the Indus Civilization. In China "A prominent feature of urban design throughout the whole Chou period was the raising of important buildings on platforms of *hang-t'u* construction. At Niu-Ts'un such a platform was located at the geometrical center of the city" (Wheatley, 1971:186).

The temples of the Maya and the precursors of the Inca reflect celestial alignment, but it is questionable that the intellectuals of these societies had formulated an integrated system of geometric patterns. However, in the Yucatan, rectangles have been uncovered that are formed on the basis of alignments of shadows cast by the sun as it rises and sets at the Winter and Summer solstices; there are also markings of the equinoxes (Leon-Portilla, 1973:129).

Before these centers could be geometrically planned it was necessary that complex patterns of alignments were noted and formalized by observers of celestial events. It was only after some persons had acquired command of patterns of alignments that cities or centers could be designed that reflected geometric patterns. The formulation of these principles was first achieved by those who made note of celestial events. Then subsequent generations used these principles in elaborating and refining their observatories and monuments.

Directionality

The most primitive spatial dimension is directionality. The simplest form of directionality is the specification of the location of some event or object in relation to self. The development of an abstract procedure for specifying directionality independent of the immediate location of self requires the consensual establishment of direction on the basis of the location of some significant object. For a group located at the base of a mountain range "over the mountains" is an abstract, although crude, specification of direction.

The locations on the horizon of the heliacal rising and setting of the major stars have served as a means for the specification of direction in many societies. "Where the Pleiades rise" has provided a directional reference point for many ancient civilizations. The heliacal rising and setting of stars remains relatively constant, although their location on the horizon slowly changes. The detection of the changes requires sustained careful and precise observation from a stable location. For practical purposes, directionality based on the heliacal risings and settings of stars provides a stable and relatively precise system of orientation.

The location of the sun and moon on the horizon changes throughout the year. However, the sun appears to stand still for a few days at the solstices. Both the Winter and the Summer risings and settings of the sun at the solstices have been widely used as primary reference points. These locations are significant events in the temporal systems in all solar-lunar calendars and served as significant points of orientation for nearly all, if not all, sedentary groups. Many groups used both the heliacal risings and settings of stars and the solstices as reference points. The Pre-Socratic Greeks used a mixture of stellar points of references and the solstices to specify direction. They were not capable of specifying the "cardinal" directions (Dicks, 1970). Many systems for specifying directions have been developed that did not establish the cardinal directions of north, east, south and west currently employed by modern societies.

The streets of the ceremonial center of Teotihuacan are aligned 15° 28' east of north and 16° 30' south of east. "The archaeological evidence suggests that the deviation of 1° from a perfect right angle between the two is probably not accidental" (Aveni, 1980:223). In fact, it might be questioned that they even had the concept "right angle." Thompson thought the Maya were incapable of making a right angle. It does not seem unreasonable that an orientational system or set of them were developed that were not tied to celestial north.

Some of the more complex systems for specifying directionality were developed by seafarers. The navigators of the South Seas sailed hundreds of miles from one small island to another. They accomplished these feats without benefit of maps, or at least, maps in the form of diagrams that they carried with them. They had a rich body of astronomical lore that was transmitted orally which provided them with an orientational system that allowed them to sail with certainty from one island to another.

The content of these "maps" of the South Sea navigators was similar to the "portolan" maps (from port-to-port maps) that were developed by the seafarers of the Old World. Portolan maps were widely used in the ancient Mediterranean by the Phoenicians and they probably have a much more ancient history (Hapgood, 1979). Portolan maps do not have the cardinal directions, nor do they specify latitude or longitude. They simply provide directions between a series of ports. Many were very complex. Some provided an elaborate set of directions for sailing between many different ports.

Portolan maps do not specify area; they are only directional. However, they were based upon astronomical phenomena. The location of the risings and settings of major stars and the zenith passage of stars provided the key reference point for the navigators of the South Seas. Some also incorporated the solstices and the equinoxes. These maps are multidirectional, but they do not constitute a grid system.

The determination of latitude can be rather easily accomplished by making careful note of the position of the stars. However, the determination of longitude requires precise notation of the time and precise observations of the angles of celestial bodies. All groups with a tradition of long-distance sea travel developed procedures for specification of latitude. The calculation of longitude by seafarers was not possible until after the clock was invented.

It is impossible to determine when procedures for the determination of longitude were first established. Strabo, who lived about the time of Christ, noted that longitude can only be determined by observing eclipses. The determination of longitude in this manner requires considerable astronomical sophistication. It is possible that astronomers of the third millenium B.C. had procedures for the specification of longitude. If they did, the calculations were limited to land-based observations. Observations made at sea would not have been precise enough to allow for the computation of longitude in this manner.

Two-Dimensional Forms

The first geometric form was a straight line—the line formed when observers established a fixed point of observation and a series of locations on the horizon. The transition from establishing a series of straight lines to two-dimensional forms was a major achievement. How and when it first occurred is unknown—perhaps unknowable. The presence of houses with a rectangular shape at some of the ancient trade centers suggests that the residents had acquired a crude mastery of the rectangular shape before agricultural communities were established. It is likely that mastery of two-dimensional geometric forms was first achieved at the early trade centers. Their refinement and elaboration was accomplished by communities dependent upon agriculture who made precise observations of the alignments of celestial events for timekeeping purposes.

It is possible that the first two-dimensional geometric forms emerged as the consequence of noting both sunrise and sunset at different times of the year. If observations are made of sunrises and sunsets at the Summer and Winter solstices from an established observational site, the alignments are close to reciprocals. The sunrise of the Winter Solstice is close to the reciprocal of sunset of the Summer solstice and sunrise at the Summer solstice is close to the reciprocal of sunset of the Winter solstice. Then if note is taken of the interrelation between markers placed an equal distance from the observational site a "rectangular" form is produced. The creation of two-dimensional alignments—trapezoids, parallelograms, and rectangles—probably was first achieved by making a set of reciprocal observations of the location of the sun on the horizon. The exact form created by making this set of observations depends upon the latitude of the observations and the morphological features of the landscape. If the horizon is uniform the result approaches a rectangle.

Systematic notations by a body of specialists of a series of reciprocal alignments would provide the foundation for noting that the line between the markers of the Summer solstice sunrise and the Summer solstice sunset was "parallel" to the line created by the markers of the sunrise and sunset of the Winter solstice. The original formulators of this observation, of course, did not have the concept "parallel." The symbol parallel emerged from their efforts to develop systematic procedures for making observations. Noting the relative position of the markers for the two sunrises and the two sunsets provided the foundation for noting the "parallelism" of these two sets of markers. When the sets of lines are combined a trapezoid is created.

The detection of trapezoidal forms necessarily preceded the formation of two-dimensional forms that consisted of four equal corners or right angles. Upon becoming aware of a series of trapezoids and noting their variations, attempts could be made to create a "perfect" trapezoid or a rectangle. The creation of a square was a subsequent development. Rectangles and squares are more abstract forms than are trapezoids and parallelograms.

Triangles as a distinctive form may have emerged in conjunction with rectangles, or they may have emerged independently and then were incorporated with rectangles. Careful observation of the sunrise and sunset at the solstices and equinoxes would create reciprocating triangles if the eastern and western horizons were equally free of obstructions. For example, if on flat terrain markers were placed to specify the Summer solstice sunrise and sunset and the sunrise and sunset at the equinoxes from a stable observation point, the result would yield two triangles whose apexes would meet at the point of observation. At any latitude except the equator, the resulting triangles formed by the Summer solstices risings and settings in conjunction with the risings and settings at equinoxes in comparison to the risings and settings at the Winter solstices and the risings and settings at the equinoxes will be unequal.

Both right angles and isosceles triangles are prominent in the design of the monuments of the earliest Egyptian dynasties. Right-angle triangles were probably extracted from rectangles. Once the rectangle had been detected and articulated then subsequently two right-angle triangles could be abstracted. The formulation of an isosceles triangle probably occured by placing markers equally distant from an observation point and then connecting the observation points. The result is a triangle with two sides of equal length.

The circle as a geometric form may have emerged either in conjunction with the shadows cast by gnomons or in conjunction with a series of markers depicting the alignment of a series of celestial bodies on the horizon. The shape created by the shadow of a gnomon during the day forms an arc, but it is not half of a circle. The length of the shadow during the early and late part of the day is greater than during midday. The result is an elongated arc. The specific form of the arc varies with the latitude and the time of the year the observations are made. However, it is conceivable that on the basis of extensive observations of the arcs created by a series of gnomons, the concept of circle might have been formulated.

If a series of locations of the sun, moon, and major stars are made and the markers are placed at equal distances from the observational site, then an arc forming part of a perfect circle is created. If markers are placed to note both the risings and settings of several bodies including stars in the northern- and southernmost regions of the sky a complete circle is formed.

The circle was known by the Egyptians of the early dynasties, but was not widely employed in their architecture (Badawy, 1965). The Sumerians made infrequent use of the circle; the Chinese employed the circle to construct some of the monumental centers. The builders of the megaliths of Britain were capable of constructing circles, but more commonly constructed oval-shaped observatories and monuments.

The formation of the concepts rectangles, right-angle triangles, and circles appear to be closely associated with the development of an integrated set of directions. To establish an abstract set of integrated directions it is necessary to formulate procedures for designating locations relative to each other. The formulation of due north, or celestial north, is dependent on establishing the central point among the circumpolar stars. Once that has been accomplished then the reciprocal can be established as south, and the midpoints on the horizon are equivalent to the sunrise and sunset at the equinoxes.

The specification of direction on the basis of a 360° compass may have been an elaboration of the four cardinal directions, or it is possible the 360° compass emerged from the specification of a series of equally sized isosceles triangles. The Egyptians had command of both right-angle and isosceles triangles early in their history. The Sumerians may have established an integrated system for designating direction prior to the Egyptians.

Three-Dimensional Forms

The development of symbols for three-dimensional forms necessarily followed the elaboration of two-dimensional forms. Three-dimensional forms may have emerged directly from concerns that centered on timekeeping and the heavens. It seems certain that the pyramid form emerged from efforts to construct monuments that dramatically displayed key celestial events.

By the Fourth Dynasty the Egyptians had command of the pyramid form. The Step Pyramid was constructed during the second dynasty. Its mode of construction is very similar to the ziggurats of Mesopotamia. However, the Great Pyramid of the Fourth Dynasty demonstrates that by then Egyptian intellectuals had command of the pyramidal form. It is conceivable that other groups may have preceded the Egyptians in acquiring command of the pyramid.

Other three-dimensional forms such as the cube, cylinder, cone, and sphere may have been spinoffs of intellectual activity that centered on timekeeping. However, it is also possible that much of the stimulus for the development of three-dimensional forms came from concerns with storing food. The original development of three-dimensional geometric forms and their quantification was undoubtedly an achievement of an agricultural society. The Sumerians probably took the first steps in this direction. It appears the Egyptians were the first to construct an integrated system of thought of forms.

QUANTIFYING SPACE

All who have mastered the rudimentary procedures for the computation of the area of geometric forms take for granted the processes of combining numeric and geometric symbols. However, the merging of these two symbol systems is not an automatic outcome of their presence. Just as some groups have complex numeric systems, but do not use them to keep track of the number of days that have transpired since the last Winter solstice, there are groups with primitive geometric forms and numeric symbols who have not combined them into a unified set of procedures that allow for the quantification of forms.

The term trigonometry originally referred to procedures for the computation of unknown dimensions of triangles from known dimensions. It refers to the computation of unknown lengths, angles, areas, and volumes of various forms from known dimensions. Trigonometric procedures necessarily developed when persons first achieved command of the means to quantify simple forms and then more complex forms. The first step was the quantification of distances, then the quantification of area, and lastly the quantification of volume.

Quantifying Distances

The simplest form of measuring distance is noting the relative space between two points. When it is noted that it is further between one set of two points than it is between two other points a primitive form of measurement is established. The quantification of distance may have been stimulated by a concern on the part of those who routinely traveled between one location to other locations with the specification of the different distances. However, it is more likely that distance was originally quantified by those who directed the construction of observatories and monuments.

The most primitive specification of long distances is in terms of temporal units—the number of days it takes to travel from one point to another. Both land and overseas distances were commonly quantified by specifying the number of days required to travel from one location to another. In ancient China long distances were specified by a unit equal to "a day's travel time." The unit of distance varied by terrain. The distance from one location to another was shorter for rough terrain than for smooth terrain.

It appears that short distances, those used in construction, were the first that were quantified by the formulation of standard units of measurement. A wide variety of units have been devised. Many, perhaps all, of the more primitive ones emerged from the use of certain features of the human body or human action to specify distance. They include the "digit" based on the width of the thumb, the palm, the foot, and the pace. The standardization of these units required their sustained use by a stable group who repeatedly dealt with recurring problems. Their standardization was closely intertwined with the construction of large communal centers and monuments.

There are indications that the units for measuring distance in the Old World stemmed from a common source. One standard unit of measuring distance in ancient Britain was the megalithic yard. Interestingly, the standard unit of measurement associated with the Indus civilization is almost equal to the megalithic yard of ancient Britain. Their similarity suggests that both may have stemmed from a common source. It is extremely doubtful that men of knowledge of such widely separated societies had direct contact with each other or even indirect contact through a third party.

The two units of measurement may have emerged from a common unit established earlier in western Asia. The Sumerian standard unit for distance was a *shusi*. Fifty *shusi* are equal to the traditional Indian *gaz*. Given the evidence of trade contacts between the civilizations of the Indus Valley and lower Mesopotamia, it is likely the two units of distance stem from a common source.

It is unlikely that standard units for the measurement of distance were developed at centers that were primarily dependent on trade. The primary orientation of traders to distance is the effort and time required for the transportation of goods from one location to another.

Quantification of Area

Long before procedures for the quantification of area were invented, persons characterized areas as larger and smaller. However, when the two areas in question have a different form, it is often difficult to achieve consensus. It was the development of the ability to quantify various geometric forms that allowed for the precise specification of the size of areas.

The Sumerians measured the area of their fields (Kramer, 1959); they therefore had developed at least crude procedures for the quantification of space. Not all agricultural groups measured the area of their fields or even used geometric forms to form boundaries. The ancient Britons do not appear to have quantified the area of their fields. Their fields were marked by boundary stones and other devices, but there is no evidence of a concern with straight lines or other geometric forms in the layout of their fields. The boundaries were irregular (Fowler and Evans, 1967) and tended to follow "natural" dividing lines. The fields of many groups who practiced agriculture are delineated in a similar manner.

Simple geometric forms were probably used to design the monuments of ancient societies long before they were used to mark off boundaries of fields. Despite the fact that the first meaning of the term geometry was the specification of procedures for surveying fields, it seems likely that geometric and trigonometric procedures were first employed to construct observatories and monuments. Once developed in that context, the procedures were extrapolated and used to design cities, construct geometrically patterned roads, design irrigation systems, and finally to survey fields.

It may be that the Pythagorean Theorem was the first trigonometric function formalized. As used by the Egyptians it was essentially a constructional triangle for establishing right angles by using a rope of twelve units in length. The rope was knotted at intervals of three, four, and five units (Badawy, 1965:23). The Pythagorean Theorem was used by the Egyptians during the early dynasties. It probably has an even more ancient history. Some of the monuments of ancient Britain incorporate both cardinal directions and the Pythagorean triangle (Hadingham, 1975:162). The Sumerians had command of the principle as did the designers of the cities of the Indus Valley.

Command of the Pythagorean Theorem allows one to lay out the foundation of a rectangular building with the minimal amount of effort and great precision. A rectangle can be accomplished in other ways. One is to use a compass to specify one-fourth of a circle, then draw two straight lines of the desired length and width of the proposed structure, then use the compass again at the end of the two straight lines to determine one-fourth of a circle and from those points draw another set of matching lines. If the procedures are carefully followed, when the second set of lines intersect, a rectangle is established. This procedure presumes command of a compass to establish one-fourth of a circle; such knowledge was not available to those who first designed rectangular structures.

A rectangular structure can also be created by trial and error. To construct a retangular building in this manner one first measures ten units in one direction and twelve units in another at an approximate right angle from the end of the ten-unit line, and ten units at a right angle from the end of the twelve-unit line. A parallelogram is a far more likely result than a rectangle, but through a series of realignments a rectangular structure can be achieved.

Given the tremendous utility of the Pythagorean Theorem for construction, it may be that it was the first trigonometric function that was widely employed. However, it is possible that primitive trignometric functions were first used to quantify the area of rectangles. The simplest computation involves the multiplying of the length of an area by its width. A plot of land five units by twelve units contains sixty square units. While this is child's play for those embued with basic trigonometric procedures, is not at all obvious to those who have not been taught the principle.

The computation of the area of a circle posed special problems. The Sumerians may have mastered it, but the Babylonians used the crude approximation of three times the radius squared to compute the area of a circle. The builders of the megaliths of Britain may have mastered it, but it is doubtful. The Egyptians formulated a procedure with an error of less than 0.6 percent (Gillings, 1975:140).

The quantification of area was an invention of the first magnitude. Complex number systems provided a base for the specification of large quantities of events and objects; the development of two-dimensional forms provided a necessary condition for the quantification of area. By combining these two sets of abstract symbols human beings acquired a set of procedures that allowed for the formulation of complex and precise programs of action. It is likely that a procedure of this complexity was invented only once, although it could have been created independently by more than one group.

The precise computation of the area of all circles and many other two-dimensional forms requires command of fractions. Similarly the precise computation of the volume of all cylinders, spheres, and cones requires command of fractions. Without command of fractions it is possible to compute crude approximations, but impossible to specify the quantity of these forms with precision.

The intellectuals of ancient civilizations had their difficulties with fractions, as do most when they are first introduced to them. With the exception of the fraction of $\frac{2}{3}$ the Egyptians expressed all fractions as $\frac{1}{n}$ or a series of $\frac{1}{n}$s. For example, the fraction of $\frac{2}{5}$ was expressed as $\frac{1}{3}$ plus $\frac{1}{15}$ and the fraction $\frac{2}{7}$ was expressed as $\frac{1}{4}$ plus $\frac{1}{28}$. The procedure, while rather cumbersome, provided a means for dealing with parts. The Chinese, Sumerians and perhaps the builders of the megaliths of western Europe were capable of managing fractions. However, it is not an ability easy to come by and is far from universal.

Quantification of Volume

The quantification of two-dimensional space was an intellectual achievement of the first order. The subsequent quantification of volume, while an extremely significant accomplishment, was not of the same magnitude. It only required persons to extrapolate from principles already formulated and to make one additional computation that was parallel to computations already in practice.

Once the ability to compute the area of a square has been devised, all that is necessary to compute the volume of a cube is to multiply the product of the width and length by the height. In a similar manner the volume of a cylinder can be computed with only one additional step after procedures for the computation of the area of a circle have been established.

The computation of the volume of pyramids involves combining procedures for the computation of the area of triangles with procedures for computing the volume of cubes; the computation of the volume of cones involves combining the procedures for computing the volume of cylinders with those of computing the area of triangles. The steps are rather complex, but rather easily derived from the more basic procedures. The Egyptians mastered procedures that allowed for the rather exact computation of both pyramids and cones, including the volume of a truncated pyramid (Gillings, 1972).

The computation of the surface area and volume of a sphere is more complex. Credit for this achievement is usually given to the Greeks, but Gillings (1972) offers evidence indicating that the Egyptians mastered the ability to compute the surface of a hemisphere. If they were capable of computing the surface area of a hemisphere, it is likely they were capable of computing the volume of a sphere as well.

Number versus Forms

There was considerable variation between ancient societies in the stress placed on numeric versus geometric systems. The Maya and the Chinese stressed numeric formula; in contrast others stressed geometric formula. The builders of the Western European megaliths had command of a complex system of geometric forms. Thom (1971 and 1976) presents considerable evidence and a forceful line of reasoning indicating that they had command of a complex numeric system that was applied to space. But there is only inferential evidence that they applied numeric system to two-dimensional geometric forms. There is no positive evidence that they used a numeric system to quantify area, although there are strong indications that they quantified distance (Atkinson, 1974:130). Their mode of thought appears to have been primarily geometric as opposed to numeric.

In a somewhat similar manner the Egyptians emphasized geometric thought and minimized numeric thought, or at least subordinated their numeric formula to geometric formula. For example, the square root of a number was called the "corner" of the number. "This term was clearly derived from the notion of a square cut diagonally" (Taton, 1963:25). The Egyptians' stress on area is also indicated by their procedure for demonstrating the Pythagorean Theorem. They "proved" the theorem by displaying a three-by-three set of squares and a four-by-four set of squares on the two right-angle sides of a right triangle and a five-by-five set of squares along the hypotenuse.

The integration of geometric forms and numeric symbols was accomplished in Egypt prior to the formation of the dynastic period. At Abydos during the first dynasty a "magnificent monument shows a maturity and elegance in design and sculpture hardly surpassed later. The constructional diagram of the internal panel is a square topped by an 8:5 triangle. ... The harmonic analysis of the palace facade (also) reveals the 8:5 triangle (Badawy, 1966:1970).

In addition the 8:5 triangles were integrated with the Fibonacci series at least as early as the Third Dynasty (Badawy, 1965:183). The Fibonacci series consists of a series of numbers wherein each number is the summation of the two preceding numbers—3, 5, 8, 13, 21, 34—. The numbers retain this ratio as they approach infinity. This suggests both that the intellectuals who developed this formula had formulated the concept infinity and were intrigued by the constancy of the relation between the numbers. The formula was displayed in the monuments of the Egyptians.

The Egyptians, perhaps more than any other ancient civilization, stressed the relations between forms. For example, Problem 48 of the Rhind Mathematical Papyrus offers a numeric procedure of "squaring" the circle (Gillings, 1972:145).

The unification of numeric systems and geometric form was likely the consequence of the unification of two modes of complex thought developed somewhat independently of each other. There are suggestions that the residents of the Upper Nile had developed a complex calendar and a considerable body of astronomical thought keyed to the sun (Horus). This body of thought stressed alignments and geometric forms. In contrast, the residents of the Lower Nile appear to have developed a complex body of thought based on a sidereal calendar with only a minimal amount of emphasis given to alignment, but had elaborate numeric cycles. The residents of the Lower Nile had more extensive trade contacts with western Asia where a complex numeric system was first developed.

The most ancient precise calendar of Egypt is a numeric one keyed to the heliacal rising of Sirius. Subsequent to the unification of the Nile an integrated system of numeric and geometric thought was developed. During the same period they devised the 365-day calendar consisting of 12 months of 30 days each for a total of 360 days with 5 days left over and a 360-degree circle. In constrast the Chinese developed a 365¼ day calendar and a circle of 365¼ degrees. They defined a degree as one day's mean solar motion. Both systems were based on celestial observations, but the Egyptians developed a neat symmetrical system, whereas the Chinese allowed theirs to reflect the "imperfections" of celestial movement.

The Egyptians rounded off the rough spots of sensate experiences and provided the useful fiction of perfect forms. This allowed for the development of a level of abstract thought not possible when observed regularities are precisely noted and adhered to. No two empirical events are ever identical. But when empirical events are approached with the belief that some of them can be expressed formally—in perfect forms—then it is possible to search for and detect patterns of regularities that otherwise might not be observed. This premise (fiction) underlies all modern scientific efforts.

Not all ancient civilizations developed highly elaborate procedures for the management of space. For example, the Maya with their highly complex system of temporal sequences seem to have been only incidentally concerned with the quantification of space. "Time, not space, is the principle medium of expression for all the astronomy gleaned from the Maya codices" (Aveni, 1979:85). There is little evidence that the Maya quantified geometric forms; they may have. If they did not, perhaps the stumbling block was their failure to develop a system of fractions. They had elaborate celestial sequences, but these were always expressed in whole numbers. One of their sequences combined the 365-day solar calendar with the Venus cycle of 484 days to achieve a cycle of 176,660. They were aware that 365 days was not a "true" measure of the solar year. Each fourth year they adjusted their agricultural festivals a day to maintain synchronization of celestial and terrestrial seasons. But they never used fractions to express the quantity of time.

SUMMARY

The quantification of geometric forms provided the foundation for all complex construction efforts. These formulae still lie at the base of all major construction efforts of human beings. Skyscrapers, highway systems, factories, and space travel rest upon the ability of human beings to perform basic trigonometric functions.

These principles were not originally formulated to achieve these objectives. Rather they were first formulated to acquire more precise measures of sequences of events and to dramatize the events. In their concern with temporality human beings devised procedures that allowed them to develop precise and elaborate procedures for the management of space. Some ancient societies developed highly abstract and integrated systems of thought that centered on space. The Egyptians of the Old Kingdom were probably the first to develop an integrated system that combined numeric and geometric functions. They used these concepts to construct monuments, map their world, and to organize their society.

The accepted myth is that the basic principles of geometry, which lie at the heart of engineering, were formulated by a few geniuses of Greek ancestry a few centuries before the birth of Christ. The myth is an attractive one. It credits a few individuals with providing the basis for a revolution in human thought and action. However, the myth rests upon a shaky foundation. The geometric forms and trigonometric functions that underlie the complex engineering and scientific efforts of modern man required millennia of development. It probably began in western Asia and was elaborated and modified many times in different regions. It achieved its first integrated expression during the unification of Egypt that culminated in the construction of the Great Pyramid.

The development of these symbolic systems allowed human beings to subsequently order a wide variety of experiences into a unified whole, to formulate complex programs of action to modify their environment, to build complex edifices, and last but not least to develop complex social structures. These systems of thought and their derivations are used today to design skyscrapers, plan international traffic systems, and formulate complex bureaucratic structures.

Of all the experiences of human beings, only those associated with celestial movement are sufficiently stable to allow for the construction of abstract and precise procedures for structuring of space. When combined with numeric symbols they allow for formulation of complex programs of social action coordinated by a centralized administration. The construction of large-scale coordinated activity requires that this form of thought be combined with complex temporal structures. This level of complexity was achieved by several different ancient civilizations.

The magnitude of these achievements is difficult to overemphasize. It is only a slight overstatement to say that, "The complex activity which we call civilization (is) a concerted effort to force upon Nature, irregular in her deeds and unruly in her moods, the acceptance of these forms preferred by man" (Dantzig, 1955:85).

Chapter XIV

Were They Scientists?

Students of ancient civilizations who are not professional anthropologists or historians of science often credit ancient scholars with sophisticated bodies of knowledge of celestial phenomena (Lockyer, 1894/1973; Tompkins, 1971; Hawkins, 1968; Thom, 1971 and 1976; and Aveni, 1979 and 1980). In contrast, professional students of ancient civilizations have been reluctant to accept the idea that ancients accumulated bodies of scientific knowledge. They have been especially resistant to crediting the ancients with undertaking "scientific" study of celestial phenomena. The Hellenists in particular have been vehement in their efforts to discredit the scientific accomplishments of the ancients. In the words of one, "Equally misguided are the attempts made to impute complicated astronomical motives to the builders of ancient monuments such as Stonehenge; such fantasies are reminiscent of the 'pyramid literature'— and equally valueless, despite the modern trappings of computer calculations with which they are invested" (Dicks, 1970:249).

The difference in standpoint taken by the "amateur" and the "professional" students has been acutely expressed in the two different traditions that focus on the ancient Britons. Lockyer, Thom, Hawkins, and Newham are all essentially amateur students of the ancient Britons. They have demonstrated many astronomical alignments for the megaliths of Briton and implied that the ancient intellectuals were engaged in the scientific study of celestial phenomena. The professional students of the ancient Britons almost uniformly reacted to such imputations with cries of heresy. Daniels, Atkinson, Hawkes, and others have accused the amateurs of projecting a scientific mode of thought onto the ancients when it was well established that these monuments were centers of ritualistic activity. One implication of the reaction is that scientific and ritualistic activity were mutually exclusive, a highly questionable position. A second implication is that evidence supporting the proposition the megaliths were centers of ritualistic activity is overwhelming. Whereas in fact, the evidence that the megaliths served as ritual centers is less than the evidence that they served as observatories.

Recently some anthropologists who specialize in the study of the ancient Britons, including Atkinson, have acknowledged the astronomical alignments of the megaliths. MacKie (1977) has offered an interpretation of the ancient Britons that incorporates both the evidence generated by the archaeoastronomers and traditional archaeologists.

A similar difference between the amateurs and professionals holds for students of ancient Egyptians. Lockyer's study of the astronomy of the Egyptians which was completed in the last century, has been completely ignored by Egyptologists. Some of the specific alignments claimed for the Egyptians by Lockyer are incorrect. However, his thesis that the Egyptians made extensive study of celestial phenomena and aligned their monuments to key celestial events is valid. Tompkins (1971) and Stecchini (1971) offer an elaborate account of the astronomical knowledge of the Egyptians. No professional Egyptologist has given any recognition of the effort. Tompkins does make some rather silly statements, but his theme that the Egyptians made extensive studies of celestial phenomena and developed a sophisticated body of thought tied to empirical observations is well founded.

The standpoint taken by professional scholars toward the astronomy of the Maya and ancient Chinese has been different. From the beginning, scholars of these civilizations have acknowledged that the intellectuals of these ancient societies made accurate observations of celestial phenomena and developed complex bodies of knowledge. Most of the early students of the Maya were amateurs; they were not professionally trained archaeologists. They set the tone for subsequent studies of the Maya. The early scholars of ancient China regarded ancient savants of China capable of developing complex bodies of thought. In a series of publications Needham has advocated the complexity of thought of the ancient Chinese, although he has expressed his reservations about the "scientific" nature of their efforts.

There are several reasons why some modern scholars have been reluctant to accept the proposition that the ancients made scientific studies of celestial phenomena, not the least of which is ethnocentrism. Most western scholars implicitly accept the idea that scientific studies are a unique achievement of western Europeans. If one acknowledges that some ancients made scientific studies of the heavens, then the uniqueness of the achievement of western European intellectuals would lose some of its mystique.

A second reason for resistance is that the scholars of the Middle Ages established the tradition that the Greeks were the first philosophers. In addition, the earliest modern western European astronomers were stimulated by and built on the astronomical knowledge of the Greeks. Modern philosophers of science, historians of science, and Hellenists have promulgated the tradition that philosophy and science began with the Greeks. Most of them credit the Greeks with being the first reflective and detached students of the environment. The intellectual elite of all prior civilizations supposedly were captives of myths and rituals.

A third reason that many fail to acknowledge the sophisticated bodies of knowledge of the ancient scholars is the implicit acceptance of an evolutionary model of unilineal and cumulative growth of knowledge. However, the research of archaeastronomers has demonstrated that the evolution of human knowledge has experienced several flowerings and setbacks. There have been many explosions of knowledge, followed by dark ages. The stagnation of intellectual activity that followed the classical Greeks was not the only dark age.

Many ancient civilizations had centers of knowledge—universities. The nature of these centers of knowledge and the specific content of the knowledge developed varied greatly. However, one common concern of all ancient centers of knowledge was celestial phenomena. The heavens were studied and there are many indications that elaborate integrated bodies of knowledge were formulated. Nor were astronomical events the only phenomena that were systematically studied. The Egyptians of the Old Kingdom also formulated medical principles. A statement on surgery formulated in the Old Kingdom is "remarkable for its empirical approach to the subject" (Aldred, 1965:63-64). The complexity and correctness of a statement instructing physicians on how to treat head fractures has only been recently recognized (Ralston, 1977). The reanalysis of the statement leading to an appreciation of its correctness was made by a surgeon, not an Egyptologist.

Most of the content of the bodies of knowledge generated by ancient intellectuals has been lost. The evidence we have of their achievements is reflected in the ruins of their observatories and monuments. However, there is considerable circumstantial evidence, in addition to the observatories and monuments, that indicates that in some of these societies there were sophisticated students of celestial phenomena who formulated abstract and empirically grounded bodies of knowledge.

Nearly all acknowledge that some ancient societies accomplished engineering feats of considerable complexity. Despite this some still maintain that the knowledge that allowed for the engineering feats did not constitute scientific knowledge. This position reflects a lack of understanding of the complexity of knowledge and mathematical principles necessary for the successful completion of major engineering endeavors.

Scholars of science are almost in unanimous agreement that scientific activity is a distinctive form of human activity, yet there is little consensus on what constitutes scientific activity. For the purpose of discussion it is presumed that scientific activity is: (a) an effort to formulate abstract assertions based upon sustained and precise observations of selected phenomena (science is empirical), (b) the construction of interrelated abstract assertions based upon sets of observations, (c) the deduction of additional regularities from established principles that can be verified by additional observations, and (d) the continual modification and elaboration of assertions through empirical studies.

EMPIRICISM

The cornerstone of scientific endeavors is empiricism. However, the empiricism is of a special sort. In the organization of most of their activity human beings are empirical. To be empirical simply means to assign significance to sensate experiences. Most of us do that routinely. If we did not assign significance to our sensate experiences, we would not survive. We note events, take them into account, and adjust our activity to events we note. If we did not, we would soon have a fatal accident, unless we were continually watched over and protected by others. Children have to learn to assign significance to their sensate visual and auditory experiences before they can act autonomously.

The empiricism that is the foundation of scientific activity is of a different order than the day-to-day empiricism of all human beings. It entails the systematic and precise observation of selected facets of the sensate world from a stable standpoint or a limited number of standpoints for the purpose of formulating a general (abstract) proposition. The empirical efforts of scientists are given direction by their interest in and belief that if careful observations are made, regularities can be detected and articulated.

The development of the lunar calendars of the paleolithic peoples that have been analyzed by Marshack (1972) required sustained observations of celestial phenomena. Before awareness of a yearly cycle could be achieved, at least some persons made sustained notations of the order of celestial events. The observations leading to the formulation of a yearly cycle need not have been precise or very systematic. All that was required was the notation of some regular and dramatic events and the keying of the lunar sequences to those events. These observations were not made to formulate general principles of celestial phenomena, but to allow for the accurate anticipation of significant terrestial events. Nomadic life prevents precise observations of celestial phenomena.

The detection of precise regular patterns of movement by the heavenly bodies could not have occurred until after sedentary communities were established. Only then was it possible to note the systematic patterns of solar, sidereal, and lunar movement. For example, if one retains a constant geographic position and makes observations of major stars and the solstices, it can be detected that at each Winter solstice the same heliacal rising of a star will occur more or less simultaneously year after year. Actually there is a slight variation, but the variation would not have been noted by the first students of celestial movement.

Once a pattern had been discovered between the movement of the sun on the horion and the reappearance of a star in the heavens then additional regularities could be sought. It is very likely that some imprecise regularities were detected prior to the establishment of sedentary communities. Even after the establishment of sedentary communities, it is doubtful that much effort was exerted to specify precise regularities between solar and stellar movements.

The precision of the early students of celestial movement was limited to "naked eye" observations. However, many ancient groups refined their observations. For example the residents of ancient Britain and western Europe built observatories that contained foresights and backsights that were several miles apart. One complex observatory on the coast of western Europe continued a series of foresights that were up to nine and ten miles from the backsight. The observers located themselves at the backsight and sighted the various locations of the sun and moon over the foresights at different times of the year. This allowed them to make very precise observations of solar and lunar movement.

It appears that the astronomers of ancient Britain detected the perturbation of the moon (Thom and Thom, 1978). The perturbation of the moon from its ellitipcal orbit is caused by the variation in the gravitational pull of the sun on the moon. It achieves its maximum value when the moon is directly between the earth and sun or when the moon is opposite the side of the earth from the sun. Its maximum value is 5° 08' 43". Tycho Brahe was the first modern European to detect the perturbation of the lunar orbit.

The detection of a pattern of this sort requires sustained and precise observation from a constant standpoint. Furthermore, it is necessary to make careful notation of a large number of lunar cycles before the pattern can be ascertained.

Many other ancient agricultural societies made extended precise observations of various celestial patterns. It was these observations that provided the empirical foundation for the formulation of the statements specifying the patterned movements of celestial bodies. The original impetus for the systematic study of the movement of heavenly bodies was not to formulate astronomical principles. The early observers were unaware that such patterns existed. However, in their concern with specifying more precisely the occurrence of critical celestial events, they acquired a body of data that allowed them to also specify the patterns of celestial movement. The most ancient students of celestial movement were not interested in formulating abstract assertions based on their observations. But there is considerable evidence that many of the later students of celestial movement did formulate abstract assertions.

ABSTRACT ASSERTIONS

The formulation of a series of names in a definite order specifying the sequences of days of each moon and the sequences of moons of each year in conjunction with the recognition that the cycles were repetitious constituted a primitive form of abstraction. Nearly all human groups achieved this level of abstraction. These sequenced names organized experiences based upon observations of celestial phenomena. They characterized sets of past experiences into a unified whole and provided a framework for observing future sequences of experiences. Primitive calendric systems that were limited to the specification of the sequences of moons following the Winter solstice or the heliacal rising of a star were imprecise abstractions, but nonetheless they were abstract propositions based upon empirical phenomena.

When sequences of names were replaced by numbers, propositions were formulated that were both more precise and more abstract. The fact there are fewer moons per year than days per moon, plus the condition that terrestrial conditions change more from moon to moon than from day to day, suggest that the specification of moons by numbers preceded the numeric specification of the days of each moon and year.

It is impossible to state when the numeric specification of the sequential order of celestial phenomena was first achieved. It is likely that the early Sumerians achieved this level of sophistication. It may have been achieved long before. The numeric specification of the length of the lunar cycle and solar year was definitely achieved by the Egyptians by the Old Kingdom.

The specification of the Egyptians that an extra moon was to be intercalated if the heliacal rising of Sirius occurred on or before the eleventh day of a given moon necessarily required that previously they numerically specified both lunar and sidereal sequences. The numeric specification of both sets of sequences provided the foundation for the formulating of a general numeric principle for the introjection of an extra moon.

Several of the ancient civilizations developed numeric formulae that asserted the interrelations between several celestial cycles. The Egyptians of the Old Kingdom noted that 309 lunations were equivalent to 25 civil years (Taton, 1963). The Maya constructed a cycle of 1,359,540 days that was the multiple of 7 celestial cycles. The ancient Chinese were aware of the Metonic cycle of 19 years and 235 lunations. They also had a cycle of 76 years that consisted of 4 Metonic cycles and another cycle of 513 years. The designers of Stonehenge apparently had detected a 56-year cycle that was used to predict lunar events (Hawkins, 1965). Many different "theories" were constructed that consisted of sets of propositions that specified the patterns of movements of celestial bodies.

The detection of extended patterns of interrelations between lunar, solar, and sidereal movement was first achieved by persons who were unaware of their existence. The detection of the first extended pattern, a pattern with a duration of several years, must have been a eureka experience of the first order. Once the first extended pattern had been detected then observers could intentionally organize themselves to detect additional extended patterns. For example, once the Metonic cycle had been detected, then additional sets of cycles could be sought.

These extended sequences were a form of abstract thought. One might quarrel with their accuracy, but the effort resulted in the formation of sets of interrelated propositions that characterized complex series of empirical experiences. Concrete events were arrayed on the principle of a never-varying set of repetitious cycles.

The formulation of extended cycles provided a foundation for an indefinite temporal frame. Once the idea was established that extended cycles could be projected into the future and the past, it likely generated a consciousness that the future and the past were never ending. The concept infinity was probably first formulated by persons who projected repetitious cycles into the future and the past.

A complex set of principles specifying the numeric order of cycles can be formulated from a single location. All that is required is sustained observations, an accurate set of notations of past events, and an interest in relating series of observations to each other. Efforts of this sort had an empirical base and constituted a form of abstraction.

If the system of thought was based upon the observations from a single location, the principles formulated were provincial. They were principles that "held" for only a specific location. Provincially based principles allow for a form of deduction, namely the deduction of extended sequences of future and past events. Provincially based abstract propositions do not allow for the deduction of experiences that will be generated if one changes his location and then makes observations from the second location. Before deductions of this type can be undertaken, it is necessary to be aware of sets of observations made from other locations. Then a cosmopolitan system of thought can be formulated. A cosmopolitan system of thought allows for the specification that if one has observed a series of events at X location, then when observations are made at location Y, a different set of experiences will be generated. Some ancient intellectuals appear to have achieved this level of sophistication.

DEDUCTION FROM INTERRELATED PRINCIPLES

The term deduction is used in several different ways. One use of the term refers to the activity of mathematicians when they attempt to deduce specific numeric and geometric relations from known values. A second use refers to specification of empirical regularities not yet observed by extrapolation from principles based upon prior empirical observations. It is the second use of the term that is of concern here.

A simple prototype of mathematical deduction is the computation of the hypotenuse of a right-angle triangle when the length of the other two sides is known. The formula is a^2 plus b^2 equals c^2. The Greeks are commonly credited with developing this form of deduction. However, they were not the first to take up such problems.

The second form of deduction is the extrapolation from a series of established principles of additional regularities that will prevail if observations are made from a different standpoint or location. The prototype of this form of deduction was Newton's hypothesis that as a consequence of the centrifugal force created by the rotation of the earth on its axis, the earth is not a perfect sphere, but is slightly flattened at the poles. Measurement of the curvature of the earth has validated Newton's deduction.

It is extremely doubtful that the intellectuals of ancient societies made deductions as complex as those of Newton. However, there are indications that they did make complex deductions that were based upon established regularities. The Egyptians probably deduced that the earth was a sphere; the residents of ancient Britain may have.

If observations were from a single location it is unlikely that students of celestial movement would conclude the earth was a sphere. However, when they became aware that the observations made at location X were of a different order than the observations made at location Y, then a foundation was provided that might entice them to resolve the incongruities. For example, if the stars are observed from 30° latitude approximately one-third of the stars of the northern hemisphere are circumpolar—stars that never set. However, if the observations are made at 45° latitude then approximately one-half of the stars of the northern hemisphere are circumpolar. In addition, some of the southern stars that are visible at 30° latitude are not visible at 45° latitude.

There were several observatories in Egypt prior to the Old Kingdom. The northernmost was located at the apex of the Delta; the southernmost approximately 500 miles to the south. Observations of the stars, sun, and moon made at the apex of the delta yielded quite a different set of experiences than those made 500 miles to the south.

There is no direct evidence that the men of knowledge associated with the various observatories compared observations. However, it is extremely likely that they did. There was extensive boat traffic on the Nile. Goods were transported from one location to another primarily by boat. Political figures routinely traveled on the Nile. It is almost certain that the men of knowledge of the various locations were aware of the observations made at other locations, at least by the time Egypt was unified, if not earlier.

On the basis of comparing the observations made at different latitudes it was apparent that a greater number of circumpolar stars were visible at the northern locations. The differences in the alignments formed by the sun at sunrise and sunset at the solstices also systematically vary with the latitude of observation. Given the extensive attention the Egyptians gave to both sidereal and solar movement it is very likely that they deduced the earth was a sphere.

Another indication that they made this deduction is one of the tales of Herodotus. He related the story of the Egyptians employing Phoenicians to circumnavigate Africa. Herodotus was writing over 2,000 years after the building of the Great Pyramid and the supposed event may have occurred shortly before his time. Nonetheless it indicates an awareness on the part of some Egyptians that the earth was a sphere.

As Herotodus related the tale, he stated that it was claimed when the sailors rounded southern Africa the sun was on their right as they proceeded in a westerly direction. Herodotus indicated that he doubted this aspect of the story. A recent analysis of the tale and its historical context casts doubt on the circumnavigation of Africa. However, the more significant point is that the content of the tale indicates that either circumnavigation was achieved or there was a body of thought in Egypt that specified the earth was a sphere. It is likely that either the Egyptians were aware of observations of solar movement from south of the Equator or that in their efforts to fit together a series of observations made along the Nile, they had deduced the earth was a sphere.

The Egyptians probably constructed an integrated system of thought to account for the observed movement of the planets as well as the stars and moon. Macrobius, a Roman scholar of the fourth century A.D., reported that the Egyptians had a formulation that stated the sun circled the earth, that Mercury circled the sun, and that the cycle of Venus enclosed both the sun and Mercury (as quoted in Dreyer, 1953:129-130).

The Egyptians displayed the planets on some of their monuments. When they did, the planets Jupiter, Saturn, and Mars were frequently separated from Venus and Mercury. In the Egyptian formulation the planets Mercury and Venus were considered as adjuncts of the sun (Parker, 1974:60).

The Egyptian "theory" of celestial movement was not correct, but nonetheless it indicates a sophisticated body of thought based upon detailed and systematic observations. It cannot be determined exactly when the theory was first formulated, but given other developments in Egypt, it is likely that the theory was formulated during the Old Kingdom. If and how they accounted for the movements of the exterior planets is unknown, although it is likely that the system of epicycles popularized by Ptolemy was first formulated by the Egyptians (Newton, 1978).

Other indications that the Egyptians formulated a comprehensive body of principles of celestial events are some of the features of the Great Pyramid. The Great Pyramid reflects both solar and sidereal events. Lockyer suggested that the intellectual activity of the period was the consequence of astronomers who focused primarily on sidereal events and those who focused primarily on solar events becoming aware of each other's system and resolving incongruities. This seems highly probable. It is likely that they constructed a theory of celestial events that incorporated lunar, planetary, and stellar movement.

The Great Pyramid is located almost exactly on 30° latitude. It is 1'9" to the south of 30°. The error is equivalent to the error resulting from refraction based on naked eye observation of the sun. The concepts ⅓ and ⅔ occupied a central position in Egyptian mathematics. It seems reasonable that they selected the location for the Great Pyramid to reflect the ⅓ and ⅔ distance between the equator and pole and then selected the specific location on the basis of empirical observations.

It also seems likely that the ancient Britons developed a comprehensive system of thought to integrate their observations. One indication of this is that one of their megalith monuments is located on the relatively barren island of Unst. Unst is the northernmost island of the British archipelago. It lies just short of 61° latitude. At the time of the construction of the megalith the moon was circumpolar for a day or two each month (Thom and Thom, 1978:168). It is likely that this particular megalith was constructed to make observations of the moon when it was circumpolar. These observations in conjunction with observations made from observatories further south may have stimulated the men of knowledge to deduce a system of thought that led to the conclusion that the earth was a sphere.

The Maya were aware that eclipses were the consequence of conjunctions of the sun and moon. It is likely that they were also capable of predicting eclipses. They had calculated the solar year as 365.2420 days in length; the modern figure is 365.2422. However, the Mayan system emphasized sequential order. There is no evidence that they developed a sophisticated system of thought that specified the relative spatial position of the earth, moon, sun, and planets. They did make a series of systematic observations from different locations and late in the classical period Copan was established as a center for astronomical studies. It is certainly conceivable that they developed an astronomical theory that specified the positions of the heavenly bodies in relation to one another.

There is considerable circumstantial evidence that the ancient time-keepers of at least some societies were aware of observations made at other locations, and further, that some attempted to resolve different sets of observations and formulated comprehensive systems of thought to integrate disparate sets of observations. That they formulated principles from which they made deductions cannot be ascertained but seems likely.

MODIFICATION OF PRINCIPLES

In the history of humanity there has been a general movement from a state of ignorance to knowledge. However, this movement has suffered from many setbacks and stagnations. Sometimes the setbacks have been in the form of destruction of knowledge centers. In other instances the inquisitiveness that underlies scientific investigations faded from the scene as dogma replaced inquiry.

The observatories and monuments of some of the ancient civilizations indicate that many times societies proceeded through a phase of growth and liberation that was followed by stagnation. There are several indicators that the first generations of a newly established civilization actively sought knowledge. Then in some cases stagnation followed as the intellectuals became transformed into priests. The production of rituals replaced activity designed to test, modify, and elaborate established principles.

When communities were established in new territories the residents quickly became aware that the timekeeping principles that had served them well in their native communities were not adequate. They found it necessary to formulate a new calendar. Their observations informed them that the nature of their experiences linked to celestial phenomena were different from those of their native communities. Both the time-keepers and the rank and file were concerned with developing an adequate calendric system. The timekeepers were undoubtedly intrigued by the variations observed from location to location. Their primary interest was the formulation of a new timekeeping system. But in the process some must have been intrigued by the difference in observed patterns of celestial movement and attempted to concoct theories to explain the differences.

During the formative periods established bodies of knowledge were discarded and new resolutions were sought. Useful and intriguing knowledge was accumulated. There was probably contact with older communities and information accumulated in them was contrasted with the newly acquired information. The principles of celestial movement were in a state of flux. A liberal and inquisitive attitude predominated. The exact sequence of development varied tremendously. However, many of the newly formed civilizations experienced a bursting forth of intellectual activity.

The development along the Nile during the formative period serve as a prototype. During the early centuries there was widespread intellectual ferment. There was "an entirely unusual search for first principles" (Aldred, 1965:64). Nowhere in the ancient world prior to the Greeks was there anything comparable to accomplishments of the first generations of Egyptians (Smith, 1946). The intellectual developments of the Egyptians during this period were especially outstanding in comparison to subsequent developments in Egypt.

Subsequently the accumulated knowledge became dogma. "Truth" was formulated prior to or perhaps during the Fourth Dynasty and subsequently the primary concern was to maintain it. The truth of the Egyptians was codified in their complex numeric, geometric, and written symbols. These principles were accessible only to those indoctrinated into the system. Later generations of Egyptian intellectuals minimized the significance of sensate experience. Their astronomy, geometry, numeric systems, sculpture, paintings, and medicine changed in the following centuries. However, the intellectuals promulgated the belief that all was constant, that no new ideas were possible.

They developed and made into dogma the principle of ever-recurring cycles. They maintained that time "was without consequence through infinite ages" (Wilson, 1951:38). Utopia had been achieved; the task of the intellectuals and other elite was to maintain the established perfection. To achieve this it was necessary to discredit the empirical world. They were relatively successful.

Observations of celestial phenomena continued throughout the existence of ancient Egypt. However, the intellectuals were no longer interested in the acquisition of empirical data to acquire new understandings, but only to substantiate established truths. The reification of knowledge in Egypt was extreme. Similar developments occurred in other ancient civilizations. However, none of the others appear to have been as successful in maintaining as constant a set of beliefs about the nature of celestial phenomena as the Egyptians.

The replacement of a search for knowledge by dogma demonstrates that the continued existence of a civilization does not assure a continued search for knowledge and the modification of old principles. The stagnation of inquiry appears to have been intricately associated with bureaucratization, authoritarianism, and isolation. Egypt experienced all of these developments during the latter stages of the Old Kingdom when inquiry came to an end.

SUMMARY

Most of the evidence of sophisticated bodies of knowledge is associated with ancient societies that constructed monuments. These societies rested on an infrastructure of agriculture; many of them evolved into centralized authoritarian states. The prototype was Egypt. Similar developments occurred in Mesopotamia, China, Central America, and South America. The conjunction of complex bodies of astronomical knowledge with authoritarian states might lead one to conclude that authoritarian states were conducive to the development of abstract principles. However, the sequence of development indicates that the greatest growth of astronomical knowledge occurred during the first centuries of the foundation of civilizations in new regions. Then, with the rise of authoritarian states, these bodies of knowledge stagnated and became reified.

The creation of knowledge centers rested upon a foundation of abundant agricultural production, communal concern with timekeeping, and the maintenance of contact with other societies. The stability provided by agricultural production and the interests of farmers in acquiring knowledge of when to plant crops provided the social base to support an elite who studied celestial phenomena. The intellectuals of a few civilizations systematically observed the heavens and formulated principles based on their observations.

It is conceivable that maritime traders supported the study of celestial phenomena. The elaborate set of observatories on the island of Malta may have been supported by Mediterranean traders. It is unlikely that this set of observatories was supported by agricultural communitites of mainland Europe. It may be that the relative stability of agricultural communities in comparison to trade communities has created a bias in the preservation of ruins. The indications that knowledge centers were more closely associated with agriculture than trade may simply reflect that bias.

It is very possible that there were two relatively distinct traditions, one that focused on timekeeping associated with agriculture, and a second that concentrated on celestial phenomena for navigational purposes. The two interests are not mutually exclusive. In both cases, if there were two independent developments, the original impetus stemmed from practical concerns. But in some instances these practical concerns led to the creation of "theoretical" knowledge.

It is certain that in some ancient societies there were intellectuals dominated by a spirit of inquiry who (a) made systematic empirical observations to establish abstract propositions, (b) developed sets of interrelated assertions based upon their observations, (c) deduced from their abstract assertions additional propositions that were in principle subject to empirical verification, and (d) reformulated established beliefs on the basis of their empirical studies. They were students who were concerned with acquiring a more complete understanding of their environment.

In some instances the search for knowledge stagnated. This frequently occurred in those agricultural societies that evolved into authoritarian states. The spirit of inquiry was replaced by a concern with maintaining a social order that served the interests of the elite, including the intellectuals; in still others the economic base that originally supported them became depleted.

The knowledge acquired and the spirit of inquiry upon which it was based were often lost, but in a few instances some of the knowledge diffused to other societies. In still fewer instances the diffused knowledge collided with a new spirit of inquiry. Then new bodies of knowledge that surpassed the old were on occasion formulated.

The original impetus for the construction of complex abstract bodies of knowledge stemmed from concerns with precise timekeeping. These concerns in conjunction with the ambivalent position of timekeepers in their community stimulated some to become students of the heavens. These ancient students of the heavens provided the foundation for modern scientific endeavors. Failure to recognize their achievements provides us with a shortsighted and incorrect conception of modern scientific endeavors.

Chapter XV

Centralized Administration

Weber argued that bureaucracies were both the bane and the foundation of civilization. Nearly all students of civilizations agree that the emergence of centralized administration was a major milestone. But there is little agreement on how the first systems of centralized administration came into being. Several scholars have formulated theories of the emergence of administrative systems. Three of the more widely held theories are: (a) the conquest theory, (b) the "big man" or tyrant theory, and (c) the military transplantation theory.

Ibn Kaldun, the Arab scholar, was the first social scientist to suggest that centralized administrations were first established by nomadic groups conquering sedentary communities. According to his formulation the conquerers then established administrative systems to extract tribute. However, nomadic groups have never developed administrative specialists. A sequence similar to the one posited by Kaldun has occurred many times, but did not occur until after administrative systems had been established by sedentary groups. Then, occasionally, when nomadic groups conquered sedentary communities, the administrators of the conquered sometimes saw fit to serve their conquerers. One of the more famous and well-documented cases of this is the conquest of China by the Mongols.

The big man or tyrant theory posits that one person established himself as the focal point for the community; through diligent work he accumulated both a following and wealth. Then through a combination of coercion and careful allocation of rewards he affirmed his position. The offspring of big men tend to succeed their ancestors and eventually a monarchy is established. An integral part of the process is the emergence of a coterie of followers who administer the affairs of the community for the tyrant. Big men or tyrants have played an important part in the transformation of the political systems of many cities and nations. Examples range from the trade communities of preclassical Greece through

231

the feudal period of Europe to relatively recent transformations in underdeveloped countries.

The establishment of tyrannies supported by administrators has an ancient history. The early dynasties of Mesopotamia and Egypt were probably established in this manner. However, complex administrative systems were present in Mesopotamia and probably in other regions before tyrannies and monarchies were established. Bureaucracies provided the foundation for the emergence of monarchies; monarchies did not provide the foundation for the earliest systems of centralized administration. The dynasties of Sumer followed the establishment of administrative systems; they did not precede it.

Spencer (1972) thought that administrative systems were first founded by military units. According to his formulation, the necessity of centralized authority was first recognized by military leaders. They developed systems of administration to more effectively pursue military objectives. Then the effectiveness of the social arrangement was recognized and employed in other areas of human activity.

Modern armies are bureaucratized. However, this achievement is the culmination of millennia of developments. The complex administrative structures that frame modern military efforts did not emerge from intergroup conflict. War is highly explosive, chaotic, and destructive. Success is in part dependent upon precise and complex plans. However, once the battle is joined, affairs become chaotic. Many flee; others lose their lives. Disintegration and disorganization, not integration and organization, are the consequences of violent conflict.

All three of these general theories of the emergence of administrative systems posit conflict as an essential ingredient of the development of administrative systems. Centralized administrative systems have been imposed or adopted by all three procedures within the historical era. However, there is no evidence to indicate that the earliest systems of centralized administration were the consequence of either inter-or intragroup conflict. Rather, systems of administration developed when persons voluntarily and cooperatively established a special arrangement to meet special problems confronting their community. Specifically they were created to provide greater security and wealth for the community through the centralized accumulation of material goods.

The earliest centralized administrative systems were not exploitative of the citizens of the community. The hierarchical and exploitative features of centralized administrative system were later developments. The later developments were in part an inherent outgrowth of the system itself and in some cases the consequence of the merger of bureaucratic interests with military interests. Like most other major transformations, the establishment of administrative systems had unintended consequences.

Nearly all students of ancient civilizations implicitly, if not explicitly, regard the formation of administrative systems as a major transformation. All characterize the predynastic Sumerians, the Egyptians of the first dynastic period, the Harappans and the Minoans as civilizations. In contrast, there is considerable uncertainity among students of ancient civilizations that the Britons who constructed Stonehenge and other megaliths were civilized; many are also reluctant to classify Çatal Hüyük as a civilized community. The distinctive difference between the Sumerians and others on the one hand, and the ancient Britons, Çatal Hüyük, and other large trade centers on the other, is that there is evidence of the centralized accumulation of wealth and presence of administrative specialists for the former group, whereas the latter group appears neither to have accumulated communal wealth nor to have had administrators.

Wright and Johnson (1975) develop the theme that state structures originally emerged in Mesopotamia. As they formulate the issue, when the activity of groups of producers is supervised by specialists and the activity of these specialists in turn is supervised by a second group of specialists, a social structure that can be called a state is established. There is merit in their formulation. Further it seems that a stable three-tiered structure with the two top tiers coordinating the activity of others was established in Mesopotamia during the fourth millennium B.C.

As formulated by Wright and Johnson, the implication is that both of the two top tiers of the structure were relieved from manual labor while the bottom tier produced the material wealth of the community. The two top tiers acquired their subsistence by appropriating the fruits of labor of the producers of material goods. However, the evidence does not indicate that both of the two top tiers were relieved from manual labor. Rather what seems to have been the case was that a stable three-tiered structure was established with the top tier consisting of representatives of the community, the second tier consisting of persons charged with keeping accounts of communal wealth, and a third tier consisting of producers, including perhaps traders. During the period of the earliest systems of centralized administration, members of the top tier were not relieved of the necessity of producing their own subsistence; they remained producers. Only the administrators were relieved of manual labor. Later, as the system became more elaborate, there were several tiers of administrators, all of whom were relieved from manual labor.

THE FIRST ADMINISTRATORS

It was with the emergence of the *sanga* as a distinctive category that a stable centralized administration was first established by the Sumerians.

The *sanga* were charged with keeping accounts of the communal wealth. They first appear in the protoliterate texts about 3500 B.C. The title *sanga* is most commonly translated as priest, but some linguistic specialists think the term accountant would be a more accurate translation. Other specialists translate the term as scribe (Biggs, 1974).

Many large-scale communal efforts of various sorts had been undertaken by numerous communities long before the emergence of the *sanga*. The construction of large defensive fortifications and monuments preceded the emergence of the *sanga* by millennia. The construction of these edifices required that the activity of some be supervised and coordinated by others. The construction of observatories and monuments necessarily was supervised by timekeepers or persons closely affiliated with them. The construction of fortifications and perhaps canals may have been supervised by timekeepers, but it is more likely that these efforts were supervised by others.

The distinctive feature of the *sanga* then, was not that they were supervising the activity of others. Rather it was that they were in charge of keeping accounts of communal wealth. That function could not, of course, have been established until after the practice of centrally accumulating communal wealth was established.

The *sanga* first emerged in communities that specialized in growing grain, especially barley. The *sanga* were affiliated with the temples and administered the economic affairs of their communities. They did not have the power of initiation; they acted at the behest of the community. In principle the same relationship between administrators and the community prevails today. Public administrators serve the community; they do not command it.

The critical question is: What was the foundation for their emergence? They emerged in food producing communities that were also active in intercommunity trade. These communities, in addition to being of substantial size, had both a robust solidarity and a cosmopolitan tradition. Their solidarity stemmed from communal activities that rested on their agricultural activities and were linked to their temples. Their cosmopolitan orientation rested upon their linkage with other communities through trade.

The tradition of temple construction preceded the appearance of the *sanga* by almost two millennia. The oldest known sedentary community of lower Mesopotamia, Eridu, dates from about 5300 B.C. It was founded by intruders who brought sophisticated assemblages to the region (Jaward, 1974:23). A temple was constructed on a sandhill shortly after the community was founded. As the community grew, larger temples replaced the earlier and more modest ones. Some of the communities of lower Mesopotamia had constructed gigantic ziggurats prior to the emergence of the *sanga*.

One indication of the robust solidarity associated with the temples is that during the literate period every citizen belonged to a temple, even the slaves. The residents were referred to as the people of the god Nann, or whatever diety prevailed in the temple (Whitehouse, 1977:64). The same relationship among the citizens and between the citizens and the temple probably prevailed during the preliterate period. The attachment of the citizens seems to have been primarily to a temple not to a city.

Not all of the preliterate cities of Mesopotamia were monolithic. Some of them had more than one temple. Khafajah had three by 4000 B.C. and a fourth was added later (Hole, 1974:277). Apparently in some of the cities multiethic groups, each with their own distinctive temple, existed in harmony.

From their beginnings these communities were active in intercommunity trade. Trade was vital during the periods the *sanga* emerged. Some, perhaps most of the trade, was funneled through the temples. In the literate period both private and public economies were operative. The texts of Ur mention the *Karu*, a merchant organization, which consisted of traders who pooled their resources and shared risks and profits (Oppenheim, 1977:91). During the literate period there is an increase in the importance of private trade. If this trend is projected back into the preliterate period, it implies that early intercommunity trade was funneled through the temples and that private trade was a later development.

In any event intercommunity trade was of significance to these communities during the fourth millennium. At least some of the communities of lower Mesopotamia traded with other groups as a community. Trade between individuals or lineages of different communities may or may not have occurred simultaneously. During the period the *sanga* emerged, there was a modification and expansion of intercommunity trade. It is likely that grain, particularly barley, and other products were centrally accumulated at the temples and traded with other groups.

During the same period internal trade was of limited significance. Local markets were largely or entirely absent (Adams, 1966:92). The citizens had little reason to trade with one another. Most were farmers with the same products. On the other hand the region was deficient in wood, metal, and other resources. These were imported. At least some of the communities carried on a brisk trade with pastoralists. During the early centuries the Sumerians offered grain. Later they established elaborate trade networks based on manufactured goods as well as grain.

During the literate period the temples owned land, animals, and im-

plements. The distribution and use of these possessions were administered by the *sanga*. It is conceivable that these settlements were communally
organized from their foundation. It is also conceivable that the first
communal activity other than the activity associated with the construction
and maintenance of the temples and the celebrations linked to them was
the centralized accumulation of goods to more effectively participate in
intercommunity trade.

In either case intercommunity trade that was supervised by persons
affiliated with the temple became important. Collectives were established
that traded with other groups and communities. The *sanga* emerged
from these collectives; they maintained the accounts for the collectivities.
Specialists in record keeping were probably established before the title
appears in the texts. We first know of them in the texts. But it is probable
that individuals who were sophisticated in numeric procedures maintained communal accounts before literacy emerged. Several historical
communities that were not literate, both city-states and nations, had
public bookkeepers. A well-known case is the Inca Empire.

Complex numeric systems had been used millennia before they were
used by the sanga. The distinctive feature of the bookkeepers of Sumer
is that they were keepers of the public record. They were accountants
for the community, not for individuals or families. Consequently they
were accountable not to an individual, but to a collectivity.

THE SANGA AND THE UNKEN

The early *sanga* were not the political elite of their communities. Sovereignty was vested in the *unken*, not the *sanga*. The literal translation
of unken is "a circle of the people." A common translation is "council
of the elders." Like many other communities communal decisions were
vested in a collectivity among the predynastic Sumerians. Many societies,
both ancient and contemporary, have similar institutions. The exact nature of the arrangement varied. Groups as diverse as the Iroquois, herders of Africa, and the Mongols had arrangements wherein
representatives of lineages congregated from time to time to discuss,
negotiate, and resolve issues. The basis for membership in the councils
varied. Among those who routinely raided, the warriors were dominant;
among those who traded extensively, the wealthier merchants were dominant, and among the agriculturalists, the more successful farmers dominated these councils.

The decision-making processes of these communities was collective.
The influence exerted during these meetings was not equal, but most
of the decisions affecting the community were arrived at in public. Not

all participated, but nearly all were often in attendance when the community was confronted with an important issue. Membership in the councils in the more complex groups was rather precisely specified; however, in the simpler groups the criteria for membership on the council were not specified. Among the simpler societies the meetings of the council were not regularly scheduled; rather, meetings were held whenever an important issue confronted the community.

In the protoliterate period the *unken* of Sumer met on an ad hoc basis; whenever a crisis confronted the community a meeting of the *uken* was called. When the communities were small it is likely that nearly all were in attendance, but as the communities grew, then perhaps only the elders of the community met. At the meetings the situation was discussed, negotiated, and a collective decision was hammered out. Meetings were held at the temples—the community center. It is likely that at these meetings the wealthier merchants and the more productive farmers, who may have been one and the same, were more influential than most. Many of the issues confronting the *unken* were economic.

It was the *unken* who authorized the *sanga*; the early *sanga* were accountable to the *unken*. In principle the *sanga*, like contemporary public administrators were apolitical. They were delegates; they did not formulate policy. Their position was not unlike that of accountants employed by a governmental agency. This is indicated by one revealing case. As part of a major economic transaction between two communities the owners of the property are characterized as "men elected by the house of—" and they were hosted at a festival by another community to consummate the exchange (Adams, 1966:84). The *sanga* facilitated the transaction, but it was the elected representatives of the community who validated the exchange.

However, like all persons who occupy a critical position in the accumulation and flow of information the *sanga* had the opportunity to exercise considerable influence on the decision-making process. It is almost a certainty that by the time the title was established that the *sanga* were no longer merely acting on the basis of delegated responsibilities. By that time they were probably exercising considerable influence on the policies of their communities. They were not an aristocracy; no aristocracy was present during the period when the *sanga* were becoming focal points of the social structure of these communities. They were important persons, but they were not given special treatment at burial. At least the graves of the early *sanga* are unknown, or if known, not recognized (Adams, 1966:127).

The *sanga* became increasingly dominant in the following centuries. They allocated seeds, agricultural implements, animals, exercised considerable influence on the intercommunity flow of goods, and supervised the internal distribution of goods. In some communities a highly centralized social structure emerged with the *sanga* occupying the focal positions. Both their emergence and growth was an uneven affair. Some communities had them; others of the same size did not. However, in general the *sanga* emerged as an important category in the larger communities. Uruk became a flourishing center with a complex administrative structure surrounded by smaller towns with only minimal administrative structures (Adams and Nissen, 1972:18). Apparently some of the larger cities served as collection points for the smaller communities. Perhaps the surplus grain of the smaller communities was brought to the larger ones where they were in turn traded for imports from outside the region.

Some of the temples became industrial centers. They imported raw material and produced manufactured goods at the temples. Both the internal and external distribution of the manufactured products were administered by the *sanga*. Craftsmen were employed by the temples. Originally these craftsmen manufactured tools, clothing and other functional items. The manufacturing of military equipment and prestige items does not begin until a millennium later. In at least some of the communities the output of the craftsmen were consigned totally to the temples (Wheatley, 1971:258).

Some of the temples became wealthy. They owned large tracts of land and herds of livestock. One early dynastic text lists 9,660 donkeys belonging to a temple. One is tempted to surmise that these donkeys were beasts of burden used to transport trade goods. If such was the case, the temple was engaged in large-scale trading with other communities.

Most of the larger communities of the predynastic period had a system of central administration. However the accounting procedures and other administrative techniques were not completely uniform. Many cities had their own special mode of computation into the dynastic period. The kings of Ur attempted to impose a uniform nomenclature on their empire after the dynasty become established (Delaporte, 1925:232). Apparently during the predynastic period the relationship between the various towns and cities was a symbiotic one; they were interdependent, but maintained a fair degree of autonomy. The basic idea of centralized accummulation of goods and complex accounting systems became widespread, but each community developed its own specific procedures.

In at least some of the cities of the period the temple complex included a complex administrative apparatus. The *sanga*, who had become ranked, supervised and coordinated complex economic undertakings. They became a distinctive and dominant class. The rank and file citizenry became caught up within an all-encompassing system. They had little alternative but to subordinate themselves to the administrators of their cities or to withdraw from the system. Most preferred to remain with the system, but some migrated to other regions.

It is not certain that the first public administrators were Sumerian, although it appears likely. It is possible that similar developments were underway in other regions. The other early large social structures based upon centralized administration seem to have stemmed from Mesopotamia. The appearance of centralized administration in Egypt, India, and on Crete follows the establishment of new communities in these regions by intrusive populations that brought with them traits that probably originated in Mesopotamia. The administrative procedures of Egypt, India, and Crete were not identical with those of Mesopotamia, but they show definite signs of either stemming from Mesopotamia or their emergence was stimulated by earlier developments in Mesopotamia.

OTHER CENTERS

Once administrative structures had been developed it became easy, comparatively speaking, to introduce the system or at least elements of it into other social systems. But before that could occur the members of the adopting group had to have a social structure that was complex enough to make effective use of administrative apparatus. It is impossible for nomads to adopt a system of centralized administration. Only sedentary communities accumulate sufficient wealth to support a complex administrative system. In later millennia several nomadic groups conquered sedentary groups and employed the administrators of sedentary communities to exact tribute from the conquered. All of the early social structures with central administration were agricultural groups that also traded.

The early diffusion of administrative procedures occurred through several intertwined processes and resulted in several distinct forms. In each case the early diffusion was affiliated with the colonization of new territories by agriculturalists. In the Nile and Indus Valleys and on Crete both trade and agriculture were introduced, followed by the emergence of centralized administrative apparatus. It is possible, but doubtful, that administrative specialists migrated with the colonists who established these new settlements. It is more likely that some of the early settlers of these regions had some administrative skills and that centralized administration emerged subsequent to the establishment of large communities in these regions. The form of the administrative systems and the intertwinings between administrative procedures and other facets of the social structures of these communities varied.

The Egyptians

It is generally accepted that the Nile Valley was unified by conquest. This probably was the case. However, a foundation for the unification was provided by the earlier establishment of a relatively uniform administrative procedure in the larger settlements on the Nile. Similarity of timekeeping did not provide a foundation for the unification of the Nile. Prior to the unification of the Nile the agriculturalists of the lower Nile had a lunar calendar that was linked to stellar phenomena; those of the upper Nile had a lunar calendar linked to solar events. Unification of calendric systems was not achieved in the Nile Valley until after political unity.

There are indications in at least some of the predynastic communities that material goods were centrally accumulated and dispersed. It was once thought that the earliest hieroglyphs which appear on vases were the names of the owners. But it is now thought they specify the contents of vessels (Baumgartel, 1955:61). If these vases were labeled for their contents it suggests that they contained communal resources, not the goods of private merchants.

It is interesting that the original meaning of the term pharaoh was "big house." It was only later that the term pharaoh became attached to the king of Egypt. The "big house" may have been the administrative center of some of the early large agricultural communities on the Nile.

The administrative apparatus of Egypt emerged in close conjunction with the emergence of a warrior elite. In contrast, the administrators of Sumer were established before a military elite had emerged as part of a totalitarian system. During the early dynasties of Egypt the administrative system was in a state of flux. A rather complex administrative apparatus was established before it settled into a definite ranked structure. There were almost 2,000 distinct titles for administrators by the Fourth Dynasty. But it was not until the Fifth Dynasty that the ranking of administrators became standardized. "Under Nefirkare, third king of the Fifth Dynasty, tombs reveal for the first time a standardized bureaucratic system" (Johnson, 1978:57–58).

The Harappan Civilization

The Harappan civilization of the Indus Valley may have been founded by collectivities under the supervision of administrators. There appears to have been considerable differentiation between the elite and the rank and file of the early agricultural communities from their beginnings. The structure of the Harappan cities was keyed to central administration. As in the earlier centrally administered cities of Mesopotamia, intercommunity trade was extensive and supervised by an administrative elite.

The accumulation, dispersion, and exchange of goods was managed by administrators.

The layout of the Harappan cities indicates they were planned cities. They did not grow in the disorganized manner of the earlier trade centers. Apparently the elite designed the cities and supervised their construction and subsequent expansion. The graves of the elite of these communities have not been located. It is possible, if not likely, that the differentiation between the administrative elite of the Harappan civilization and the rank and file did not achieve the level where the elite decorated themselves with luxury items at burial.

The Harappan civilization exhibits great uniformity. The similarity of the communities to each other indicates that a common intellectual source lay behind the planning of these communities. The lack of creativity suggests communities that were bureaucratically organized. These developments may have been the consequence of stimulus-diffusion, but it is more likely that they were the consequence of the migration of collectivities that included administrators or at least some persons skilled in administrative procedures.

It is conceivable, but highly unlikely, that the Harappan civilization was entirely or largely an indigenous development. It may have begun as a series of small settlements of farmers in which a centralized administrative structure may have evolved independently. It is more likely that during the emergence of authoritarian states in Mesopotamia relatively large groups of persons, including some administrators, migrated from the lower Mesopotamia region to the Indus Valley.

The accepted date for the beginning of the Harappan civilization coincides with the emergence of authoritarian city-states in Mesopotamia. It is possible that some administrative elite of these Sumerian communities faced with an authoritarian system coordinated the migration of groups to the Indus Valley to establish new settlements. It is also possible that some of the agricultural settlers of the Indus Valley were from communities that had been defeated in war by other communities. They may have fled to another region to avoid subordination by their conquerors.

The Minoan Civilization

The evolution of civilization of Crete has several parallels with other centrally administered societies, but it also has some very distinctive differences. The earliest forerunners of the Minoans were modest settlements along the coastlines. They appear about 3500 B.C. Several different ethnic communities were established on Crete; not all the communities spoke the same language. The early communities traded.

It is impossible to determine if the early trade was centrally administered. However, given the location of Crete and the necessity of transporting goods long distances, it is likely that almost from the beginning trade was organized by collectivities of persons pooling their resources.

The classical Minoan civilization does not emerge until the middle of the third millennium B.C. When it does, it is a centrally administered economy. It is doubtful that it was a direct spinoff of the Sumerian civilization. But either techniques of record keeping were brought to these communities of Crete by specialists, or the residents of these communities on the basis of their trade contacts learned of the procedures and imported them to Crete.

The procedures have many similarities with those previously established in Mesopotamia. The craftsmen, like their counterparts in Mesopotamia, were attached to the palaces and paid from central stores (Renfrew, 1972:340). The records were similar to those of Mesopotamia. The tablets deal almost without exception with records of receiving goods, disbursments of goods, inventories of livestock, land holdings, and lists of personnel (Renfrew, 1972:296). They reveal a massive redistribution system. Like the Sumerian communities, there were no markets for the internal distribution of goods.

The palaces of the Minoans were analogous to the temples of Mesopotamia. They were not residences of monarchs. At least the rulers occupied a different position within these social structures than did the monarchs of Egypt and later Mesopotamian cities. They did not build gigantic monuments, and they did not have great ceremonial centers (Renfrew, 1972:269). They had calendric systems. They held ceremonies in conjunction with their temples, but they were not the elaborate ceremonies that were associated with some food producing societies. Nor did they leave behind elaborate monuments of calendric significance (Renfrew, 1972:411). The calendar did not dominate their lives.

Their literacy was limited to maintaining accounts at the "palaces." They developed no tradition of heroic writing, or wisdom literature, or astronomical texts. They had a social structure that was keyed to an administrative elite. They were a bureaucratized society without a foundation of solidarity based on communal celebrations tied to celestial phenomena; they did not have a warrior elite. There were no fortifications during the third millennium (Renfrew, 1972:394). Graves containing weapons of war appear in the late Bronze Age, long after the "palace economies" had been established.

The graves of the early communities contain very few artifacts. The practice of placing goods in graves began in the third millennium B.C. Most of the graves of that period contained no artifacts, but a few of them contained several items of luxury goods. Then the placement of goods in graves became common. A high percentage of these later graves contained goods of some sort. The distribution of goods in these graves indicates two very distinct populations. Some graves contain many luxury items; others usually contained only pottery bowls and cups. There were two distinct classes of Minoans. The goods that are distinctive to the elite graves are rather curious. The three items that most clearly differentiate the elite graves from the nonelite are: copper tweezers, copper spatulas, and frying pans. Other items that tend to be limited to elite graves include bone toggles, copper pins, painted pots, obsidian, and cooper needles, (Renfew, 1972:374).

The agricultural production of the earliest Minoan communities was largely limited to cereals—wheat and barley. Later they produced legumes, livestock, olives, wine, and figs (Renfrew, 1972:462). During the same period when the changes occured in the placement of goods in graves the quantity of goods that were centrally stored became less. Smaller amounts of grain were stored. Simultaneously there is an increase in the production and storage of exotic goods such as olives, wines, honey, and figs. When the production of these products became widespread in the third millennium, a system of "palace" distribution was firmly established.

The distinctive grave goods, the centralized economy without local markets, the absence of monumental centers, and the absence of a warrior class indicates a hierarchically organized social structure that was focused on an administrative elite. The administrators of Crete appear to have been more differentiated from the citizenry than were the early administrators of Sumer. They were also probably more self-serving and exploitative than the early administrators of Sumer.

A number of factors could account for the difference. Perhaps one of them was that the Mesopotamian communities had a more robust communal solidarity linked to their monuments. The administrators of Sumer emerged within the context of a centuries-long tradition of communal construction of ziggurats and holding large-scale communal celebrations to note the passage of time. Furthermore each Sumerian community was part of a larger complex surrounded by other communities with similar traditions. The Minoan civilization was a later development and relatively isolated from communities that had large monumental centers.

The Minoans had a calendric system and they held celebrations in conjunction with significant celestial events. However, their monuments did not dominate the community; they were of secondary importance. The so-called palaces, which were probably administrative and storage centers, dominated the community. The relationships between the citizenry and the palaces was largely that of administrators to administered, not one based on simultaneous celebration of significant events. The robustness of the solidarity between the elite and nonelite was probably less for the Minoans than for the Sumerians.

The relatively low level of solidarity between the elite and nonelite of the Minoans allowed the administrators to more easily disassociate themselves from the rank and file. Reciprocally the rank and file did not have sufficient solidarity to collectively call into account their administrators. The greater sophistication of the elite combined with the low level of solidarity allowed the administrators to more easily develop a differentiated and exploitative standpoint toward the rank and file. Consequently a class of administrative elite who were given differential treatment both in life and death emerged.

The rank and file citizens of an island community had fewer alternatives if they became disenchanted with their way of life. Even if they were burdened with heavy taxes they had little alternative but to continue to support the established system or to withdraw to an unsettled region and attempt to seek out an existence as subsistence farmers or as food gatherers. Only those manning the trading vessels and a few others had contact with other regions. The opportunity to migrate was very limited.

As the Minoans became more stratified they entered into a state of decadence (Hutchinson, 1974). It is commonly believed that the Minoan civilization was brought to an end by a gigantic volcanic eruption. The collapse of the Minoan civilization may have been hastened by a natural disaster, but many cities have suffered major disasters and quickly rebuilt. The collapse more likely was a consequence of the decadence of the elite and widespread alienation among the citizenry.

When the natural disaster occurred neither the decadent elite nor the disenchanted rank and file were sufficiently committed to the system to organize themselves to reconstruct their community. Not every resident was disenchanted; some attempted to reestablish the old system. Shortly after the disaster small communities were established in the ruins of the city. These communities were populated by persons with the same culture as the prior residents. They built small shrines that were similar to the earlier shrines, but they were much cruder (Hutchinson, 1974:412).

In summary, the early Minoan civilization that was established prior to the emergence of a warrior class appears to have been a prototype of a bureaucratic society. An administrative apparatus dominated the lives of the Minoans. All were linked together primarily on the basis of a bureaucratic structure. Both the internal and external movement of goods was controlled by administrators. Neither markets nor monumental centers played an important part in the lives of the Minoans.

Mesoamerica

It is difficult to determine when centralized administration first appeared in Mesoamerica. At the time of the conquest of Central America the Aztecs had a complex system of centralized administration. The system of administration of the Aztecs was much older than the Aztecs themselves. A similar condition held for the Inca. Elements of centralized administration may have been established in Mesoamerica when substantial sedentary communities were first established on the eastern coast in the third millennium. These settlements were involved in long-distance trade (Craven, Bullard, and Kamper, 1974) and they may have had a primitive form of centralized administration.

Or, it is possible that the Olmec introduced the first system of centralized administration. They began to construct large monuments about 1500 B.C. and acquired goods from long distances. Their long-distance trade may have been supervised by administrators or may have been controlled by private merchants. The fact that the Olmec monuments were violently destroyed by the Olmec themselves suggests that the citizenry had become severely disenchanted with their elite. The elite may have been timekeepers or administrators or some combination of these two.

It is possible that a centrally administered system was not established in Mesoamerica until after the collapse of the Olmec. Centralized administration may have emerged as the consequence of the fusion of the Olmec agricultural tradition and the emerging Maya trade tradition. In any event it seems that the emergence of centralized administration followed much the same path of development in Mesoamerica as in Mesopotamia. In both cases both trade and crop production were well developed before centralized administrative systems were established.

The centralized administrative systems of Mesoamerica were not direct spinoffs of the Old World systems. Although it is likely that some of the critical elements for the formation of a system of central administration stemmed from the Old World. It is very likely that the early trade communities of Central America were stimulated by Old World contact, and the Olmec probably had an Old World origin. Centralized administration then emerged after the formation of both extensive trade networks and the establishment of large-scale agricultural production. It is possible, but doubtful, that systems of administration of the New World were entirely an indigenous affair.

Summary

It is centain that several ancient civilizations had systems of centralized administration prior to the emergence of totalitarian states. These societies emerged from an infrastructure provided by food production and intercommunity trade. Agricultural production provided a stable and enduring resource that was traded with other groups. Specialists in record keeping were established, who supervised the accummulation of goods and the exchange of these goods with other groups. These specialists were experts in the management of information and the accumulation and dispersion of communal goods. They were programmers of trade for their communities. In the larger and more successful communities these specialists became categorically differentiated. They were relieved from manual labor and derived their subsistance from the contributions of others.

During the early centuries they acted primarily for the benefit of all. Many of these communities prospered due to the expertise of their administrators. However, later generations of administrators became disembedded from the rank and file and exploited their fellow citizens. They were capable of and enticed to manipulate the arrangement to serve their personal benefit. Two critical features of the developing social relationships that invited disembeddness and exploitation were the rather intense accountability directed at the administrators and the monopolies of knowledge associated with the position. These factors in turn elicited the construction of formal norms or the bureaucratization of administrative procedures.

ACCOUNTABILITY AND BUREAUCRATIZATION

The creation of the position of public administrator witnessed the emergence of a new and distinctive type of social arrangement. It vested the occupant of the position with responsibility for maintaining a record of the material resources of the community. The occupants were charged with the effective accumulation, storage, and allocation of communal resources. The resources were those of the community and the administrators were accountable to the community.

The importance of the activities of the administrators was recognized by most members of the community. They were aware that the decisions and activities of the administrators had consequences for all of them. Consequently the citizens were concerned with the competency and honesty of their administrators. It is almost a certainty that during the emergence of the *sanga*, the *unken* carefully assessed the abilities and integrity of potential occupants of the position. Those who had demonstrated an ability for numeric computations and a reputation of honesty were selected. Merit became the primary consideration for the selection of administrators.

According to Max Weber, administrative systems—bureaucracies—provide the most efficient means for the coordination of large-scale human endeavors. Administrative structures place a premium on rationality, regularity, and order. These structures assure that those with the greatest ability are selected to supervise. Merit replaces kinship, age, military prowess, and personal attachments as the criteria for authority. According to Weber the emergence of centralized administration resulted in rational authority replacing charismatic and traditional authority.

Weber was not an uncritical advocate of administrative systems; they were not an unmixed blessing. He saw them as the epitome of rationality, but at the same time recognized that within bureaucratic structures human beings become cogs in a machine. Furthermore, within these systems each person becomes primarily concerned with personal advancement within the structure and only secondarily concerned with the effective performance of his reponsibilities.

Weber's ambivalence toward administrative structures reflects the ambivalence of many members of modern societies. On the one hand most citizens rail against the inhumanity and inefficiency of bureaucrats; on the other hand, when confronted with a recurring problem they commonly advocate that an administrative unit be established to deal with the problem. It is not administrative structures per se that are the target of animosity for most, but the bureaucratization of procedures.

The early administrators were not bureaucrats; they were not encased by a set of formal norms that specified the procedures they and others were to follow. Rather they were assigned objectives and were evaluated largely on the basis of their success in the accomplishment of the objectives. The bureaucratization of procedures was a subsequent development that was an unintended consequence of centralized administration.

The focal position of administrators in conjunction with the high visibility and importance of their activity rendered them intensely accountable to the larger community. The intense accountability of public administrators encourages them to take steps that lessen their accountability to the community. It is this, more than any other factor, that leads to the development of bureaucratic procedures. Procedures were formalized to protect the administrators from calls for account. Once bureaucratic procedures were formalized, then the occupant of an administrative position could avoid some of the accountability associated with the position by rigidly adhering to procedures.

Accountability is a potential facet of all instances of coordinated activity (Weiland, 1975). Each time human beings cooperate to achieve a social objective they render themselves potentially accountable to one another. Whenever persons coordinate their activities to achieve an objective, if the objective is not obtained due to incompetence of one of them, that person is accountable to the other. All members of a hunting expedition are accountable to all others. If one makes a mistake and frightens the game away, he is likely to be the focal point of rather intense accountability. If the "incompetent one" indicates that he did not intend to frighten the game—that his act was an accident—and if his explanation is accepted, then the acting unit is "reconstituted." Of course, if a person continues to demonstrate incompetence, in due time he may be systematically avoided and in extreme cases rejected from the group.

Accountability within social units where members act in a solidary manner to achieve objectives is typically of limited duration. Furthermore, each member of solidary units recognizes that he is potentially accountable to others. Consequently the accountability between members of undifferentiated groups typically is muted by the mutual recognition that anyone can make a mistake and may be called into account.

In contrast, when there is the allocation of sustained differential responsibilities, such as one being charged with the task of collecting and storing the valuables of others, then differential responsibility and accountability are stablized. Any division of labor, even a temporary one, creates differential accountability. For example, when a group of hunters negotiate a division of labor with one segment agreeing to lie in wait while the other segment spooks the game toward the first group, each segment is differentially accountable to the other. In this and similar situations the differential accountability is short-range and framed by an immediate objective.

Sustained differential accountability was established long before the emergence of public administrators. However, the emergence of public administrators created an enduring and highly differentiated relationship that was linked to the material resources of the community. Those two features combined to intensify the accountability of the administrators. The administrators were the focal points of networks of accountability. Not only were they the targets of calls for accounts, but they were also the focal points of calls for accounts issued to other members of the community. As with all large groups, some members of these communities were less diligent than others in providing their share of produce for the central stores. Consequently norms were formulated that required all to provide their share of goods for the well-being of all. It became the task of the administrators to enforce the norms that were probably originally formulated by the community. The rank and file members of the community thereby became accountable to the administrators. The administrators thereby were both the focal points of calls for accounts stemming from the community and for issuing calls of accounts to other members of the community.

In general those communities that established an effective system of centralized administration were more successful than others. They obtained a more secure, if somewhat less exciting, life. Those systems that endured and expanded, created large social units whose social cohesion rested primarily on a foundation of differential accountability. In some cities there was a proliferation of titles within a few generations after the first appearance of the *sanga*. These communities transformed from loosely structured trade and agricultural centers into a tightly administered system.

Large populations found themselves linked together in a complex set of accountable relationships that they did not fully comprehend. As the systems enlarged they also underwent a transformation from loosely administered systems into highly bureaucratized systems. All, both the administrators and the citizenry, found themselves encased within a complex system of formal norms. Many of the consequences were neither intended nor desired.

Four of the more profound dimensions of the transformation were (a) the lessening of accountability of the administrators to the community, [b] the intensification of accountability of the rank and file to the administrators (c) the diminution of solidarity between the administrators and others, and (d) the formulation of an ideology that justified special treatment for the administrators. In the more extreme cases the administrators came to have little in common with the rank and file; bureaucratic procedures replaced solidary relationships as the primary base for social unity.

The monopoly of knowledge of the administrators during the formative period was far less than that of the timekeepers. All were aware when the harvest had been good. That information was difficult to obscure. But complex administrative procedures evolved that operated to keep the rank and file relatively uninformed. Bureaucratic regulations were developed that specified procedures to be followed. The administrators deliberately mystified the rank and file about the inner workings of the system. The administrators thereby became less accountable to the community.

Simultaneously the administrators separated themselves from those they administered. Shortly after the establishment of administrative systems in Mesopotamia, the living quarters of the *sanga* became attached to the temples; they were set aside from the larger community (Adams, 1966:135). They thereby were less visible and vulnerable to the community.

The first administrative units were created by the community; at least the community as expressed by the *unken*. Members of the community voluntarily related themselves to the administrators. They brought their produce to the central location to be managed by the administrators. It became the primary responsibility of the administrators to make certain that each citizen had contributed his fair share. The rank and file members of the community thereby became accountable to the administrators. The administrators, like most human beings, were more diligent in issuing calls for account to others than in rendering themselves accountable to others. They stressed the accountability of citizens to them and minimized their accountability to the community. The long-run impact was the bureaucratization of the relationship between the administrators and the citizenry; the citizens found themselves subordinated to the demands of their administrators.

Any division of labor tends to lessen the solidarity of a social unit. When a division of labor entails intense accountability, the undermining of solidarity is often extreme. Community members who produced barley and brought it to the central stores had an entirely different standpoint toward it than did those who administered the stores. The differentiation of activities inherent in such systems produced entirely different standpoints from the rank and file than it did from the administrators. The two sets of persons often had little in common.

As the successful communities grew they expanded their economic undertakings. One of the more significant developments was that the temples became industrial centers as well as centers of storage. The temples accumulated goods; citizens were hired to manufacture products from the raw material. They were paid in units of barley. Citizens had an alternative source of subsistence; the life of each became slightly more secure.

However, this development also had the consequence of intensifying the accountability of the rank and file to the administrators. In principle those employed at the temple worked for the community. But in practice they were employed by the administrators. They retained or lost their position as employees at the pleasure of their supervisors.

The employer-employee relationship is a distinctive form of bilateral accountability. The employer is obliged to provide items of value in exchange for the employee subordinating himself to the directives of the employer. The employer-employee relationship was established before centralized administration. But the employer-employee relationship within a context of an urban center dominated by a market is quite different from the same relationship within a community that is dominated by a centralized administration. In the former the employee is more likely to have alternative sources of employment. If he finds the directives too abrasive he may break off the relationship. Within a centralized economy the employee has only the alternatives of accepting the conditions specified by the administrators or leaving the community. The employee thereby becomes intensely accountable to the employer, both on and off the job. When a citizen was both an employee of administrators and accountable for supplying goods to the central stores, he was highly differentiated from them.

The timekeepers were also clearly differentiated from the rank and file of the large agricultural communities. However, there was a fundamental difference. Each time a celebration was held, both the time-keepers and the rank and file established shared foci and were solidarily responsive to events. Within centrally administered communities all were solidarily responsive to an excellent yield. In addition, within these same communities communal celebrations continued. These and other activities continued to provide a solidary foundation. Nonetheless, the overriding feature of the division of labor between administrators and others was their differentiation. Consequently as administrative systems became more elaborate the communal solidarity of the community lessened. Social unity was maintained more on the basis of obligations and less on the basis of mutual embeddedness.

In at least some of the totalitarian states of the historical eras the administrators developed a complex ideology justifying special treatment for themselves. This may not have occurred in the Sumerian communities of the predynastic period. However, in Egypt, China, and later Mesopotamian nations an ideology of class was formulated. This was expressed most forcefully in a well-known Chinese statement: "Great men have their proper business, and little men have their proper business. Some labor with their minds, and some labor with their strength. Those who labor with their minds govern others; those who labor with their strength are governed by others. Those who are governed by others support them; those who govern others are supported by them" (Balazs, 1967:62).

At least some of the administrators became political. They saw their interest at variance with the interests of others. They developed rationalizations justifying their special interests. They were the ones with access to the critical information and were specialists in manipulating words. They had a tremendous advantage over others in the ideological conflict. They sought and justified self-advancement at the cost of the nonadministrative members of the society. In addition, internal struggles for power and influence within the large systems became prevasive. Each unit attempted to expand at the cost of other units; and often at the cost of the tax-paying citizens.

The administrators of some of these societies became highly exploitative. They manipulated information and the dispersion of goods to their advantage. Extremely exploitative relationships do not appear to have been established until the emergence of totalitarian states. An exception may have been the Minoans. The differentiation between the administrators and rank and file seems to have been rather extreme among the Minoans in comparison to that of the Sumerian and Harappan civilizations. The administrative system of Egypt does not appear to have been highly exploitative until the the Fifth Dynasty.

It was with the merging of military and administrative interest that a highly exploitative system was established in Egypt and Mesopotamia. One of the critical facets of the development was the transformation of the nature of accountability. With the establishment of totalitarian states, the administrators became primarily accountable to the military elite. Then they became primarily concerned with pleasing the military and relatively indifferent to others. This development also enticed each administrator to become largely concerned with achieving a higher rank with the system. Each became primarily concerned with becoming a bigger cog in the machine and disinterested in the welfare of his subordinates.

The expansion and endurance of these systems was restricted by the ability of the administrators to provide viable services; their relationship with the larger community was not solely that of exploiters although in some cases that seems to have been their primary orientation. They organized transport and exchange, supervised the construction of roads, canals, dikes, and dams, and they built up reserves against famine. They simultaneously served and exploited their communities. In general the early administrators served their communities; as the systems grew and became bureaucratized the exploitation of the community overshadowed the services rendered.

SUMMARY

Before centrally administered structures could develop, a number of rather complex social relationships had to be present. Each community had to have at least a small number of persons who were numerically sophisticated and capable of long-range planning. Communal solidarity of considerable intensity that incorporated enough productive persons to provide a surplus sufficient for maintaining intercommunity trade and to support "nonproductive" specialists had to be established. Then the residents of these communities had to believe that by establishing nonproductive specialists to manage their material resources the welfare of all would be enhanced. Then, and only then, administrative specialists could be established who would endure.

The first centralized administrative systems were not imposed by violence. Rather they emerged from a base of communal solidarity in conjunction with concerns of intercommunity exchange. The presence of communal solidarity was not sufficient for the emergence of administrative specialists, at least not specialists who were continuously involved in the coordination of the communities activites. The timekeepers or their associates supervised the building of observatories and monuments, but they were not administrative specialists.

There are no indications that the earliest administrative systems were established by a small segment of the population to exploit the bulk of the population. Rather the earliest systems of central administration were established to enhance the benefit of all members of the community. However, as a consequence of some features of such systems they became bureaucratized. The bureaucratization was in large part a reaction to the intense accountability associated with the position of administrator. One of the long-range consequences of the bureaucratization of the system was the emergence of two distinct classes—the administrators and the administered. Some systems exploited the subordinates. It is certain when an administrative system was combined with a monarchy it became highly exploitative.

The emergence of totalitarian systems was dependent upon the prior establishment of centralized administration. When the centralized administrations merged with monarchies, the administrative offices tended to be inheritable. In Egypt and China, with the emergence of monarchies, many of the offices became inheritable. The inheritability of office in conjunction with the bureaucratization of the system created an arrangement wherein administrators were only minimally accountable to the community. These administrators were exceedingly corrupt and exploitative.

Weber claimed that the development of bureaucratic procedures was a part of a general evolutionary trend toward greater rationality and order, and away from mystification and disorder. He conceived the transformation as one from charismatic authority to bureaucratic authority. One presumption underlying Weber's analysis is that order is best achieved through hierarchy; that egalitarian relationships are necessarily disorderly. That assumption does not hold up under close scrutiny.

He further presumed that the establishment of formal criteria represented a movement from mysticism toward rationality. He failed to recognize that all rationality stems from a specific standpoint. Furthermore, that the administrators are the prime formulators of the formal criteria for the system. The criteria they formulate represent not the standpoint of the community in totality, but the standpoint of the administrators. Consequently, the elaboration and formalization of criteria is more often than not a movement toward mystification, not away from it.

The alternative to bureaucratic authority is not charisma as suggested by Weber, but a negotiated order. A negotiated order is constructed by persons offering alternatives and evaluating each other's alternatives. Each acknowledges the standpoint of the other as valid and treats the other as an equal. The resolution of issues and differences is a mutual construction. The program is jointly formulated and understood by all. In contrast, within administrative structures there are differences in access to information; then the one with the greater information can mystify the less informed.

Both legislative and administrative units are concerned with structuring the future. But the negotiated world of legislative bodies facilitates open awareness; the programmed world of administrative units entices administrators to release as little information as possible. Negotiations inherently call for the public disclosure of all relevant information. Negotiators must make public all the relevant information; if they do not, other members of the negotiating unit can declare invalid any commitments made.

It was the highly bureaucratized societies that were the most exploitative. Neither the Egyptians nor the Chinese had an effective legislative body. Both the administrative and political elite of these societies became highly corrupt and exploitive. They employed both ideology and coercion to subordinate the bulk of the population while deriving great personal benefit at cost to the rank and file.

The alternative to bureaucratic authority is not charisma, but a negotiated order constructed by the community at large or through representatives of the community. Legislative bodies partially control the corruption inherent to administrative hierarchies. The displacement of hierarchy through charismatic movements usually results in the replacement of one corrupt system with another almost identical system.

Chapter XVI

Conflict and Conquest

Conflict is exciting. We react more intensely to and talk more about conflictual encounters than about cooperative efforts. Legends, histories, and the news are filled with accounts of conflicts and conquests. The attention given violence has enticed some to conclude that conflict is the predominant form of social activity. Some social scientists have theorized that complex social structures rest on a foundation provided by conflict and conquest (Webb, 1975). Such is not the case. Social change often occurred as the consequence of conflict, but more often than not the change was devolution, not the emergence of more complex structures.

Complex social structures have often been imposed on others through conquest, and elements of conflict have often been a part of the processes that resulted in the elaboration of extant social structures. But in no case was conflict the foundation for more complex forms of sociation and more extended temporal structures.

Nonetheless conflict has long been and remains a prevalent form of social activity. Some of the skulls of Peking Man, which are between a half a million and a million years old, were severed from the torso and smashed. Other archaeological evidence indicates that deadly conflict has a very ancient past and was a common activity within a wide variety of societies. The myths and histories of many societies are filled with accounts that glorify violence. And, of course, modern nations have waged wars that killed and mutilated millions.

Despite the prevasiveness of conflict, the continuation of the species has not rested on conflict. Human existence is dependent on cooperation, not conflict. Conflict is destructive and chaotic. Cooperation is constructive and structured. It has been the elaboration of cooperative activities, not the elaboration of conflictual activities, that led to more complex social structures. Elements of conflict have been viable facets of some of the social changes that have resulted in the emergence of more complex

255

structures within a society. However, in these instances the conflictual elements have been subordinated to over-arching cooperative endeavors.

Many times groups with relatively simple structures but superior weaponry have attacked and scattered or destroyed groups with more complex structures. The survival of sedentary communities was often dependent upon the development of effective defensive procedures. In these instances conflict has stimulated the elaboration of social structures, but conflict per se was not the foundation upon which the more complex structures rested.

Many of the earliest sedentary communities were attacked and destroyed, some of them several times. Throughout millennia, beginning with the establishment of sedentary communities, through the emergence of large trading and agricultural communities, the more civilized were often the targets of violence from the less civilized. Many of the earliest sedentary communities were destroyed by violence, but none were founded by violence. Once sedentary communities were established, some of them appear to have expanded through a merger of sedentary communities and nomadic pastoralists.

However, there is no evidence that the earliest trade centers and agricultural societies were established by one group conquering another. Some of them were transformed through a peaceful group merging with a relatively violent group. Some of these societies subsequently extended their influence and territory by conquest. The extension of their influence through conquest was accomplished by organizing their violent activities to achieve distal objectives; violence was subordinated to centralized planning.

Nomadic food gatherers had neither the resources for violence nor the ability to project the complex futures necessary for the subjugation and control of other groups. Others could only be subjugated and controlled after violence had been structured by the centralized coordination of actions. The complex forms of sociation and temporal structures necessary for that activity first emerged in sedentary communities.

The emergence of a policy of conquest required the merger of the ability to do violence and the ability to project distal futures. Within the historical period this merger was sometimes accomplished by one group with superior military ability attacking and subjugating another with the ability to program complex and distal futures. Then if some of the members of the conquered groups saw fit to serve their conquerers as programmers, a merger of violence and centralized planning was achieved. One of the more famous and well-documented instances of this merger is the conquest of China by the Mongols. Chinese administrators merged with the conquering Mongols to found a new dynasty.

This merger on a smaller scale probably occurred prior to the historical period. It is conceivable that when a condition prevailed wherein nomadic herders had sustained contact with a sedentary community and the sedentary community was subjected to sporadic attacks from the nomadic herders this merger may have occurred. However, that merger could only have occurred after sedentary communities were established that were at least in part centrally administrated. Therefore, it probably did not occur until after agricultural communities were established; it is doubtful that it occurred by nomadic herders attacking communities that were primarily trade centers.

The raiding and looting of sedentary communities by nomadic groups preceded conquest by millennia. Raiding and looting are a much simpler form of activity than conquest. Raiding and looting are organized on the basis of a projected future of some complexity, but of far less complexity than the projected future required for conquest. Conquest, as opposed to raiding and looting, probably was first undertaken by sedentary communities, not nomadic groups.

THE ELEMENTS AND STRUCTURE OF CONFLICT

Conflict is a relatively simple form of activity. Other animals are capable of conflict. The only elements of sociation necessary for the production of conflictual encounters are reciprocal attentiveness, reciprocal responsiveness, and the projection of individual futures of each doing violence to the other. The production of conflict does not require the presence of either a shared focus or a social objective. The intensity of conflict ranges from two persons exchanging insults to attempts to kill each other; its extensiveness ranges from fights between two individuals to international wars.

The primary focus of each combatant is on the other. There is no shared focus in simple and intense conflictual encounters. Sometimes a shared focus is present at the beginning, but as the conflict is joined the shared focus disappears. For example, two children may have a toy as a shared focus, but contest for control of the toy. Once they become combatants often the shared focus is forgotten.

There is no shared future in pure conflict. Each combatant projects a future of doing violence to the other. They thereby project similar but incompatible futures. Each attempts to render the other less capable of action or to drive the other from the scene. They do not act in unison to achieve a social objective. They act upon each other to acquire their personal objectives. Each acts to adversely impinge upon the other. Each party organizes himself to inflict pain or damage on the other.

In some discussions of conflict, force and violence are equated. Force is the transfer of energy. It may or may not be violent. Force becomes violence when it adversely impinges on another. Furthermore, violence does not always lead to conflict. Human beings almost routinely violate each other. Most violations are minor and unintentional. When the infringement is minor and unintentional and one becomes aware that he has adversely impinged upon another, an apology is often offered. If not offered it may be called for. If an apology is offered and honored, that is usually the end of the affair. Sometimes an apology is not offered, or if offered not honored. Then conflict, avoidance, or flight is likely. None of these responses provides the foundation for the establishment of a stable relationship.

Whether an act is violence or not is sometimes established retrospectively. When one person playfully punches a friend with the intention of reaffirming the relationship, the recipient may regard the act as an infringement. Then the meaning of the act may be established post hoc. Most acts of violence are not ambiguous. Both the target and the initiator are usually in agreement that an act was violent.

In a similar matter the intentionality of an act is sometimes established post hoc. Although again both the recipient and the perpetrator of the act are usually in agreement on the intentionality of the act. When one group ambushes another and rains arrows on them, there is no doubt on the part of either party on the violence of the act. However, occasionally the offending party may plead that the arrows were not intended for those who received them.

Not all acts of violence lead to conflict. If the recipient of a violent act accepts the account that the act was not intended, then conflict may not ensue. On other occasions the target of the act may flee the scene. However, recipients of violence who judge themselves as equally or more capable of doing violence than the perpetrator typically respond in kind if the assessment is made that the violence act was intended.

Conflict is basically an egalitarian form of social activity. When two parties join in conflict, for the moment at least, each assesses the situation as one wherein he can do as much or more damage to the other than he will receive. When the unarmed slave attacks his armed master he makes a declaration of equality. From the standpoint of a third party, the declaration may appear foolhardy, but nonetheless the slave is declaring himself equal.

When human beings are the targets of violent acts, if they cannot flee, even if they are less powerful than the other, they often respond with reciprocating violence. The weak often respond in kind when cornered. Only those who have been repeatedly subjected to more intense violence after responding in kind learn to control their responses. Slaves must be repeatedly reminded that if they commit a violent act toward their masters it will elicit even more extreme acts of violence before they learn to control themselves. Then if the opportunity for flight is present they usually take it.

Conflict may be encased within a cooperative context. The conflict between professional prize fighters is constrained by all agreeing to abide by certain constraints and the presence of a third party to enforce the constraints. However, when conflict emerges without the presence of a third party it tends to escalate. In the early stages each party may organize itself largely on the basis of a distal future of conquering the other, but success is partially dependent upon being highly attentive and responsive to the other in the immediate present. If there is considerable difference in the ability of the combatants to do damage to each other, then the more powerful may organize his activities on the basis of a distal future. But when conflict is between parties with relatively equal ability to do damage to one another, then the party that is most attentive and responsive to the immediate situation has the greater likelihood of success.

INTERNAL CONFLICT

Violations of another commonly occur between individuals who are members of the same group. Members of families, work groups, and communities frequently, both unintentionally and intentionally, infringe upon one another. These infringements sometimes lead to conflict. Nearly all groups have procedures for settling internal disputes short of physical violence. None have developed a completely effective set of procedures for preventing and controlling internal violence. Families, lineages, small sedentary communities, and nations have often fragmented as the consequence of internal conflict.

There is great variation from group to group and society to society on the level of concern with internal conflict and the complexity of their procedures for controlling it. Some groups tolerate considerable internal conflict while others react with abhorrence to any internal conflict. Some have simple procedures for resolving disputes; others complex ones. The emergence of societies with large populations was contingent upon the development of procedures for the resolution of internal conflict short of physical violence. Those that did not fragmented.

Procedures for the control of internal conflict usually take the form of other members of the unit acting as a collectivity toward the potential combatants or representatives of the community acting in behalf of the community to restrain the intensity of the conflict. Many societies banished persons deemed responsible for internal conflict.

Most societies are more concerned with restraining the conflict between equals than the violence of a powerful person on a weaker one. When violent conflict erupts between parties with relatively equal ability to do violence to each other, it is more likely to infringe upon others than when a powerful person directs violence toward a weak person. Consequently nearly all societies, even the simplest, have procedures constraining conflict when the combatants are equal, but some do not have procedures for restraining the violence of the powerful on the weak.

Among some groups of Australian Aborigines there were no procedures to control the violence of adult males directed to females or the violence of adults toward children. However, when conflict broke out between two adult males or two adult females, then an effort to contain the conflict was usually made. When it broke out between two adult males, other males gathered around and separated them. Then each was armed with a spear. They were supposed to aim the spears below each other's waist. They did not always adhere to the rules of the game, and it seems likely that sometimes their aim was poor. In a similar manner, when two women began to fight they were separated and each was armed with a club. Then they took turns pounding each other on the head. In the cases of both the males and females, when one of the combatants fell, all, including the victor, administered first aid to the loser (Bates, 1967).

Some hunters and gatherers had no standardized procedures for controlling internal violence; individuals with a reputation of violence were simply avoided. Among some Eskimo groups, if a person came to be regarded as dangerously violent then someone might assume the responsibility for killing him. At least some of the time the person assuming the responsibility consulted with others before acting. If his actions were supported by most other members of the group the killing of the violent person did not touch off an internal feud.

Internal conflict frequently lead to the fragmentation of societies. Food gathering groups and simple agricultural groups routinely fragmented with each fragment of the original group becoming a distinct and autonomous group. Fragmentation often led to the spread of a cultural tradition over a larger territory, but not to the establishment of more complex social structures.

PRIMITIVE WAR

All or nearly all societies attempted to constrain internal conflict. However, a different state of affairs held for external conflict. Some societies actively avoided outsiders, others approached strangers with caution and peacefully but in many societies violence toward outsiders was routine. Some attacked and raided their neighbors whenever the opportunity arose.

How extensive warfare was among ancient food gatherers is difficult to assess. Most contemporary food gatherers live in marginal regions. The prototype is the Eskimo. The Eskimos were occasionally attacked by Indians and they fought to defend themselves, but they did not go to war. Violent conflict between individuals occurred, but groups of Eskimos did not attack either other Eskimos or non-Eskimo groups. Most contemporary food gathering groups do not have any established procedures for initiating intergroup conflict. However, most of these groups have been pushed to edges of habitable areas by more powerful groups. In the process they have learned that conflict with their more powerful neighbors was very likely to have disastrous consequences. Only those who have learned to avoid intergroup conflict have survived.

Perhaps the accounts of intergroup conflict among the Australian Aborigines provide a fairly accurate depiction of "war" between food gatherers prior to the emergence of sedentary communities. Before the Australian Aborigines were eradicated or controlled by western Europeans, conflictual intergroup encounters apparently occurred with some frequency. Most of the battles stemmed from some infringement by one group, real or imagined, that generated resentment within another group. They did not attack each other for plunder or to subjugate the other group. They warred for revenge. The causes of these conflicts were the same sort of events that touch off feuds between families.

The "wars" consisted of two groups confronting each other and hurling insults and projectiles at each other. The battles were not between "warriors," rather all members of each band took part. Of course, it was the hunters who were equipped with the projectiles who did the most damage. But others also hurled projectiles and shouted insults. More often than not it was a person who was not agile enough to duck the projectiles who was wounded or killed. Usually a serious injury or death on one side brought the conflict to a halt as both sides retreated from the arena to assess the significance of the wound or death.

These battles had many parallels with the "nothing fights" of the Maring (Vayda, 1976). The Maring made a distinction between the nothing fights and true fights. Nothing fights were limited to conflicts wherein the two parties confronted each other in an open area and hurled insults and projectiles at each other. During these conflicts "warriors darted out from behind the shields to shoot their arrows then darted back. Some men also emerged temporarily from cover in order to taunt their foes and to display their bravery" (Vayda, 1976:15).

During the nothing fights many other activities in addition to the hurling of projectiles and insults occurred. Each side made assessments of its relative ability to wreak havoc on the other. The contesting parties were within shouting range of each other. Consequently sometimes they "negotiated" a resolution of their dispute short of war. Simultaneously within each group some called for the escalation of the encounter to a true fight while others argued against escalation.   Sometimes both sides agreed to a true fight. Then a couple of days were taken to prepare for it. When the two sides reentered the arena the combatants brought their axes and jabbing spears as well as their bows and arrows. They armed themselves for killing, not taunting. The true fights came to an end with one side fleeing. The losers were chased and killed, the women and children were slaughtered. The villages of the losers were taken over by the victors and the huts and fields burned. Sometimes enough losers survived to reestablish a community at another location.

The nothing fights of the Maring and the skirmishes between bands of Australian Aborigines took a similar form. Deadly violence was part of these encounters, but the encounters also allowed the combatants to bring the encounters to an end short of deadly violence. The weaker party usually had the opportunity to leave the scene if they decided that they were incapable of withstanding the onslaught of the opposition.

The internal structure of these undertakings rested almost entirely on a foundation of band solidarity. Of course, there was some internal differentiation within each group, but it was largely restricted to the more powerful, daring, and better-armed individuals taking a more active part in the confrontations. There was no categorical differentiation. Each member of each side of the conflict acted in a similar manner toward the enemy. The actions stemmed from a foundation of band solidarity and if successful, enhance the solidarity of the band. The defeated were sometimes scattered. The solidarity of the defeated was attenuated.

The objective of the conbatants in these primitive wars was neither plunder nor conquest; revenge was the primary objective (Vayda, 1975). When the conflicts ended with one party fleeing from the arena, any possessions left behind were appropriated as a matter of course. And sometimes the victorious acquired access to new territories as well. The acquisition of plunder and access to territory that sometimes resulted from successful primitive wars provided the seeds for the growth of the idea that wars could be undertaken to acquire wealth as well as revenge.

RAIDING AND LOOTING

When warfare was limited to conflicts between nomadic groups, concern with the acquisition of plunder was of secondary importance. Undoubtedly some combatants were interested in acquiring goods from the enemy. But it was after the emergence of sedentary communities that a concern with plunder came to the fore. A viable tradition of raiding and looting was first established among nomads who had sustained contact with sedentary communities. The earliest raids of sedentary communities were probably motivated by a combination of revenge and a dire need for the necessities of life.

It is certain that traditions of raiding and looting did not begin by residents of sedentary communities attacking nomadic groups. The poverty of the nomads did not make such efforts worthwhile. Furthermore, the location of sedentary communities was known by the nomads, whereas the location of the nomads was often difficult to ascertain.

Conflict between sedentary communities and nomadic groups led to a transformation of the nature of intergroup warfare. Two of the more important changes were: (a) the development of defensive procedures and (b) shock weapons supplementing and replacing projectiles as instruments of war. Intergroup conflicts became more deadly.

Conflict between two nomadic groups consisted of skirmishes between two mobile groups. When one side began to get the worst of the encounter, they withdrew from the encounter. When the conflict was between a sedentary group and a nomadic group, the sedentary group was less willing and less able to withdraw from the conflict. They had their homes and possessions to defend and often they were surrounded by their attackers making flight more difficult. Nomadic groups retained the option of withdrawing.

The nomadic group was the offensive unit; they were the initiators of violence. The sedentary groups responded to the initiations of the attackers. This difference created an entirely different social context for the defenders and the offenders. Attacks elicited glorification of self among the attackers; successful raids validated self-importance. In contrast, defensive violence occurred within a context that invited the lodging of self as part of the community one defended. In the preparation for defense the primary orientation among defenders was not toward what each would do to achieve glory, but what was necessary for communal survival.

The search for personal glory became important among raiders. The same orientation was present among defenders, but to a lesser extent. A concern with personal prestige among defenders is not conducive to effective defense, while an interest in personal prestige enhances the likelihood of success by the raiders.

While the example is from a much later time, a prototype of this difference in orientation between offenders and defenders is the war between the Greeks and the Trojans. In the account provided by the

Greeks "Hector says he fights for his fatherland. How unlike the heroic ideals of Achilles who fights (or does not) only as the cause is an extension of himself. Hector is the defender of the civilized world, a truly noble man; that he falls in its name is tragic, the way of an unstable world" (Stover and Kraig, 1978:154–155).

The extraction of goods by violence and the search for personal glory became institutionalized in some societies. Obviously not all societies could acquire the necessities of life in this manner; some had to be victims. Yet, warfare became an important means for the acquisition of goods for some societies. Later both centers of trade and agricultural communities raided and looted each other as well as suffered the raids of nomadic groups.

The titles "sacker of cities," "slayer of men," and "warrior" were passionately sought by members of some societies. These groups no longer skirmished, but initiated conflict to wreak havoc and loot the opposition. Techniques of killing were refined. In the skirmishes between nomads the weapons of the hunt were the weapons of the battle. Tools of war emerged from the clashes between raiders and defenders.

Weapons designed to kill other human beings supplemented and replaced the weapons of the hunt. War axes, clubs, and tomahawks were used in hand-to-hand combat. When the conflicts were limited to nomadic groups hurling projectiles at each other, relatively little damage was done. With the establishment of sedentary communities and the invention of axes and clubs, the losers were slaughtered. Use of hand-to-hand weapons probably developed first among the defenders of sedentary communities but they became the weapons of all as communities raided communities.

The emergence of raiding and looting was accompanied by greater internal differentiation. The adult males came to occupy a more central position in the social structures of those societies that raided and looted. Furthermore, the activities provided the foundation for the emergence of intense solidarity among the males. They acted in unison in a highly exciting and significant activity, whereas the females were largely spectators. Intense bondedness among the males was generated. The intense solidary bondedness among the males in turn provided a foundation for them to become dominant within their societies; females were relegated to a secondary position in the internal structure of these societies.

Concomitantly with the emergence of male dominance among raiders was the emergence of greater differentiation among the males. Those who demonstrated their prowess in combat occupied focal positions in societies that regularly attacked and looted others. "War heroes" emerged as the elite of these societies. Aristocracies were established based on the ability to wreak havoc on others.

Many societies specialized in raiding and looting. Some of them endured for centuries; others emerged and faded from the scene in a generation or two. No known civilization emerged from a nomadic society that was heavily dependent on raiding for the necessities of life. Some acquired considerable size and wreaked widespread havoc, but most of the nomadic groups that derived a considerable part of their wealth though raiding remained rather small. The few that contained large numbers seem to have survived for only a generation or two. Attila the Hun and his followers laid waste to vast territories and scattered hundreds of communities, but no enduring complex social structure was established by the Huns. In a few other instances large nomadic groups of raiders attacked and conquered large sedentary communities and established new dynasties. However, that development seems to have been contingent upon the prior establishment of a hierarchical bureaucratic structure among the conquered.

Civilizations did emerge from a few sedentary societies that had a tradition of raiding. But in these instances raiding was gradually replaced by trade. Two of the better-known examples of this transformation are the preclassical Greeks and the Vikings. Both the early Greeks and the Vikings raided and looted their neighbors on a grand scale. However, the emergence of these societies as civilized societies occurred as trade slowly replaced raids as the common form of intergroup contact. Raiding is too chaotic and undisciplined to provide the foundation for complex social structures. The relation between raiders and their victims is that of a predator and prey; it is fragile and usually short-lived.

Not only were the relations between attacker and victim chaotic, but the internal relations of societies that routinely raided were also rife with violence and chaos. The warriors who acquired their position on the basis of their ability to do violence to outsiders also used violence on their fellow citizens to maintain their special position. Aristocratic warriors frequently used violence to dominate their fellow citizens.

TRIBUTE-TAKERS

Neither conflictual nor predator-prey encounters provide the foundation for a stable relation between individuals or groups. Before violence can be a significant dimension of sustained relations between individuals or groups the conflictual or predator-prey relation must be transformed into an enduring asymmetric relation that is based on coercion. Coercion is violence organized to subjugate another to establish a tyrannic relation. A tyrannic relation is established when both parties acknowledge that one has greater ability to do violence than the other, the more powerful party informs the weaker that violence will be withheld providing the weaker party acts as instructed, and compliance is elicited from the weaker party.

A simple tyrannic relation is established when an adult informs a child that if the child does not stop pounding his drum he will be beaten, and the child accepts the specified parameters. A viable threat of violence is a necessary party of a tyrannic relation (Miller, Weiland, and Couch, 1978). But, if the target of the threat fails to acknowledge the viability of the threat, even if the target is subsequently killed, a tyrannic relation has not been established.

The party interested in initiating a tyrannic relation does not attack victims to destroy them. Rather violence is either initiated or threatened and contextualized by the would-be tyrant indicating that violence will be witheld if the victim complies with the directives of the tyrant. Tyrannic relations may be established between individuals or collectivities. The nation that threatens another nation with pillage and plunder unless tribute is forthcoming is attempting to initiate a tyrannic relation. The master-slave relation is the prototype to tyrannic relations between individuals.

Tyrannic relations generate both fear and resentment. It is a fragile relation. It can only be maintained so long as the belief in the ability of the tyrant to do violence to the subordinate is maintained. Furthermore, its continuation rests upon the ability of the tyrant to maintain close surveillance of the subordinates, prevent flights, and restrict their access to instruments of violence (Miller, Weiland, and Couch, 1978).

Intergroup tyranny has been established many times in the historical era. Powerful groups have often attacked and subdued the less powerful and then informed the defeated that they would not be subjected to further destruction if they agree to pay tribute to the victors. The Romans and the Aztecs specialized in establishing this relation. The emergence of this form of intergroup relation transformed some raiders and looters into tribute-takers (Lind, 1982).

Tyrannic relations require the use of disciplined violence, violence that is constrained by a projected future wherein one party subordinates itself to the interest of another. It is a less chaotic social relation than conflict and predator-prey relations. The actions of tyrants are temporally structured and a temporal structure is imposed on another. So long as the superordinate constrains his behavior on the basis of the future projected and the subordinate accepts the parameters specified, their relations remain constant; an order is established.

The imposition of an enduring tyrannic relation to extract tribute could not have occurred until after sedentary groups were well established. For the first several millennia of sedentism neither nomadic nor sedentary groups had the sophistication to impose a tribute-extracting relation on another collectivity. The earliest tribute-extracting relations may have been established by pastoralists attacking and subduing sedentary communities. Webb (1975) theorizes that the earliest authoritarian states emerged in this manner. That is possible, but unlikely.

Nearly all, perhaps all, nomadic herders of the historical period had sustained trade relations with sedentary communities. For the most part these relations were peaceful, but many were interlaced with violence. The pastoralists both traded with and preyed upon sedentary communities. As the consequence of sustained trade relations between sedentary communities and pastoralists, the pastoralists could have acquired the sophistication necessary to impose a tribute-extracting relation on sedentary communities.

Jacobs (1970) suggests that the ancient pastoralists, nomads with domestic animals, were groups that had at one time been sedentary. She thinks that ancient pastoralists had earlier been sedentary groups who either as the consequence of ecological changes or defeat by raiders were forced to become nomadic herders. If such was the case their tradition may have provided them with the sophistication necessary for the establishment of a tribute-extracting relation with sedentary communities.

Either their sustained trade contact with sedentary communities or their own tradition or both may have provided the sophistication necessary for the establishment of a tyrannic relation between themselves and sedentary communities. The fact the imposition of a tyrannic relation generates resentment among the subordinates, in conjunction with the sedentary community retaining its distinctive collective identity, rendered such relations very fragile. In addition, the pastoralists were at least semi-nomadic. The requirements of their herds for food necessitated that the herds be moved from one location to another during various parts of the year. Furthermore, some years it was necessary to move the herds to distant locations to provide them pasture. These conditions and constraints provided a context wherein the members of the subordinated community could harbor their resentment, and on occasion they had the opportunity to cast off their tyrants.

Complex large-scale tyrannic tribute-extracting relations have been constructed many times in the historical era. However, most of these have been between two sedentary groups. On occasion nomadic groups have attacked and subjugated large communities, but in most of these instances the subjugated community had a well-established hierarchy with the rank and file of the conquered group in an extremely subordinate position prior to their conquest. These conditions allowed for the attackers to displace the established elite and found new dynasties. The attackers and the subjugated merged into a single entity; they did not retain their distinctive collective identity.

When the subjugated group is allowed to retain its distinctive identity and required to pay tribute, the relation allows for the nurturing of resentment toward their tribute extractors. When this condition prevails the subordinated group usually takes any opportunity that arises to prepare itself for casting off their tyrants. Rebellions are common.

A famous example of this type of relation is that between the Hyksos and the Egyptians. Their relation was a very complex one with many dimensions. But it was in part a tribute-extracting one. The Hyksos acquired command of the lower Nile and they required the Egyptians who retained control of the upper Nile and their distinctive collective identity to pay tribute. A critical facet of the success of the Hyksos in establishing the relation was their military superiority that rested in part on their war chariots. The Egyptians nurtured their resentment for generations. They acquired mastery of the military technology of the Hyksos. After over a century of paying tribute they reorganized themselves and drove the Hyksos from the Nile Valley. When they did, they did it with vengeance, chasing them into western Asia.

Most of the ancient pastoralists probably had weaponry that was superior to that of the sedentary communities and a more viable warrior tradition. Some probably established a tribute-extracting relation with sedentary communities. But it is likely that like the later Egyptians, the subjugated, intensely resented their tyrants. If and when the opportunity presented itself, they probably drove off their tyrants or created so many difficulties that it was impossible for the pastoralists to maintain the relation.

It is conceivable that some pastoralists did establish a tribute-extracting relation with sedentary communities by subjugating them, followed by the two traditions merging into one. However, it is more likely that if a merger did occur, it was a more peaceful one than that of a pastoral group establishing and maintaining a tribute-extracting relation.

MERGER

The emergence of the Romans may offer an instructive example of a merger of a sophisticated trade and agricultural tradition with a pastoral tradition. The precursors of the Romans were two distinct pastoral groups that had established settlements on two hilltops near where the Tiber flowed into the sea. The settlements were established prior to 800 B.C.

The social structure of these two pastoral groups was probably similar to that of most other pastoral groups. There are no indications that they had a social structure of any great complexity. They raided and were raided.

About 700 B.C. the Etruscans, who probably originated in western Asia, established settlements in Italy. They were literate traders and agriculturalists. They pushed aside the indigenous populations of nomads and simpler agriculturalists. Shortly before 600 B.C. some Etruscans began to settle in the area occupied by the pastoral precursors of the Romans. Rather rapidly Etruscan craftsmen, merchants, builders, religious experts, and doctors established residency among the natives (Ogilvie, 1976:3). At least some of the traders appear to have been attracted to the region by the salt marshes near the sea on the Tiber. Salt from the marshes was widely traded.

The settlements of the pastoralists underwent a transformation between 625 and 575 B.C. The settlements became a city. The city was laid out in a geometric patern. Prior to the Etruscan presence the settlements were scattered clusters of huts; they became a city with public buildings, streets, and markets. The sophistication required for this transformation did not emerge from the pastoralists, it was imported.

Not all of the older Etruscan cities were laid out in a geometric pattern, but some were. The Etruscans had a sophisticated solar-lunar calendar; they noted eclipses of the sun and moon. They were capable of complex engineering feats. All of the early engineering undertakings of Rome were Etruscan.

According to legend, an Etruscan monarchy was founded about 616 B.C. It is difficult to discern exactly what occurred. But it seems that large numbers of Etruscans acquired important positions within the settlements. They were more sophisticated and became wealthier than most of the natives. There was probably at least some ill-will between the natives and the Etruscans. The first "king" probably was a tyrant who represented the emerging interests of the Etruscan merchants, craftsmen, and intellectuals. The natives were relegated to a secondary position in the decision-making process. The Etruscans were the dominant political group until approximately 507 B.C. Then the Etruscan rulers were cast off and a republic was established.

It is of more than passing interest that prior to the dislodging of the Etruscan monarchy, calendric affairs were in the hands of Etruscan priests. When a new moon appeared it was the priests who had the task of informing the king. The calendar was secret; a priestly elite had command of the calendar. It specified the days on which assemblies could be held, the days for legal transactions, festivals, and the days the king appeared before the assembly. The uniformed citizens were at a tremendous disadvantage whenever they confronted the Etruscan elite in public disputes.

When the monarchy was overthrown, one of the reforms was making the calendar public. The Praetor Maximus was to affix a nail on a public building at the end of each year. Timekeeping was made public; the priests were partially stripped of their monopoly of knowledge. Other files of the government were also made public.

Despite the fact the ruling Etruscan elite were deposed, early Rome was composed of several ethnic groups who existed in relative harmony. In addition to the native pastoralists and Etruscans, Greek and Phoenician enclaves were present. Trade expanded. Rome became an urban center.

One of the distinctive features of the transformation was the merger of the warrior tradition of the pastoralists with the organized military procedures of the Etruscans. Warriors are embedded with their fellow warriors and they fight as the spirit moves them; their violence is not coordinated by centralized discipline. In contrast, soldiers are subordinated to a central command and fight in formation. The Etruscans introduced centralized coordination of violence to the Romans. The savage warrior tradition of pastoralists was combined with disciplined organization; an army was established.

The Roman soldiers were controlled by vicious discipline. The commanders of each unit were vested with the authority to whip and execute any who showed cowardice or failed to adhere to the discipline. Decimation was standard practice. Any military cohort that failed its task might be decimated. All soldiers of a unit to be decimated were lined up and each tenth one was beheaded. Nor was this the only form of savage discipline. One early legend relates that a military dictator (general) had his own son killed for leaping from the ranks to attack the enemy. The truthfulness of the legend is less significant than that it reveals the importance placed on fighting in formation.

The military units from the earliest times cut across ethnic divisions, kinship lineages, and residential areas. The military units practiced outside of the city. They became very viable political units; they were probably quite viable social units from the earliest years. The cohorts developed solidarities that to an extent supplemented and replaced family, residential, and ethnic solidarities. To a large extent Roman politics were the politics of military units.

The popular image of the Roman civilization is that it rested on conquest and slavery. The later Roman civilization conquered on a grand scale and enslaved millions. However, these activities did not provide the foundation for the Roman social structure. As Rome became a wealthy city, she was an attraction to surrounding poorer pastoral and agricultural groups. The relations between Roman and the wealthier Etruscan cities were relatively peaceful during the early centuries. During the fifth century there were almost annual rumors of attacks and attacks by Rome's less wealthy neighbors. Skirmishes were frequent. The Romans were on the defensive. They fought to save the city and its wealth from the attackers. Later Rome warred upon and conquered Etruscan communities.

Slavery played a relatively minor part in the early centuries. The first auction of slaves by Romans occurred in 396 B.C. following the defeat of a large city (Ogilvie, 1976:69). The first slave market was established in 259 B.C. The emergence of slavery as a significant feature of the Roman social structure was the consequence of a militaristic political system that was first organized to defend the city. Only later did it become transformed into a conquest society.

Early authoritarian social structures may have emerged from a merger of pastoralists and sedentary communities. This merger may have been effected on the upper Nile prior to the dynastic period. During that period there was extensive trade between pastoralists of the Sahara and the residents of the valley. If the merger occurred, it is very likely that it occurred in somewhat the same manner as the merger that took place between the Etruscans and the precursors of the Romans. Then after the merger occurred, a policy of conquest led to the unification of the Nile. But it is doubtful that the original merger was the consequence of pastoralists conquering sedentary communities.

CONQUEST

Before a society could establish a policy of conquest, administrative and military specialists had to be merged. Undisciplined warriors are capable of attacking, destroying, and scattering communities. They might even establish a tribute-extracting relation. But the conquest and occupancy of a community, city, or territory requires complex centralized planning. Only after the merger of militarists and administrators could a society expand its territory through conquest and maintain a stable exploitative relation. A policy of conquest requires that both the attacks and the subsequent occupancy of territory be centrally coordinated.

Once administrative specialists had emerged, some societies exanded through conquest. However, that policy had rather distinctive features. First, conquest typically was not directed toward nomadic food gatherers or herders. Their mobility, poverty, and inability to subordinate themselves made such groups unlikely candidates for conquest. The Australian Aborigines were not conquered so much as scattered, eradicated, and absorbed. There was conflict between the western Europeans and native North American Indians but it was primarily directed toward driving the Indians from the territory desired by western Europeans. A similar condition prevailed between ancient complex societies and simpler nomadic ones.

Ancient conquest was primarily directed toward other complex sedentary societies. Only they were wealthy enough to make the effort worthwhile. Furthermore, the more successful conquests were those directed toward established hierarchical bureaucratic societies. Those directed toward groups of simple agriculturalists and trade centers often were costly endeavors. The resistance and poverty of the Britons rendered the Roman effort to conquer them a failure. Those civilizations that rested primarily on a foundation of trade were often extremely resistant to conquest. The Romans had great difficulty in subordinating both the Jews and the Carthaginians. They defeated them, looted their cities, enslaved or scattered their populations, and occupied their territory, but they did not conquer them.

In contrast the Romans conquered and established a tribute-extracting relation with the Egyptians quite easily. The Romans merely replaced the ruling Ptolemic dynasty. The Egyptian populace offered little resistance, despite their large numbers. There have been many instances of relatively small groups with superior military ability conquering large bureaucratic societies and installing themselves as the political elite. What is often overlooked in these instances is that the conquered society already had an extremely authoritarian, if not totalitarian, social structure. From the point of view of the conquered populace, the displacement of the extant elite with a new elite was a difference that did not make a difference. The Mongols who conquered China were greatly outnumbered. One estimate is that after the conquest the ratio of Chinese to Mongols was a thousand to one. Yet the Mongols displaced the ruling elite and established a new dynasty. In all cases when a relatively small number of militarists have attacked and subdued nations with large populations, the conquered nation was highly authoritarian with a complex bureaucratic apparatus. Not only did the rank and file of these societies often fail to actively resist the conquest, but the bureaucratic elite often readily served their conquerers. The Mongols could not have administered China without the active support of Chinese bureaucrats.

In a similar manner the Persians who were relatively unsophisticated but very militaristic, conquered large bureaucratic societies. Early in their expansionist period they conquered the Babylonians. At least some of the Babylonian administrators and intellectuals found it profitable to serve their conquerers. The first major palace built by the Persians was "surrounded by seven walls each, in imitation of the Babylonians, of a different hue, thus symbolizing the sun, the moon and the planets" (Bausani, 1962:13). In all probability the palace was designed by Babylonian engineers and its construction supervised by Babylionian administrators.

In many instances after the merger of the conquering militarists and the conquered administrators, more conquests were undertaken. The Mongol dynasty attempted to conquer all of Asia. The Persians conquered vast territories; the Inca established a conquest nation reaching for the northern to the southern regions of South America.

Centralized hierarchical structures that contained a system of centralized violence often expanded through conquest. The expansion often blessed the conquered with the benefits of a more complex social structure. In each case these nations had a complex centralized administrative system. Many of the conquests were undertaken by civilizations that had experienced a relatively recent merger of warrior militarism and bureaucracy. The armies of the conquerers underwent a transformation. Warriors became soldiers. Warriors defeat others; but it requires soldiers to conquer nations.

SUMMARY

Conflict is a simple and chaotic form of social activity. It preceded the emergence of human societies. The growth of human societies required that procedures be devised that controlled internal conflict. Those societies that did not control internal conflict either fragmented, destroyed themselves, or weakened themselves and became vulnerable to destruction by others. To an extent the movement from simple and small social systems to large and complex ones rested upon the development of procedures for containing internal conflict.

Conflict is temporally structured. Each party projects a future of defeating the opposition. The futures are incompatible. Furthermore, the futures projected are immediate ones. Conflict is present-centered, not future-centered, activity. Consequently intense conflict tends to be chaotic and destructive.

Intergroup conflict is a composite form of social action. It requires members of each party of a conflictual encounter to act in unison with other members of their group. When conflict was between small nomadic groups, the members of each group oriented primarily to the enemy while they simultaneously aligned their actions in a parallel manner with their fellow combatants. But there was little internal coordination of actions. Each person within the group acted largely as an individual, but with the social support of his fellow band members.

The emergence of sedentary communities was followed by the establishment of more complex forms of intergroup conflict. The mounting of a successful raid on a sedentary community of any size required that members of the raiding group coordinated their actions with one another; reciprocally the successful defense of the community required the coordination of action among the defenders. The efforts of both the raiders and defenders were organized on the basis of a communal objective. The temporal structures of both the attackers and the defenders became more complex than those of nomads who sporadically skirmished with each other.

The development of procedures for extracting tribute instead of loot required the subordination of violence to a distal communal objective. The content of the projected future also changed from one of destroying the enemy to that of subjugation. The maintenance of a tribute-extracting relationship required that both the attackers and the victims agree that the attackers had greater ability to wreak havoc than the victims and that violence would be withheld providing the subjugated acted as directed.

Conquest is based on violence that is organized to achieve control of territories and populations. The defeated are required to become part of the social structure of their conquerers. Conquest had incorporated many primitive societies into larger and more complex structures. Conquest emerged as a distinctive form of intergroup relations after the formulation of complex administrative programs and the merger of military and administrative specialists. Conquest presupposes the organization of violence on the basis of a complex distal future. It required the coordination of large bodies of people by an administrative elite.

Primitive war, raiding and looting, tribute extraction, and conquest have been and remain prevasive human activities. Each has contributed to the spread of ideas from society to society. However, it is doubtful that conflict in whatever form was the foundation for the emergence of complex structures from simpler structures. It is possible that the earliest authoritarian societies were the outcome of conflicts between nomadic raiders and sedentary communities with the two populations subsequently merging. If the earliest authoritarian societies emerged in this manner the original merger of nomadism and sedentism was probably rather peaceful. The tremendous resentment that is generated among the conquered when either a tribute-extracting relation or a conquerer-conquered relation is established makes it unlikely that the earliest enduring authoritarian states were the consequence of conquest.

Chapter XVII

Totalitarian States

A major step toward totalitarianism was the creation of monarchies. The commonly accepted date for the beginning of the monarchy of Egypt is 3050 The first dynasty of Mesopotamia was established about 2900 The first totalitarian states emerged from these monarchies. Within totalitarian structures a monopoly of knowledge, a hierarchical administrative structure that controls communal wealth, and centralized violence are unified. The degree of centralization of these activities and the completeness of the merger varied. But some ancient civilizations approached perfect totalitarianism.

Neither monarchies nor totalitarianism were created through the efforts of a single person or a small group of persons. Their emergence rested upon a foundation provided by a number of prior developments. Two of the more important developments that preceded the rise of monarchies were the asymmetrical relationships that focused on timekeepers and the administrators of the communal wealth. When these relationships were combined with monarchy the foundation was laid for totalitarianism.

The first monarchies were not intentionally created, nor did they emerge overnight. They were the consequence of a series of incremental changes that probably spanned generations. The office of king and divine lineages were the culmination of a series of historical accidents that occurred within a particular social context. Both internal processes and transactions between societies contributed to the formation of kingship. In some cases kingship merged with other social relationships to establish totalitarian societies. It is likely that many tyrannies were established long before monarchies were established in Egypt and Mesopotamia. But it appears that the first totalitarian social structures were established in either Egypt or Mesopotamia.

Complex monumental centers and administrative apparatus were in place in Mesopotamia long before a monarchy was established. They provided two of the conditions necessary for the establishment of enduring monarchies but by themselves were not sufficient. The emergence

275

of monarchies and the subsequent establishment of a totalitarian structure took a somewhat different form in Egypt. There the three sets of relationships may have been established more or less simultaneously, although it seems that rather complex timekeeping systems and administrative apparatus were established in many of the communities on the Nile before monarchies emerged.

The rise of monarchies was dependent upon communities having to defend themselves from raiders. Some of the agricultural communities with a centralized timekeeping system were repeatedly successful in repulsing raids. Intense fear and hatred were directed at the raiders. An intense communal solidarity that focused on the military elite emerged as these raiders were beaten off. The successful repulsion of the raiders elicited a response of thankfulness toward the military elite. They became war heroes. The solidarity that focused on the military elite both supplemented and competed with the solidarity that focused on their monuments and temples.

All three categories of people—the intellectuals, administrators and war specialists—were focal points of the social structure of their communities. A monarchy was established when the war leader was provided with a permanent title. In turn the title became inheritable and divine lineages were established. These social structures became totalitarian when the three sets of elites were merged into an organic whole and these specialists were categorically differentiated from the rank and file. The earliest enduring monarchies emerged from within large communities; they were not formed by foreign militarists imposing their will on conquered communities. The rank and file members of these communities contributed to the establishment of totalitarian systems by supporting and showing deference to the elite. The result in some cases was that the ideas of the intellectuals, the skills and resources of the administrators, and the violence of the military elite merged and were presented as a united front to the rank and file.

The use of violence on fellow citizens played a relatively minor part during the first few generations of monarchs. Subsequent to the establishment of a fairly high degree of totalitarianism, violence was employed to control and subordinate the rank and file members. Violence was then used to maintain the established hierarchy, but it is unlikely that it played a major part in the establishment of the earliest monarchies.

THE FIRST MONARCHIES

A monarchy apparently was established on the Nile a century or two earlier than in Mesopotamia. There was trade contact between the two regions during the critical period. The formation of the monarchical structures in Mesopotamia may have been in part the consequence of stimulus-diffusion, but it is possible that the parallel developments occurred independently in the two regions. The communities of the Nile and Mesopotamian valleys had similar social structures and were confronted by similar problems.

Monarchies did not emerge in identical fashion in Mesopotamia and Egypt, although their emergence shared many similarities. The differences are indicative of various paths followed by societies who constructed totalitarian structures. There is more information available on the emergence of monarchy in Mesopotamia than on its emergence in Egypt. Therefore, the material on Mesopotamia is presented first.

Mesopotamia

The cities of Mesopotamia were routinely confronted by raiders. When a city was threatened with an attack, the *unken* met and selected someone to lead the defense of the community. The title *lugal* was bestowed on him. It was not a permanent title, but was conferred for a limited duration. The practice was similar to that of the Romans of the republican period. When confronted with an emergency the Romans selected someone to serve as dictator for a specified duration.

Prior to the dynastic period the title *lugal* was not conferred for life; nor was divinity conferred to a lineage. "During the Early Dynastic period no kings seem to have been regarded as gods during their own lifetime but some were posthumously elevated to that position" (Adams, 1966:138). Later the office of *lugal* acquired divine characteristics and divinity was subsequently conferred upon their descendents. The title came to be that of king.

The city of Nippur played a special role in conferring the title of king from the earliest periods. Even later kings of Sumer derived their authority in part by eliciting recognition from Nippur (Jacobsen, 1970:139). Yet there are no indications that Nippur ever exercised military control over other Sumerian cities. Apparently her special position was derived from her reputation as an intellectual, administrative, and festival center. It is likely that citizens, or at least the elite citizens, of other communities congregated at Nippur for special festivals and when they were confronted by problems.

At the meetings at Nippur, the authority of the assemblies was derived from "An, god of heavens and 'father of the gods'" (Jacobsen, 1970:165). That suggests that men of knowledge affiliated with the temple of Nippur occupied a central position in the selection and validation of a person as war leader or king.

The early war leaders were clearly subordinate to the assemblies. When the older material is consulted, "We find the ruler scrupulously refraining from action in the matter of peace or war until he obtains consent of the assembly, in which, therefore, internal sovereignty of the state would seem to be vested" (Jacobsen, 1965:162). The early war leaders then were not sovereigns; they were delegated responsibilities by assemblies representing the will of the community.

Even after the *lugal* had taken on the meaning of king, the earliest "palaces" were not ostentatious. They were relatively modest-sized buildings structured along the lines of a household, but organized for military purposes (Jacobsen, 1970:148). The temples remained the dominant buildings of the communities for the first few generations of kings. Later the palaces competed with the temples for dominance and the wealth of the community.

The terms *lu* for full and free citizen and *mashen-kak* for commoner of subordinate status emerged simultaneously with or shortly after the establishment of kingship. These terms "do not occur in any presently known documents before the Early Dynastic period in spite of the presence of the term 'slave' " (Adams, 1966:97). The citizens of communities became categorically differentiated with the emergence of kingship. The presence of two distinct categories of citizens indicates that an aristocracy had emerged who had prerogatives denied other citizens.

After the emergence of monarchies in Mesopotamia there was an increase in strife between the city-states. Wars between cities became commonplace as monarchies attempted to extend their influence and dominate other cities. Territorial disputes and other infringements frequently led to clashes between cities. The spread of intercity wars was accompanied by the spread of monarchy as the dominant political structure. The merger of the military, administrative, and intellectual elite seems to have been less complete than that achieved by the Egyptians. A series of monarchies rose and fell. Some acquired control over vast territories, others were limited to a single city-state.

Egypt

The communities of the upper Nile developed somewhat differently than those of the lower Nile in the centuries immediately following the colonization of the Nile. The residents of the upper Nile had more contact with pastoralists; the communities of the lower Nile had more extensive contact with traders from Asia. It is likely that in one or more of the cities of the upper Nile there was a merger of the pastoralist tradition with the agricultural and trade tradition. The two traditions may have combined in much the same way the Etruscans merged with the pastoralists on the Tiber to found Rome. The predynastic communities of the upper Nile were more stratified than those of the lower Nile.

Militarism pervaded at least some of the predynastic communities of he upper Nile. The predynastic art stressed the brute power of arms, muscles, jaws, and teeth. In one instance the "king" is shown as a lion tearing open the enemy's stomach. Another displays him as a rampart bull, goring his foes (Johnson, 1978:45). Warriors, or perhaps soldiers, seem to have been the focal point of the social structure of these communities. There were wars with both nomadic raiders and between sedentary communities on the Nile.

Prior to unification, at least some of the communities on the Nile had monumental and administrative centers. However, these centers do not appear to have dominated the communities as much as they did in Mesopotamia prior to the dynastic period. Militarism, centralized administration, and the construction of monuments and temples became more significant as more regions of the Nile Valley were brought under cultivation. The merger of these three sets of relationships probably was not completed prior to the Third Dynasty. It may not have been consummated until the Fifth. When it was consummated the intergration was greater than that achieved in Mesopotamia and far more enduring.

The earliest kings of Egypt, like their Mesopotamian counterparts, were not divine. The office of king was divine before divinity was conferred on the king as a person. The early Egyptians made a distinction between the divinity of the office and the human nature of the king himself. "Thus *hm* of 'majesty' really meant the king's body; *miswt* meant the 'bearer of the office' and implied divinity" (Johnson, 1978:42). The kings of Egypt may not have become divine persons until the Fifth Dynasty. The worship of Re became the dominant religion among the nobility with the establishment of the Fifth Dynasty and the king was defined as Re's earthly representative.

Somewhat earlier, by the Fourth Dynasty, a uniform style of thought and a hierarchical political structure was established. The art of the predynastic and early dynastic period varies; it was not stylized. There was a transformation of art between the First and Fourth Dynasty. The art of the Fourth Dynasty expresses both changelessness and hierarchy. The king is shown towering over both his fellow Egyptians and the enemy. It also displays serenity, not violent emotions.

There was also a tremendous proliferation of titles during the same period. There were almost 2,000 distinct titles by the Fourth Dynasty, but the titles were not ordered in a consensual hierarchy. The rank of each functionary during the early dynasties probably reflected both the whim of each particular king and the abilities of each functionary to advance himself in the bureaucratic structure. By the Fifth Dynasty, the ranking of the bureaucratic elite was standardized (Baer, 1960).

The social distance between the king and his subordinates increased. By the Fifth Dynasty he held life and death power over them. One tale of the Fifth Dynasty relates how a functionary was struck on the foot by the king's scepter during a ceremony. That could have meant death for the functionary, but the king apologized and assumed responsibility for the *faux pas* and the functionary was spared. The same king twice allowed his subordinates to kiss his foot instead of the dust in front of his feet. These stories may have little basis in fact. Nonetheless the recording of the events depict the nature of the relations between the king and his subordinates.

The extreme power of the king over subordinates is but one side of the story. During the same period the king became subordinated to *Ma'at*. He not only ruled in accordance with *Ma'at* but his actions were synchronized with *Ma'at* to assure the continuation of order. The intellectuals developed the ideology that it was "unthinkable that nature and society should follow different courses, for both alike were ruled by Ma'at—'right, truth, justice, cosmic order' " (Frankfort, 1948:277).

The pyramid texts of one king includes the statement, "I sit before Re. I open his portfolios. I break the seals of his decree and seal up his dispatches. I send forth his tireless runners. I do whatever he dictates to me" (Jordon, 1976:129). That the king was as subordinated to the movement of the cosmos as this passage indicates is highly questionable. Yet the statement offers what was regarded as the ideal relation between king and the cosmos.

The military, administrative, and intellectual elite of Egypt appear to have merged into a firmer organic whole than was the case for Mesopotamia. That may have been a consequence of the fact that the three sets of elites emerged about the same time in Egypt whereas the intellectual and administrative elite had a far more ancient tradition than the military in Mesopotamia.

The Mesopotamians had an equivalent to *Ma'at*. "To the Sumerians the universe and everything in it, including the activities and institutions of man, was immutable. The functioning of this unchanging universe was governed by a series of divine laws known as *mes*" (Whitehouse, 1977:97). However, the intercommunity wars that continued to plague the Mesopotamian region frequently disrupted the merger of the elites. The wars often ended with one city almost literally destroying another. During the wars and immediately following them the military rose to a predominant position. Only in times of relative stability would a merger of the military and other elites be achieved.

The relative isolation of the Egyptians from other complex societies lessened the likelihood of widespread war that disrupted the internal structure of their society. Once unification was achieved there was no other group that could seriously threaten the Egyptians during the Old Kingdom. In addition, quite early in her history Egypt restricted contact with foreigners. During the predynastic period and for the first dynasty or two, trade with foreigners continued, but then foreign trade was brought under the control of the palace.

The establishment of monarchies was not limited to the Nile and Mesopotamia Valleys. Similar structures were established in China, Mesoamerica, and South America. The emergence of monarchies among the Maya was associated with the rise of the term *tecpan*, which referred to a community building that served as the storehouse for weapons and also the palace of the ruler (Thompson, 1966:124). The words for "fortified town" and "glory" appear at the same time.

The earliest monarchies emerged within agricultural communities. This despite the fact that trade centers had a much longer history of being raided by surrounding groups. Subsequent to the rise of monarchies, totalitarian structures were on occasion imposed on urban centers. Marketplaces populated by diverse ethnic groups are inherently antiauthoritarian; they could not have provided the foundation for the emergence of the first totalitarian states.

Those who constructed the first monarchies were not conscious that they were creating a novel form of authoritarianism. Monarchies emerged as communities confronted communal problems and attempted to resolve them. The novel developments were viewed by all, or at least nearly all, as necessary to achieve peace and security. The construction of these systems was aided and abetted by the rank and file. During the formative periods the military elite did not abrogate for themselves the wealth of the community. Class-consciousness was only minimally present.

However, classes were formed. The elite came to see themselves as distinct and deserving of special treatment. The first generations did not siphon off large quantities of material wealth for their personal glorification, nor did they severely exploit the rank and file. But many of their descendents did.

INTENSIFICATION OF SOLIDARITY

The gigantic monuments of these societies were built during the concluding phases of their formative period. "Classical Teothihacan and Protoliterate Uruk both rise in one incredible burst to a plateau that, according to these criteria was not demonstrably surpassed during the remainder of the sequence that has been presented for each area" (Adams, 1966:172). In a similar fashion the five largest pyramids of Egypt were all built within one century during the Fourth Dynasty (Mendelssohn, 1947b). The monuments reflected the culmination of the integration of these societies. The monuments and other larger-scale constructions were communal efforts; they were not the consequence of an autocratic elite forcing their will on a downtrodden and servile population.

They were mammoth undertakings; the extreme case is probably the pyramid construction age of Egypt. The size of the effort would have been impressive if accomplished by a nation with a population of a hundred million, but it was the accomplishment of a much smaller population. The population of the Nile Valley at the time did not exceed a few million and may not have exceeded two million. The efforts of large numbers was focused on the communal objective of constructing monuments that expressed the pride, glory, and knowledge of the society. It is estimated that over a hundred thousand workers were congregated yearly for from ten to twenty years when the Great Pyramid was built. The sustained coordination of that large number of persons over that extended a period could not have been accomplished by a small autocratic elite imposing their will on hundreds of thousands of persons.

The precision of the efforts reflect an enthusiastic community. Very few public buildings of any subsequent civilization, including our own, exhibit the quality of workmanship of the Great Pyramid. "This awesome fact itself provides a clue to the spirit in which the pyramid was built, and the religious fervor of the Old Kingdom society, especially during the Fourth Dynasty" (Johnson, 1978:50). The precision of the Great Pyramid and other artifacts constructed during the formative periods reflects more than a robust communal solidarity. It also reflects an intellectual sophistication capable of careful and precise planning that was integrated with an administrative unit capable of precise guidance and supervision of large-scale human endeavors.

The monuments were the community's statement of their communal solidarity, administrative integration, and intellectual sophistication. The robustness of the solidarity of these societies in part rested upon the population having gone through a set of exciting transformations that made their lives more secure and satisfying than the lives of their immediate ancestors. The intellectuals, administrative elite, and military elite were viewed as having made significant contributions to the successful transformation from an insecure and difficult life to security and plentitude. A complex set of intertwined developments culminated in the establishment of a tightly integrated social system.

The cohesion of these societies was mutually constructed; it was not imposed. Not all members of these ancient nations were equally committed to their social systems, but the overarching ethos was an extensive and intensive communal solidarity. To an extent the social unity achieved by these ancient nations probably was deliberately engineered by the elite. The elite probably instituted public works with the intention of expanding and reaffirming both the communal solidarity of these nations and their own special position within the established structure. They organized undertakings that appealed to the rank and file, and most of rank and file willingly accepted the programs offered by the elite. Coercion was of minimal importance; communal pressures were sufficient to assure that most would lend a hand to the projects.

It is widely accepted that the Egyptian pyramids were constructed at the behest of the kings and for their glorification. However there is only very shaky evidence supporting that interpretation. The pyramids of the Fourth Dynasty do not have any declaration of the name of their builders or their occupiers (Ruffle, 1977:25). Nor is there any evidence that they were designed to serve as the tombs for kings (Mendelssohn, 1974). Kings may have been buried near the monuments, but this only indicates that both they and the monuments occupied a central position in the social structure.

There is little evidence of ostentatious consumption of the nation's wealth by the kings of the early dynasties. The graves of the nobility of these dynasties contain only the scantiest equipment. Further, the grave goods of this period were of poor quality. "When the central government had collapsed during the First Intermediate period, both the quality and the intrinsic value of the grave goods at Qua increased greatly" (Frankfort, 1951:93). The military elite occupied a focal position during the formative periods of these nations, but there are few indicators that they dominated and systematically exploited their fellow citizens.

The military of the early dynasties, from the point of view of their communities, provided the very real function of protecting the civilized world from the onslaught of the noncivilized. The populace of these ancient nations must have been very self-conscious about their distinctiveness. Both the conflicts between the emerging nations and surrounding groups, and the changes that had recently occurred within their own societies informed them of their distinctiveness. These societies were not traditional societies; they were novel social structures. Conflicts between them and the less civilized and the construction of monuments that announced their achievements affirmed the differences between them and others and reaffirmed their internal solidarities.

Simultaneous with these developments, the structures of these societies became more hierarchical; the social distance between the elite and the rank and file grew. The elite became representatives of the the cosmos with the responsibility of assuring that the established order would be maintained. Their structures rigidified and stagnated; they became traditional societies. But that did not occur until the intellectual, administrative, and military elite became integrated and had developed an ideology justifying special treatment for themselves. Then the military became parasites of their own societies.

THE RATIONALIZATION OF ORDER

The intellectuals, especially the timekeepers, provided complex programs of action that linked the kings, the administrators, the rank and file, and the intellectuals themselves to the repetitious movements of celestial bodies. All became merged into one coherent whole. The king served to link human action with the cosmic movement. He became responsible for assuring that social affairs remained in synchronization with celestial affairs. Reciprocally, the king was allocated the honor of having the closest contact with the heavens. The linkage was made part of the communal celebrations. The celebrations united cosmic order, communal solidarity, social order, and hierarchy. The social order of these societies was keyed to celestial events. A centralized timekeeping system was established for the nation, and the military elite were the earthly representatives of cosmic order.

In Egypt a series of critical changes occurred with the establishment of a civil calendar during the Old Kingdom. Prior to the establishment of the civil calendar the Egyptians used either a sidereal-lunar or solar-lunar calendar. During the Old Kingdom a calendar of 365 days was instituted. The new calendar and the old calendars existed simultaneously for centuries. But "As the centuries passed the civil year became more and more the important year in the life of the people" (Parker, 1950:45). The earlier festivals had been keyed to heliacal risings of stars (especially Sirius), the solstices and equinoxes, and moons. They served as the focal points for the reaffirmation of communal solidarities. These events were slowly replaced by holidays specified by the civil calendar. The apex of the political structure replaced celestial events as the focal points for the reaffirmation of communal solidarity. To an extent this transformed communal celebrations into political obligations that had to be fulfilled to maintain order.

The activities of the central political figures were tied to celestial events; they too had to respect the cosmic order. The installation of a new king had to wait for the beginning of a key series of events in the celestial world. "For kingship, not being merely a political institution, had to conform with the cosmic events no less than the vissitudes of the community" (Frankfort, 1948:102). The death and burial of the king was linked to celestial events by the Fifth Dynasty. The seventy days of preparation of the king's body for final burial paralleled the seventy days Sirius disappeared from the sky each year at the thirtieth parallel of latitude where the Great Pyramid was located. Then after seventy days the king, like Sirius, was reborn. He then joined the never-setting circumpolar stars where like them he would never die.

The linkage of the king's action to cosmic events was extremely elaborate and precise in Egypt. But the same type of linkage was forged in many other ancient monarchies. The specific nature of the linkage and the content of the rituals varied greatly, but in all the king served as the conduit who linked celestial movement to the social structure of his society. The intellectuals, especially the timekeepers, provided the programs of action that tied social structure to cosmic structure.

There was a close affiliation between the military elite and the timekeepers of China. "The astronomer was not a citizen on the outskirts of the conventions of his society, as perhaps in the Greek city-states, but a civil servant lodged at times in part of the imperial palace, and belonging to a bureau that was an integral part of the civil service" (Needham, 1969:24). The rituals of the political elite that reaffirmed the established order were important ones that were programmed by the timekeepers. "The most important of all the state observances (in China) was the sacrifice at the winter solstice, performed in the open air at the south altar of the Temple of heaven, December 21st" (Edkins as quoted in Lockyer, 1894/1973:88). The emperor knelt before the altar and performed rituals that assured the continuation of both cosmic and social order.

The same general state of affairs prevailed among the Maya. The "emergent picture suggests that the Maya rulers, consciously and directly linked events of their own lives with eclipses and planetary movements" (Kelly and Kerr, 1975:57). Furthermore, the titles of the Mayan monarchs were derived from their calendar.

Some of these rituals continued to serve to inform the populace when to undertake planting and harvesting of the crops. The planting, care, and harvesting of crops had been linked to celestial events long before the emergence of monarchies. But with the emergence of monarchies the military elite became an integral part of the celebrations that informed all when to plant and harvest. For example, the Inca maintained sacred fields near the major plaza of the capitol. It was in these fields that the king opened the respective seasons by "his ritual first plowing and first harvesting" (Zuidema, 1975:257).

The daily lives of the intellectuals and bureaucrats were also encased within elaborate programs of action keyed to celestial events. It pervaded the lives of all. The priest made sacrifices as dictated by the communal calendar. In China among the bureaucratic elite, "once summer had officially begun it would have been an unthinkable affront to Heaven and Earth to wear the green robes appropriate to Wood, the element of Spring" (Needham, 1969:22). The celestial sequences provided order for all.

The repetitious order of celestial events stands in marked contrast to the comparative chaos of human action, especially the chaos associated with conflict. In their studies of celestial movement the intellectuals had concluded that much of the chaos of human life could be removed if human affairs were subordinated to celestial events. With the rise of military specialists the intellectuals were confronted with a segment that could wreak havoc on social order. The establishment of an orderly system necessitated the subordination of the military elite to the order they had formulated. They were not always successful in enticing the other elite to accept the programs of action they had to offer. But some, by offering the military elite a special place in the rituals, enticed them to accept the structure the timekeepers had formulated. It seems likely that at least some of the time the military elite may have demanded a special place in the established ceremonies and order.

Those who formulated and offered these programs of action were not necessarily acting either to promote their personal well-being or in bad faith. They were intrigued with the repetitious order of the cosmos and probably viewed the subordination of human action to celestial movement as a necessary condition for the continuation of social order. "The rhythm of time enchanted the Maya; the never ending flow of days from the eternity of the future into the eternity of the past filled them with wonder" (Thompson, 1966:14). A similar orientation probably prevailed among the intellectuals of most ancient totalitarian societies. From that point of view it was only reasonable to order the affairs of their communities in the same manner as the cosmos was ordered.

The formulations specifying the nature of the relations between human activity and the cosmos varied. In some societies the formulation stressed that human beings must subordinate themselves to the cosmos. But in others the belief that some control could be exercised over the heavens was part of the ideology. For example, the Inca recognized that if seeds were planted too early the young plants might be destroyed by a frost; and if too late the crop might not mature. Yet at the same time they thought it necessary to sacrifice to the sun to solicit it to arrive at specific locations on the horizon so that the planting of the maize could take place at the proper time. While they subordinated themselves to the sun they also thought they could influence the sun's movement.

A critical facet of the ideology offered by the intellectuals of these societies was the promulgation of a cyclical conception of time—that each present and future was the repeat of some past. Various complex celestial cycles had been computed. Then the ideology was developed that, like celestial affairs, human action was also cyclical; that what was present today among human beings had prevailed at some prior period. Change did not occur, only cycles. The future was equated with the past. This paradigm of thought was established with varying degrees of completeness in ancient totalitarian societies.

The cyclical paradigm implicitly denies the possibility of reform and innovation. Once it became the established mode of thought the closest any could come to instituting reform was to advocate a return to the "old" ways from which society had strayed. Chinese reformers never projected their ideals into the future; they conceived of the ideal as having existed in the past (Balazs, 1967:117). When the cyclical paradim was the predominant mode of thought, the concept of progress was not viable. The primary concern was to keep events in tune with the established order; any innovation was *ipso facto* a threat to social order. More than that, innovations threatened cosmic order.

The establishment of the cyclical paradigm also offered a formulation that freed rulers of responsibility. In Egypt if the king followed protocol "if disaster struck, no blame fell on the crown" (Johnson, 1978:97). The intellectual elite of China offered the definition of the ideal ruler as one who "should sit simply facing south and exert his virtue in all directions so that Ten Thousand Things would automatically be well-governed" (Needham, 1969:212). To the extent monarchs could be enticed to accept the definitions of order and the place in that order offered to them by the intellectuals, they posed no threat to the intellectuals and bureaucratic elite. If the king accepted the dictums offered, it allowed the intellectuals and administrators to coordinate the affairs of the nation without interference. In the extreme case the ideal ruler was merely a passive figurehead.

Once established and fully rationalized these systems had tremendous durability. Yet despite the efforts to maintain constancy, changes occurred. Given the fragility of human beings, deviants might become king or chief bureaucrat and now and then disasters beyond human control struck. These catastrophies disrupted the established order. On occasion they enticed some to be reflective. But most found the disruptions disconcerting and yearned for the reestablishment of order.

The maintenance of the cyclical paradigm made it necessary to discredit all novelties. This was accomplished in a number of ways. It was accomplished in part by simply denying that any changes had occurred or by designating changes as mere epiphenomena. Other times the past was reconstructed to fit into the established cycles. The purpose of records in Egypt was not to provide a historical record, but to demonstrate continuity of the present with the past. If the accomplishment of this task required rewriting the past, so be it. In general, novelty was reacted to with abhorrence or defined as reinstituting what had once been the case. The past was not used to inform the present and the future, but to constrain the future.

The maintenance of a consensual belief in constancy is difficult in the best of circumstances. It is especially difficult if a number of sources of information are available. Then alternative definitions of past and current affairs are more likely to be formulated. The formulation of alternative definitions is especially likely to occur during times of crisis. To lessen the likelihood of alternative formulations being offered the elite instituted monopolies of knowledge.

CONTROLLING KNOWLEDGE

The continuation of extremely asymmetrical structures with the minimal use of violence requires rather effective monopolies of knowledge. The flow of information within ancient totalitarian societies was systematically regulated. The effective assessment of the adequacy of a given program requires access to information upon which the program is based. When decisions affecting the communal welfare are made in open assemblies, others have the opportunity to acquire the relevant information. But when decisions are made behind closed doors, those not privy to the information have little alternative but to accept the decision or disaffiliate from the community.

Official secrecy appeared in Egypt by the Fourth Dynasty. One of the senior officials of that dynasty had the title "Master of Secrets of Things that Only One Man Sees" (Johnson, 1978:44). The king may have been the person referred to who was the ultimate recipient of the information, although he may not have been. In ancient China an imperial edict stated, "If we hear of any intercourse between astronomical officials and their subordinates and the officials of any other government departments, or miscellaneous common people, it will be regarded as a violation of security regulations which should be strictly adhered to" (Needham, 1974:79).

The Inca had two versions of their past. "The official, censored version presumably is that which was recorded in song and legend and repeated at public ceremonies. The other, involving recognition of fraud practiced upon the people, is presumably that which the Inca class believed" (Gibson, 1948:47). After the Aztecs became dominant in Mesoamerica they systematically rewrote their past to legitimate their rule.

The flow of information was officially controlled in many, if not all, ancient totalitarian societies. The internal dissemination of information necessary to structure the day-to-day activity of the nation was a state monopoly. The monopoly was not complete, there was always some leakage. But in most instances the leakage was small and had no consequences. Egypt established and maintained a state monopoly on the manufacture and distribution of papyrus. In China "publishing, as the official almanacs which told the farmer the proper dates for beginning and ending the various operations of the agricultural year, and of simple written illustrated handbooks on rice cultivation, serculture, spinning and weaving" was a state monopoly (Berkelback, 1967:56).

The techniques of writing that developed within these societies supported the maintenance of monopolies of knowledge. The writing became highly stylized and very complex. It required years of study to master it. In Egypt there are "examples of cursive writing that mostly date from the first and second dynasties, but by the Fourth Dynasty hieratic writing had developed" (Lauer, 1976:133). In neither Egypt nor China was there any movement to simplify writing. Rather writing became more complex, making it extremely difficult for those not exposed to years of training and official indoctrination to acquire information from written material. On occasion there may have been something equivalent to an underground press, but the size and impact of such undertakings, if they occurred, were minimal.

The monuments continued to serve as communal timepieces and promoted the established order. The palace architecture, sculpture, and art conveyed a unified message to all. All modes of communication were used to convey the message that the established order was perfect and further, that it was in tune with the cosmos. The monumental architecture, sculpture, and art were centrally located to effectively provide uniform information for all. It displayed and glorified the established order, both the cosmic and the political.

Artists were an integral part of the political order. The artists were not individuals offering distinctive standpoints. Rather they were obedient and submissive to the divine order; Egyptian artists sought to convey a universal order—*Ma'at*. They idealized the established order (Johnson, 1978:180). For example, Egyptian artists depicted the royalty as blessed with perfect bodies; the bodies of others could be displayed as less than perfectly proportional (Michalowski, 1969:188). The king was displayed on the walls of temples destroying enemies, conquering foreigners, and performing pious rituals to the gods (Schmandt-Besserat, 1978:20).

A monolithic and integrated message was conveyed to all. Most citizens had little interest in acquiring any information other than that provided by the official statements; most were unaware of the presence of any other information. So long as affairs were run in a reasonable fashion there was little threat to the monopoly of knowledge. Furthermore, those in control of the flow of information were in league with those in control of violence. Any effort by the uninitiated to acquire such information unleashed punishment. The rank and file did not pose a threat to the intellectual and bureaucratic elite.

Threats to their security and special positions stemmed from those in control of violence. To make their position secure it was necessary for the intellectuals and bureaucrats to construct a relation between themselves and the king that made him dependent on them. This they managed with varying degrees of success. They kept the king uninformed, misinformed, and attempted to indoctrinate him with the official ideology.

The deliberate withholding of knowledge from the monarch appears to have been standard practice in Egypt by at least the Fifth Dynasty. The king was misinformed as to the true length of the solar year. The swearing-in ceremony for each new monarch included an oath by the king to protect the 365-day year (Parker, 1950; Lockyer, 1894/1973). The timekeepers of the time were well aware of the exact length of the solar year (Krupp, 1977:207). The 365-day year was used for governmental record keeping. It served that purpose quite well. But it did not allow for the accurate prediction of celestial events. The information necessary for that was retained by the intellectuals.

Once a totalitarian structure was established, the education of the royalty included indoctrination into the temporal structures and associated rituals that had been formulated. Most of the royalty took what was offered as the "natural order" for granted. Only those exposed to alternative paradigms of thought could have had a base for questioning the order offered. Most of the time the intellectuals were successful in enticing their rulers to accept their formulations. Even when these societies were conquered by uncouth and uneducated barbarians and a new dynasty was founded, within two or three generations the new royalty usually accepted the formulations offered by the conquered.

For example, the Aztecs established themselves as the new rulers of a totalitarian society. They did not completely destroy the intellectual centers or bureaucratic apparatus. After the first generation or two the Aztec rulers accepted the frame of thought offered by them. By the time of the conquest of the Aztec by the Spaniards, the Aztec king had become encased with the frame of thought offered by his intellectuals. He "tore down and reconstructed at least one building so that its alignment would correspond with the sunrise of the equinoxes" (Aveni, 1975a:xiii). In addition, he "was required to arise after dusk, at about 3 , and immediately before dawn to offer incense to certain principal stars" (Aveni, 1975b:167). Montezuma was so imbued with the frame of thought offered by his intellectuals that he never resolved whether he should treat the approaching Spaniards as gods or enemies or both. His indecision contributed to the destruction of his empire. He had accepted such large amounts of the teachings of his priests that he was incapable of effective action. His grandfather would probably have marched out his troops and destroyed the approaching enemy forthwith.

From time to time individuals became aware of the frauds, but most were relatively powerless to expose them. Few had the ability to detect fraudulent information; of the few with the ability, far fewer had the resources to expose it to the populace. Most of those who became aware of fraud were not interested in exposing it to the populace. To do so would only threaten their own special position.

However, on occasion an effort was made to expose fraud. Perhaps the most famous example is the heretic king of Egypt in the Fourteenth century The heretic king is most famous for a revolution in art and his challenge to the priesthood. But he may have attempted an even more profound revolution. It seems that he also had the temerity to tamper with the Egyptian calendric system which had been in operation for well over a thousand years. He thereby was attacking one of the basic canons of truth upon which the official social structure of Egypt rested.

One part of the new center that he established was a great temple with a narrow rectangular enclosure oriented east-west. It contained six successive courts with parallel rows of offering tables. "The total number of offering tables on either side of the longitudinal axis for the first five courts is 365, and for the first four courts plus the sixth is 366, which would correspond to the number of times that the daily ritual was performed during one normal year and during a leap year, respectively" (Badaway, 1965:40).

Many characteristics have been offered of the heretic king. But running through all is a concern with *Ma'at*—truth, order, and justice. It is conceivable that he had become aware of the fraud that had been established practice since the Old Kingdom and attempted to introduce a new system based on "truth." When he attempted to make the official calendar one of 365 1/4 days he was making public one of the key bits of knowledge that had been kept from monarchs for over a thousand years. He disturbed the established hierarchy for a short time, but in the long run his reform efforts had no impact on structure of the Egyptian society.

The special position of the intellectuals of these societies was largely dependent upon their control of information that was deemed important by other elites. In this manner they could assure themselves a special position within the structures of their societies. Most of them probably truly regarded the calendric system and its associated festivals as the foundation of social order. They therefore promulgated the dogma that all, including the king, must subordinate themselves to the orderliness of the cosmos. To the extent they were successful, it provided them with a foundation for directing the behavior of all—including the activity of the king.

CENTRALIZED ACCUMULATION OF GOODS

The integration of a communal timekeeping system, a centralized administration and the military elite created a totalitarian system. However, the endurance of these systems for generations required that, in addition, the elite to establish procedures for assuring that all would be provided the basic necessities for life during periods of shortage. This they accomplished with varying degrees of success by the practice of saving some of the harvest from the good years for anticipated famines. The elite, of course, controlled both the accumulation of these goods and their dispersal.

The centralized storing of food and other communal resources was established in Mesopotamia long before the monarchy emerged. It was probably practiced from at least the time of the establishment of the first public administrators. How these goods were accumulated by the temples is unknown. But it is likely that the stores were replenished by tithing. All members of the community were expected to contribute. Communal pressures led most to contribute. The early palaces of Mesopotamia were organized in much the same manner as the temples. However, whereas the temples had probably relied on voluntary contributions, the palaces "exacted military service, enforced labour on communal projects and levied direct taxes" (Whitehouse, 1977:71).

During the predynastic period of Egypt the storage of grain surpluses was a household affair (Hoffman, 1979:201). The storage of surplus grains became a communal enterprise during the early dynasties. More than 40,000 stone vases used to store food in subterranean warehouses were found at one location with a Third Dynasty date (Barocas, 1976:24). The centralized accumulation of surpluses probably preceded the Third Dynasty. An elaborate census had been established by the Second Dynasty. Biennial records were kept of people, cattle, donkeys, fish ponds, and fruit trees. The grand vizier, the nation's chief bureaucrat, supervised the census and the accumulation of wealth. A central treasury appears during the Third Dynasty. It was located at Memphis and was independent of the royal palace (Janssen, 1978:224). Apparently it was controlled by administrators who may have been acting in behalf of the king, although it is possible the king did not control the treasury of the nation at that time. Once the centralized accumulation of surpluses was established as official policy, officials were fed and clothed from these storehouses (Janssen, 1978:228).

The Chinese invented, "The so-called 'ever-normal granaries', designed both to facilitate the control of agricultural prices and provide emergency stocks for relief of famines" (Berkelback, 1967:56). All, or nearly all, totalitarian societies established procedures for the centralized accumulation of goods. Those that did not were far less stable than those that did.

The centralized accumulation of goods allowed the elite to establish a paternal relation with the rank and file. Those in dire straits during times of shortage were fed from these stores. That elicited a response of gratitude from the recipients. Of course, it also made the life of the rank and file somewhat more secure and reaffirmed the asymmetrical relations between them and the elite.

In times of plentitude these stores also provided one of the necessary features for marshalling large numbers to work on communal monuments. Undertakings such as the pyramid construction period of the Fourth Dynasty would have been impossible without centralized stores that contained large quantities of goods.

USE OF VIOLENCE

Violence was used to maintain order in these societies. However, during times of stability internal violence was of minimal significance. The extensive communal solidarity linked to the monuments, the rationalizations provided by the elite, and their control of the accumulated goods enticed most to comply with the dictates of the elite. Any deviation, at least public deviation, from the established order elicted disapproval from one's friends and neighbors. That enticed most to adhere to the established order.

One of the most impressive features of these societies is the relative absence of "revolutions from below." In Egypt there is no evidence of a revolution of the masses during her 3,000 years of existence (Frankfort, 1948). Other totalitarian societies were less stable. Occasionally China experienced rebellions that were in part fueled by intense dissatisfaction among the masses. There were conflicts within these societies, but most internal conflicts were between elites struggling for control of the political apparatus.

The almost complete lack of awareness among the rank and file of any viable alternative prohibited any large-scale uprising. The lack of revolutions in Egypt stemmed in part from her geographical isolation. That isolation was enhanced by the restrictions placed on foreigners entering the country and the control of international trade by governmental functionaries. Other totalitarian societies were less self-contained.

Yet now and then malcontents and other deviants appeared on the scene. Then violence was used to assure all that the established order was the natural order and obedience was the preferred form of conduct. Once a rigid hierarchy had been established and rationalized, the elite of these societies were not averse to using violence to maintain order. In general, violence, or at least public violence, was used on only the common people. In China violence was "a means for coercing those unable to reach the necessary moral standard. The social group of *chum-tsu*, i.e., the upper class, was practically immune from the law because of its supposed high standards" (Pokora, 1978:201).

All members of these totalitarian societies became potential targets of violence as differentiation between the ranks increased. The king held life and death power over his immediate subordinates; they in turn held equal power over their subordinates. Each official, so long as he retained his official position, could threaten his subordinates with extreme violence. Within such systems "an official in his capacity as a representative of the state is sacrosanct, but as an individual he is nothing" (Balazs, 1967:63).

The functionaries of these societies were in constant fear that their superior might find them deficient. If they were found deficient they were stripped of their official position and in many cases put to death. They became extremely responsive to their superiors and in turn became tyrannic toward their subordinates. Within the multitiered structures the subordinates to the king could not effectively be called into account by their subordinates. They were in a situation where, "provided they did not violate tradition or the interests of the ruler, their control over their subject population is absolute, and as arbitrary as the ruler's is toward them" (Wheatley, 1971:72). All superordinates tended to become tyrannic; they treated their subordinates as instruments. Fear replaced solidarity as the foundation for communal action.

AN UNEASY COALITION

While the elite of these societies had many common interests, they also had their differences. The unity of the military, intellectuals, and bureaucrats of Egypt seems to have been more constant and secure than that between most other sets of specialists of other totalitarian societies. In later Egypt there were occasional struggles for power among the elite, and at least some of these struggles pitted the military elite against the bureaucratic elite. In the short run the military elite were usually victorious, but in the long run the interests of the intellectual-bureaucratic elite held sway.

One of the most ancient legends of Mesopotamia depicts conflict between the military and other elites. The legend of Gilgamesh dating from the early dynastic period recounts how he pleaded with the elders to declare war on Kish and was turned down. He then convened a meeting of young men who supported him and forced his will on the assembly (Adams, 1966:141). Later when Babylonia had arisen to the fore in Mesopotamia, there was at least an incipient conflict between the military elite and the priests in charge of the most important rituals. Only on the New Year's festival could the king enter the innermost sanctuary of the central temple. Before he could do that, a high priest removed all of his insignia and humiliated him by slapping him in the face and pulling his ears (Oppenheim, 1977:122).

During the Hun Dynasty some of the Chinese bureaucrats and intellectuals contested with the military for power. The military became disenchanted with them and had large numbers of them killed. Literate persons were searched out and put to death. Of course, the military elite soon found that the continuation of the system required administrators, so a new cohort of them emerged. But the punishment served as an object lesson; the following generation of bureaucrats remained in their proper place.

A limited form of political consciousness emerged in these societies. For the most part it was limited to mutual awareness among the sets of elites that while all were part of the same social system they had somewhat different interests within the system. The common people were largely devoid of political consciousness. They may have become disenchanted, but with no awareness of alternatives and no power to take action to modify their position, they could only choose between apathy and enthusiasm.

Most of the time the different sets of interests of the elite were encased and constrained by an overarching monolithic ideology. But on occasions their different interests provided the seeds for some of the elite to take action to improve their position within the system. Most such efforts were unsuccessful; if they were successful, they seldom transformed the social structures. A new set of elite with the same programs of action simply replaced the old elite. The uprisings were merely palace revolutions. The most common justification for these palace revolutions was not to move toward a new and better way of life, but to reinstitute the traditional way of life from which the old elite had strayed.

During the formative periods of totalitarian societies, communal solidarity provided the foundation of communal action. But as hierarchies emerged, mutually recognized interdependency between categories tended to replace communal solidarity as the foundation for communal action. Members of these societies became disembedded and unity was maintained largely by each segment recognizing its dependency on the other. The king recognized his dependency on his intellectuals, bureaucrats, and the common people; they in turn recognized the necessity of supporting and placating him if their security was to be maintained.

Placating the king became a pervasive concern. He was enticed to indulge in ostentious consumption. Luxury and prestige items were manufactured for the king and other elites. The first luxury and prestige items were commissioned for royal lineages (Wheatley, 1971:74). The development of this mode of production was "a response to, not a determinant of, the emergence of social class" (Wheatley, 1971:76). The administrators not only encouraged the military elite to consume the nation's wealth, but they in turn imitated the behavior of the kings.

One consequence of that development was the further exploitation of the rank and file. In some instances the production and consumption of wealth by the elite reached gigantic proportions. The elite feasted on gold plates while the rank and file starved. The elite became decadent and the rank and file alienated. Most continued to publicly support the established order, even if somewhat indifferently.

SOME CONSEQUENCES

The establishment of the belief that the king derived his power from the heavens and was thereby superior to all others created a dilemma for those who associated with him. He was the source of recognition and rewards, but he was also beyond human accountability. Those with such powers, if they decide to act tyrannically, are uncontrollable. They have at their command a complex social arrangement that when activated can wreak havoc on persons and social structures. The disturbance created by the heretic king of Egypt could only have occurred within a context where a monarch had a complex social apparatus at his command to do with as he wished.

These social structures became interlaced with tyranny, fear, and egoism. Communal objectives receded to the background as individual desires and the interests of special categories came to the foreground. The wealth of the nation came under the control of persons in critical positions. Members of the elite competed with each other for personal glorification. As these social structures were transformed, the monuments and other public works became shoddier.

Corruption became the mode. Those in official positions had the greatest opportunity to be corrupt. Those at the bottom of the hierarchy had neither the resources nor the opportunity to siphon off wealth for their private use. Bribery and the black market became taken for granted. Officials simultaneously fulfilled their public duties and extracted wealth from the communal coffers for their private consumption. Publicly they supported the extant system while manipulating it for their private benefit.

The black market became an institution in Egypt. Bureaucratic functionaries were the focal points of the black market activity. A papyrus of the Twentieth Dynasty reveals monstrously dishonest dealings. About 90 percent of a temple's grain disappeared into private warehouses (Johnson, 1978:203). Most pretended to regard the established system as sacred, yet there was more or less universal awareness that all with the opportunity took advantage of their special position.

The level of corruption seems to have achieved even greater heights in China during some periods. Whereas in Egypt merchants never became an important class until toward the end of her existence, a wealthy merchant class emerged in China. The Chinese merchants had the wherewithal to bribe officials. The main form of contact between the merchants and officials was through bribery. "The merchants could not have operated their policy of bribery if it had not been for the practices of embezzlement and 'squeeze' on the part of the officials" (Balaza, 1967:108).

Despite the fact these systems became tyrannic, highly corrupt and stagnant they usually endured unless disturbed by an invasion. So long as there were no foreign instrusions, the systems were quite stable. However, they were very vulnerable to foreign intrusions. Some were destroyed by invaders; others absorbed their invaders.

SUMMARY

Enduring social structures that were based in part on centralized violence first emerged within relatively wealthy societies who were exposed to repetitive raids. They were indigenous responses to external impingements. The societies were heavily dependent upon agricultural production, had an elaborate timekeeping system, a complex administrative apparatus, and experienced sustained harassment from surrounding groups. Military specialists emerged as a consequence of repetitive conflicts with surrounding groups.

The differentiation between the men of knowledge and administrators on the one hand and the rank and file on the other preceded the aristocracy-commoner differentiation based on military powers by millennia. When the military specialists emerged and were merged with the other elite, the foundation was provided for the establishment of totalitarian systems. A coalition was formed between those with a monopoly of knowledge, those in control of the community's material resources, and those with special ability to do violence. The coalition was probably not the consequence of explicit negotiation or conspiracy. Rather the sets of elite simply came to recognize that they stood apart from the rank and file and therefore had a common interest in maintaining their special position. The promotion of their elitism detracted from communal concerns, subordinated the rank and file, and established a system wherein some segments systematically exploited other segments.

The communal temporal structures and administrative procedures were linked to the emerging political hierarchy. The monarchical system like the temporal structures became sacred. Hierarchical modes of sociation were blended with the temporal structures. In a few instances the political hierarchy and temporal structures became a divine order that was beyond questioning. The merger linked social order, political order, and celestial movement into an organic whole. The consequence was a hierarchical society that was programmed in elaborate detail. A key to making these systems stable was the subordination of the military elite to temporal structures offered by the intellectual elite. When that was accomplished, the social structures of these societies were stabilized, barring intrusions.

The artifacts of ancient totalitarian states have led some to conclude that the earliest city-states and nations rested upon a foundation of centralized violence. The palaces, rich burial sites, and luxury items associated with these societies are stark reminders that an elite minority consumed much of the wealth of these societies. However, these artifacts do not demonstrate that the successful accumulation of vast amounts of wealth was dependent upon the establishment of centralized violence. Rather it demonstrates the establishment of and rigidification of a class system wherein the elite consumed much of the surplus production to the detriment of other members of the society. Monopolies of knowledge and violence were unified for the benefit of a few at the cost of many.

Totalitarian societies did not evolve in a straightforward and unilineal fashion, nor rapidly. There were many fits and starts. Nor does it seem they were the outcome of deliberate planning. Rather they were the products of a complex series of historical accidents interacting with extant complex social structures. The merger seems to have reached an epitome in Fifth Dynasty in Egypt. No other nation seems to have constructed as tight and as enduring a totalitarian structure as the Egyptians.

The opulent and ostentatious consumption of the nation's wealth and corruption that later became the hallmark of these societies did not develop until after a totalitarian system had been well established. Once they became totalitarian then decadence and alienation became pervasive. Some of them collapsed under their own weight; others were conquered. Some of those conquered faded from the scene; others were interjected with novel ideas and embarked on expansionistic enterprises.

Chapter XVIII

Literacy and History

Literacy, the rendering of discourse into a series of inscriptions that can subsequently be translated back into discourse by another person, was a relatively late development. Inscriptions in the form of pictographs have been used to display information for tens of millennia. They may have been used by some groups as early as 150,000 years ago (Forbes and Crowder, 1979). It is certain that lunar sequences were rendered into a stylized system of notations by 30,000 years ago. Traders were making numeric notations of quantities by 9000 B.C. Each notation system increased the capacity of human groups to accumulate, retain, and share information. However, these systems of notation were aids to discourse; they were informative only within an oral context.

The development of literacy allowed human beings to share information across time and space independent of an oral context. When all or nearly all of what could be offered orally was written and capable of being read by others, the amount of information accumulated and retained was drastically increased. Furthermore, information became far more durable. Whereas oral accounts are extremely responsive to current affairs written accounts remain relatively constant.

The development of written histories was contingent on combining literate descriptions with an established chronology to array past human affairs in a sequential order. All human groups, including nonliterate ones, can sequentially array some of their past. Some nonliterates have an extremely limited past that is sequentially ordered; others with a rich oral tradition had rather elaborate pasts. Written accounts of past human endeavors provided large quantities of information that could be chronologically ordered. The historical depth of societies was then greatly extended.

The most ancient notation systems were memory aids. What was inscribed was intended for the writer. The notations enlarged the amount of information available to the writer. Then the notations of earlier generations were used by later generations. When subsequent generations used the notations of prior generations' past experiences it enriched the current knowledge of a group. The earliest notations spanned time.

The use of writing to span space was a later development. It was not until a rather mature system of writing had been established in a plurality of groups that writing could be used to communicate across space. The earliest use of notations to span space was as a memory aid for messengers who carried information from one location to another. After literacy was established in a plurality of groups, it became possible for one person to communicate with another at a different location without the messenger being privy to the information.

The most ancient notation systems were linked to specific activities. The earliest standardized notation systems apparently were developed in conjunction with the study of celestial phenomona and economic transactions. However, literacy and history did not emerge directly from either astronomic or economic concerns. Rather they emerged from a complex interfacing between elaborate oral accounts of past human exploits and systems of notation that had been developed in conjunction with astronomic and economic activity.

For millennia after the emergence of literacy only a very small percentage of the population of the "literate" societies was able to read and write. Universal literacy within a society is a very recent accomplishment. Nonetheless, the emergence of literacy and history radically transformed societies even when only a small percentage of the population was literate. It was the literate members of civilizations who were primarily responsible for programming the activity of their societies. Only they had access to large bodies of information. Literacy emerged in conjunction with the activities of some focal persons and in turn strengthened their focal position.

Those societies with literates in general have far more information available than those composed solely of illiterates. Consequently literate societies are capable of more complex social structures. However, a few nonliterate societies with a rich oral tradition constructed complex social structures. Within these societies some persons specialized in learning and retaining information in the oral form.

THE ORAL TRADITION

Rich oral traditions were developed in many of the ancient societies long before the emergence of literacy. The amount of information that can be retained in regular discourse is severely limited. However, if information is rendered into verse then the amount and complexity of the information that can be retained is greatly enhanced, especially if the oral tradition is supplemented with brief notations. Persons who are trained in the tradition are capable of reciting poems of two, three, and four hours' duration. The *Iliad* was orally transmitted for centuries before it was written.

Many lengthy oral compositions were developed in conjunction with a heroic tradition. However, there are indications that other oral traditions were also developed. Several ancient civilizations had oral traditions linked to astronomical knowledge. The Incas had astrologer-poets who knew "the round of the Sun and Moon, eclipses and of stars and comets, hour, Sunday and month of the year and the four winds of the world for sowing food since of old" (Ascosta as quoted in Zuidema, 1975:219). The Druids of Caesar's time spent up to twenty years learning verses of astronomical knowledge. Both the navigators and the astronomers of the South Seas retained their knowledge in verse form. A study of the tale of Senuhe, one of the most ancient tales of Egypt, has demonstrated that some of the wisdom literature of Egypt was originally in oral form.

The transmission of these poems from one generation to another was facilitated by memory aids and demonstration props. For example, the young men of the South Seas were taught sets of poems by older navigators while at the same time shown the relative position of islands and stars by arrangements of pebbles. Each poem contained the information necessary for sailing from one island to another. To sail from island X to island Y one poem was used; to sail from island X to island Z another poem was used.

The men of knowledge of ancient Britain may have produced star charts that were used in association with an oral tradition. Carvings on a rock have been found that are the mirror image of eight first-magnitude stars of the northern hemisphere. The markings on the rock have the same relation to each other as the stars in the heavens. It is likely "the stone was used to 'print off' star charts onto skins laid face downwards" (Hadingham, 1975:173).

Many complex oral traditions have been developed that were based on the heroic exploits of previous generations. The *Iliad* is the prototype of an oral rendition of past exploits of warriors. This particular genre of oral composition emerged within several societies that had a political system that focused on warriors. The accounts were first composed orally, and then, in some cases as with the Greeks, put into writing. The *Iliad* was transformed into writing after the Greeks acquired literacy from the Phoenicians.

The oral tradition leaves no artifacts, or at least only artifacts that are very difficult to recognize. It is impossible to make an accurate assessment of the importance of an oral tradition for the emergence of literacy. However, many large social structures rose and fell long before literacy was established. The information necessary for the construction of ancient monuments and the coordination of complex endeavors was probably retained and transmitted orally.

The Inca had a complex governmental system, built huge monuments, constructed complex road and irrigation systems, and coordinated the activities of large armies and work gangs. They had elaborate systems of notation that specified astronomical sequences, quantities, and the relative spatial position of both celestial and terrestrial objects. But they did not have a system for rendering discourse into notations; they relied on their oral tradition in conjunction with a series of memory aids to preserve the necessary information. The Britons who built Stonehenge and other gigantic monuments were probably illiterate.

These and other examples indicate that large and complex social structures emerged without the benefit of the written word. Literacy emerged from complex social systems and in turn allowed for the construction of more complex social structures. Nonetheless, complex social structures encompassing hundreds of thousands and in some cases a few million were established and maintained by illiterates.

EARLY LITERACY

It is possible that the first system that allowed for a more or less complete rendering of discourse into writing was developed in the urban centers of western Asia. The Sumerians are commonly designated as the first literate civilization. It may be that, "The first application of writing was, in fact, the keeping of economic records within the temple" (Adams, 1966:125). However, there is considerable circumstantial evidence that literate traditions were developed earlier in other regions and that the establishment of a literate tradition rested in part on a foundation provided by an oral tradition of heroic exploits.

The earliest Sumerian writing was limited to nouns and numbers. The early texts of the temples seldom used verbs. The two earliest verbs were "received" and "gave out" which noted transactions between temple functionaries and citizens. A third verb that probably meant "remains on hand" also appears in the early texts (Biggs, 1974:43). This system of writing was used by the Sumerians for a considerable period before literacy emerged. Literature may go back as early as 2650 B.C., perhaps somewhat earlier (Biggs, 1974:31). The Sumerians of approximately 3200 B.C. who organized the complex temple-centered trade networks apparently were not literate.

A heroic tradition emerged among the Sumerians during the period when there was considerable conflict between the city-states. The heroic period probably peaked about 2750 B.C. (Kramer, 1959:200). The Sumerian sagas that recounted these conflicts "were composed when writing was either altogether unknown, or, if known of little concern to the illiterate minstrel" (Kramer, 1959:202). These sagas teem with static epithets, lengthy repetitions, and other features common to oral renditions of heroic affairs composed by later societies. The epics of the Greeks, Indians, and Teutons all have many features similar to the sagas of the Sumerians. The sagas of the Sumerians were written on clay by scribes attached to the temples about 500 or 600 years after their composition in the oral form (Kramer, 1959:202).

It seems that both a complex oral tradition of heroic sagas and a complex system of notations of economic transactions were developed during the later part of the fourth and early part of the third millennia in Mesopotamia. The two traditions were probably developed by two quite distinct sets of specialists. One the one hand, the minstrels related their accounts of the heroic exploits of past generations; on the other hand, the *sanga* developed systems of notation to facilitate transactions associated with the temple. Then subsequently, perhaps with the emergence of monarchies, the two traditions were combined to produce written descriptions of past human actions.

But it is possible that the rendering of past human activities into discourse developed earlier outside of Mesopotamia. It is of more than passing interest that the ideogram for a writing table that first appears about 3000 B.C. in Mesopotamia is a representation of a wood tablet, not a clay tablet, despite the fact the Sumerians of the time wrote on clay. That strongly suggests that either writing or an elaborate notation system was borrowed from groups that wrote on wood. Wood was in short supply in the Mesopotamian region. However, in other areas of western Asia there were complex trade centers that had a plentiful supply of wood.

Wood was widely used as a medium by ancient civilizations. Both the Greeks and Romans wrote on wood during their earliest literate periods, as did the Vikings. The Cuna of Central America and the Easter Islanders also wrote on wood. Other ancient civilizations used material similar to wood. The early Maya wrote on bark. One of the earliest specialists among the Maya were the bark beaters (Hammond, 1977:63). The Egyptians, who had almost no wood available, first wrote on sheets that were produced by pounding together bundles of the papyrus plant. The widespread use of wood as a medium suggests it was a very ancient practice.

In addition, many of the ancient systems of writing took the same form. One line was written from left to right, with the following line from right to left, the next left to right and so on. This system was widely used in the eastern Mediterranean area. Later the Greeks, Romans, and Vikings used the same system as did the Cuna and Easter Islanders. The widespread dispersal of this system also suggests an ancient past.

Sustained conflict was a major stimulus for the composition of sagas. These sagas in turn then provided one of the necessary ingredients for the emergence of a literate tradition. The cataclysmic, violent, and exciting nature of combat makes a profound impression. Warriors and those who witnessed or heard of the battles were stirred. They attempted to share the experiences with others. When the accounts were transmitted through regular discourse much of the excitement and many of the details were lost. However, when tone and rhythm were combined with discourse, more excitement could be conveyed and more details retained. The most ancient sagas developed independently of notation systems. Inscriptions were not an integral part of the emergence of ancient sagas. However, in some societies complex notations of astronomic and economic events were also developed. In some cases these systems of notation were modified and elaborated to allow for rendering sagas into writing.

Literacy seems to have emerged from two rather different heroic traditions. Both reach back into a distant past of conflict. One literary tradition emerged among societies that fought and traded with others, the other, from societies with an agricultural base who repetitively drove off intruders. The oral compositions of the warrior-trader traditions served largely as entertainment. The oral compositions of the defender-farmer tradition were also entertaining, but also justified the emerging hierarchy.

The literacy of Mesopotamia rested largely on a foundation of conflicts between city-states whereas that of the Egyptians rested largely on a foundation of conflict between the civilized and uncivilized. Both types of warfare were present within each region; the two forms of conflict are not mutually exclusive. However, in following generations one of the two traditions of oral sagas recounting these conflicts tended to become dominant.

It is doubtful that the Egyptians of the First Dynasty were literate. "The difference between the First and Second Dynasty scripts is so marked that at one time Egyptologists thought they were separated by hundreds of years" (Johnson, 1978:45). The predynastic residents of the Nile had a notation system. The same system of notation was used during the early dynasties. By the Second Dynasty the Egyptians had developed a system of writing that allowed for elaborate descriptions of human affairs.

The literate accounts of the Egyptian formative period were probably based on earlier oral accounts of the conflicts. These written accounts of the earliest period offered rationalizations of the emerging monolithic structure. It is possible that the original oral sagas from which these accounts were derived also rationalized the emerging hierarchy. However, a more likely development was that these accounts were composed first in the oral form, much like the sagas of other civilizations with a heroic period. Then, when the monarchy was established and the Egyptians became literate, the sagas were rendered into writing; in the process the content of the sagas was transformed to provide a rationalization for the monarchy.

The first literate persons of civilizations tended to be either scribes or performers. The prototype of early literates of the scribe tradition is the scribes of Egypt; the prototype of early literates of the performer tradition is the minstrels of preclassical Greece. The scribes' basic relationship was with their authorities; the performers' basic relationship was with the community at large. The written accounts provided by the two types of literates reflected their position within their respective social structures. The scribes composed tales that tended to justify an extant order; the performers composed tales that tended to reflect the interests of the community.

The position of the scribes was like that of modern accountants and "official" biographers. The validation of their efforts came from the elite. Their task was to provide information that was useful and pleasing to the authorities. The scribal tradition was well established in Egypt by the Fourth Dynasty, perhaps earlier. Statues of scribes appear during the Fourth Dynasty. That indicates scribes were important persons in the social structure of Egypt by that time. The statues display the scribes as alert, attentive, and subordinate to the authorities. The scribes kept the accounts of the nation, including descriptions of the exploits of the ruling elite.

The earliest literate persons of the Greeks were minstrels who performed before audiences. The literate minstrels emerged from an oral tradition. The *Iliad* had been performed for centuries before it was written down. Later literate Greeks composed new poems and then plays. The early plays were in verse form. Prose accounts were not composed until still later. Herodotus is representative of the last development. His histories are entertaining tales of past events and the affairs of foreign socieites. These compositions occasionally justified the position of the current elite, but their primary objective was to entertain. The composers of these poems, plays, and histories made assessments of events and sometimes made evaluations of conditions that were contrary to the interests of the elite.

The performer, like the writers of popular novels, is primarily dependent upon the reactions of an audience. Validation of his efforts stems from the audience. Those who are successful in eliciting widespread approval continue their literary efforts; the unsuccessful discontinue. The content of their tales is also influenced by reactions to their efforts. But the nature of the influence is quite different from the influence of the authorities on scribes. Disbelieving and negative responses from the audience enticed performers to modify the content of their tales to fit with the beliefs and wishes of the audience.

The sagas of the Greeks underwent a series of transformations as a consequence of the interplay between the performer and the audience. One example of this transformation is the descriptions of war chariots in battles of the *Iliad*. The version of the *Iliad* that has survived has warriors driving their war chariots to battle and then dismounting to fight the enemy. The original oral sagas probably recounted battles where men fought from chariots. But chariot warfare was not current among the Greeks during the generations that the *Iliad* was popular. Both the composers of the tales and the audience had difficulty visualizing fighting from chariots. Therefore, the content of the saga was modified to reflect the current styles of fighting.

The performer has greater autonomy but less security. The scribe has little autonomy, but so long as his authority retained his position and he pleased his authority, he had a relatively secure life. Performers were more innovative than scribes. Innovations often enhanced their reputations. Novelty generated excitement. The innovations of scribes tended to be limited to techniques that allowed for more complete and accurate retention of information and the development of procedures that made the information less available to others. The security of their position rested in part on the development of techniques that made it difficult for others not trained in the intricacies of inscribing accounts to decipher them.

One consequence of the difference in their position was that the performers tended to develop simplified techniques of writing whereas the scribes tended to develop complex techniques. All the earliest systems of writing were ideographic. Later, a general transformation of the ideographic systems into phonetic systems occurred. However, within the civilizations that developed a totalitarian political structure, scribes occupied a central position and there was little or no movement from their ideographic systems. Egypt and China maintained ideographic systems for millennia. The earliest writing of the Egyptians was rather crude and simple. Then early in the dynastic period, the scribes developed a complex ideographic system. Its served as the official language of the Egyptians throughout their history. Its constancy was so great that an Egyptian scribe of the time of Christ was capable of reading inscriptions from the Old Kingdom. Two other systems of writing developed in Egypt during the intervening period. Both were simpler forms, but they did not replace the official language.

Phonetic systems of writing developed within contexts where traders used notation systems to facilitate economic transactions and minstrels performed for audiences. Traders were primarily concerned with keeping an accurate record; they had little interest in developing a system of notation that allowed for elaborate descriptions of human endeavors. The minstrels found phonetic systems useful. They allowed them to retain in writing complete descriptions of human endeavors.

The modern phonetic system of writing is derived from the Phoenicians. They were primarily traders. Their system stems from Egypt. They did not take over the system of writing of the Egyptians. They borrowed some of the characters and the system slowly was transformed into a phonetic system. The Greeks acquired the phonetic system from the Phoenicians and completed the process of rendering it phonetic.

It was the minstrels of Greece who elaborated the phonetic system. They used it to give rich and detailed accounts of various human endeavors. The early Greeks did not have a standardized system of writing. There was neither a standardized alphabet nor a standardized spelling. Systems of notation varied from region to region, across time, and from person to person. The alphabet was standardized in Athens about 400 B.C. The Greeks of that period had neither a monarchy nor a bureaucracy. Each user of the alphabet exercised his autonomy.

The percentage of a population of societies with an ideographic system that was literate always was quite small. The development of a phonetic system did not assure universal literacy, but phonetic systems make it more difficult to maintain monopolies of knowledge. It requires years of study to become fully literate in an ideographic system, but one can become literate in a phonetic system in a few months.

The retention of written descriptions of human activity requires a system of notation that specifies action and quality, as well as number and relative location of objects. A system that names objects, quantifies objects, and specifies relations between objects is quite adequate for retaining the information necessary for a complex calendar, the construction of monuments, specifying the spatial position of objects, and recording goods on hand. The retention of descriptions of human activity requires a more elaborate system. Both an ideographic and a phonetic system can be used to provide accounts of human endeavors. However, when an ideographic system prevails, it inherently is conducive to monopolies of knowledge and totalitarian structures. Phonetic systems are inherently antithetical to monopolies of knowledge and totalitarian systems.

Written accounts of past human endeavors were a necessary precursor to the development of an historical consciousness with temporal depth. The nature of the historical consciousness that developed within societies was in part a function of the system of writing that prevailed within the society. Ideographic systems were associated with a cyclical conception of the past and phonetic systems were associated with the development of linear histories.

ANCIENT HISTORIES

The adults of all human groups can sequentially array some of the past activities of their groups. However, in many groups little attention is given to the past; in others the past is a significant part of their lives, but there is little interest in sequentially ordering it. In most nomadic food gathering groups there is little concern with retaining a complex account of the past and even less with sequentially ordering it. Some nonliterate groups had a richly textured past that offered elaborate details, but their past had little chronological depth. Other nonliterate groups had oral traditions that offer a past that was sequentially arrayed for several generations.

The adults of food gatherers had an awareness of events that occurred in their parents' and perhaps in their grandparents' day. However, their short life span and nomadic life made it difficult to develop a past of great complexity. Grandparents were relatively uncommon; most were deceased before the grandchildren achieved maturity. Furthermore, the pervasive fragmentation of nomadic groups inhibited the development of richly textured pasts. Chronological depth seldom extended beyond two or three generations.

When groups became sedentary then more elaborate pasts were constructed. The surrounding environment remained relatively constant and tales became attached to families, objects, and locations. Grandparents were more common. The elders provided more elaborate tales of the past than the elders of nomadic groups. Sedentism did not automatically lead to the development of extended histories. During the first several millennia of existence residents of sedentary communities had neither the ability nor interest to develop and retain a sequentially ordered past. Some sedentary groups developed oral traditions that provided them with richly textured pasts. However, the earliest oral accounts were not chronologically ordered.

Those who composed these oral accounts of past human endeavors had little interest in providing an "accurate" account of the past, nor were they concerned with arraying them in a chronological order. Their prime interest was to entertain. When inconsistencies were noted in either the events described or in the sequential order, it might elicit comments. But so long as the accounts remained in the oral form, it was difficult to assess the accuracy of the accounts even if inconsistencies were noted.

When accounts of the past are in the oral tradition, they are highly receptive to influence. If the accounts are at variance with current conditions they are often modified to make them more consistent with current conditions. For example, during the eighteenth century, one African group had an oral account of their origin that stated their society was formed by seven brothers. In the twentieth century the same group gave an account of five brothers founding the society. When the account of their origin was first recorded, the society was composed of seven clans; only five clans remained in the twentieth century.

Written accounts are less subject to current conditions. Literacy was necessary for the development of an interest in the "accurate" reconstruction of the past. Literacy did not assure the emergence of historical analysis, but it provided material that could be systematically examined when inconsistencies were noted in two or more accounts. Then efforts could be made to resolve inconsistencies.

CYCLICAL HISTORIES

The earliest histories, the chronological ordering of past human actions in writing, were probably composed by the Egyptians of the Second Dynasty. The Egyptians are frequently characterized as nonhistorical (Toulmin and Goodfield, 1962: Fehl, 1964). However, they had rather elaborate records that sequentially ordered some of the activities of their ancestors. They have been characterized as nonhistorical on the grounds that their accounts of the past denied social change. Nonetheless they had written accounts of considerable temporal depth.

Their histories were distinct from modern histories. The affairs of human beings were linked to the ever-recurring cycles of celestial events. The constancy of both the cosmos and the social structure was stressed. Current situations were regarded as a reconstruction of a past condition. Both the cosmos and human affairs were conceived of as having been set in motion sometime in the past and to have remained constant.

The frame of thought used to order the past in this manner was derived from astronomical studies. Elaborate chronologies of cyclical celestial events had been constructed long before chronologies of human affairs were kept. The chronologies of celestial events indicated the world consisted of repetitious movement. The intellectual elite, in league with the military elite, linked human affairs to celestial affairs. They developed a rationalization claiming a similarity for the two realms. The subordination of complex human endeavors to celestial events provided the foundation for the development of cyclical histories, histories that stated nothing had changed since the beginning.

The students of the heavens were not interested in chronologically ordering human affairs; they were interested in the heavens and in retaining their position. In ancient agricultural civilizations it was consensually acknowledged that it was necessary to subordinate some human activity to celestial movement if the society was to survive. Crops had to be planted as specified by the calendar. A cyclical mode of thought was first developed to order the future, not the past. Then the recognition emerged that the past, like the future, was repetitive. The culmination of this mode of thought was that all was constant.

Some of the literate elite of societies that developed a cyclical paradigm had to have been cognizant that changes occurred. Even in a society as tightly administered and isolated as Egypt, changes occurred. Some distinctive events were recorded. For example, the Egyptians recorded the construction of naval fleets and the "hacking of the intruders." However, as these events are offered they are not conceptualized as distinctive. Rather they were regarded as revalidation of an established order, not as changes in the social structure. When the king performed a function, whether chasing intruders from the valley or honoring the sunrise of the Spring equinox, he was reasserting once again the established order.

Their records emphasized constancy. The yearly height of the Nile at flood stage was noted and annual festivals and other cyclical events were recorded, as were the installations of new monarchs. Lists of kings and priests were kept. These accounts contained information about persons and their activity, but little information about changes in the social structures. Any information that may have indicated changes in the social structures was ignored or discredited; it was the repetitious events that were the significant ones.

The stress on constancy justified the extant political order. New dynasties were established, but new dynasties were linked to prior ones and displayed as representing a constant world. Undoubtedly in many instances the intellectual elite were cynical. They had to have been cognizant of discrepancies between what was recorded and what had occurred. They also had to know that accounts of the past were sometimes systematically manipulated to justify the current hierarchy.

However, the cyclical mode of thought was probably taken for granted by most intellectuals. Sometimes their reordering of the past was a conscious effort to "rewrite" history to serve the ruling elite. But often the past was manipulated to make it consistent with the cyclical paradigm of thought, quite independent of influence from the authorities. Whenever a given frame of thought is widely accepted, facts are often juggled to fit into the established paradigm. No cynicism need be involved.

The Egyptians developed a very refined and elaborate cyclical history. However, the application of this frame of thought, which was derived from astronomical studies, was not limited to the Egyptians. It was present in various degrees among the Sumerians, Chinese, Maya, Inca, and others. The early Chinese historians were a subsection of the department of astronomy. They established a department of historiography about 100 A.D. Historical studies, as a distinctive intellectual activity, were never established in Egypt. The historical analysis, if it can be called that, of these societies was for the most part carried out by court functionaries. The relationship between the historians and the political elite varied. In some instances they had a degree of autonomy. The Chinese historians theoretically were "free from the manipulations of the reigning monarch or officials of the day" (Needham, 1969:234). In practice they devoted considerable effort to justifying the current ruling elite.

The historical studies of ancient totalitarian societies were not completely dominated by the cyclical paradigm. In some instances attention was given to unique and distinctive events. For example, the Chinese historians fitted many of their observations to a cyclical mode of thought, but they were attuned to some forms of change. "No classical literature of any civilization paid more attention to the recording and honouring of ancient inventors and innovators than that of the Chinese" (Needham, 1969:267).

The cyclical paradigm was not limited to societies with totalitarian social structures. Intellectuals of other societies sometimes used the cyclical paradigm to order human affairs. Aristotle regarded it as a viable mode of analysis. He thought he might be living before the Trojan War as well as after it. Traces of the cyclical paradigm remain in some modern historical efforts.

When the cyclical mode of thought prevails, it serves to conserve the extant social structure. The past is used to justify the present. If conditions in the present are different from the past, they inherently are out of order. The primary task of cyclical historians is to record the ever-recurring sequences. Disturbances and changes are taken as indications that something is amiss. During times of changes the Egyptian literates made strong negative evaluations of current conditions. The Hyksos intruders were cursed with vengeance. They created chaos; it was a time of "seventy kings in seventy days." Among other crimes, they upset the established hierarchy.

During periods of internal stability cyclical historians kept records of the recurring social occasions. Often the records consisted of nothing more than a listing of important events. If evaluations were made, they typically praised the elite for either maintaining the established order or for reestablishing what was regarded as the proper order.

The cyclical paradigm stands in marked contrast to a linear conception of the past and future. For cyclical historians recurring events are the significant ones; distinctive and unique events are the significant ones for linear historians. Both attend to movement, but cyclical historians stress movements that supposedly are identical to past occurrences; linear historians, in contrast, give emphasis to transformations and emergences.

EARLY LINEAR HISTORIES

The emergence of linear history rested upon the tension between the descriptions of the repetitious order of celestial events and written accounts that indicated variability of human affairs. The chaos of human affairs, especially the changes and transformations associated with warfare, stand in stark contrast to the recurrent cycles of celestial movement. Linear history acknowledges cataclysmic transformations and uses a chronology based upon astronomical observations to sequentially order major modifications of the social structures and the relative predominance of different societies.

Linear history seems to have first emerged in Mesopotamia. The world of the Mesopotamians was far less constant than that of the Egyptians. The floods were less certain and conflict between regions more common. One Sumerian city-state would achieve predominance, but then it would decline or be defeated by another in war. They another city would rise to prominence. The fluctuations in the relative power of cities led some to serious reflection about major social changes.

One of the earliest accounts that hints at a linear history is an inscription from Mesopotamia of about 2400 B.C. A boundary stone has been uncovered that refers back to earlier battles and covers about 150 years. A pictorial display of one of the battles between two communities is offered. The account includes "a series of inscriptions that describe a long-standing conflict over the frontier between Lagash and the neighboring city of Umma" (Butterfield, 1981:29).

While there are hints of linear history for the third millennium , it is during the second millennium that linear history clearly emerged. Its emergence was closely affiliated with large-scale intercommunity conflict throughout the eastern Mediterranean and Mesopotamian regions. The Hittites with their iron weapons and war chariots entered the region. The Sea People raided Egypt and other civilizations; there was sporadic but prolonged conflict between Egypt and the western Asians. The Mesopotamian region was rife with conflict. The period is marked by "the development of the narrative treatment of events and the emergence of history as a literary genre" (Butterfield, 1981:44). The accounts focused on cataclysmic consequences of war.

A new type of record keeping was established. Previously records, to the extent they were kept, were of economic transactions, celestial phenomena, the listing of rulers, and oral compositions of the glories of war. The clash of imperial social systems that contained literates led to the formulation of self-conscious struttings in writing. Written descriptions of the conflicts proclaimed the accomplishments of the political elite. A written heroic tradition emerged. These boastful accounts were not recorded to challenge cycical thought, nor to establish linear histories. The inscribers did not know that they were providing information that would challenge cyclical thought. But by rendering past accomplishments into writing, diverse descriptions became available for study. Different accounts could then be compared and contrasted and, if a chronology was available, sequentially ordered. It slowly became apparent to some that not all of the events of the past occurred in a cyclical manner.

The early descriptions that provided the information necessary for the development of linear histories were not accurate accounts; they were not made to provide material for later analysis. They were attempts to frighten enemies, intimidate the masses, elicit approval from the gods, and to reassure the elite they were in fact all-powerful. Despite their boastful and inaccurate qualities, they informed all who could read them that what had transpired was a distinctive, if not a unique, set of events. The presence of more than one account of a past event informed all that it was possible to take more than one standpoint toward a given set of events.

Traces of linear history appear in Egypt during the second millennium. One inscription of that period reads in part "I swear as Re (loves me and) as my father Amon favours me, all these things happened in truth; I have not presented fictitious things as things that happened to me" (Butterfield, 1981:55). The composer of this statement recognized that more than one account was possible and that not all accounts were an accurate reflection of what had transpired. Some of the monarchs upon having a statue built to honor them, instructed later generations not to erase the inscribed names or to claim credit for the accomplishments of their ancestors. More often than not the pleas were ignored. The rewriting of history to demonstrate all was constant and that the present elite derived from the old elite continued. Cyclical history remained the dominant mode of thought in Egypt.

The early linear histories, like the earlier cyclical ones, were highly ethnocentric. The accounts do not concern themselves with justifications of conflict; they were all written from the point of view of the victorious party; at least those who ordered the inscriptions claimed victory. They reflect, not the standpoint of a detached observer, but the standpoint of persons completely imbued with the culture of their native society. No effort was made to assess past events from a neutral or third-party point of view. The early historians did not have the cross-cultural experience that allowed for the development of a detached point of view.

The Hittite accounts of the past, in comparison to those of Egypt and Mesopotamia of the same period, were offered in a linear format and were far less ethnocentric. Their accounts often dealt with the ethics of a conflict and offered descriptions of what occurred first, second, and so on. The Hittites were illiterate when they entered the region. Their social structure was in a state of flux. Their newly emerged intellectuals were not imbued with a cyclical frame of thought and they were exposed to multiple points of view.

A series of cataclysmic transformations is conducive to the development of linear histories. Cataclysmic events shake the consciousness of all; all seems chaos. All societies experience cataclysmic events. However, if there are no written records of the events, no extended chronology that can be used to retrospectively order the events, or if a cyclical mode of thought is completely dominant then cataclysmic events are not sufficient for the emergence of a linear conception of the past.

The Hittites experienced a series of cataclysmic events (many of their own making) within a few generations as they became one of the most powerful societies in the region. In the process they became literate and acquired an extended chronology from established civilizations. They did not have a well-articulated cyclical frame of thought. Their written accounts of their transformations as they conflicted and competed with other societies allowed them to construct a linear and nonethnocentric account of their past that gave primary emphasis to distinctive events and major transformations. They produced the first "modern" historians.

AN ANOMALY

The Jews were among the first to develop a complex linear history that had no traces of cyclical thought. Their history was a series of unique and linearly ordered cataclysmic events. There was but one exodus from Egypt, only one Moses, one period of wandering in the desert, and a series of other distinctive events. Written accounts of these events were sequentially ordered. In addition, the duration of important experiences, such as the length of their stay in Egypt, were specified.

Many other earlier civilizations had greater economic and intellectual resources, more detailed accounts of their past, and more elaborate chronologies. In comparison to other early histories, theirs was a modest one, not a boastful account of conquest. Jews were instructed to confess, "A wandering Aramean was my father; and he (the tribe) went down into Egypt and sojourned there, few in number; and there he became a nation, great, mighty and populous" (Deuteronomy as quoted in Butterfield, 1981:82). The distinctive feature of their history was not its complexity or precision, but its linear order and its modesty.

Prior to their attachment to Egypt, the Jews were nomadic herders who had sustained, if sporadic, contact with sedentary groups. There are no indications that they were militarily significant or economically important. They were probably illiterate without an extended chronology. During their stay in Egypt they acquired both literacy and a chronology. In the Old Testament it is claimed that a Jew instructed the Egyptians to plan for the future by saving grain from the years of plenty for the years of need. It is far more likely that they acquired a conception of distal futures from the Egyptians than that they taught it to the Egyptians.

Their distinctive position vis-à-vis the Egyptians while residents of the Nile Valley provided a foundation for the emergence of an intense self-consciousness. They were segregated from the Egyptians by the Egyptians. The Egyptians treated them as inferiors, restricted their movements, and required them to pay taxes. The sedentary and constrained life clashed with their tradition of nomadic herders. They experienced a series of cataclysmic transformations within a few generations.

Their early history stands in marked contrast to that of other ancient civilizations. It begins with them leaving their nomadic ways to acquire the necessities of life, followed by a period of dependency upon a wealthy and more powerful group. They then reasserted their autonomy. The past of the Egyptians and the Sumerians did not reach back beyond the origin of the state; the Hittites had no tales of the period preceding their arrival into Asia Minor. However, the Jews had a linear history that reached back into their nomadic days, through a period of sedentarism, into another nomadic period. Their history was unpretentious but variable and vibrant.

Furthermore, it projected a future of hope. Prior to, during, and following their attachment to Egypt, they had contact with sedentary groups who were wealthier than they. They longed for the land of milk and honey possessed by the sedentary communities. This yearning was transformed into a promise from their god that a land of milk and honey was forthcoming. This belief justified their subsequent conquest of wealthy cities. Their god awarded them.

Their history was ethnocentric. Like the earlier cyclical histories, other societies are only acknowledged in terms of their impingements upon the Jews. Yet in contrast to the historians of older and wealthier groups they recorded and assessed the unbecoming behavior of their own. They applied standards of proper behavior to themselves and noted deviations. They were not above judgement.

They acquired literacy and a chronology from others but used them in a distinctive manner. They constructed and maintained a history, based not on conquest, but upon the trials and tribulations of a modest group maintaining a distinctive collective identity while surrounded by more powerful groups. They had a linear historical consciousness far superior to that of other societies of the period. As with the Hittites, their historical consciousness rested upon a foundation provided by literacy, a command of an extended chronology, exposure to multiple points of view and a series of cataclysmic transformations. It differed by offering accounts not of exploits and conquest, but of wanderings and sufferings.

Their earliest history provided them with a chronological account of their transformation from an inconsequential subordinate group to a relatively wealthy and autonomous group. In contrast, the Egyptians did not have written accounts that sequentially arrayed their past until after they had become the dominant society in the region. They did not have written accounts of their past until after their social structure was stabilized. The same condition appears to have been the case for many other ancient civilizations preceding the emergence of historical accounts.

The early history of the Jews informed them that their current life was different from that of their ancestors. Once they had become autonomous and relatively wealthy they were aware that their current way of life was an improvement over that of their ancestors. Their history informed them that not all was constant in human affairs, that a better life was possible. Within that context progress can emerge as a viable concept. Their subsequent defeats and victories exposed them to a series of cataclysmic changes. That provided a foundation for the emergence of a frame of thought quite different from the cyclical paradigm. All was not constant.

GREEK HISTORY

It is frequently claimed that the Greeks were the first historians. Herodotus, who wrote during the latter part of the fifth century B.C., is commonly referred to as the father of history. However, the historical consciousness of the Greeks was greatly stimulated by their contacts with others. The debt of the Greek historians to other societies, especially to the Phoenicians, is much greater than is usually acknowledged. During the centuries preceding Herodotus, the Greeks traded and frequently warred with the Phoenicians.

They acquired literacy from them; it is also likely they originally acquired an interest in sequentially ordering the past from the Phoenicians. Philo, who lived between 64 and 141 wrote a history of the Phoenicians, only fragments of which survive. He claimed that his history was a Greek rendition of a history originally written in the fourteenth century by a Phoenician. Hellenists have given little credence to the claim. However, "Among the Ugaritic clay tablets found at Ras es Shamra are texts dealing with mythology that strikingly resemble what Philo had set forth" (Wunderlich, 1974:275). Josephus, who wrote during the first century , reported the that Phoenicians had records that dated from the tenth century , 500 years prior to Herodotus.

Whether acquired from the Phoenicians or elsewhere, there is little doubt that the Greeks were indebted to others for their awareness that the past could be sequentially ordered by an extended chronology. Herodotus was acutely aware that the Egyptians regarded the Greeks as mere children in the field of history. Nonetheless the early histories of the Greeks were markedly different from that of the earlier histories of the Egyptians, Sumerians, Hittites, and Jews.

Like the earlier historical efforts it concentrated on conflict. Greek history emerged within a context of an extremely rich oral tradition that had been transformed into a written one. Their rich oral tradition provided large bodies of information about the past affairs of the Greeks. In addition, the Greeks of the period had, through their trade, established sustained contact with a variety of others. Their written materials provided them with exciting accounts of the exploits of their ancestors; the trade contacts provided them with awareness of variation. The past was an intense one, like that of the Jews, but their awareness of variation was far greater than that of the Jews. It was similar to the breath of awareness of the Hittites.

However, the early Greek historians had only an extremely limited chronology at their command. Herodotus' lack of command of a chronology is so great that he does not even make a sustained effort to chronologically order the past. In contrast, Thucydides, who follows him by a generation, attempted to specify with exactness the chronological order of events. However, he did not have available an established chronology that allowed him to give a precise and extended history of Greek affairs prior to his own lifetime. Josephus noted the lack of command of a chronology by the Greeks. "We therefore (who are Jews) must yield to the Grecian writing as to language and eloquence of composition; but then we shall give them no such preferences to the verity of history" (Josephus, 1960:608).

The distinctive feature of Greek history was not that it was the first, but rather its breadth of perspective. The Greek historians' accounts of other civilizations display an attitude of wonderment, not one of condemnation. The affairs of others, as well as the affairs of the Greeks, are a source of excitement and entertainment. Both Greeks and others alike were praised for proper behavior and condemned for improper behavior. There are traces of ethnocentrism, but comparatively speaking, these historians were students of the world, not of their own society. Greek history may have suffered from a lack of an adequate chronology, but it had breadth and intensity.

The Greek historians also made critical assessments of the validity of accounts of the past. Neither oral nor written descriptions were automatically assumed to be accurate. Each source of information was evaluated. Accounts were compared with each other, assessments were made of the reasonableness and truthfulness of the accounts. Descriptions of events that were regarded as beyond what was possible for human beings to accomplish were discredited. Reports of direct communication between human beings and gods were ridiculed. The Greeks were seekers of truth about the past, not scribes who justified the extant order.

SUMMARY

The only evidence we have of the existence of societies prior to literacy is the artifacts and tracings they left. With the emergence of writing a new source of information becomes available. It provides us with information about those who produced the writings and those written about. We know of the Trojans both through archeaological research and the writings of the Greeks. Literacy increased the amount of information available to us about ancient societies; it also transformed the nature of the information.

Of even greater importance, literacy increased and transformed the information available to members of these societies. Some nonliterate societies composed verses to more effectively retain and transmit information. These poems served as the medium for the retention of information. The amount of information contained in these poems was much greater than that possible in regular discourse. However, the content of these poems was highly responsive to current conditions.

Information inscribed on a material medium was less responsive to current conditions. By inscribing information on a material medium a series of events—talk—was transformed into a series of objects—written words. Written material is a static entity. It can be inspected, examined, and analyzed. The written word provides an "objective" description of events.

After written materials are available, disagreements and uncertainties of whether an event occurred in the past may still arise. The presence of written accounts changes the nature of the resolution of disagreements. Once information is written, the written account is available for inspection. If accounts differ, then each account can be assessed for its completeness and veracity; new accounts that attempt to incorporate the diverse information may then be offered.

Written accounts themselves do not provide a sequenced past. The development of history required that the literate accounts of past affairs be placed in sequence. The chronologies used to sequentially order the past were developed by those who studied and articulated the repetitious cycles of celestial events. The earliest histories were cyclical. They sequenced human affairs by applying the paradigm developed in the study of celestial events to human affairs. This development first occurred in agricultural societies with a totalitarian social structure.

Linear histories were first developed by the intellectuals of societies with extensive intercommunity contacts acquiring and applying the extended chronologies developed in the totalitarian context. They used these chronologies to order past cataclysmic events, many of which were associated with warfare. Linear historians acknowledge transformations; they are not captives of a static mode of thought. Both the past and the future are conceived of as subject to reformulation.

Within totalitarian societies knowledge of the past was in the hands of an intellectual elite subordinate to the authorities. They formulated an official history. The extant social order was conceptualized as everlasting. The past was fitted into a static mode of thought; it was not available for reformulation. In contrast, in societies where the literate were not affiliated with the ruling elite, there often were competing written accounts of the past. The intellectuals disputed the past and the past was open to reformulations.

In some instances the written accounts acquired the status of "reality." What was written was regarded as having greater validity that the empirical world. When the written word achieved this status it was no longer a liberating factor, but had become a means of social control. The written word achieved this status among the intellectuals of the totalitarian societies. In some other societies, the written word served to expand and extend the consciousness of all.

Chapter XIX

A Special Case?

Since the enlightenment, most western European scholars have presumed the foundation for western European civilization was laid by the Greeks. The transformations that occurred among the Greeks during the first millennium B.C. are often referred to as the "miracle of Greece." The flourishing of the Greeks is often discussed as if it were unique. The emergence of the Greek civilization is better documented than the flourishings of more ancient civilizations, but it shared many features with other flourishings. The uniqueness of the changes wrought by the Greeks has often been overemphasized.

The emergence of the Greek civilization is frequently described as if it occurred in a very short period of time. The so-called classical period of Athens, which is roughly coterminus with the life of Socrates, is usually emphasized. Socrates was put to death when he was about seventy years old in 399 B.C. Some scholars date the beginning of the classical period with the defeat of the Persians in 478 B.C. A remarkable series of events did occur in Athens during the fifth century. However, many other significant developments occurred centuries earlier in other locations while Athens remained an agricultural village. Samos and Corinth were trade and intellectual centers before the "miracle of Greece" touched Athens. Athens emerged as the center of intellectual activity during the fifth century B.C. and Alexandria became the center of intellectual activity in the third century.

The emergence and spread of the Greek civilization occurred between approximately 1000 B.C., when some Greek communities became involved in intercommunity trade, through the classical age, to the conquest and absorption of the Greeks by the Romans. A period of approximately 1,000 years transpired from the time the Greeks stirred from their life as illiterate farmers and raiders to their destruction by the Roman Empire. Some activity continued in the fields of mathematics,

321

astronomy, and other sciences in some locations for a century or two after Rome occupied Alexandria.

There was considerable variation among the Greek communities in when and how they experienced the changes. Some underwent profound transformations in a short period. Sparta blossomed early, but then deliberately rejected the developments that most other communities welcomed. Athens was slow in entering the international commercial network, but became both the commercial and intellectual center of the Greeks. Agriculture remained important in most regions, and raiding continued to be important in some regions into the classical period.

The Greeks composed poetry, plays, and histories that constitute a significant part of our modern western European heritage. The foundation for modern science was laid; mathematic principles were acquired and diffused. The accomplishments were Greek, but they could only have occurred by the Greeks borrowing practices that had been formulated by other civilizations. The Greeks acquired ideas from others, reformulated some of them, and put some of them to new uses.

The debt of the Greeks, and thereby western civilization, to the Phoenicians and Egyptians was considerable. Through their contact with the Phoenicians, they became involved in international trade and were transformed from illiterates to literates. Their contacts with the Egyptians provided them with the opportunity to expand their trade, acquire geometric principles and astronomical knowledge and stimulated a frame of thought that has culminated in modern science.

The "Greek miracle" included the acquisition of ideas from others in addition to the Phoenicians and the Egyptians. Yet the debt of western European civilization to those two ancient civilizations is greater than to any others. As in other cases when there is the founding of a new civilization, those constructing the civilization borrow ideas from many sources. Some of these ideas are taken over in toto; others are radically transformed when they are put into practice by the emerging civilization. The acquisition of a variety of cultural elements from others provided stimuli for many inventions among the Greeks.

THE PHOENICIAN INFLUENCE

The Phoenicians had an urban civilization of considerable substance while the Greeks were small impoverished agricultural villagers who raided their wealthier neighbors. The Phoenicians established large trade centers in many areas of the eastern Mediterranean. Their civilization rested upon an infrastructure of long-distance trade. Their trade was primarily, but not solely, maritime. They also manufactured many commercial products.

The original Phoenicians were nomads who specialized in the overland transportation of goods. In the second millennium they developed maritime trade networks. They emerged as a significant and distinctive civilization during the last half of the second millennium B.C. Their emergence as a major maritime power was quite distinctive. Most of the ancient maritime trade centers were first established as urban centers and then became involved in long-distance trade. In contrast, the Phoenicians were first long-distance traders and then established large urban centers.

Phoenician communities appeared on the Syrian coast shortly after the expulsion of the Hyksos from Egypt. Some of the early Phoenicians may have been descendents of the Hyksos. Their early successes in trade seem to have been linked to their trade contacts with the Egyptians. In the latter part of the second millennium there were Phoenician cities at numerous locations on the coastlines of western Asia, northern Africa, and southern Europe. By 1000 B.C. Tyre, Sidon, Byblos, and other Phoenician cities were important centers of commerce.

Their cities were all essentially ports of trade. They were fortified against land attacks, but were oriented to the sea. They traded within inland groups, but the bulk of their trade was maritime. They sought out new materials and markets. The societies they traded with ranged from the most complex civilizations to primitive groups. They had little interest in territory, other than that necessary for the establishment of a port. Some farmed, but their agricultural efforts were limited. On occasion they warred, but most of their wars were defensive or attacks on pirates who threatened their shipping lanes. Their life revolved around long-distance maritime trade and the manufacturing of goods.

They accumulated a rich lore associated with their long-distance trade which they jealously protected. One of their legends relates that a captain, upon learning a foreign ship was following him, deliberately wrecked his own ship to prevent the foreigners from learning his destination. According to the legend, other Phoenician merchants reimbursed him for his losses. The truthfulness of the legend is less significant than what it reveals about Phoenician ideals of behavior.

They transported both raw and manufactured goods. The timber from the forests of Lebanon was a major source of wealth for some. Others transported metals from western Europe to eastern Mediterranean cities. They became famous as the source of esoteric goods. They maintained a rather effective monopoly of knowledge on the techniques for manufacturing glass and purple dyed cloth. Both of these items were avidly sought by the wealthy of other civilizations.

The Phoenicians adopted many practices from older civilizations. The wealthier communities built temples and palaces in imitation of the edifices of older civilizations. However, their civilization was neither temple- nor palace-centered; it was centered on the marketplace. Theirs was a commercial civilization. The wealthier merchants were the focal persons of their communities, not priests or kings.

Early Greek-Phoenician Contact

Contact between the Greeks and Phoenicians was established by 1000 B.C., perhaps earlier. About that time the pottery of some of the Greek communities changed from the crude and slipshod imitation of the old Mycenaean pottery to a new and distinctive form of pottery with abstract geometric decorations. Greek pottery was widely traded.

The earliest contacts between the Greeks and the Phoenicians may have been Greeks raiding Phoenician communities, or Phoenician traders seeking out new markets. The two forms of contact remained closely intertwined for centuries. There was probably an intermixture of trade and raiding from the earliest days of their contact. The name Phoenician was given to them by the Greeks in reference to the purple cloth they traded. That indicates that trade was a significant form of contact from the earliest days. But the Homeric tradition suggests the earliest significant contact between the Greeks and the commercial cities was accomplished through raiding and looting.

The oral tradition of the Greeks indicates that the preclassical Greeks were extremely violent. The heroic ideals portrayed in Homer are those of pirates, raiders, and destroyers of those who dared to stand in the way. The pottery of the Greeks of 750 B.C., which is about the time the Greeks were becoming literate and intensely involved in intercommunity trade, was decorated with warships manned by armed sailors. Apparently raiding and piracy was an important and honored way of life at that time.

The warrior tradition receded in importance as the Greeks became involved in trade. Thucycides claims that the first Greeks to discontinue the practice of going about the streets armed were the Athenians. It is very likely that other Greek communities that had become involved in trade prior to the Athenians had discontinued parading about dressed to kill before the Athenians did. In general as the marketplace achieved a position of dominance in Greek communities, violence receded. The Spartans, who rejected commercialism, remained exceedingly violent throughout the classical period.

The Greek attitude toward the Phoenicians was ambivalent. On the one hand they were wealthy and the source of desired goods, but on the other hand they were mere traders lacking the "heroic qualities" of raiders. The attitude of the Greeks toward the Phoenicians is indicated by the tale that Ulysses was moved to enter an athletic contest, after first declining, because of an insult that referred to him as a merchant. The Phoenicians were equally ambivalent toward the Greeks. On the one hand the Greeks were uncouth and violent barbarians who attacked the more civilized and looted whenever they could. Yet the Greeks offered an opportunity for trade. Among other items the Greeks had to offer in trade was the loot they had acquired from their raids.

Trade between the Greeks and the Phoenicians was relatively insignificant for the first few centuries of contact. The Greeks had little to offer; they were simple farmers. They were not important centers of the commercial network during the Homeric period. "There is no single word in either the Iliad or Odyssey that is in fact a synonym for merchant" (Finley, 1967:415). Intercommunity trade appears to have emerged as a relatively important activity about 825 B.C. when literacy first appeared among the Greeks.

The earliest Greek markets were located on the edges of their communities; they were not in the center of their towns and cities. The earliest trade was between residents of the villages and aliens. Later the markets became the centers of some of the Greek cities. The earliest commercial centers were on the coast of Asia and nearby islands. Later it spread into the European communities. Even then some, like the Spartans, maintained their traditional way of life. When money became popular among the Greeks, the Spartans attempted to retain their purity by prohibiting the use of money. Consequently many hoards of coins have been uncovered at Spartan sites.

As the markets expanded the Greeks took on Phoenician ways. They were self-consciously aware of their lack of wealth and sophistication in comparison to the Phoenicians. They regarded the Phoenicians with disgust, but that did not prevent them from adopting many of the Phoenician traits. They learned how to trade, what items were in demand at other locations, the marvels of other societies, and importantly, the locations that held promise for the establishment of colonies. They slowly became urban sophisticates and put aside their rustic days of raiding and farming. Prestige based on wealth slowly replaced prestige based on heroic endeavors.

Literacy

The literacy of the Greeks did not descend from the earlier literacy of the Minoan and Mycenaean civilizations. Mycenaean writing was still in use on the island of Cyprus while the Greeks were acquiring literacy from the Phoenicians. But the literacy of the Minoan and Mycenaean civilizations did not contribute to emerging phonetic literacy. The last vestige of Minoan and Mycenaean literacy disappeared as the new literacy emerged.

According to Greek legend a Phoenician—Cadmus—taught the Greeks the alphabet. It is more likely that the acquisition of literacy was a diffuse process. The original literacy of the Greeks was "the cursive writing used in business activity rather than monumental characters of, for example, Byblos. Al Mina may have been the point of contact" (Finley, 1971:87). Al Mina was a trade center on the Asian coast populated by both Greeks and Phoenicians. The early literacy of the Greeks emerged in the markets and was used to facilitate trade.

By 725 B.C. there were several different alphabets in the various Greek communities. The variation in alphabets may indicate a variety of sources, or it is possible that all stemmed from a single source and then evolved in distinctive fashions in various Greek communities. By 700 B.C. the alphabet was used in a number of locations to decorate and enhance Greek pottery. By 660 B.C., if not earlier, some communities used their literacy to publish their laws (Hammond, 1967:92). The laws were engraved on wooden posts at the marketplace. The use of the written word in this manner indicates that literacy was pervasive enough in some communities that universal literacy was presumed. Of course, not all were literate, but a sufficient percentage must have been literate for the communities to use the written word to display their laws.

The alphabet was widely used to inscribe couplets and grafitti. About the same time the compositions of Homer were transformed from the oral to the written form. Shortly afterwards or perhaps simultaneously a new genre appears, namely poems composed in writing. This poetry reflected changes in the Greek social structure. These poems attended to current conditions, they did not glorify the days of old. Hersiod, Archilochus, and Sappho were among the first to gain fame by using the alphabet to compose the new poetry.

All three of these poets were affiliated with trade. Hersiod who probably wrote his poems about 725-700 B.C. was a farmer, but his father had been a merchant. Archilochus was probably born shortly before 700 B.C. He was a native of the island of Paros—an early trade center. He was soldier, sailor, and merchant. Sappho was a native of the island of Lesbos and born about 618 B.C. Lesbos was a center of foreign trade; merchants of the island hawked their wares in Egypt. Her brother was a wine merchant who traveled to Egypt, and she married a merchant.

The compositions of Homer reveled in the glories of combat. There are few traces of this in the compositions of Hersiod. He attends to the concerns of a farmer attempting to eke out an existence in a difficult world. He is aware of the more sophisticated world outside the farming community, but it did not appeal to him. The world of Hersiod was not romantic; he had little sympathy for either war or distant parts.

Archilochus wrote of war, but his war was "Dirty, dangerous, vivid, uncomplicated, (and) often boring...(with) corpses drying to parched mummy in the summer sun, and men who prefer to throw away their shields and live rather than be carried home dead with honour" (Green, 1972:166). His poetry reflected the turmoil of the period. Violence was significant, but it had lost the glorious and exciting overtones of Homer.

Sappho was fascinated with and glorified love, not war. She was acutely aware of the larger world. Compared to Homer, she was a cultural sophisticate. She was knowledgeable about foreign ways. Homer was aware of foreigners, but only as enemies or as mysterious peoples and places. Her poetry reflected a self-conscious hedonism and an adventurous life associated with overseas travel.

The poetry of these writers was a break from the Homeric tradition. It was a genre of literature that reflected the changes of Greek communities were undergoing and current affairs. It did not glorify war; nor did it reflect the tribal solidarity of the poetry of Homer. Rather these poets focused upon individuals coping with a changing world laced with problems and conflict. It reflected the egoism of the marketplace, not the solidarity of raiders.

The literacy of the Greeks had none of the secrecy and sacredness of the temple or palace writings of totalitarian civilizations. It was not the literacy of priests, bureaucrats, and political elite. It appeared and flourished at the marketplace. It was available to anyone frequenting the markets who had the time, talent, and resources to acquire it.

The emergence of the Greek civilization followed much the same pattern as the emergence of several earlier civilizations. It rested on an infrastructure of intercommunity trade. The stimulus for the trade was provided by Phoenician contact. Through their trade and raiding the Greeks became aware of the larger world about them. Then when established communities experienced times of stress, colonists left to found new communities. Some of the first new communities were established on the eastern coastlines of the Mediterranean Sea. This brought them into more intense contact with the Phoenicians and others. They colonized these regions; they farmed as well as traded. Their violent tradition stood them in good stead. They drove out more primitive groups and conquered some sites previously occupied by other civilized groups.

The establishment of new Greek settlements gave further stimulus to trade. Later some communities were established for the expressed purpose of stimulating trade. The Ionian communities were the first to become heavily dependent on trade; they were also the first to become literate. The colonization of Italy was accomplished by groups from Ionia as well as from the older Greek settlements. The colonization of Italy and other western regions was similar to the colonization of North America by western Europeans. Large areas of land were brought under civilization. These agricultural communities provided a firmer foundation for the intercommunity trade of the Greeks.

The growth and expansion of the Greek civilization then took much the same form as the growth and expansion of earlier civilizations. Perhaps the most distinctive feature of the early Greek civilization was the high level of literacy. They became literate simultaneous with becoming civilized. Furthermore the literacy was phonetic. Anyone could acquire command of it in a relatively short period. Phonetic writing was easily mastered; it facilitated the acquisition of large amounts of knowledge by all. The phonetic system was a powerful medium that released constraints on the amount of information that could be accumulated and transmitted.

A wealth of material from the oral tradition was available among Greeks when they became literate. That stimulated some to use their literacy to compose original works. The literacy of the Phoenicians was also phonetic, but the transformation of the Phoenicians from illiterates to literates required centuries. They had inherited a system of writing that was essentially ideographic. It was slowly transformed into a phonetic system. In contrast, the Greeks acquired a mature phonetic system, and some communities were transformed from illiterates to literates in decades. Furthermore the transformation occurred within a context of a rich oral tradition. The oral tradition contained many ideas that could be transformed into writing.

Literacy entered the Greek world from the fringes; it was not affiliated with either a temple or a palace elite. The rank and file became literate as quickly as the elite; they may have become literate earlier. Secondly, the Phoenicians did not dominate the Greeks. They were superior to the Greeks in material wealth, but they were not militarily superior. The Greeks were more than their equals on the battlefields.

Perhaps the most distinctive feature of the acquisition of literacy by the Greeks was that they became literate prior to or simultaneous with becoming sophisticated in the management of numbers and geometric forms. The earliest numeric system of the Greeks was a base twenty-seven system. Their numbers were the same as their alphabet. Alpha was both a letter and the number one; beta was both a letter and the number two, and so on. Geometric forms were displayed on their early pottery as they became involved in trade, but geometric forms were not used to design monumental buildings until after literacy was well established in the Greek communities. Mathematics and astronomy developed after phonetic literacy was well established.

In the long run the Phoenicians were relegated to a secondary position in the eastern Mediterranean; the Greeks acquired the dominant position. The Phoenician cities of western Mediterranean continued to flourish until they were destroyed by the Roman Empire. The hegemony of the Greeks in the eastern Mediterranean was aided by their adoption of money. Money, a standardized coin of the realm, entered the Greek communities about 625 B.C. The Phoenicians did not adopt money. They continued to conduct their trade by barter. Money provided a fluid medium of exchange and facilitated the storage of wealth. Money and military might allowed the Greeks to replace the Phoenicians as the dominant civilization in the eastern Mediterranean.

As the Greeks expanded they established contact with the Egyptians. They served as mercenaries for the Egyptians and subsequently acquired a favored position in trade with the Egyptians. These developments opened new vistas for the Greeks. They learned first hand of the marvels of Egypt and avidly sought them.

THE EGYPTIAN CONTACT

Greeks probably had contact with the Egyptians as early as the eighth century B.C. There are references in the *Iliad* and *Odyssey* to Egypt. However, the references do not indicate that Homer had any direct knowledge of Egypt. "For him Egypt is just a distant and wonderful land, full of marvels and wealth" (Austin, 1970:12). The Egyptians appear to have established a fort on the delta to keep out Greek raiders in the late eighth or early seventh century (Austin, 1970:12). But then Greek mercenaries were hired by the Egyptians during the early seventh century, about 660 B.C.

The employment of Greek mercenaries by Egyptians was closely associated with the emergence of the Saite Dynasty, which held sway between 663 and 525 B.C. The Saite Dynasty was established with the aid of mercenaries, many of whom were Greek. Several of the military outposts in Egypt were manned by Greek mercenaries under the command of Egyptian officers. Greek inscriptions that date about 600 B.C. were scratched on a statue 700 miles up the Nile. The inscriptions are in six different handwritings which indicates that literacy was rather widespread among the Greek soldiers.

The Saite Dynasty was a time of internal turmoil among the Egyptians and a period of revival. Shortly after it was established, the king disrupted the sacred bureaucracy. In 648 B.C. he appointed a female relative to the post of high priest of Amon at Thebes. That he could impose both an outsider and a female upon the priests indicates that for the moment at least the bureaucratic elite did not have the influence they usually exercised in Egypt. As part of the revival, the dynasty attempted to resurrect the glories of ancient Egypt. They "consciously imitated the past, in art, in literature and in the reconstruction of old official titles" (Jordan, 1976:113). It was an age of prosperity; foreign trade flourished and the Greeks were the primary beneficiaries of the trade.

By late in the seventh century B.C. trade between the Greeks and Egyptians had acquired a position of some significance. About 615 B.C. the port of Naukratis, populated by Greeks, was established on the delta. Naukratis soon became Egypt's most important commercial center (Jordan, 1976:114). From then on there was sustained peaceful contact between the Greeks and the Egyptians.

In 575 B.C. the Egyptian king used Greek mercenaries as his body guards. Nonetheless the Greeks were not welcomed into Egypt with open arms. They were uncouth foreigners. The Greeks, while tolerated, were not given unrestricted access to Egypt and Egyptians. They were not to marry Egyptians or to eat with them. Trade at Naukratis was closely regulated. According to Herodotus' account, when a Greek ship arrived at any other location on the delta, the captain of the ship had to swear that he had not come of his own free will, but had been brought to the location by contrary winds. Then he had to go around the delta in barges to Naukratis.

It is doubtful that any of the elite of Egypt had sustained contact with the barbarian foreigners. Nonetheless Naukratis became a city of considerable significance where Greeks and Egyptians had routine dealings with one another. Naukratis was only ten miles from the city that served as the capital of Egypt during the Saite Dynasty. Some of the more curious Greeks must have traveled to the capital and made at least incidental contact with some Egyptians.

The majority of the earliest Greek residents of Naukratis were from Ionia; the influence of the Milesians was dominant during the early decades of its flourishing (Austin, 1970). Greek hoards of coins that date from the sixth century have been uncovered. After about 500 B.C. there is a sharp increase in the proportion of Athenian coins (Austin, 1970:38). Simultaneously Athens was emerging as the dominant trade and intellectual center.

The Egyptian riches and knowledge awed the Greeks. Some of them consciously imitated the Egyptians—a tyrant of Corinth named his son after an Egyptian king. The nature of the relationship between the Greeks and Egyptians was like that common whenever two societies of different levels of complexity and wealth have sustained peaceful contact. The elite members of the less advanced frequently attempt to imitate the elite of the superior society. Both historical and archaeological data indicate that this was the nature of the relationship between the Greeks and the Egyptians in the seventh, sixth, and probably the fifth century B.C.

The Greek written sources referring to contact between the two societies date from the later part of the critical period. It is unanimous in claiming that Egypt was the source of ideas that served as the foundation of mathematic and astronomic developments among the Greeks. Despite these facts, many contemporary scholars of ancient Greece are reluctant to assign any significance to Egyptian-Greek contact.

Some historians of science, philosophers, and Hellenists have been vehement in their denial of importance of the contact between the Greeks and Egyptians for subsequent developments among the Greeks. Even many of those who acknowledge trade between the Greeks and Egyptians deny that the contact had a significant impact on the development of mathematics and astronomy among the Greeks. The following are but a sample of those who take this position. "Egyptian astronomy had much less influence on the outside world for the very simple reason that it remained through all its history on an exceedingly crude level which had practically no relation to the rapidly developing mathematical astronomy of the Hellenistic age" (Neugebauer, 1957:80). "Egyptian astronomy never rose above the level of crude observation to develop into a science" (Dicks, 1970:28). "The stories current in antiquity about Thales and other Greeks learning Geometry from the Egyptians are beyond doubt false" (Toomer, 1971:145). One suspects they protest too much.

A few historians of science have argued that the development of mathematics and science among the Greeks was influenced by Egyptian contacts. "It is childish to assume that science began in Greece; the Greek 'miracle' was prepared by millennia of work in Egypt, Mesopotamia and possibly in other regions. Greek science was less an invention than a revival" (Sarton, 1952:ix). "The eight-year cycle that Eudoxus brought in, the Octaeteris, was really precise. Of its stemming back to Egypt there is no question. He actually fitted the beginning of his own Octaeteris to the start of the Egyptian Teraeteris" (Santillana, 1963:826).

That Egyptian intellectuals of the period were involved in scientific pursuits is questionable. It depends upon one's definition of science. There is no evidence that during the period in question Egyptian intellectuals were making sustained observations of the empirical world with the objective of formulating general principles. The evidence points in the opposite direction. Egyptians had long since discontinued studying the empirical world for the purposes of formulating principles. Their knowledge had stagnated; it had become encased within an authoritarian bureaucracy and was treated as sacred canon.

However, intellectuals, especially astronomers, occupied an important position in the social structure of Egypt. There was variation from one dynasty to the next in the relationship between the bureaucratic-intellectual elite and the king, but usually they were focal persons. There is every reason to think they were critical members of the social structure during the Saite Dynasty with its concern with reviving the ancient traditions. Strabo, who wrote about the time of Christ, reports "The priests (of Egypt) devoted themselves both to philosophy and to astronomy and they were companions of the King" (Strabo, 1932:9). After sustained peaceful contact was established, many Greeks traveled to Egypt to examine and learn about Egyptian marvels. Thales may have been the first to expose Greeks to the mathematic and astronomic knowledge of the Egyptians.

Thales

Thales, the first Greek philosopher, was a native of Miletus, the first Greek city to have extensive trade with the Egyptians. He was a merchant who reportedly returned to Egypt to learn from the Egyptians. His most famous feat is his supposed prediction of an eclipse. He could not have made the prediction on the basis of astronomical knowledge present among the Greeks at that time. The Greek communities had a variety of calendars. One of the more complex Greek calendars of the period was an eight-year cycle, which was not an indigenous development (Nilsson, 1920). The eight-year cycle was not a very precise calendar. Each year had a discrepancy of about 1.585 days (O'Neil, 1975:42). At that time the Greeks did not have the equinoxes located (Dicks, 1970), nor were they aware that the morning and evening stars (Venus and Mercury) were planets. That knowledge became established in Greek communities about the time of Pythagoras.

Such crude astronomical knowledge would not have allowed Thales to make his famous prediction. The question then is: Where did he acquire the necessary information? The most likely source was Egypt. He may have acquired it from some other source. It is possible that Thales' prediction was a fabrication, but at least he acquired the reputation of being able to predict eclipses.

A second "famous accomplishment" of Thales was instructing the king of Egypt how to compute the height of a pyramid. That he solved the problem for an Egyptian king can be readily dismissed. It is unlikely that an Egyptian king surrounded by Egyptian intellectuals called upon a barbarian Greek to solve such a routine problem.

The legend informs us that Thales accomplished this feat by measuring his own shadow and height, then the shadow of the pyramid and through calculating the ratio determined the height of the pyramid. One problem with the legend is that the procedure does not provide the correct answer. At the minimum Thales would also have had to calculate the base of the apex of the pyramid, a procedure that was beyond the ken of Greeks of the period. Furthermore, "The Greek word *pyramis* was an adaptation of the Egyptian word *pyremus* which curiously enough, denoted neither an imperial tomb nor a geometrical solid. Pyremus was Egyptian for altitude" (Dantzing, 1955:44). It is much more likely that Thales learned to calculate the height of tall objects, such as an obelisk, by computing ratios, and then instructed other Greeks how to perform the task. They marveled at his ability.

A third feat credited to Thales was computing the distance at sea of a ship by noting the proportion of the ship that had disappeared from sight. That he accomplished such a task is doubtful. It requires very precise observations, observations that the Greeks were not capable of making. It is more likely that he learned that such a feat was possible and related the tale to other Greeks.

Some historians of science recognize the crudity of mathematic and astronomic thought current among the Greeks in the sixth century B.C. Those who recognize that condition and also deny any significance to Egyptian-Greek contact for the mathematic and astronomic developments among the Greeks are forced to conclude "that the traditional stories of discoveries made by Thales or Pythagoras must be discarded as totally unhistorical" (Neugebauer, 1957:148).

However, if one acknowledges that the Egyptians had a sophisticated system of mathematics and made precise observations of celestial phenomena, although this body of knowledge had long been stagnant, then it seems likely that Thales' feats were made possible by his traveling to Egypt and learning some of their principles. He then used his knowledge (bag of tricks) to impress and entertain others. Thales' reputation was similar to that of outstanding minstrels. He provided entertainment. Simultaneously he introduced into the Greek communities some mathematical principles and an interest in making observations of celestial phenomena.

Pythagoras

According to the accounts of the Greeks, Thales was the first philosopher. However, it was the interjection of Pythagoreanism that is generally regarded by students of Greek intellectual history as a major turning point. It is reported that Pythagoras spent twenty-two years in Egypt and two years in Babylonia. It is doubtful he stayed that long in Egypt, but he may have. While there he reportedly learned the language, adopted their customs, and entered the holiest parts of the temples.

The details of Pythagoras' visit to Egypt are questionable. But it seems likely that his contact with the Egyptians was more intense and of greater duration than most Greeks who toured Egypt. He was a native of Samos. Many of the mercenaries of Egypt were Samian. The tyrant of Samos had a treaty or pact with the king of Egypt. Pythagoras reportedly carried a letter from the tyrant of Samos to the king of Egypt. He was a visiting scholar sponsored by his government. That accounts for his greater familiarity with Egyptian knowledge than other Greeks of the period.

When he returned among the Greeks he founded a cult. Among other things he stated the earth was a sphere and that "all was number." Aristotle credits him with elevating Greek mathematics from the arithmetic of the marketplace. His most famous contribution was the Pythagorean theorem, a principle of construction that had been in use for at least 2,000 years in Egypt. It is suggestive that the meaning of the word theorem among the Greeks at that time was not that of a scientific law or an established principle. Rather, it had the meaning of a sight, something to contemplate, something to examine in its own right. In short, a theorem was a marvel.

In Southern Italy, where Pythagoreanism was strong, archaeologists have uncovered a set of gold plates upon which is inscribed the *Book of the Dead* from Egypt in Greek (Burn, 1966:141). Pythagoras and his followers acted toward his knowledge in a manner consistent with the Egyptian tradition. They surrounded it with mysticism and secrecy. This behavior stands in marked contrast to the prevailing stance among the Greeks.

Most Greeks with special talent and knowledge appeared at the marketplace, the most public place available, to demonstrate their wares. They treated their knowledge much as the grower of wool treated his excess shearings; something to be sold to anyone interested. The story of Hippocrates, a geometer, illustrates the conflict between the two stances toward knowledge. "While on a visit to Athens he (Hippocrates) came in contact with a group of Pythagoreans who taught him what they knew of geometry and arithmetic; that having subsequently lost his fortune, he was reduced to selling these mathematical secrets to anyone who could and would pay the price, thus betraying his mentor's trust" (Dantzing, 1955:121).

Plato

The writings of Plato indicate he was heavily influenced by Egyptian traditions. He was aware of the teachings of Pythagoras; he claimed it was necessary to understand mathematics before one could pursue other intellectual endeavors. Strabo, writing about four centuries later, states that Plato studied in Egypt. Strabo reported that on his own visit to Egypt "the houses of the priests and schools of Plato and Eudoxus were pointed out to us; for Eudoxus went up to that place with Plato, and they both passed thirteen years with the priests, as is stated by some writers" (Strabo, 1932:83). The phrasing suggests that Strabo may have had his doubts about Plato spending thirteen years in Egypt. It is possible Plato only knew of Egypt through the accounts of others. Strabo also states the Egyptian priests were secretive, but Eudoxus and Plato courted their favor and the Egyptian priests "did teach them the fractions of the day and night, which running over and above the three hundred and sixty-five days, fill out the time of the true year. But at the time the true year was unknown among the Greeks" (Strabo, 1932:85).

A few of Plato's statements suggest that he traveled to Egypt. In one he states "If you inspect their paintings and reliefs on the spot, you will find that the work of ten thousand years ago—I mean the expression not loosely but in all precision—is neither better nor worse than that of today" (Plato, 1934:33-34). The phrasing suggests that Plato had examined the paintings and carvings. Plato admired the constancy of the Egyptian world. In his ideal world, Plato too would have practiced deception and brought human action in tune with the cosmos.

Eudoxus

Eudoxus lived from about 408 to 355 B.C. He may have journeyed to Athens to study with Plato. The relationship between Eudoxus and Plato is uncertain. However, there is little doubt that he traveled to Egypt. Like Pythagoras, when he went to Egypt he carried with him a "letter of introduction" from his tyrant to the king of Egypt. Pythagoras and Eudoxus developed the most elaborate "theories" of the nature of the universe. They were also the two Greeks who are reported to have been sponsored by their rulers, who in turn had a relationship with the king of Egypt. They established closer contact with Egyptian intellectuals than other Greeks who traveled to Egypt prior to the founding of Alexandria.

Eudoxus constructed more elaborate and accurate statements about the solar system than did other contemporary Greeks. He specified the duration of the synoid cycle of Mars—thirty years. "Modern astronomers,..., who examined the 'sphere of Eudoxus', found that his model represents the motion of Saturn and Jupiter perfectly" (Ley, 1963:30). Before Eudoxus could construct such a complex and accurate model either he had to have access to information about the cycles of these planets, or was exposed to a model developed by someone else that displayed the movements, or had to have accumulated an extremely complex, precise, and sustained series of observations of planetary movement. It is extremely doubtful that the latter alternative was the case. It is very likely that he acquired the principles for constructing the model when in Egypt. According to one report Eudoxus acquired astronomical knowledge from the priests of Heliopolis. In the time of Christ, an observatory near Heliopolis was pointed out as the one used by Eudoxus (Heath, 1921).

The sudden appearance of mathematic and astronomic thought as complex as that offered by Thales, Pythagoras, and Eudoxus was an amazing development. The mathematic principles and astronomic theories they offered were constructed without benefit of support by the community. They did not constitute an elite group who rested upon a foundation of communitywide support. Rather they were enterprising individuals who sought out information from others and in turn offered it to their native society. That was possible only by making extensive use of knowledge that had been previously accumulated. Later Greek intellectuals, especially those affiliated with Alexandria, were supported by the ruling elite. However, the early philosophers and scientists had no such support. Some of them derived a livelihood from their special knowledge, but only by making it available in the marketplace.

Other Developments

There were many other developments among the Greeks that indicate the substantial influence of the Egyptians on the development of mathematic and astronomic thought among Greeks. Most of the later mathematic and astronomic developments occurred at Alexandria, which became the intellectual center of Greece. Not all the later developments were mathematic or astronomic but many of them were.

About 300 B.C. Euclid offered the elements of geometry. They remain the foundation for modern elementary geometry. It is often presumed that Euclid formulated the principles. A more likely development is that he learned geometric rules formulated by the Egyptians over two thousand years earlier, then offered a summary of them to the Greek community. "There is irrefutable evidence that a substantial portion of the material recorded in the Elements (of geometry) was known before Euclid, and there is nothing in either the style or in the plan of the treatise to suggest that it was intended as a collection of original contributions" (Dantzing, 1955:37). It is possible that the principles of Euclid were developed by earlier Greeks, but a more likely explanation is that Euclid attempted to summarize what he had learned from the Egyptians.

Eratosthenes of the third century B.C. is credited with computing the size of the earth. Supposedly he accomplished this task by noting that in southern Egypt at Syene, which is located on the Tropic of Cancer, on the day of the summer solstice the sun casts no shadow. He also noted the length of the shadow cast at Alexandria on the same date. Then by computing a ratio based on the difference, he computed the size of the earth. This feat is similar to that of Thales computing the height of a pyramid. It is doubtful that Eratosthenes traveled to southern Egypt, dug a pit, noted the lack of a shadow, noted the shadow cast by the sun at Alexandria, measured the distance between the two locations and then computed the size of the earth. It is more likely that Eratosthenes was instructed about these phenomena by Egyptians and wrote an amount of them for his fellow Greeks. It is possible that he did make the observations himself. But if he did, it was only after being instructed in the procedures by the Egyptians.

The astronomical efforts of the Greeks culminated in the formation of the Ptolemaic System during the second century A.D. It has long been assumed that Ptolemy's theory of the solar system was based upon observations made by Greeks, if not by Ptolemy himself. However, it has been demonstrated that his reported observations were largely fabricated (Newton, 1977). Newton claims that Ptolemy deliberately manufactured data and concocted a system that misled astronomers for centuries. He characterizes Ptolemy's work as an intellectual crime.

Ptolemy was strongly influenced by the Egyptian intellectual tradition. He used the Egyptian system of fractions for his calculations. It is possible that he acquired a theory of the solar system from the Egyptians and constructed an alternative theory that he offered to the Greek-speaking community. The Egyptians had developed a system wherein the planets Mercury and Venus circled the sun while the sun circled the earth. It is conceivable that Ptolemy was imbued with the idea that the earth was the center of the cosmos and formulated an alternative theory that placed the earth in the center of all celestial movement. Then he may have fudged his data to save the theory. He gave priority to the system; he subordinated his observations (if he made any) and those of others, to his theory. That mode of relating data to theory is still practiced in some scientific endeavors.

The Greeks acquired ideas from the Egyptians in fields of endeavor besides mathematics and astronomy. The developments of the Greeks in art, engineering, and medicine were stimulated by ideas from Egypt. In contrast to historians of science, most historians of art acknowledge that developments in Greece were heavily influenced by ideas from Egypt. "The idea of making life-size colossal statues came to Greece from Egypt" (Beazley, 1966:11). One of the first large statues built by the Greeks was on the island of Samos. It was a statue of Apollo made in the Egyptian style. The Greek artists were knowledgeable of the Saite cannon and acknowledged their Egyptian origin (Iversen, 1971:74). The procedures of the Saite cannon were complex. "Its stylistic characteristics could not be caught and reproduced without an intimate knowledge of the canonical principles and rules, which were complicated and difficult to apprehend, (they) could only be taught in Egypt" (Iversen, 1971:73). A Samian also "invented ways of polishing precious stones and brought the art of bronze casting from Egypt to Greece" (Sarton, 1952:191). At least some artisans from Samos traveled to Egypt to acquire Egyptian techniques for the production of statues and metal work.

There are several engineering efforts by the Greeks following the period that indicate Egyptian influence. One of the more famous is the tunnel through a mountain on the island of Samos. The tunnel was built by two crews digging from opposite sides of the mountain. "The crews missed making a perfect join in the middle by 20 feet horizontally and 3 feet vertically" (DeCamp, 1963:100). Herodotus was awed by the effort and characterized it as "the greatest engineering work of any Greek land." It probably was the greatest engineering effort of any Greek community of that date. In the words of a modern engineer, Herodotus "is entitled to his opinion and so are modern archaeologists who have become interested in the tunnel and think highly of it. Nonetheless, the first European attempt to conduct water underground shows so many elementary technical defects that it is difficult to share their views" (Sandstrom, 1970:81). The feat was extraordinary only in comparison to other Greek engineering efforts of the period. In comparison to the engineering efforts of the Egyptians of 2,000 years previously, it was an extremely modest endeavor. Many other ancient civilizations were capable of undertaking far more complex engineering efforts.

It is possible that the designer or designers of the tunnel acquired the idea of constructing a tunnel to conduct water from Phoenician or other sources. However, the Egyptians were far more sophisticated engineers than the Phoenicians. Given that many Samians had served as mercenaries in Egypt, that the tyrant of Samos had a treaty with the king of Egypt, and Samians were involved in trade with Egyptians, Egypt is the more likely source. The designer of the tunnel had probably journeyed to Egypt to learn engineering. His first effort, like that of some contemporary engineers of underdeveloped nations who learn elementary engineering principles while students in developed nations, was less than a complete success.

Egyptian men of medicine had an international reputation. Their medical knowledge, like their knowledge in other fields, had long since stagnated, but was superior to that of most other societies of the time. "Egyptian influence on Greek medicine in particular may be detected in the widespread resort to incubation as a means of irrational therapy from the fifth century B.C. onwards" (Harris, 1971:118).

CONCLUSIONS

The flourishing of the Greek civilization that began about 1000 B.C. was stimulated first by their contacts with the Phoenicians and later by their contacts with the Egyptians. Contacts with other societies also contributed. The emergence of Greek civilization, like all flourishings, rested upon the establishment of new sets of social relations. The creation of intercommunity trade networks and markets transformed many Greek communities from clusters of homogeneous, illiterate, and self-sufficient farmers who preyed upon their neighbors into urban centers of considerable size and wealth.

The transformation was quite rapid. However, the transformations that occurred when the Sumerian, Egyptian, Maya and other civilizations emerged were also quite rapid. One of the distinctive features of the Greek transformation was the early acquisition of more or less universal literacy. Literacy was so common in those communities with large markets that by the seventh century B.C. it was presumed all could read.

The phonetic alphabet allowed the Greeks to retain and accumulate large bodies of information, information that was available to anyone interested in it. The transformation of the rich oral heritage into writing provided an exciting account of their past. It provided all with a body of thought that stressed the distinctiveness of the Greek tradition. The heroic sagas remained viable despite the fact that simultaneously the Greeks were entering a new age. These sagas, festivals, and tales of ancient gods were preserved in writing and continued to serve as a foundation for communal solidarity while the marketplace was emerging as the dominant institution. Communal solidarity and the egoism of the marketplace existed simultaneously. The detribalization that is usually a consequence of the expansion of the market was counteracted by their rich heritage preserved in writing. The *Iliad* and the *Odyssey* were their bible.

The Greeks' extensive foreign trade contacts made them sophisticated urbanites, yet they preserved their tribal heritage in writing. That allowed them to retain an intense communal identity. They may have been the first civilization to combine the urbanism of the marketplace with an intense communal solidarity. Perhaps it was a unique combination never before or after achieved.

They then established a close link with the Egyptians. Their mercenaries who served in Egypt informed them of the wonders and wealth of Egypt. Sustained trade contact was established. Some travelers acquired ideas from Egyptians that they brought back to the native communities. The Egyptian ideas had become encased within the Egyptian bureaucracy and were treated as sacred dogma by the Egyptians. These ideas were part of the monopolies of knowledge controlled by the palace and temple. When they were introduced to the Greek communities they entered via the marketplace. The ideas were available to all who were interested in acquiring them. Some were intrigued by the tales of marvels and traveled to Egypt to acquire more ideas. Some learned that one could earn a living by becoming an expert and selling one's knowledge. The Sophist tradition emerged. The Sophists offered their knowledge for money. They taught everything from how to compute the area of a circle to how to curry favor from the powerful.

The Egyptian intellectual elite would have been aghast at the treatment their ideas received. Ideas that the Egyptians regarded as divine were vulgarized, bandied about, and ridiculed in the marketplace. It was as if the Vatican sold the sacred relics of early Christianity to illiterate pagans. Pythagoras tried to instruct his fellow Greeks in the proper standpoint to take toward the sacred knowledge, but without success. He was ridiculed for his efforts.

The spread of these ideas among the Greeks was facilitated by their literacy. Their phonetic literacy made it relatively easy for anyone interested to retain the ideas in writing. The first philosophers were also the first to write prose. Numeric and geometric thought was encased by a previously established literacy. Many were capable of writing down these ideas, then examining them, and offering reformulations of the original ideas.

One of the critical elements brought to Greece was the fiction of perfect forms. The Egyptians had concluded that *a* truth, if not *the* truth existed in repetitious cycles, geometric forms, and numeric formulae. Pythagoras, Plato, and others attempted to instruct their fellow Greeks on the validity of this formulation. They, like the Egyptians, were confused. They had concluded human beings were capable of thought independent of an environment. In constrast, other Greeks insisted on giving primacy to phenomena. They concluded that all was flux, that everything changed, that nothing was constant. They perversely insisted upon pointing to the inadequacies of the perfect forms.

The Pythagoreans demonstrated the validity of their position by noting the constancy of numeric formulae and geometric forms. Each and every right-angle triangle could be used to show the validity of the Pythagorean theorem. So long as attention was directed at geometric forms the Pythagoreans could carry the day. However, when these ideal forms were used to display regularities of the empirical world, difficulties emerged.

Many of the arguments centered on the issue of the adequacy of these forms to characterize empirical phenomena. The pungent phrase of "saving the phenomena" became viable. The empiricists insisted the critical test was not the internal consistency of the numeric and geometric statements, but their adequacy to characterize empirical events.

Much of the intellectual ferment that constituted the miracle of Greece was the consequence of interjecting the reified principles that had been preserved within a bureaucratic context into the bargained and negotiated world of the marketplace. Bureaucratic principles derive much of their validity from endorsement by the elite. These same ideas, when offered at the marketplace, must stand on their own merit. They cannot be validated by either a temple or palace elite. Those imbued with the marketplace ideology regard themselves as capable of assessing the worth of all things, including ideas.

Those with ideas to offer at the marketplace must entice others to accept their ideas. In constrast, intellectuals who are part of a bureaucracy are primarily concerned with pleasing the elite of the bureaucracy. This difference was recognized by later Greek intellectuals. After a center of intellectualism was created at Alexandria it was maintained by endowments from the political elite. Greek intellectuals who were not part of the Alexandrian establishment jeered at those who were. They referred to them as "fowls in a chicken coop" (Burn, 1966:357).

The tension created when persons with a belief in perfect forms were confronted by those who were not imbued with that frame of thought was a catalyst for the reformulation of abstract ideas among the Greeks. The tension created by acceptance of the concept of perfect forms and the variability that is experienced when the empirical world is given significance continues to inform modern science.

Copernicus gave priority to phenomena and developed a theory that replaced the Ptolemaic system. Yet Copernicus allowed his belief in perfect forms to influence his formulation of an abstract account of the movements of the planets. He altered his observations in order to offer a system wherein the planets moved in perfect circles. Perhaps he believed in the perfect circles and doubted his own observations, or perhaps he recognized that others believed them and that by displaying the movement of the planets in perfect circles his theory would be more acceptable. "Even Galileo came to grief by trying to fit into his new method the idea of perfect circles and circular inertia that he thought necessary to preserve the order of the cosmos. There was a Pythagorean in him that would not die" (Santillana, 1963:824).

The objective of placing diverse observations into an abstract form informs all modern scientific theories. That objective may have structured the efforts of the Egyptian intellectuals of the first few dynasties.

Subsequent generations of Egyptians presumed that all had been ordered. The Greeks became aware of perfect forms. They attempted to use them, but found them inadequate for some observations. The tension created by the clash created a climate that enticed many to attempt to resolve the lack of fit. Those Greeks most imbued with the Egyptian frame of thought preserved the forms; others treated them as other human products—something to be assessed and evaluated.

New understandings have not been achieved by the elaboration of forms per se, or by the "uninformed" examination of phenomena. Rather it has been the interface between forms and phenomena that is the foundation of modern science. The conflict between form and phenomena was one of the major contributions, if not the major one, of the Greeks to modern civilization. That same tension between perfect forms and the messy empirical world continues to stimulate modern scientists. A concern with form and saving the phenomena has provided the foundation for many drastic reorderings of human thought. Examples range from Copernicus' efforts, through Darwin's *Origin of Species* (forms), to Simmel's formal sociology.

DATES OF SOME IMPORTANT DEVELOPMENTS AMONG THE GREEKS

11,000 B.C.	Early trade with the Phoenicians
825–725	Spread of literacy
725–700	Hersiod's poetry
660	Publication of laws in some communities
625	Money enters some Greek communities
615	Greek trade center on Nile delta
590	Sappho acquires fame Greek mercenaries at second cataract of Nile
585	Thales predicts eclipse
575	Greek mercenaries serve as body guard of Egyptian king at Memphis
530	Pythagoras founds school (cult) in Italy

478	Persian invasion repulsed
399	Socrates put to death
300	Alexandria flourishes
	Euclid publishes elements of geometry
146	Romans sack Corinth and Carthage

Chapter XX

The Mechanization of Time

One of the most distinctive features of modern civilizations is the pervasive use of precise temporal structures. Several have asserted that the clock is the foundation of industrial societies. It is not the clock per se that is significant. Rather it is the formulation and use of very precise temporal structures that distinguishes modern civilizations from ancient ones. The clock is merely an instrument that has facilitated the formulation of distal futures that are more precise than those of any ancient civilization. The clock, when combined with a precise calendar, allows for the specification of long-range futures in an extremely precise manner.

Space probes are the prototype of modern undertakings that use mechanical timing to specify a long-range and precise future. A distal future was projected when the objective of exploring space was established. Then, the period between the formulation of the objective and the launching of the space vehicles was sequenced. The countdown for each launch epitomizes the precise temporal structures that underlie space travel. The temporal precision of space probes is but an example of many finely timed activities that pervade modern civilizations. The administration of factories, massive transportation of people and goods, and international warfare all rest upon a foundation of precise temporal structures. These activities were only possible after human beings had acquired command of precisely sequenced futures.

Some appreciation of the importance of precise timing for modern civilization can be acquired by noting how frequently administrators refer to their calendars and clocks. If one were to remove the calendars and clocks from any large modern organization, the coordinated activity of that unit would disintegrate. Chaos would reign in an organization like General Motors if by magic all their clocks and calendars disintegrated. Clocks and precise numeric calendars are artifacts that are distinctive to modern civilization; they provide the means for formulating the temporal structures that are necessary for the maintenance of the social structures of modern civilizations. They are not incidental; they are prerequisites of modern civilizations.

The importance of clocks and calendars is not restricted to the co-ordination of behavior in large organizations. Citizens of industrial societies look at the clock to see if they should get up, go to work, dismiss class, take a break, eat, go home, catch a bus, and go to bed. The clock and calendar are used to arrange meetings of families, friends, and work associates. Nearly all adult members of modern societies use them to structure their lives.

The importance of precise temporal structures is recognized by those who work in the field of economic and social development. Those who work in underdeveloped countries often complain that citizens of non-industrialized societies lack a conception of time. Of course, all human beings have a conception of time. But many members of nonindustrial societies lack the precise and complex temporal structures that most citizens of industrial societies take for granted. The correlation between industrial development and the pervasiveness of numeric calendars and clocks within a society is not perfect, but it approaches it.

Many ancient civilizations had very complex temporal structures; some of them with multiple calendars may have had temporal structures as complex as those of modern industrial societies. The Egyptians, Chinese, Maya, and others had elaborately intertwined temporal structures. However, they lacked mechanical instruments of timing. The behavior of large numbers of persons was coordinated by someone serving as the timer for those providing the energy. The shouts of the foreman co-ordinated the efforts of the workmen on the Great Wall; the beats of the drummer coordinated the strokes of the galley slaves of the Romans. This form of coordination is present in modern industrial societies. However, it has been supplemented and to a large extent replaced by me-chanical timing.

The development of mechanical timing spanned a long period. Its development was closely intertwined with the emergence of other ma-chines with cogs and gears. The Greeks of Alexandria may have taken the first steps toward mechanical timing. The earliest evidence of ma-chines with cogs and gears is from that period. Water-driven machines that ground grain appear in Europe about the same time. Water-driven machines appeared in China almost as early. But grinding mills first became common in Europe. They developed and spread as the Roman Empire of the west collapsed. During the same period trade networks and urbanism expanded in Europe.

Grinding mills were in widespread use in central and western Europe prior to the appearance of clocks. Their refinement provided the tech-nological foundation for the development of mechanical instruments that "told" and "measured" time. Mechanisms that told the time of day and measured off units of duration appeared in various parts of Europe by the thirteenth century. They became common, at least in some regions, during the seventeenth century.

Like many other transformations of social structures the invention of the clock had unanticipated consequences. Those who invented clocks were not aware that they were laying the foundation for a distinctive civilization. Like most other major transformations of social structures, the preliminary developments spanned a long period, but then within a relatively short period the social structure of European civilizations underwent a major transformation. The transformation wrought by the development of mechanical timing required the presence and widespread use of a precise calendar. Long-range futures that are precisely sequenced require the use of both a numeric calendar and a clock. A clock allows for the precise sequencing of the future, but unless it is integrated with a precise calendar no long-range precisely sequenced futures can be projected.

REFINEMENT OF THE CALENDAR

The first steps toward the mechanization of time were not taken in societies with a consensually accepted precise calendar. Rather they were taken by persons who were citizens of societies where vague solar-lunar or sidereal-lunar calendars held sway. The Greeks probably took the first steps. The Greeks familiar with the astronomical lore of the Egyptians knew that the Egyptian calendar was more precise than those of their native communities. Some attempted to entice their fellow citizens to adopt a more precise calendar, largely without success. A few city-states reformed their calendar, but most did not. The adoption of an innovation like a refined calendar by a society requires intellectual or political centralization, or both. The Greeks established neither.

Alexander's armies conquered immense areas. Had he lived a normal life span, he might have established a centralized political structure. Upon his death the incipient political unity of the Greeks fragmented. Greeks retained control of Egypt after Alexander's death. It became the commercial and intellectual center of the eastern Mediterranean. Greek and other intellectuals congregated there. Some made astronomical studies and acquired or formulated a fairly precise calendar. They determined that the Egyptian civil calendar of 365 days was not an accurate reflection of solar movement. In the early part of the third century B.C. an edict was issued by the Greek authorities that the 365 1/4 day calendar was the official calendar. The edict was strongly resisted by the Egyptian priests. The reform seems to have had little immediate consequences outside of Egypt. It may have had little consequence in Egypt outside of Alexandria.

Alexandria was the dominant commercial center of the eastern Mediterranean in the two centuries before Christ. But neither political unity nor intellectual hegemony prevailed. The region was rife with large-scale conflict. The Greeks, Phoenicians, Romans and others clashed on the battlefields and in naval engagements. The Romans prevailed. They conquered most centers of civilization. The Romans were relatively unsophisticated. They were regarded by the Greeks and Phoenicians as crude barbarians. Their dominance was based upon techniques of warfare that they had perfected. Nonetheless it was the Romans who introduced the numeric calendar of the Egyptians into Europe.

The military activity of the Romans was highly structured. Their camps were laid out in a geometric pattern; they used complex and precisely coordinated military maneuvers to conquer other groups. An ancient legend reports that a Roman general pointed to the order displayed in the format of a Roman military camp and asked the rhetorical question: Does that look like barbarians? The legend indicates both that the Romans were self-conscious about their lack of sophistication and the pride they took in the orderliness of their military activity.

After the overthrow of the Etruscan elite the Romans established a republic. In the early centuries the Romans were on the defensive as they were attacked by others. They then adopted a policy of preventive war and conquered and looted on a grand scale. They established tyrannic relations with many other civilizations. Other civilizations were either subdued or destroyed. The conquest of Alexandria gave the Romans access to the material wealth of Egypt and exposed some of her citizens to the intellectuals of Alexandria. Alexandria rapidly declined as an intellectual center; her library was burned; yet it was the source of the calendric reform of Caesar.

Prior to Caesar's time the Roman calendar was a relatively simple lunar one. The beginning of each year was established by an edict from the Roman senate. The specification of the start of a new year had become a political controversy. Those in office often extended the year in order to retain their positions longer. The official (civil) calendar fell into disrepute. Farmers ignored it and relied on the heliacal risings of stars (Bardis, 1978).

Caesar became dictator and the Roman republic was transformed into a totalitarian system. He ordered the adoption of the 365 1/4 day calendar that had been established in Alexandria. The Roman months (moons) were rearranged. The first months of the year were named after Roman gods. Caesar gave his own name to July. In the next generation Augustus decided that he too deserved to have a month named after him. The remaining months were numbered. The calendar served as the civil calendar for the Roman Empire.

The Roman calendar was a rather precise one, but it was not widely adopted. Most of the cities and countries that came under Roman control retained their local calendars. However, Roman festivals were set by the civil calendar. As Roman influence became dominant in other regions their calendar tended to replace the local ones. The political hegemony of the Romans in the west collapsed and political fragmentation followed.

In the intervening years the Catholic Church had emerged as a viable institution in western Europe. It was the church that maintained the Roman calendar. Scholars of the church wrote histories of the church. They established the practice of dating affairs from the birth of Christ. The Roman calendar achieved hegemony among the literate. However, it was a long, drawn-out process before the Julian calendar was widely accepted.

There were many controversies that centered on the calendar between the church officials and local groups. Two of the more controversial issues were Easter and Christmas. These two festivals and midsummer's day—the summer solstice—were widely celebrated in Europe. Easter was a fertility festival that was linked to the spring equinox and Christmas was originally the celebration of the sun beginning its northward movement after the winter solstice. The church officials vacillated between condemning these celebrations as pagan and incorporating them as Christian festivals. The latter alternative prevailed in the long run.

Complications arose when the church attempted to resolve inconsistencies that emerged between the Christian scholars, most of whom used the Julian calendar, and the agricultural festivals of western Europe. In 325 A.D. Easter was fixed on the first full moon on or after the spring equinox and the spring equinox was defined as occurring on March 21 by the Julian calendar. In the following centuries the Julian calendar slowly spread across Europe. During that period local groups continued to celebrate their yearly festivals by solar-lunar calendars. In addition, nearly all monarchies dated events by the year of reign of the current monarch. There was no universal calendar in Europe.

The Julian calendar of 365 1/4 days was far more precise than the solar-lunar calendars, but it was not self-adjusting. By the thirteenth century European astronomers were aware that the Julian calendar did not accurately reflect celestial movement. They advocated calendric reform. Roger Bacon called upon the church to adjust the calendar. He noted, "this year (1267) the winter solstice was on the Ides of December, twelve days before our Lord's nativity and the vernal equinox on the third day before the Ides of March. This fact cannot only the astronomer certify, but any layman with an eye can perceive it" (as quoted in Gimpel, 1976:190).

Bacon and other students of the celestial bodies either made quite precise measurements of the solar year or had access to the precise observations of others. Bacon claimed the 365 1/4 day calendar was in error one day for each 130 years, a rather accurate observation. His formulation may have been derived from ancient Alexandria through the Arabs, or it may have been an indigenous development that was stimulated by contact with Arabic intellectual centers in Spain. In either event astronomical knowledge was available among European intellectuals by the thirteenth century for the formulation of a rather precise calendar.

Bacon's call for reform was echoed by others in the succeeding generations. In 1582 the church reformed the calendar. Subsequent minor modifications have resulted in the calendar currently used by most modern civilizations. In 1884 the mean solar day was adopted as the universal day at the International Meridian Conference (Howse, 1980). Both commercial and intellectual interests advocated the establishment of an international calendar.

Several ancient civilizations had calendars as precise as the one used to make the 1582 adjustment. The distinctive feature of the calendric system adopted in 1582 was not its precision. Rather the distinctive development was that the calendar became combined with precise mechanical procedures that measured short durations. The calendar and clock became a unified system that allowed for the precise specification of extended temporal sequences.

ORIGIN OF CLOCKS

Many ancient civilizations had procedures for specifying the time of day and night and for measuring units of duration smaller than a day. But none developed procedures for mechanically specifying the "time of day" or to measure short units of duration. The mechanized specification of duration was largely a European development. The first steps toward the mechanization of time may have been taken elsewhere, but the invention was brought to its fruition by Europeans.

Several procedures for the specification of the "hours" of the day had been developed previously. Our current twenty-four-hour system is derived from the Egyptians. They selected twenty-four stars at approximately the same latitude as Sirius that were about equidistant from each other. They first used these stars to divide the night into twelve units;

later they were used to divide the daylight period as well as the night. They also had a variety of sundials. The Great Pyramid served as a sundial in addition to its other functions (Tompkins, 1972). They also developed other devices to measure periods of short duration. One was a bowl with a small hole in the bottom that was floated in water. The sides of the bowl were sloped to compensate for the variation in the rate of water intake as the bowl filled. Refined bowls of this type were in use by 1400 B.C.

Sundials became popular instruments among the Greeks and Romans about the time of Christ. Some were finely worked and elaborately decorated. In many ways they were like finely crafted modern clocks. Portable sundials were common; they were adjustable for latitude. Some told the season of the year as well as the time of day. They were rather accurate instruments for the measurement of short periods of duration. However, these sundials were not the precursors of mechanical time.

The mechanisms that were the precursors of clocks were devices designed to display the dynamic relations between the earth, moon, sun, planets, and stars. The earliest literary reference to these models is by Cicero about 60 B.C. He related that when the city of Syracuse was sacked by the Romans in 212 B.C., two celestial globes that had been constructed by Archimedes were included in the loot (King, 1978:3).

The Greeks associated with Alexandria constructed several different mechanical devices. One was a steam-powered device that opened and closed doors. They also constructed several water clocks, many of them were complex mechanisms. One that was recovered from the Mediterranean Sea, which dates about 80 B.C., displayed solar, lunar, and planetary movement (Price, 1974). The mechanism had differential gears. Some of these machines also had a dial that "told time."

During the following centuries of Roman rule, interest in these machines declined in the west. The mechanical devices that were the precursors of the modern clock did not emerge from the mechanical devices of the Roman Empire. They faded out of existence. An interest in the mechanical display of time was revived in Europe through contact between the Arabs and the Europeans. In 807 A.D. an ambassador from the Arabs presented Charlemagne with a water clock. An inscription of 1142 A.D. from southern Italy recites in Latin, Greek, and Arabic the installation of a clock (Kurz, 1975).

The Arabs built finely crafted and complex mechanisms that told time before the Europeans. One Arabic clock of 1315 was known as the elephant clock. Each half-hour it put on a small circus act. The bird on the top began to sing, the cupola turned, a man on the left moved his arm, a falcon dropped a metal pellet from his beak into the mouth of a dragon, two dragons moved, the pellet found its way to a vase, the mahout on the elephant beat his drum, and a scribe indicated the hour (Kurz, 1975:9).

The tradition of mechanical display of time that appears to have originated in Alexandria was not maintained in either Greece or Italy. The Persians may have maintained it for several centuries, but it was the Arabs who reintroduced the technique to Europeans.

About the same time the Arabs were constructing their complex mechanisms, timekeeping mechanisms appeared in China. The Chinese constructed a large water clock in 1090 A.D. It was over thirty feet tall with a celestial globe in the upper story. The construction of a clock of this size and complexity indicates either that there was a long history of clock construction among the Chinese or through foreign contact, perhaps with the Persians, the Chinese acquired a complex set of ideas about mechanical time. It seems unlikely that there was a long tradition of clock construction in China. The tradition of clock construction was not maintained by the Chinese. When the Ming dynasty was established, the clock was either destroyed or became dysfunctional. "By an extraordinary coincidence the greatest Chinese astronomical clock had disappeared just four years after the birth of the greatest European astronomical clock" (Gimpel, 1976:121). Jesuit missionaries reintroduced the clock to China in the sixteenth century. They used it and other devices to capture the good will of the Chinese elite. The ultimate objective, of course, was to convert the heathens.

The appearance, disappearance, and reappearance of clocks in western Europe and China is but another example of the uncertainty of cultural continuity. The construction of mechanical timekeeping devices seems to have been continuous from the time of their earliest construction in Alexandria to modern Europe, but it was not continuous in all societies that at various times built them. By the thirteenth century, the same century Bacon called for reform of the calendar, clocks and devices that displayed astronomical phenomena were being manufactured in Europe. In 1338 a clock manufactured in Venice was shipped to Asia. During the fourteenth century Europe surpassed the Arabs in the construction of clocks.

In some urban communities there was an intense interest in clocks. Communities sponsored the construction of large clocks. Some debated whether or not to build a clock. Some regarded them as a foolish expenditure of wealth; others regarded them as the source of communal pride and as attractions that would benefit the community. A 1335 statement reads in part that Milan has "a wonderful clock, with a very large clapper which strikes a bell twenty-four times according to the twenty-four hours of the day and night and thus at the first hour of the night gives one sound, at the second two strikes, and so distinguishes one hour from the other, which is of greatest use to men of every degree" (Gimpel, 1976:168).

The earliest European clocks were poor timepieces. They had only one hand to tell the hour. Their inaccuracy was so great that someone was appointed to correct the clock each day. Sundials were more accurate and were used to correct them. It was not until late in the seventeenth century that clocks became accurate timepieces. As late as the mid-seventeenth century, clocks commonly were in error about fifteen minutes per day, but by the later part of the seventeenth century some did not vary more than ten seconds per day (Macey, 1980:33).

European clocks were of interest to both astronomers and laypeople long before they became accurate timepieces. One 1385 letter noted that a clock of a community was such a marvel "that solemn astronomers came from far regions to see (it) in great reverence" (Gimpel, 1976). Many regarded clocks as the source of communal serenity and order. Citizens of the western cities were more supportive of clock construction than communities of eastern Europe. The Church of Rome was receptive to the new measures of time, but the Greek Orthodox church resisted the new contraption. "Until the twentieth century Orthodox priests never allowed a mechanical clock to be installed in an Orthodox church. For them it would have been blasphemy" (Gimpel, 1976:169).

As clocks spread through western Europe, the clock makers attempted to outdo each other. Considerable mechanical ingenuity was directed toward building larger, more accurate, and more distinctive clocks. Many of the leading scientists of the period worked on the perfection of the timepieces. Miniaturization led to the production of watches. The early watches were conversation pieces for the wealthy. They were decorations, provided mechanical music, made astronomic predictions, and some were miniature theaters. Timepieces became smaller, more accurate, and cheaper.

SCIENTISTS AND TIMEKEEPING

The intertwining of research by scientists of the Middle Ages and the development of precise timekeeping procedures is so complete that the two developments might be regarded as a single effort. From Roger Bacon to Newton, intellectuals actively sought both more knowledge of the empirical world and more accurate means for the measurement of duration. Bacon, Copernicus, Kepler, Galileo, Huygens, and others made astronomical observations, formulated principles, and made strides toward more accurate measurement of duration. The developments culminated in Newton's statement that the universe was but God's timepiece.

The re-emergence of empirical science proceeded simultaneously with the development of both a more precise calendar and the manufacturing of mechanical timepieces. Roger Bacon was one of the first of western Europe to articulate the belief that knowledge was to be derived from the study of phenomena. He stated there were two ways of knowing: one was reason, the other, experience. Reason might provide an answer, but only experience could provide truth. He was anti-Pythagorean. Other leading intellectuals affiliated with the church stressed the importance of reason and faith in arriving at truth. The latter position became the official position of the church.

Bacon, Copernicus, and other empiricists were in conflict with the official position of the church. The conflict between the two positions was not readily apparent to most. Bacon, Copernicus, Kepler, Galileo, Newton, and most others who conducted empirical studies thought of themselves as promoting both knowledge and Christianity. The work of Copernicus that culminated in the heliocentric theory of the universe was originally directed toward improving measures of duration. Many of the early researchers were either priests or supported by the church and supportive of the church. The incongruity between the two positions only flared into the open on occasion. It was not a sustained conflict.

The construction of accurate clocks was motivated in part by a concern with precise procedures for making comparable astronomic observations. However, there were other factors that contributed to the refinement of clocks. Overseas traders were intensely interested in mechanical timekeeping. It was recognized that if an accurate mechanical procedure for specifying duration was available, navigators would be capable of computing longitude as well as latitude. Trading interests offered rewards to the person who could solve the problem. One of the earliest offers was by the king of Spain. Galileo submitted a claim for the reward, but his claim was not accepted. Holland and Britain also offered rewards.

Clocks provided a means for the standardization of periods of short duration. They made "equal hours" a common concept. Long before clocks it was recognized that the duration of days and nights varied. Those familiar with elementary astronomy knew that only on the equinoxes were the day and night of equal duration. Equinoctial hours had been in common use among astronomers for centuries. But it was the development of clocks that made the concept a popular one. Subsequently equal hours was adopted as the standard measure of duration by civil authorities.

A second development was the spread of awareness that there were minor variations in the durations from one noon meridian passage to the next. Astronomers had been aware of the variation for centuries, but it was a rather shocking fact that became widely known in the seventeenth century (Bruton, 1979:225). Mechanical devices came to be regarded as the personification of order; they offered a more finely tuned order than the movement of the sun itself.

The movements of the "perfect" machine came to represent the greatest order possible. Order became equated with mechanical movement. Only the machine was ever-constant. Scientists propagated the belief that mechanized movement was the ultimate measure of duration. This frame of thought implicitly called for human beings to subordinate themselves to the machine. It was parallel to the thought which prevailed among the intellectuals of ancient societies who formulated the principle that all were to subordinate themselves to celestial movement.

The refinement of the calendar and mechanical timepieces slowly pushed other procedures for noting duration and structuring the future into the background. It was no longer necessary to make observations of the sun on the horizon to decide when to plant wheat, or to note the sun's location in the sky to determine the "time of day." Celestial observations were replaced by the calendar and clock. The changes were made possible and advocated by the men of knowledge. They provided two of the foundation stones for modern civilizations. The refinement of the calendar and the mechanization of time were two prerequisites for the industrial revolution. However, they were not sufficient for the emergence of the industrial revolution. Additional sources of energy had to be harnessed.

THE HARNESSING OF ENERGY

Prior to the industrial revolution human effort provided most of the energy for the manufacturing of goods. Human beings hammered metals into kettles and knives; human energy turned the potter's wheel and moved the loom. The harnessing of additional sources of energy for the manufacturing of goods was necessary before mass production could become the dominant mode of production. The harnessing of new sources of energy was largely a European development.

The use of animals to provide energy for the transportation of goods and the cultivation of crops has an ancient history. However, the use of animals in the manufacturing process is a relatively recent development. Donkey-powered mills predate water-powered mills. The energy provided by animals in the manufacturing of goods brought about some changes, but it was not a major transformation. The first major step toward harnessing the energy necessary for the mass production of goods was harnessing water power. Wind-driven machines were also developed, but they were and remained a limited source of energy. It was the harnessing of water power that made possible major transformations of the manufacturing process.

Water-powered grinding mills were built in the second century B.C. The output of the earliest water-driven machines was about one-half that of a donkey-powered mill. But two centuries later mills with six times as much power were built. The energy output of these machines was very low in comparison to modern machines. Yet in comparison to the energy output of human beings, it was tremendous. Forty persons had to work ten hours a day at grinding grain to match the output of a single water-powered grinding mill.

In the following centuries, water-powered grinding mills became common in many regions of western Europe. Some of them produced large quantities of ground grain. One built during the Roman Empire in Arles was capable of producing flour for 80,000 people. When the *Doomsday Book* was compiled in 1086 there were 5,624 water driven mills in England (Gimpel, 1976:12). The early millers served the surrounding farmers; they did not accumulate large quantities of raw material that were transformed into manufactured goods. Farmers brought their grain to the mills and had it ground into flour. Payment was usually in the form of the mill owners taking a percentage of the farmer's grain. The mill owner sold some of the flour he accumulated to town and city residents. Later millers purchased and ground large quantities of grain.

Water-driven mills also were used in the manufacturing of several other products. Textile mills were constructed. Other mills specialized in tanning, and a few in the production of paper. Most of the mills were concentrated near the emerging urban centers. After the flour mills, the cloth industry was one of the first to undergo a major transformation. The earliest water-driven textile mills were modest affairs. But in the thirteenth and fourteenth centuries large textile mills were established in Italy and Flanders. The mills of Flanders imported large quantities of wool from England; factory-manufactured cloth was widely traded in Europe. Woven materials replaced hides as the common form of clothing.

The growth and spread of mills transformed the manufacturing process. Factories had long been an integral part of commercial civilizations. But the factories of ancient civilizations consisted of clusters of workers attached to merchants, temples, or palaces. The early water-driven grinding mills were mostly family enterprises. But the textile mills and some others became major centers of production. The owners of the mills acquired large quantities of raw materials and employed persons to man the mills and sell the manufactured goods.

The overall impact of harnessing water power was to relieve human beings of some of the drudgery of providing the energy for the manufacturing of goods. The traditional production systems could not compete with the mills. Cottage production of cloth receded in importance. Mill-woven cloth rather quickly became a major item of trade. Some of those with the resources and skills to design and administer these factories became wealthy.

The maintenance of the textile mills and other factories required that large numbers of persons be enticed or coerced into subordinating themselves to the machines. The energy expenditure of these workers was relatively small in comparison to that required to produce the same amount of cloth by the hand- or foot-driven loom. However, the attentiveness and responsiveness demanded was great. Some weavers were almost literally harnessed to the machines. The transformation of the manufacturing process was not limited to the textile industry, but the textile industry led the way in the establishment of large mass production centers.

When weaving was a cottage industry each person was subject to the pressures and demands of his employer and other members of his family. The worker in a textile factory was subject to the same pressures and demands. In addition, the mill worker had to subordinate his actions to the machine. When a person is part of a cottage industry there is some opportunity for bargaining and negotiating with others. But when a person is part of a factory complex and the flow of energy is machine-controlled, there is little room for bargaining and negotiating. The worker must be responsive to the machine, but the machine is not responsive to the worker. Those who could not or would not subordinate themselves to the machine were discharged or punished. Many refused; some fled. The least powerful, the children and women, were those most frequently subordinated to the machine in the early centuries.

With the emergence of water-driven mills, the nature of the relation between the owners and employees underwent a profound change. In cottage and craft industries there is at least some direct contact between the owner and the workers. They often worked side by side in the same shop. Sometimes they were of the same lineage. They often had contact with each other when not at work. In contrast, in the mills there was almost no direct contact between the owners and the workers. The owners designed and administered the mills, the workers related to the machine. They did not act in unison with either the owner or fellow workers, but with the machine.

The percentage of persons who were subordinated to the machines was small, but steadily increased. They provided goods that facilitated the expansion of trade. Urban centers and factories grew. The number of merchants, craftsmen, artists, and literate also grew. Commercial interests became dominant in the urban centers. They formed competing, cooperative, and ambiguous relations with the church and the totalitarian feudal units. Numerous coalitions between these interests were formed as each interest competed for hegemony. Conflict between the different interest groups was common, but trade based on mass production steadily expanded and commercial interests rose to the top at the expense of the church and manor.

URBANISM AND LITERACY

Prior to its collapse the Roman Empire contained several large urban centers. These centers did not disappear when the empire disintegrated. Many cities of substantial size endured. The emergence of water-driven factories stimulated population growth and increased the wealth of the cities. As the cities grew, the incipient conflict between them on the one hand and the feudal system and church on the other hand burst into the open. The church had established a temple-centered hierarchy with a partial monopoly of knowledge. The unity of the church was far from complete; it was rife with factions. Simultaneously many small totalitarian mini-nations had been established by warriors. The warriors were the aristocrats of the feudal system. However, no large-scale totalitarian system based on centralized coercion was established. The feudal units routinely warred with one another. The church was generally supportive of the feudal aristocracy, but the two sets of interests were not completely unified. The interests of the warriors often collided with the church.

The interests of the church elite, the feudal lords, and the merchants of the urban centers interfaced in many ways. Sustained contact between the emerging urban centers and the feudal units was the consequence of the feudal elite establishing trade contact with traders. The feudal elite were attracted to the wares offered by the merchants. Many small markets—*urbs*—were established that were attached to feudal manors. In many cases the *urbs* grew rapidly and in some instances absorbed the feudal manor, both the buildings and the feudal way of life.

The *urbs* provided an entry point into the commercial world for many of the subordinates of the feudal world. Many of the serfs took advantage of the opportunities provided by the markets and trade networks. They fled to the cities; trade networks became escape routes. Feudal lords almost routinely searched the marketplaces for the runaway serfs. "The air of the town makes one a freeman" became a cliché. Many cities passed an edict stating that a person who had been a resident of the city for a year and a day was a free man, an edict that was ignored by the feudal aristocracy. Wars broke out between the feudal lords and the cities. Usually the church sided with the feudal aristocracy.

Clerics often served as rationalizers and administrators of the feudal manors. Rationalizations justifying the feudal hierarchy were offered by the church. In a few instances the administrative skills provided by persons trained by the church were combined with the violence of the warriors to establish monarchies. The monarchies and the commercial interests of the cities were in sustained conflict. In some regions the monarchy prevailed; in others the commercial interests prevailed; and on occasion, a working coalition was established between the elite of the manor-church groups and the commercial groups to effectively exploit the rank and file citizenry.

From the time of the collapse of the Roman Empire, a literate tradition had been maintained by both the church and trade centers. The percentage of people who were literate was very small, but when paper became available there was a marked increase in the percentage of literates in the cities.

Paper had been invented in China. It was brought to Europe by traders and entered the social structure of Europe in the urban communities. In China the manufacture and distribution of paper was controlled by the palace; its control was part of the Chinese effort to maintain a monopoly of knowledge. Furthermore, the manufacturing of paper in China was accomplished by human energy. When paper entered Europe there was no control of its distribution; it was put on sale at the markets. In addition, shortly after appearing in Europe, large quantities of paper were manufactured in water-powered mills. The appearance of factory-produced paper greatly enlarged the amount of written materials available. Nonetheless written material remained a luxury item until the invention of the printing press.

Printed materials were first produced by wine merchants. They modified their grape presses to mass produce written material. Written material lost its status as a luxury item. Prior to the printing press one book was worth one good cow; in a few decades several books could be acquired for a single cow. A substantial percentage of the merchants, craftsmen, and others associated with the urban centers became literate. Literacy became the mode among the priests. Most of the elite associated with the feudal manors became literate.

Literacy may have been as common in a few ancient civilizations as it was in Europe in the century or two following the invention of the printing press. At least a high percentage of the adult males of the Jewish and Greek civilizations were literate. A few other ancient civilizations may have had a literate citizenry. However, none of the nation states, such as Egypt, China, and the Inca, had a literate citizenry. Those civilizations were based upon centralized temple and palace hierarchies that maintained a rather thorough monopoly of knowledge. The literate elite were primarily administrators. Those nations achieved unity by the bulk of the citizenry subordinating themselves to the programs of action formulated by the literate elite.

It is difficult, if not impossible, to maintain monopolies of knowledge when written material is mass-produced by persons whose primary interest is making a profit and phonetic literacy is widespread. The merchants who first produced and sold printed material were unaware that they were implicitly challenging the church and feudal hierarchy. Nor were the church officials or feudal elite aware that the printing press was a threat to their position.

Nonetheless the spread of printed material and literacy undermined the hierarchical structures of the church and manor. The number of Bibles in circulation increased tremendously in the following generations. In addition, printed copies of the Greek classics, scientific treatises, and perhaps most importantly, tales of exploration were widely circulated. Literacy was concentrated in the urban centers, but reached into the feudal communities. Both the elite and the subordinates of the feudal units learned about the world outside their immediate community. Many left their native lands to begin life anew in the colonies.

Urban life and literacy eroded the hierarchy of the church. The availability of printed Bibles and other material provided many with a foundation for making their own interpretations of current social conditions and formulating alternatives. The church was slow to recognize the threat of literacy to the hierarchy. Once it was recognized that many persons were reading printed material that offered alternatives to the accepted dogma, the church took steps to control the spread of ideas. In some regions ownership of the Bible by lay persons was made illegal; the index was established to prohibit the manufacture and sale of unapproved books. Underground publications made it impossible to reinstitute the crumbling monopoly of knowledge. Utopian literature, descriptions of other worlds, accounts of ancient societies, and alternative interpretations of the sacred literature abounded. The universal church fragmented. Heresies were widespread. Drastic measures were taken to reestablish unity of belief, but it was too little and too late.

Most, perhaps all, of the precise calendars developed by ancient civilizations were part of a larger body of thought that promulgated a cyclical conception of the past, present, and future. The literacy of the western European civilization, in contrast, was combined with a frame of thought that espoused a linear conception of the past, present, and future. The Christian histories were attached to the Jewish histories that stressed cataclysmic and nonrecurring changes. Christ had appeared but once, although some developed the belief that he would reappear. Nonetheless progress was a viable concept. The current world was superior to the preceding one, and the future was to be better yet. Rationalizations were developed that justified blessing those not as advanced with the benefits of the new civilization.

COLONIZATION

In the fifteenth century sustained overseas explorations fueled by the commercial interests of western Europe began. The early explorations were directed toward Asia. The political and intellectual elite as well as the commercial elite were intrigued with Asia. It was a land of marvels, wealth, heathens, and exotic goods. Interest in Asia was almost universal among the western European elite, but it was the merchants who provided the wherewithal and driving force for the explorations. Europeans discovered the Americas. Their consciousness was shaken. The world was far larger than imagined. New vistas awaited.

The spread of western European civilization over much of the earth followed a pattern similar to earlier colonizations by several ancient civilizations. In the sixteenth century many ports of trade were established in foreign lands. Adventurers in pursuit of wealth and glory quickly went forth in search of their fortunes. Soldiers of fortune blessed by the palace and temple elite of their native land ventured forth to raid and loot wealthy civilizations.

Western Europeans clashed with older civilizations. The civilizations of Mesoamerica and South America were destroyed. Other civilizations were subjugated. India became dotted with trading posts manned by Europeans and protected by soldiers. China and Japan resisted the encroachment with a minimum of success, but ultimately they too became part of the international trade network.

The early adventurers carried tales of the foreign lands back to their native lands. They were followed by agricultural colonists. The colonists settled in the Americas, Australia, and large parts of Africa. They either pushed aside or destroyed the indigenous primitive groups of food gatherers and simpler agriculturists. Some of the natives were absorbed into the social structure of the western Europeans, often as slaves. Neither other civilizations nor the primitive groups could successfully conflict or compete with the western Europeans. Both civilizations and primitive groups disintegrated and disappeared under the onslaught.

The subjugation and destruction of other societies rested in part on the superior military might of the western Europeans. Their superior military powers in part, but only in part, stemmed from gunpowder, which had diffused into Europe via the trade networks from China. The rapid spread of western European civilization into vast regions would not have been possible if the western Europeans had not been militarily superior. However, that factor by itself does not account for the Europeans' success in bringing a new civilization to vast regions of the world. Their administrative and commercial skills were equally important. It was these skills that allowed them to construct elaborate new trade networks and the administrative structures necessary to establish and maintain their dominance. The opportunities offered by the European traders enticed many to voluntarily establish enduring contact with western Europeans.

The superior farming and military technology of European settlers allowed them to rather easily displace simpler agriculturalists. Natives who resisted the encroachment of European colonists were attacked and destroyed or subjugated. Large tracts of virgin land were brought under cultivation. Large plantations were established in many regions. The colonization of vast new tracts of land expanded and gave greater stability to the international trade networks.

Europe was the intellectual center of the world. Europeans provided the knowledge base for improvements in farming, trade, and administration. Natives of the foreign land were enticed to attend the European knowledge centers and were socialized into the European culture.

All of these factors and others contributed to the rapid spread of western European civilization. However, none of these factors made the spread of western European civilization distinct from the spread of several ancient civilizations. The factor that made the spread of western European civilization distinctive was the mass production of manufactured trade goods. Mass production provided western European traders with goods that allowed them to entice natives to trade with them. The textile industry, the first industry to develop large-scale mass production techniques, provided large quantities of goods—blankets—that the natives found desirable.

The mass production of goods rapidly expanded as the international trade network grew. The use of fossil fuels as a source of energy was combined with mechanical timing. Subsequently there was an explosion in the spread of mass production in those regions controlled by western Europeans. Large numbers of western Europeans quickly became part of the mass production complex. Non-Europeans were slower in accepting the mass production system. The spread and growth of mass production factories incorporated large numbers into a new and distinctive type of social relation.

THE STRUCTURE OF MASS PRODUCTION

As with all major transformations, the construction of the social relations that are the foundation of mass production both removed and imposed constraints. It has allowed for far greater productivity of factory workers than ever before achieved. Mass production has allowed for the satiation of some human desires on a scale beyond that of any previous civilization. In the process new desires have emerged. The operation of a mass production system requires that large numbers of persons subordinate themselves for extended durations to precise and repetitious mechanical movement. The mass production worker is severely constrained by mechanical timing.

The linkage of human activity to celestial movement is far more refined in western civilization than ever before. The linkage is indirect; it is mediated by the calendar and clock. The location of the sun on the horizon at sunrise and sunset, the position of the sun in the sky and the reappearance and disappearance of stars in the heavens are seldom noted by urban residents of modern civilizations. Rather, human action has become closely regulated by reifications of celestial movement—the calendar and clock on the wall. Modern western Europeans monitor, not the sun nor the stars, but their calendars and clocks. These artifacts allow for the precise coordination of behavior of large numbers of persons. Furthermore, the coordination is achieved without human beings acting in unison with others.

Specialists in programming use the calendar and clock to project complex and precise long-range programs of action, some of which are brought to fruition. The formulation of these programs requires that the planners have command of complex and precise temporal structures that are used to project complex and precise futures. The achievement of a mass production system requires that many persons subordinate themselves to the precise temporal structures formulated by the planners. In some instances, especially for those employed in mass production systems, the subordination is extreme.

The administrators of ancient civilizations formulated programs of great complexity and duration, but the subordination of human efforts to precise temporal structures was far less than that current in modern industrial societies. The undertakings that produced the pyramids of Egypt, the Great Wall of China, the gigantic irrigation projects, and similar artifacts required the specification of long-range and complex futures. Those programs were brought to fruition by large numbers of persons subordinating themselves to the plans of action specified by an administrative elite. However, there is a profound difference in the relations among those who coordinated their activity to construct the Great Wall of China and those who coordinate their activity on an assembly line of General Motors.

Mass production requires uniformity of precision. Hand-crafted items may be precisely manufactured, but each producer produces a somewhat different artifact. In contrast, in an effectively organized mass production system each worker produces an almost identical artifact. The large-scale production of interchangeable parts requires that each member of the productive unit subordinates himself to the repetitious movement of the machine. Each worker must repetitiously produce the same sequence of behavior vis-à-vis the machine. This degree of precision can more readily be achieved if each worker is assigned responsibility for the production of a simple sequence of behavior. The prototype of this form of production is the assembly line.

One of the distinctive features of assembly line production is the coordination of the behavior of large numbers of persons without any of them attending to anyone else. No attention is given to other persons; only the machine is given attention. In the extreme case each worker acts in isolation from all others. Others may be in his perceptual field, but no attention need be given them. Attention is riveted on the machine; the assembly line worker is responsive to the machine, not to other human beings. Each time the machine produces a sequence of movement, each worker produces a reciprocal and complimentary sequence of acts.

The only necessary linkage between workers of the assembly line is an indirect one. Each is attentive to the centralized timing mechanism of the factory, but none need be attentive to other human beings. On the ideal assembly line each worker is isolated from both his fellow workers and the administrators of the activity. Other forms of production often take the form of individuals acting in isolation. Game may be hunted by the lone hunter; the family plot may be worked by an individual. However, much of the productive activity of nonindustrial societies was achieved by persons acting in unison. The productive process of groups in nonindustrial societies may or may not have been coordinated by an authority, but in all instances each worker had some direct contact with some other members of the productive unit. Assembly line production is based upon each individual subordinating himself to the authority of the administrator as transmitted by the machine. On the perfect assembly line the workers have no direct contact with the authorities or fellow workers.

The coordination of behavior may be achieved through an extremely asymmetrical relationship in other forms of production. The master dictates to the slave what the slave is to do. Nonetheless there is a degree of reciprocity in even the most asymmetrical forms of interpersonal coordination. The master is at least minimally attentive and responsive to the slave. On the ideal assembly line there is no immediate reciprocity, only a delayed and often, very indirect reciprocity. The alignment of action is almost completely unilateral. The worker must be responsive to the machine; the machine is unresponsive to the worker.

On the assembly line every few minutes, or in some cases, every several seconds the worker is required to reproduce the same or at least a nearly identical sequence of action. As long as the machine continues to operate as designed there is no variation. The worker can anticipate with exactitude the movements of the machine; there are no surprises. It is a completely structured world; all chaos has been removed. Each future sequence is identical to the past sequence. The sequences are of relatively short duration and redundant. All is predictable and extremely boring.

Once the necessary sequence of action has been mastered no thought is required; only a habitual response. When there is no variation there is no consciousness. Workers become mindless robots. It is impossible to completely subordinate human beings to the extreme repetitiousness of mechanical movement. Consequently one of the universal activities generated on the assembly line is daydreaming. Daydreaming is not unique to the assembly line, but it is pervasive on them. Assembly line workers became more involved in their dreams than in their work; work loses meaning. Holding a job to acquire the necessities of life remains meaningful, but the activity itself becomes meaningless. Assembly line workers are not emotionally attached to their work.

The mass relation of the assembly line generates a highly egoistic orientation. Individualistic futures, not communal futures, predominate among assembly line workers. The worker subordinates himself to the machine to acquire the means to fulfill his individualistic objectives. The dreams of the assembly line worker may be past- or future-oriented, but in either event they tend to be highly egoistic. It is his future that is projected; not the future of a group. Both individualistic and communal objectives are projected in most human endeavors. One of the distinctive features of assembly line activity is that the objectives are almost entirely individualistic. The owner and workers may share a vague communal objective of producing marketable items. However, for the most part their interdependence is not based upon shared objectives. Each is largely interested in only his personal objectives; they often have little or no interest in whether the other achieves his objectives. Their relation is similar to that of bargainers. When bargained exchanges are consummated, some minimal recognition of the other's interests is usually acknowledged. In the mass relation, not even that is present. Alienation from others is complete.

Some insight into the distinctive qualities of assembly line activity can be acquired by comparing assembly line workers with the activities of a construction crew. Both the workers on the Great Pyramid and road building work crews work in unison. The objective of a construction crew is programmed by others and an authority oversees their effort. However, their effort to achieve the objective is coordinated in part by each attending to and being responsive to others. They fit their behaviors together into a unified effort. Furthermore, they continually assess their joint efforts as they move toward the projected objective.

When members of a construction crew achieve an objective there is usually at least a minimal level of solidary responsiveness to their effort. They recognized that they as a unit have achieved an objective. The enterprise is communal, not solely individualistic. In contrast, despite the tremendous commonality of action by assembly line workers no solidary responsiveness is generated on the assembly line as long as the line continues to operate as designed. On occasion, when the assembly line breaks down, solidary responsiveness is elicited from the workers. Assembly line workers usually cheer when breakdowns occur; they are momentarily relieved of constraints and boredom.

Communal solidarity does emerge among assembly line workers, but it is constructed in opposition to the assembly line. Assembly line work per se does not generate communal solidarity. Solidary responsiveness is not built on the assembly line, but in opposition to it. Unions are formed to constrain the degree of subordination to the machine and increase the rewards for subordination to it. They are not formed to promote the effectiveness of assembly line production.

The assembly line worker is twice subordinated. First he is subordinated as a wage-laborer. That form of subordination is similar to the subordination of the employees of the ancient Sumerian temples and the employees of cottage and craft industries. In addition, the assembly line worker is subordinated to the mechanical sequences. Furthermore his subordination to the mechanical movement is experienced in isolation. While at work he receives no stimulation that entices him to formulate alternatives, nor does he have the opportunity to become embedded with either fellow workers or with the authority who coordinates the efforts.

The mass relation of the assembly line has allowed for the production of trade goods on a level that no other civilization approached. Precise and complex temporal structures are the basic features of this relation; interconnectedness between persons is minimal. No communal solidarity is generated. Interdependence is extreme, but embeddedness is absent.

The mass relation of the assembly line is not the only relation experienced for citizens of industrial societies. Only a minority of the citizens of industrial societies are part of the mass relation of the assembly line; even those are not continuously part of the mass relation. Much of their time is spent in a host of other forms of sociation. However, the mass relation has become predominant in other areas of activity. It is not limited to productive activity. Much of the distribution of goods and their consumption takes place within a mass relation. The prototype of mass distribution is the vending machine. Exchanges are consummated without any mutual attentiveness or responsiveness. Even when purchases are made in modern stores, there is only a minimal relation between the exchangers. They typically do not bargain with each other. The salesclerk serves largely as an instrument of distribution. There is little bargaining and therefore few reciprocating activities between the salesclerk and the purchaser.

Information and entertainment are also commonly distributed through mass relations. They, too, have become goods that are exchanged without human beings being simultaneously attentive and responsive to each other. In contrast to the dullness of the mass production system, the mass distributed information and entertainment provides awareness of alternatives and stimulation. The assembly line calls for no thought; the mass communication systems provide the opportunity for thought. However, much of the information distributed by the mass communication systems informs the recipients of new and attractive goods that have been produced by the mass production system. For many the most promising way of acquiring these goods is to subordinate oneself to the assembly line. The lives of assembly line workers who also expose themselves to the mass distribution of goods and information are paradoxical. They have far greater awareness of an opportunity to acquire a wealth of goods, but to satiate their desires they must continue to subordinate themselves to the machine.

The mass production, distribution, and consumption processes supplement each other to create a form of sociation wherein persons have little contact with each other. One works on the assembly line in isolation, acquires goods in relative isolation (in complete isolation when the purchase is made via a vending machine), and consumes the goods in isolation. Intertwined interpersonal relationships have to a large extent been replaced by man-machine relations. Many have a multitude of foci in common, but they have few or no shared foci as each relates to the common foci as individuals. Communal concerns and objectives have been partly replaced by atomized individualistic concerns and objectives.

The mass relation has not replaced all other forms of human sociation; nor can they. The emergent quality of the world assures that if human beings are to survive as a species they must continue to organize some of their activities by directly attending to and being responsive to each other. However, given the inventiveness of the human species, social arrangements may be created wherein each person lives a life of almost complete isolation. Then the claim "NBC brings you today" may be a true characterization of human life.

CONCLUSIONS

Mechanical timing and vast new sources of energy have been combined with complex administrative skills and communication networks to create relations between human beings far more complex than ever before achieved. Every human group is linked, however tenuously, with every other group into a vast network. Despite differences in language, productivity and consumption, and political structures each nation and each group within each nation has some communication and trade with others. Isolated and self-sufficient groups have almost completely disappeared. Even the simplest nomadic hunting and gathering groups that continue have some relatively sustained communication with other groups and acquire at least a few incidental items through trade.

The world has not yet been transformed into McLuhan's global village; worldwide communal solidarity has not been achieved. However, mass production and consumption have promoted great similarity of sentiments and interest. Persons in all regions of the world have very similar desires. Nearly all desire the material benefits that are offered by mass production. The factory workers of Japan, the Soviet Union, Kenya, and elsewhere all have very similar sentiments and interests, but they are not shared. Each desires personal benefits; they have little or no communal solidarity. Egoistic concerns, not communal ones, predominate. They are only minimally embedded in their communities. Their relation with others is largely competitive. Each strives to acquire personal recognition and private possessions.

A few enclaves endure that are populated by persons who actively avoid the egoism and individual striving of the world of mass production, distribution, and consumption. In most of the enclaves the adults have difficulty convincing their young that a life that stresses communal concerns is superior to the individualistic strivings of the modern industrial world. Some young persons socialized in the mass production and consumption world yearn for an alternative. Some form communes; nearly all of them fail to endure.

Communists call for the establishment of international communal solidarity. They call for all to subordinate themselves to the communal welfare. However, the production process of the communist nations are the same as those of the capitalistic world. Their political elite and public administrators are as self-serving as those of other nations. The social relations of the productive process are far more significant than an appeal to subordinate individual concerns to communal objectives.

A counterposition is offered by those developing new technologies. The inventors of new communication systems, record keeping procedures, and production methods are offering the possibility of all human transactions taking the form of mediated contact. One talks with his friends via the telephone or radio, conducts economic exchanges through electronic media, and works in complete isolation. Automated production, mediated communication, and mediated economic exchanges are offering a world wherein no one becomes implicated with another. More and more coordinated action is action that is subordinated to machines. All are becoming machinelike. Rationality is equated with subordination of human activity to machines. Newton equated cosmic movement with the tick-tock of clocks. Some modern intellectuals have developed theories of human life that equate human action, thought, and emotion with the electronic impulses of the computer.

References

Aaboe, A.
1974 "Scientific astronomy in antiquity." Pp. 21–42 in F.R. Hodson (ed.), The Place of Astronomy in the Ancient World. London: Oxford University Press.
Adams, Richard E.W.
1977 The Origins of Maya Civilization. Albuquerque, N.M.: University of New Mexico Press.
Adams, Richard E.W., and T. Patricia Culbert
1977 "The origins of civilization in the Maya lowlands." Pp. 13–24 in Richard E.W. Adams (ed.), The Origins of Maya Civilization. Albuquerque, N.M.: University of New Mexico Press.
Adams, Robert McC.
1966 The Evolution of Urban Society. Chicago: Aldine Publishing Company.
1981 Heartland of Cities. Chicago: University of Chicago Press.
Adams, Robert McC., and Hans J. Nissen.
1972 The Uruk Countryside. Chicago: University of Chicago Press.
Akerblom, Kjell
1968 Astronomy and Navigation in Polynesia and Micronesia. Stockhom: The Ethnographical Museum.
Aldred, Cyril
1965 Egypt to the End of the Old Kingdom. New York: McGraw-Hill.
Allchin, Bridget and F. Raymond Allchin
1968 The Birth of Indian Civilization: India and Pakistan before 500 B.C. Harmondsworth: Penguin Books.
Allchin, F. Raymond
1969 "Early cultivated plants in India and Pakistan." Pp. 323–329 in Peter J. Ucko and G.W. Dembleby (eds.), The Domestication and Exploitation of Plants and Animals. Chicago: Aldine.
Ammumon, A.J.
1971 "Measuring the rate of spread of early farming in Europe." Man 6:674–688.
Anderson, Edgar
1952 Plants, Life, and Man. New York: Harcourt, Brace.

Atkinson, R.J.C.
 1974 "Ancient astronomy: unwritten evidence." Pp. 123–131 in F.R. Hodson (ed.), The Place of Astronomy in the Ancient World. London: Oxford University Press.
Austin, M.M.
 1970 Greece and Egypt in the Archaic Age. Cambridge: University Printing House.
Aveni, Anthony F.
 1975a Archaeoastronomy in Precolumbia America. Austin Texas: University of Texas Press.
 1975b "Possible astronomical orientations in ancient Mesoamerica." Pp. 163–190 in Anthony F. Aveni (ed.), Archaeoastronomy in Precolumbia America. Austin, Texas: University of Texas Press.
 1979 "Old and new world naked eye astronomy." Pp. 81–89 in Kenneth Brecher and Michael Feirtage (eds.), Astronomy of the Ancients. Cambridge, Mass: The MIT Press.
 1980 Skywatchers of Ancient Mexico. Austin, Texas: University of Texas Press.
Aveni, Anthony F. and R.M. Linsley
 1972 "Mound J, Monte Alban: possible astronomical orientation." American Antiquity 37:528–531.
Aveni, Anthony F., and Sharon L. Gibbs
 1976 "On the orientation of precolumbian buildings in central Mexico." American Antiquity (October):510–517.
Badawy, Alexander
 1965 Ancient Egyptian Architectual Design. Berkeley, CA: University of California Press.
Baer, Kaus
 1960 Rank and Title in the Old Kingdom. Chicago: University of Chicago Press.
Bahn, Paul G.
 1980 "Crib-biting: tethered horses in the Palaolithic?" World Archaelogy (October):212–217.
Baikie, James
 1929 A History of Egypt, Vol. I and II. Freeport, NY: Books for the Libraries Press.
Baity, Elizabeth Chesley
 1973 "Archaeoastronomy and ethnoastronomy so far." Current Anthropology (October):389–449.
Balazs, Etieme
 1964 Chinese Civilization and Bureaucracy. New Haven, CT: Yale University Press.
 1967 "Evolution of landownership in fourth- and fifth-century China." Pp. 117–124 in S.N. Eisenstadt (ed.), The Decline of Empires. Englewood Cliffs, NJ: Prentice-Hall.
Bardis, Panos D.
 1978 "Cronus in the eternal city," Sociologia Internationalia. (Heft ½):1–54.
Barocas, Claudio
 1976 Egypt. New York: Grosset & Dunlap.
Bates, Daisey
 1967 The Passing of the Aborigines. New York: Praeger.
Baumgartel, Elsie J.
 1955 The Culture of Prehistoric Egypt. Oxford: Oxford University Press.
Bausani, Alessandro
 1962 The Persians. Translated by J.G. Donne. London: Weatherbys.

Beazley, John David
   1966   Greek Sculpture and Printing to the End of the Hellenistic Period. Cambridge: University Press.
Bender, Barbara
   1978   "Gatherer-hunter to farmer: a social perspective." World Archaeology, (October):204–222.
Benson, Elizabeth P.
   1971   Dumbarton Oaks Conference on Chavin. Washington, D.C.: Dumbarton Oaks Research Library and Collection Trustees for Harvard University.
Berkelback Van Der Sprekel, Otto P.N.
   1967   "The Chinese civil service." Pp. 50–61 in S.N. Eisenstadt (ed.), The Decline of Empires. Englewood Cliffs, NJ: Prentice Hall.
Bibby, Geoffrey
   1969   Looking for Dilmun. New York: Knopf.
Biggs, Robert
   1974   Inscriptions from Tell Abu Salabikh. Chicago: University of Chicago Press.
Blanton, Richard E.
   1978   Monte Alban: Settlement Patterns at the Ancient Zapotec Capital. New York: Academic Press.
Bokonyi, S.
   1969   "Archaeological problems and methods of recognizing animal domestication." Pp. 219–229 in Peter J. Ucko and G.W. Dimbleby (eds.), The Domestication and Exploitation of Plants and Animals. Chicago: Aldine.
Brambaugh, Robert S.
   1961   "Plato and the history of science." Studium Generale, 14:520–527.
Brunner-Traut, Emma (ed.)
   1974   "Epilogue." In Heinrich Schafer, Principles of Egyptian Art. Translated and edited with an introduction by John Bains. Oxford: Clarendon Press.
Bruton, Eric
   1979   The History of Clocks and Watches. New York: Rizzoli.
Buchanan, J.
   1976   Theorika: A Study of Monetary Distributions in the Athenian Citizenry During the Vth and IVth Centuries. Revised edition. Locust Valley, NY: Augistin.
Bullard, William R., Jr.
   1973   "Postclassic in central Peten and adjacent British Honduras." Pp. 221–242 in T. Patrick Culbert (ed.), The Classic Maya Collapse. Albuquerque, NM: University of New Mexico Press.
Burford, Alison
   1969   The Greek Temple-builders at Epidauros: A Social and Economic Study of Building in the Askepian Sanctuary during the 4th and Early 3rd Centuries. Liverpool: University Press.
Burgess, Colin
   1974   "The Bronze Age." Pp. 165–232 in Colin Renfrew (ed.), British Prehistory: A New Outline. London: Duckworth.
Burle, Aubrey
   1976   The Stone Circles of the British Isles. New Haven: Yale University Press.
Burn, Andrew R.
   1966   The Pelican History of Greece. Middlesex, England: Penguin Books.
Butterfield, Herbert
   1981   The Origins of History. New York: Basic Books.

Carney, T.F.
1962 "The administrative revolution in Rome of the 1st century B.C." Proceedings of African Classical Associations 5:31–42.

Carter, George F.
1977 "A hypothesis suggesting a single origin of agriculture." Pp. 89–133 in Charles A. Reed (ed.), Origins of Agriculture. The Hague: Mouton.

Caso, Alfonso
1965 "Zapotec writing and calendar." Pp. 931–947 in Gordon Willey (ed.), Handbook of Middle American Indians, Vol. 3, part 2. Austin, Texas: University of Texas Press.

Ceci, Lynn
1978 "Watchers of the Pleiades: ethnoastronomy among native cultivators of northeastern North America." Ethnohistory, (Fall):301–317.

Chaplin, Raymond E.
1969 "The use of non-morphological criteria in the study of animal domestication from bones found in archaeological sites." Pp. 231–245 in Peter J. Ucko and G.W. Dimbleby (eds.), The Domestication and Exploitation of Plants and Animals. Chicago: Aldine.

Chapuis, Alfred, and Edmond Droz
1958 Automata. Translated by Alex Reid. Neuchatel: Editions du Griffon.

Charlton, Thomas H.
1978 "Teotihuacan, Tepeapulco, and Obsidian exploitation." Science 200(June):1227–1236.

Childe, V. Gordon
1936 Man Makes Himself. London: Watts.

Clagett, Marshall
1959 The Science of Mechanics in the Middle Ages. Madison, WI: University of Wisconsin Press.

Clark, Grahame
1977 "The economic context of dolmens and passage-graves in Sweden." Pp. 135–150 in Vladimir Markotic (ed.), Ancient Europe and the Mediterranean. Warminster, England: Aris and Phillips Ltd.

Coe, Michael D. and Richard Diehl
1980 In the Land of the Olmec: Vols. I and II. Austin, Texas: University of Texas Press.

Cohen, Mark N.
1977 "Population pressure and the origins of agriculture: an archaeological example from the coast of Peru." Pp. 135–177 in Charles A. Reed (ed.), Origins of Agriculture. The Hague: Mouton.

Collingwood, R.G.
1929 "Town and country in Roman Britain." Antiquity 3:361–376.
1946 The Idea of History. London: Oxford University Press.

Cook, J.M.
1961 "The problems of classical Ionia." Proceedings of the Cambridge Philological Society 7:9–12.

Couch, Carl J.
1982 "Temporality and paradigms of thought." Pp. 1–33 in Norman K. Denzin (ed.), Studies in Symbolic Interaction, Vol. IV. Greenwich, CT: JAI Press.

Couch, Carl J. and Robert A. Hintz, Jr.
1975 Constructing Social Life. Champaign, IL: Stipes.

Couch, Carl J., Marilyn G. Leichty, Leigh Anderson and Robert Hintz, Jr.
1975 "Time and social life." Pp. 120–138 in Carl J. Couch and Robert A. Hintz, Jr., (eds.), Constructing Social Life. Champaign, IL: Stipes.

Florence H.
75 "A thousand years of the Pueblo sun-moon-star calendar." Pp. 59–87 in Anthony Aveni (ed.), Archaeoastronomy in Pre-Columbian America. Austin, Texas: University of Texas Press.

s, John C.
58 Indian Life on the Upper Missouri. Norman, OK: University of Oklahoma Press.

Noah
54 History and Society. Hong Kong: Chinese University of Hong Kong.

y, Moses I.
67 Studies in Land and Credit in Ancient Athens, 500-200 B.C. New Brunswick, NJ: Rutgers University Press.
70 Early Greece: The Bronze and Archaic Ages. New York: Norton.
73 The Ancient Economy. Berkeley, CA: University of California Press.

nery, Kent V.
69 "Origins and ecological effects of early domestication in Iran and the near east." Pp. 73–100 in Peter J. Ucko and G.W. Dimbleby (eds.), The Domestication and Exploitation of Plants and Animals. Chicago: Aldine.

nery, Kent V.
74 "The Olmec and the valley of Oaxaca: a model for inter-regional interaction in formative times." Pp. 64–83 in C.C. Lamberg-Karlovsky and Jeremy A. Sobloff (eds.), The Rise and Fall of Civilizations. Menlo Park, CA: Cummings.

es, Allen Jr. and Thomas R. Crowder
79 "The problem of Franco-Cantabrian abstract signs: agenda for a new approach." World Archaeology (February):350–366.

er, John L.
80 "Sinuhe: the ancient Egyptian genre of narrative verse." Journal of Near Eastern Studies (April):89–118.

ler, P.J., and J.G. Evans
67 "Plough-marks, lynchets and early fields." Antiquity 41:289–301.

kfort, Henri
48 Kingship and the Gods. Chicago: University of Chicago Press.
51 The Birth of Civilization in the Near East. London: Williams and Norgate.

d, Morton H.
67 The Evolution of Political Society. New York: Random House.

enkamp, Charles
76 Maya: The Riddle and Rediscovery of a Lost Civilization. New York: D. McKay.

lner, Percy
18 A History of Ancient Coinage 700-300 B.C. Oxford: Clarendon.

net, Jacques
62 Daily Life in China. Translated by H.M. Wright. New York: MacMillan.

s, Sharon L.
75 "Mesoamerican calendrics as evidence of astronomical activity." Pp. 21–35 in Anthony F. Avenie (ed.), Native American Astronomy. Austin, Texas: University of Texas Press.

on, Charles
48 The Inca Concept of Sovereignty. New York: Greenwood Press.

ngs, Richard I.
72 Mathematics in the Time of the Pharaohs. Cambridge, MA: The MIT Press.

pel, Jean
76 The Medieval Machine. Middlesex, England: Penguin Books.

dwin, Thomas
70 East is a Big Bird. Cambridge, MA: Harvard University Press.

Cranston, B.A.L.
   1069   "Animal husbandry: the evidence from ethnography." Pp.
           Ucko and G.W. Dimbleby (eds.), The Domestication and E:
           and Animals. Chicago: Aldine.
Craven Roy C., Jr., William R. Bullard, Jr., and Michael E. Kampen
   1974   Ceremonial Centers of the Maya. Gainesville, FL: The U
           Florida.
Culbert, T. Patrick
   1977   "Early Maya development at Tikal, Guatemala." Pp. 27–
           Adams (ed.), The Origins of Maya Civilization. Albuquerqu
           New Mexico Press.
Dalton, George
   1975   "Karl Polanyi's analysis of long-distance trade and his wide
           132 in Jeremy A. Sobloff and C.C. Lambert-Karlovsky (eds.
           and Trade. Alberquerque, NM: University of New Mexico
Daniel, Glyn
   1968   The First Civilizations. New York: Thomas Y. Crowell.
Dantzig, Tobias
   1938   Number: The Language of Science. New York: Macmillar
   1955   The Bequest of the Greeks. New York: Charles Scribner's
Darlington, C.D.
   1969   "The silent millennia in the origin of agriculture." Pp. 6'
           and G.W. Dimbleby (eds.), The Domestication and Expl
           Animals, pp. 67–72. Chicago: Aldine.
David, Rosalie
   1980   Cult of the Sun. London: J.M. Dent & Sons Ltd.
Davies, Nigel
   1977   The Toltecs. Norman, OK: The University of Oklahoma
Davis, Whitney M.
   1981   "Egypt, Somus, and the archaic style in Greek sculpture." T
           Archaeology 67:61–81.
DeCamp, L. Sprague
   1963   The Ancient Engineers. New York: Doubleday & Comp;
Delaporte, Louis Joseph
   1925   Mesopotamia: The Babylonian and Assyrian Civilization
Dicks, D.R.
   1970   Early Greek Astronomy to Aristotle. Ithaca, NY: Cornel
Divine, Arthur D.
   1973   The Opening of the World. New York: G.P. Putman.
Dodds, E.R.
   1951   The Greeks and the Irrational. Berkeley, CA: Universit
Dreyer, John L.
   1953   A History of Astronomy from Thales to Kepler. New Y
Eddy, J.A.
   1979   "Medicine wheels and Plains Indian astronomy." Pp. 1-
           and Michael Feirtag (eds.), Astronomy of the Ancients
           MIT Press.
Edgerton, William F.
   1967   "The government and the governed in the Egyptian en
           Eisenstadt (ed.), The Decline of Empires. Englewood, (

Goody, Jack
1977   The Domestication of the Savage Mind. Cambridge: Cambridge University Press.
Graulich, Michel
1981   "The metaphor of the day in ancient Mexican myth and ritual." Current Anthropology (February):45–60.
Green, Peter
1972   The Shadow of the Parthenon. London: Maurice Temple Smith Ltd.
Hadingham, Evan
1975   Circles and Standing Stones. New York: Walker.
Hadingham, Evan
1979   Secrets of the Ice Age. New York: Walker.
Hammond, Mason
1972   The City in the Ancient World. Cambridge, MA: Harvard University Press.
Hammond, Nicholas G.L.
1967   A History of Greece to 332 B.C. Oxford: Clarendon Press.
Hammond, Norman
1977   "The earliest Maya." Scientific American (March).
1977   "Ex oriente lux: a view from Belize," Pp. 45–76 in Richard E.W. Adams, (ed.), The Origins of Maya Civilization. Albuquerque, NM: University of New Mexico Press.
Hapgood, Charles H.
1979   Maps of the Ancient Sea Kings. New York: E.P. Dutton.
Harlan, Jack R.
1967   "A wild wheat harvest in Turkey." Archaeology 20:197–201.
1977   "The origins of cereal agriculture in the Old World." Pp. 357–384 in Charles A.Reed (ed.), Origins of Agriculture. The Hague: Mouton.
Harlan, J.R. and D. Zohary
1966   "Distribution of wild wheats and barley." Science 153:1074–1080.
Harris, David R.
1969   "Agricultural systems, ecosystems and the origins of agriculture." Pp. 3–15 in Peter J. Ucko and G.W. Dimbleby (eds.), The Domestication and Exploitation of Plants and Animals. Chicago: Aldine.
1977   "Alternative pathways toward agriculture." Pp. 179–243 in Charles A. Reed (ed.), Origins of Agriculture. The Hague: Mouton.
Harris, John R.
1971a   "Technology and materials." Pp. 83–11 in John R. Harris (ed.), The Legacy of Egypt. Oxford: Clarendon.
1971b   "Medicine." Pp. 112–137 in John R. Harris (ed.), The Legacy of Egypt. Oxford: Clarendon.
Hartner, Willie
1965   "The earliest history of the constellations in the near east and the motif of the lion-bull combat." Journal of Near Eastern Studies 24:1–16.
Hasebroek, Johannes
1933   Trade and Politics in Ancient Greece. Translated by L.M. Fraser and D.C. Macgregor. New York: Biblo and Tannen.
Hawkins, Gerald L.
1965   Stonehenge Decoded. Garden City, NY: Doubleday.
1973   Beyond Stonehenge. New York: Harper & Row.
Heath, Thomas
1921   A History of Greek Mathematics. Oxford: Clarendon.

Herman, Zvi
  1966 Peoples, Seas and Ships. London: Phoenix House.
Herodotus
  1954 The Histories. Translated by Aubrey de Selncourt. Middlesex, England: Penguin Books, Ltd.
Herre, World and Manfred Rohrs
  1977 "Zoological considerations on the origins of farming and domestication." Pp. 245–280 in Charles A. Reed (ed.), Origins of Agriculture. The Hague: Mouton.
Heyerdahl, Thor
  1978 Early Man and the Ocean. New York: Vintage Books.
Higgs, E.S. and M.A. Jarman
  1972 "The origins of animal and plant husbandry." Pp. 3–13 in E.S. Higgs, (ed.), Papers in Economic Pre-History. Cambridge: Cambridge University Press.
Hintz, Robert A. Jr.
  1975 "Foundations of social behavior." Pp. 47–64 in Carl J. Couch and Robert A. Hintz, Jr. (eds.), Constructing Social Life. Champaign, IL: Stipes.
Hintz, Robert A. Jr. and Carl J. Couch
  1975 "Time, intention and social behavior." Pp.27–46 in Carl J. Couch and Robert A Hintz, Jr. (eds.), Constructing Social Life. Champaign, IL: Stipes.
Ho, Ping-Ti
  1977 "The indigenous origins of Chinese agriculture." Pp. 413–484 in Charles A. Reed (ed.), Origin of Agriculture. The Hague: Mouton.
Hoffman, Michael
  1979 Egypt Before the Pharaohs. New York: Alfred A. Knopf.
Hole, Frank
  1974 "Investigating the origins of Mesopotamian civilization." In C.C. Lamberg-Karlovsky and Jeremy A. Sabloff (eds.), The Rise and Fall of Civilizations. Menlo Park, CA: Cummings.
Holmberg, Allan R.
  1969 Nomads of the Long Bow. Garden City, NY: The Natural History Press.
Howse, Derek
  1980 Greenwich Time and the Discovery of Longitude. New York: Oxford University Press.
Hoyle, Fred
  1977 On Stonehenge. San Francisco: W.H. Freeman.
Hutchinson, Richard W.
  1974 "The decadence of Minoan Crete: the Mycenaean Empire." Pp. 412–423 in C.C. Lamberg-Karlovsky and Jeremy A. Sabloff (eds.), The Rise and Fall of Civilizations. Menlo Park, CA: Cummings.
Innis, Harold Adams
  1951 The Bias of Communication. Toronto: University of Toronto Press.
  1972 Empire and Communication. Revised by Mary Q. Innis. Toronto: University of Toronto Press.
Iverson, Erik
  1971 "The canonical tradition." Pp. 55–82 in John R. Harris (ed.), The Legacy of Egypt. Oxford: Clarendon.
  1974 Canon and Proportions in Egyptian Art. Warminster, England: Aris and Phillips.
Ivimy, John
  1974 The Sphinx and the Megaliths. London: Turnstone.
Jacobs, Jane
  1970 The Economy of Cities. New York: Vintage Books.

Jacobsen, Thorkild
　1970　Toward the Image of Tammuz. Cambridge, MA: Harvard University Press.
Janssen, Jack J.
　1978　"The early state in ancient Egypt." Pp. 213–234 in Henri J.M. Claessen and P. Skalnik (eds.), The Early States. The Hague: Mouton.
Jawad, Abdul Jalil
　1974　"The Eridu material and its implications." Sumer 30:11–46.
Jennings, Jesse D.
　1978　Ancient Native Americans. San Francisco: W.H. Freeman.
Johnson, Paul
　1978　The Civilization of Ancient Egypt. New York: Atheneum.
Jordon, Paul
　1976　Egypt: The Black Land. New York: E.P.Dutton.
Josephus
　1960　Josephus, the Complete Works. Translated by William Whiston. Grand Rapids, MI: Kregel.
Karder, Lawrence
　1978　"The origin of the state among the nomads of Asia." Pp. 93–107 in Henri J.M. Claessen and P. Skalnik (eds.), The Early State. The Hague: Mouton.
Kees, Herman
　1961　Ancient Egypt, A Cultural Topolography. Chicago: University of Chicago Press.
Kehoe, Alice B.
　1981　"The cultural significance of the Moose Mountain Observatory." Archaeoastronomy (January-March):8–9.
Keil, Dana
　1977　"Markets in Melanesia?" Journal of Anthropological Research. (Fall):258–276.
Kelley, David H. and K. Ann Kerr
　1975　"Mayan astronomy and astronomical glyphs." Pp. 179–215 in Elizabeth P. Benson (ed.), Mesoamerican Writing Systems. Washington, D.C.: Dumbarton Oaks Research Library and Collection.
King, Henry C.
　1978　Geared to the Stars. Toronto: University of Toronto Press.
Knorr, Wilbur Richard
　1975　The Evolution of the Euclidean Elements. Dordrecht, Holland: D. Reidel.
Kohl, Philip L.
　1981　The Bronze Age Civilization of Central Asia. Armonk, NY: M.E. Sharpe.
Kracke, E.A., Jr.
　1967　"Sung society: change within tradition." Pp. 140–150 in S.N. Eisenstadt (ed.), The Decline of Empires. Englewood Cliffs, N.J.: Prentice-Hall.
Kramer, Samuel Noah
　1959　History Begins at Sumer. Garden City, N.Y.: Doubleday.
Kraybill, Nancy
　1977　"Pre-agricultural tools for the preparation of foods in the old world." Pp. 485–521 in Charles A. Reed (ed.), Origins of Agriculture. The Hague: Mouton.
Krupp, E.C.
　1977　"Astronomers, pyramids, and priests." Pp. 203–239 in E.C. Krupp (ed.), In Search of Ancient Astronomies. Garden City, N.Y.: Doubleday.
Kurz, Otto
　1975　European Clocks and Watches in the Near East. London: Warburg Institute.
Landstrom, Bjorn
　1970　Ships of the Pharaohs. Garden City, NY: Doubleday.

Langdon, Stephen
  1933   Babylonian Menologies and the Semitic Calendars. London: Oxford University Press.
Lathrap, Donald W.
  1977   "Our father the cayman, our mother the gourd: Spinden revisited, or a unitary model for the emergence of agriculture in the new world." Pp. 713–752 in Charles A. Reed (ed.), Origins of Agriculture. The Hague: Mouton.
Lauer, Jean-Phillippe
  1976   Saqqara. New York: Charles Scribner's Sons.
Leach, E.R.
  1954   "Primitive time-reckoning," Pp. 110–127 in Charles Singer, E.J. Homyard, and A.R. Hall (eds.), A History of Technology, Vol. 1. Oxford: Clarendon.
Lee, Richard B.
  1972   "Work effort, group structure and land-use in contemporary hunter-gatherers." Pp. 177–186 in Peter J. Ucko, Ruth Tringham and G.W. Dimbleby (eds.), Man, Settlement and Urbanism. Hertfordshire, England: Garden City Press.
Lee, Richard B. and Irven DeVore
  1968   "What hunters do for a living, or how to make out on scarce resources." Pp. 30–48 in Richard B. Lee and Irven DeVore (eds.), Man the Hunter. Chicago: Aldine.
  1968   "Problems in the study of hunters and gatherers." Pp. 3–12 in Richard B. Lee and Irven DeVore (eds.), Man the Hunter. Chicago: Aldine.
Legrain, Leon
  1922   Historical Fragments. Philadelphia: University of Pennsylvania Press.
Leichty, Marilyn G.
  1975   "Sensory modes, social activity and the universe of touch," Pp. 65–79 in Carl J. Couch and Robert A. Hintz, Jr. (eds.), Constructing Social Life. Champaign, IL: Stipes.
Leon-Portilla, Miguel
  1973   Time and Reality in the Thought of the Maya. Boston: Beacon Press.
Lewis, David
  1972   We, The Navigators. Honolulu: The University Press of Hawaii.
  1978   The Voyaging Stars: Secrets of the Pacific Navigators. New York: W.W. Norton.
Ley, Willy
  1963   Watchers of the Skies. New York: The Viking Press.
Lind, Joan D.
  1982   "The organization of coercion in history: a rationalist-evolutionary theory." Sociological Theory I.
Lloyd, Alan B.
  1976   Herodotus Book II, Vols. I and II. London: E. J. Brill.
Lockyer, J. Norman
  1894   The Dawn of Astronomy, 2nd printing, 1973. Cambridge, MA: The MIT Press.
Lofland, Lyn H.
  1973   A World of Strangers. New York: Basic Books.
Macey, Samuel L.
  1980   Clocks and the Cosmos. Hamden, CT: Archon Books.
MacKie, Euan W.
  1974   "Archaeological tests on supposed prehistoric astronomical sites in Scotland." Pp. 169–190 in F. R. Hodson (ed.), The Place of Astronomy in the Ancient World. London: Oxford University Press.
  1977a   Science and Society in Prehistoric Britain. New York: St. Martin's Press.
  1977b   The Megalith Builders. Oxford: Phaidon.

MacNeish, Richard S.
   1977   "The beginning of agriculture in central Peru." Pp. 753–802 in Charles A. Reed (ed.), Origins of Agriculture. The Hague: Mouton.
Maistrov. L. E.
   1974   "Contributions to the discussion of ancient astronomy: the unwritten evidence." Pp. 267–268 in F. R. Hodson (ed.), The Place of Astronomy in the Ancient World. London: Oxford University Press.
Malmstrom, Vincent H.
   1978   "A reconstruction of the chronology of Mesoamerican calendric systems." Journal for the History of Astronomy (June): 105–116.
Marshack, Alexander
   1972   The Roots of Civilization. New York: McGraw-Hill.
Maspero, G.
   1897   The Dawn of Civilization. Translated by M. L. McClure, third edition. London: London Society for Promoting Christian Knowledge.
Matossian, Mary
   1980   "Symbols of seasons and the passage of time: barley and bees in the new stone age." Griffith Observer (November):14–20.
Matthiea, Paolo
   1981   Ebla. Garden City, NY: Doubleday.
McCluskey, Stephen C.
   1977   "The astronomy of the Hopi Indians." Journal for the History of Astronomy (October):174–195.
McLuhan, Marshall
   1962   The Gutenberg Galaxy. New York: New American Library.
   1965   Understanding Media; The Extensions of Man. New York: McGraw-Hill.
Mead, George Herbert
   1932   Philosophy of the Present. Chicago: Open Court.
   1934   Mind, Self and Society. Chicago: University of Chicago Press.
Mellaart, James
   1967   Çatal Hüyük: A Neolithic Town in Anotolia. London: Thomas and Hudson.
   1975   The Neolithic of the Near East. New York: Charles Scribner's Sons.
   1978   The Archaeology of Ancient Turkey. Totowa, NJ: Rowman and Littlefield.
Mendelssohn, Kurt
   1974a   The Riddle of the Pyramids. New York: Praeger.
   1974b   "A scientist looks at the pyramids." Pp. 390–402 in C. C. Lamberg-Korvalsky and Jeremy A. Sabloff (eds.), The Rise and Fall of Civilizations. Menlo Park, CA: Cummings.
Michalowski, Kazimierz
   1969   Art of Ancient Egypt. Translated by Norbert Guterman. New York: Harry N. Abrams.
Miller, Dan E., Robert A. Hintz, Jr., and Carl J. Couch
   1975   "The elements and structure of openings." Pp. 1–24 in Carl J. Couch and Robert A. Hintz, Jr. (eds.), Constructing Social Life. Champaign, IL: Stipes.
Miller, Dan E., Marion W. Weiland and Carl J. Couch
   1978   "Tyranny." Pp. 267–288 in Norman K. Denzin (ed.), Studies in Symbolic Inter-action. Greenwich, CT: JAI Press.
Millon, Rene
   1976   "Social relations in ancient Teotihuacan." Pp. 205–248 in Eric Wolf (ed.), The Valley of Mexico: Studies in Pre-Hispanic Ecology and Society. Albuquerque, NM: University of New Mexico Press.

Moseley, Michael E.
1975 The Maritime Foundation of Andean Civilization. Menlo Park, CA: Cummings.
Murray, Jacqueline
1970 The First European Agriculture. Chicago: Aldine.
Needham, Joseph
1969 The Grand Titration. Toronto: University of Toronto Press.
1974 "Astronomy in ancient and medieval China." Pp. 67–82 in F. R. Hodson (ed.), The Place of Astronomy in the Ancient World. London: Oxford University Press.
Neugebauer, Otto
1957 A History of Ancient Mathematical Astronomy. Berlin, NY: Springer-Verlag.
Newham, C. A.
1973 The Astronomical Significance of Stonehenge. Leeds: John Blackburn.
Newton, Robert
1977 The Crime of Claudius Ptolemy. Baltimore and London: John Hopkins University Press.
Nichols, Marianne
1975 Man, Myth, and Monument. New York. William Morrow and Company.
Nilsson, Martin P.
1920 Primitive Time Reckoning. London: Oxford University Press.
Oates, David and Joan Oates
1976 The Rise of Civilization. New York: Dutton.
Oates, Joan
1979 Babylon. London: Thames and Hudson.
Ogilvie, R. M.
1976 Early Rome and the Etruscans. Atlantic Highlands, NJ: Humanities Press.
Oldfather, C. H.
1933 Diodorus of Siciliy. Cambridge, MA: Harvard University Press.
O'Neil, William
1975 Time and the Calendars. Sydney: Sydney University Press.
Oppenheim, A. Leo
1954 "The sea-faring merchants of Ur." Journal of the American Oriental Society 74:
1964 Ancient Mesopotamia. Chicago: University of Chicago Press.
1967 "A new look at the structure of Mesopotamian society." Journal of Economic and Social History of the Orient 10:1–16.
Otterbein, Keith F.
1970 The Evolution of War: A Cross-Cultural Study. New Haven, CT: Human Relations Area Files Press.
1979 "Huron vs. Iroquois: a case study of inter-tribal warfare." Ethnohistory (Spring):141–152.
Pannekoek, Antonie
1961 A History of Astronomy. New York: Interscience.
Parker, Richard A.
1950 "The calendars of ancient Egypt." The Oriental Institute of the University of Chicago Studies in Ancient Oriental Civilization, No. 26. Chicago: University of Chicago Press.
1971 "The calendar and chronology." Pp. 13–27 in John R. Harris (ed.), The Legacy of Egypt. London: Oxford University Press.
1974 "Ancient Egyptian astronomy." Pp. 51–66 in F. R. Hodson (ed.), The Place of Astronomy in the Ancient World. London: Oxford University Press.
1977 "The lithic dating of the twelfth and eighteenth dynasties in studies in honor of George R. Hughes." Studies in Ancient Oriental Civilization 39:177–189.
Parsons, James B.
1967 "The culmination of a Chinese peasant rebellion." Pp. 150–159 in S. N. Eisenstadt (ed.), The Decline of Empires. Englewood Cliffs, NJ: Prentice-Hall.

Perkins, Dexter, Jr.
1966   "The fauna from Madamagh and Beidha." Palestine Exlorer. Q:66–67.
1969   "Fauna at Çatal Hüyük: Evidence for Early Cattle Domestication in Anatolia."
        Science 164:177–179.
Pickersgill, Barbara, and Charles B. Heiser, Jr.
1977   "Plants domesticated in the new world tropics." Pp. 803–836 in Charles A. Reed
        (ed.), Origins of Agriculture. The Hague: Mouton.
Pirenne, Henri
1925   Medieval Cities. Princeton, NJ: Princeton University Press.
Plato
1934   The Laws of Plato. Translated by A. E. Taylor. London: J. M. Dent & Sons, Ltd.
Pokora, Timotius
1978   "China." Pp. 191–212 in Henri J. M. Claessen and Peter Skalnik (eds.), The Early
        State. The Hague: Mouton.
Polanyi, Karl
1957   The Great Transformation. Boston: Beacon Press.
1963   "Ports of trade in early societies." Journal of Economic History 23:30–45.
Praeux, Claire
1971   "Greco-Roman Egypt." Pp. 323–354 in John R. Harris (ed.), The Legacy of Egypt.
        Oxford: Clarendon.
Price, Barbara J.
1978   "Secondary state formation: an exploratory model." In Ronald Cohen and Elman
        R. Service (eds.), Origins of the State. Philadelphia: Institute for the Studies of
        Human Issues.
Price, Derek de Solla
1974   Gears from the Greeks. Philadelphia: The American Philosophical Society.
1975   Science Since Babylon. Enlarged edition. New Haven, CT: Yale University Press.
Ralston, Bruce L.
1977   "A medical re-interpretation of case four of the Edwin Smith surgical paprus."
        Journal of Egyptian Archaeology. 63:116–121.
Rathje, William L.
1975   "The last Tango in Mayapan: a tentative trajectory of production-distribution
        systems." Pp. 409–448 in Jeremy A. Sobloff and C. C. Lamberg-Karlovsky (eds.),
        Ancient Civilization and Trade. Albuquerque, NM: University of New Mexico
        Press.
Ray, Arthur J.
1978   "Competition and conservation in the early subarctic fur trade." Ethnohistory
        (Fall):347–357.
Redman, Charles L.
1978   The Rise of Civilization. San Francisco: W. H. Freeman.
Reed, Charles A.
1969   "The pattern of animal domestication in the prehistoric near east." Pp. 361–380
        in Peter J. Ucko and G. W. Dimbleby (eds.), The Domestication and Exploitation
        of Plants and Animals. Chicago: Aldine.
1977   "Origins of agriculture: discussion and some conclusions." Pp. 879–953 in Charles
        A. Reed (ed.), Origins of Agriculture. The Hague: Mouton.
Reinhold, Meyer
1970   History of Purple as a Status Symbol. Bruxelles: Latomus Revue D'Etudes Latines.
Renfrew, J. M.
1969   "The archaeological evidence for the domestication of plants: methods and prob-
        lems." Pp. 149–172 in Peter J. Ucko and G. W. Dimbleby (eds.), The Domestication
        and Exploitation of Plants and Animals. Chicago: Aldine.

Renfrew, Colin
  1972   The Emergence of Civilization. London: Methuen and Company, Ltd.
  1979   Before Civilization. Cambridge, MA: Cambridge University Press.
Reyman, Johnathan E.
  1980   "The predictive dimension of priestly power." Transactions of the Illinois Academy of Science Vol. 72, No. 4:40–59.
Ruffle, John
  1977   The Egyptians. Ithaca, NY: Cornell University Press.
Sahlins, M.
  1972   Stone Age Economics. Chicago: Aldine.
Sandstrom, Gosta E.
  1970   Man the Builder. New York: McGraw-Hill.
Santillana, Giorgio de
  1963   "On forgotten sources in the history of science." Pp. 813–829 in A. C. Crombie (ed.), Scientific Change. New York: Basic Books.
Sarton, George
  1970   A History of Science. New York: Norton.
Schaedel, Richard P.
  1978   "Early state of the Incas." Pp. 289–320 in Henri J. M. Claessen and P. Skalnick (eds.), The Early State. The Hague: Mouton.
Schafer, Heinrich
  1974   Principles of Egyptian Art. Translated and edited with an introduction by John Bains. Oxford: Clarendon.
Schegloff, Emanuel A.
  1968   "Sequencing of conversational openings." American Anthropologist 70:1075–1095.
Schmandt-Besserat, Denise
  1976   "Sumer—art in an urban context." In Denise Schmandt-Besserat (ed.), The Legacy of Sumer. Malibu, CA: Undena.
  1977   "An archaic recording system and the origin of writing." Syro-Mesopotamian Studies (July):1–32.
  1979   "An archaic recording system in the Uruk-Jemdet Nasr Period." American Journal of Archaeology (January):19–84.
Schneider, Wolf
  1963   Babylon is Everywhere. Translated by Ingebork Sammet and John Oldenburgh. New York: McGraw-Hill.
Sehested, Glenda J.
  1975   "The evolution of solidarity." Pp. 199–118 in Carl J. Couch and Robert A. Hintz, Jr. (eds.), Constructing Social Life. Champaign, IL: Stipes.
Service, Elman R.
  1975   Origins of the State and Civilization. New York: W. W. Norton & Company.
Simmel, Georg
  1950   The Sociology of Georg Simmel. Translated by Kurt Wolff. New York: The Free Press.
Singh, Purushottam
  1974   Neolithic Cultures of Western Asia. London: Seminar Press.
Sivin, N.
  1969   Cosmos and Computation in Early Chinese Mathematical Astronomy. Leiden: E. J. Brill.
Smith, Adam
  1937   The Wealth of Nations. New York: The Modern Library.

Smith, W. W.
  1946   A History of Egyptian Sculpture and Painting in the Old Kingdom. Oxford: Oxford University Press.
Soustelle, Jacques
  1961   Daily Life of the Aztecs. Translated by Patrick O'Brian. New York: MacMillan.
Spencer, Herbert
  1972   On Social Evolution. Chicago: University of Chicago Press.
Spinden, Herbert J.
  1957   Maya Art and Civilization. Indian Hills, CO: Falcon's Wing Press.
Spores, Ronald
  1967   The Mixtec Kings and Their People. Norman, OK: University of Oklahoma Press.
Starr, Chester G.
  1961   The Origins of Greek Civilization. New York: Knopf.
  1977   The Economic and Social Growth of Early 800-500 B.C. New York: Oxford University Press.
Stecchinni, Livio Catullo
  1971   "Notes on the relation of ancient measures to the great pyramid." Appendix, in Peter Tompkins, Secrets of the Great Pyramid. New York: Harper and Row.
Steiger, George Nye
  1966   China and the Occident. New York: Russell and Russell.
Stover, Leon E. and Bruce Kraig
  1978   Stonehenge: The Indo-European Heritage. Chicago: Nelson-Hall.
Strabo
  1932   The Geography of Strabo, Vol. VIII. Translated by Horace Leonard Jones. New York: G. P. Putman's Sons.
Taton, Rene
  1963   Ancient and Medieval Science. Translated by A. J. Pomerans. Bristol: Western Printing Services.
Theocharis, Demetrios R.
  1973   Neolithic Greece. Athens, Greece: National Bank of Greece.
Thom, Alexander
  1967   Megalithic Sites in Britain. Oxford: Clarendon.
  1971   Megalithic Lunar Observatories. Oxford: Clarendon.
Thom, Alexander, and A. S. Thom
  1978   Megalithic Remains in Britain and Brittany. Oxford: Clarendon.
Thompson, J. Eric S.
  1966   The Rise and Fall of the Maya Civilization. Norman, OK: University of Oklahoma Press.
  1974   "Maya astronomy." Pp. 83–98 in F. R. Hodson (ed.), The Place of Astronomy in the Ancient World. London: Oxford University Press.
Thucydides
  1934   The Peloponnesian War. New York: The Modern Library.
Thurnwald, Richard C.
  1932   Economics in Primitive Communities. Oxford: Oxford University Press.
Todd, Ian A.
  1980   The Prehistory of Central Anatolia: The Neolithic Period. Goteborg: Paul Astroms Forlag.
Tompkins, Peter
  1971   Secrets of the Great Pyramid. New York: Harper and Row.
  1976   Mysteries of the Mexican Pyramids. New York: Harper and Row.

Toomer, G. J.
  1971   "Mathematics and astronomy." Pp. 27–54 in John R. Harris (ed.), The Legacy
         of Egypt. Oxford: Clarendon.
Toulmin, Stephen, and June Goodfield
  1962   Architecture of Matter. London: Hutchins University Library.
Tringham, Ruth
  1971   Hunters, Fishers and Farmers of Eastern Europe: 6000–3000 B.C. London:
         Hutchinson University Library.
Turton, David and Clive Ruggles
  1978   "Agreeing to disagree: the measurement of duration in a southwestern Ethiopian
         community." Current Anthropology (September):585–600.
Umberger, Emily
  1981   "The structure of Aztec history." Archaeoastronomy (October-December):10–
         18.
Van Seters, John
  1966   The Hyksos. New Haven, CT: Yale University Press.
Vayda, Andrew Peter
  1976   War in Ecological Perspective. New York: Plenum.
Wallace, Anthony F. C.
  1972   The Death and Rebirth of the Senca. New York: Vintage Books.
Ward, William A.
  1965   The Spirit of Ancient Egypt. Beirut: Khayats.
  1968   The Role of the Phoenecians in the Interaction of Mediterranean Civilizations.
         Beirut: American University of Beirut.
Wasserstein, A.
  1955   "Thales' determination of the diameters of the sun and moon," Journal of Hel-
         lenic Studies, 75:114–116.
Waters, Frank
  1975   Mexico Mystique: The Coming Sixth World of Consciousness. Chicago: Sage.
Watson, William
  1961   China before the Han Dynasty. London: Thames and Hudson.
  1966   Early Civilization in China. New York: McGraw-Hill.
  1969   "Early animal domestication in China." Pp. 393–395 in Peter J. Ucko and G. W.
         Dimbleby (ed.), The Domestication and Exploitation of Plants and Animals. Lon-
         don: Gerald Duckworth.
Webb, Malcolm C.
  1974   "Exchange networks." Pp. 357–384 in Bernard J. Seigel, Alan R. Beals, and
         Stephen A. Tyler (eds.), Annual Review of Anthropology. Palo Alto, CA: Annual
         Reviews, Inc.
  1975   "The flag follows trade: an essay on the necessary interaction of military and
         commercial factors in state formation." In Jeremy A. Sobloff and C. C. Lamberg-
         Karlovsky (eds.), Ancient Civilization and Trade. Albuquerque, NM: University
         of New Mexico Press.
Weeks, Albert L.
  1979   "The spectacle of Chicken Itza." Flying Colors (8):22–25.
Weiland, Marion W.
  1975   "Forms of social relations." Pp. 80–98 in Carl J. Couch and Robert A. Hintz, Jr.
         (eds.), Constructing Social Life. Champaign, IL: Stipes.
Wheatley, Paul
  1971   The Pivot of the Four Quarters. Chicago: Aldine.

Wheeler, Mortimer
  1966 Civilization of the Indus Valley and Beyond. New York: McGraw-Hill.
Whitehouse, Ruth
  1977 The First Cities. New York: E. P. Dutton.
Willey, Gordon R. and Demitri B. Shimkin
  1973 "Maya collapse: a summary view." Pp. 457–501 in T. Patrick Culbert (ed.), The
         Classic Maya Collapse. Albuquerque, NM: University of New Mexico Press.
Wilson, John A.
  1951 The Burden of Egypt. Chicago: University of Chicago Press.
  1967 "Authority and law in ancient Egypt." Pp. 12–18 in S.N. Eisenstadt (ed.), The
         Decline of Empires. Englewood, Cliffs, NJ: Prentice-Hall.
Wing, Elizabeth S.
  1977 "Animal domestication in the Andes." Pp. 837–860 in Charles A. Reed (ed.),
         Origins of Agriculture. The Hague: Mouton.
Wittfogel, Karl A.
  1957 Oriental Despotism. New Haven, CT: Yale University Press.
Wittry, W. L.
  1964 "An American Woodhenge." Cranbrook Institute of Science Newsletter 9:102–
         107.
Wolf, Eric R.
  1969 "Society and symbols in latin Europe and in the Islamic near east: some com-
         parisons." Anthropological Quarterly 42 (July):287-301.
Wood, John
  1978 Sun, Moon and Standing Stones. London: Oxford Press.
Wright, Henry T.
  1977 "Toward an explanation of the origin of the state." Pp. 49–68 in Ronald Cohen
         and Elman R. Service (eds.), Origins of the State: The Anthropology of Political
         Evolution. Philadelphia: Institute for the Study of Human Issues.
Wright, Henry T. and Gregory A. Johnson
  1975 "Population, exchange and early state formation in southwestern Iran." American
         Anthropologists (June):267–289.
Wunderlich, Hans Georg
  1974 The Secret of Crete. Translated by Richard Winston. New York: MacMillan.
Zohary, Daniel
  1969 "The progenitors of wheat and barley in relation to domestication and agricul-
         tural dispersal in the old world." Pp. 47–66 in Peter J. Ucko and G. W. Dimbleby
         (eds.), The Domestication and Exploitation of Plants and Animals. Chicago: Aldine.
Zuidema, R. T.
  1977 "The Inca calendar." Pp. 219–259 in Anthony F. Aveni (ed.), Native American
         Astronomy, Austin, Texas: University of Texas Press.

Author Index

389

Subject Index